WHAT CAN THIS BOOK DO FOR YOU?

WITHIN A FEW YEARS, YOUR HIGH SCHOOL EXPERIENCE WILL LEAD YOU INTO THE ADULT WORLD OF WORK. THIS MAGAZINE IS DESIGNED TO GIVE YOU GUIDANCE, IDEAS, AND ANSWERS ABOUT THE MANY OPTIONS LIFE OFFERS AND THE STEPS YOU WILL NEED TO TAKE FOR EACH.

WHAT FIRST?

TAKE A FEW MINUTES TO CLAIM OWNERSHIP OF THIS BOOK. WRITE IN YOUR NAME. IN PENCIL, LAY OUT YOUR CAREER AND LIFE GOALS AS YOU SEE THEM TODAY. CONSIDER THE OBSTACLES YOU MAY HAVE TO OVERCOME IN ORDER TO ACHIEVE THEM. IF YOU DON'T HAVE A FORMAL PLAN, THAT'S OK. ANSWERING THESE QUESTIONS WILL HELP YOU MAKE ONE. THE FIRST STEPS MIGHT NOT BE EASY, BUT THERE ARE NO RIGHT OR WRONG ANSWERS. AS YOU CONTINUE WORKING THROUGH THIS MAGAZINE, REFER BACK TO THESE GOALS AND FEEL FREE TO FILL IN ANY BLANKS YOU LEFT OR TO CHANGE YOUR IDEAS.

WHAT NEXT?

YOUR NEEDS, GOALS, IDEAS, AND TALENTS ARE UNIQUE TO YOU. WHAT IS RIGHT FOR YOU MAY NOT BE RIGHT FOR OTHERS. BUT THE STEPS IN THE PROCESS OF CHOOSING A CAREER DIRECTION (AND UNDERSTANDING WHAT EDUCATION YOU MIGHT NEED TO GET THERE) ARE THE SAME WHETHER YOU ASPIRE TO REPAIR CAR ENGINES OR DESIGN THE NEXT GENERATION OF SPACE SHUTTLES.

THINK OF THIS MAGAZINE AS A ROAD MAP

KNOWING WHERE YOU WANT TO GO AND WHAT ROADS WILL LEAD YOU THERE IS THE FIRST STEP IN THE PROCESS. YOU CAN ALWAYS CHANGE YOUR DESTINATION AND CHART A NEW COURSE. HERE'S THE MAP. THE REST IS UP TO YOU.

GETTIN THE ROAD TO SUCCESS

NAME _____

AGE _____ GRADE _____ DATE STARTED _____

MY CURRENT GOAL AFTER I GRADUATE FROM HIGH SCHOOL IS TO:
_____
_____

STEPS AT SCHOOL TO REACH MY GOAL:

❑ CURRICULUM PLANNING: _____
_____

❑ CLUBS, TEAMS, ASSOCIATIONS: _____
_____

❑ CAREER RESEARCH: _____
_____

STEPS OUTSIDE OF SCHOOL TO REACH MY GOAL:

❑ VOLUNTEER WORK: _____
_____

❑ SHADOWING/MENTOR PROGRAM: _____
_____

❑ JOB EXPERIENCE: _____
_____

❑ EXTRACURRICULAR ACTIVITIES: _____
_____

CHALLENGES MY GOAL PRESENTS: _____
_____
_____

IDEAS TO OVERCOME THESE CHALLENGES:
_____

About Peterson's

Founded in 1966, Peterson's, a division of Thomson Learning, is the nation's largest and most respected provider of lifelong learning resources, both in print and online. The Education Supersite℠ at petersons.com—the Internet's most heavily traveled education resource—has searchable databases and interactive tools for contacting U.S.-accredited institutions and programs. In addition, Peterson's delivers unmatched financial aid resources and test-preparation tools. Peterson's serves more than 100 million education consumers annually.

Thomson Learning is one of the world's leading providers of lifelong learning, serving the needs of individuals, learning institutions, and corporations with products and services for both traditional and distributed learning. Headquartered in Stamford, Connecticut, with offices worldwide, Thomson Learning is a division of The Thomson Corporation (www.thomson.com), one of the world's leading e-information and solutions companies in the business, professional, and education marketplaces. For more information, contact Peterson's, 2000 Lenox Drive, Lawrenceville, NJ 08648; 800-338-3282; or find us on the World Wide Web at: www.petersons.com/about.

ISBN 0-7689-0824-8 (Middle Atlantic)
ISBN 0-7689-0827-2 (Midwest)
ISBN 0-7689-0825-6 (New England)
ISBN 0-7689-0830-2 (New York)
ISBN 0-7689-0828-0 (South)
ISBN 0-7689-0826-4 (Texas)
ISBN 0-7689-0829-9 (West)

Printed in the United States of America

10 9 8 7 6 5 4 3 2 1

Dear Student:

Whether graduation seems light years away or alarmingly close, it's never too early—or too late—to think about what comes after high school. Do you know what your next step will be? *Get a Jump* (*GAJ*) can help you figure that out. This magazine is designed to help you launch your career, whether this means going on for more education or directly entering the work force. You have a multitude of options and some crucial choices to make. In the pages that follow, we have tried to give you a jumpstart on planning the future that's right for you.

The magazine is divided into four parts. Part One looks at how to use your high school education to plan for the next phase of your life. Part Two offers information about all the different kinds of postsecondary education available to you. Part Three provides useful information about the world of work and how to handle stress, peer pressure, conflict, and other obstacles you may encounter in the real world. Finally, Part Four contains appendices for each state in your region, including valuable information on two- and four-year colleges and universities in your area as well as internships, scholarship and financial aid programs, summer opportunities, and vocational schools.

This year, *GAJ* features two exciting partnerships. American Education Services (AES) is *GAJ*'s exclusive sponsor for higher education financial aid information. At the back of your copy of the magazine, you'll find the AESMentor CD-ROM, which will guide you through the process of financing your postsecondary education. AES has also written a special article about financial aid; it appears in Section 8, Financial Aid Dollars and Sense.

The other partnership is with *TIME* Magazine. The editors at *TIME* have searched their archives for recent articles on topics as varied as the dreaded SAT exam, the top jobs for the twenty-first century, and distance learning. You'll find these articles placed throughout the magazine, complementing the *GAJ* material.

We hope you find this publication helpful as you begin thinking about the rest of your life. If you have questions or feedback, please e-mail us at getajump@petersons.com.

Sincerely,
Peterson's Editorial Staff

Acknowledgements

Peterson's would like to acknowledge the following authors for their contribution to this publication: Kenneth Edwards, Michele Kornegay, Emily Law, and Charlotte Thomas.

Table of Contents

PART 1

EXPLORE YOUR OPTIONS

Come on, admit it.... You know that big question—what will I do when I graduate from high school—is right around the corner. And even if you know the answer, most of you are probably somewhere on the worry scale in between "Oh my gosh, this is totally freaking me out" and "I know what I want to do with my life, but it's still a little scary leaving high school."

You've got a lot of possibilities from which to choose. Some of you will attend a two-year or four-year college or vocational or technical school. Some will join the armed forces. Some will go right into the workplace and start full-time jobs. But before you march across that stage to get your diploma, Get a Jump (GAJ) will help you to begin thinking about your options and to open up doors you may have never known existed.

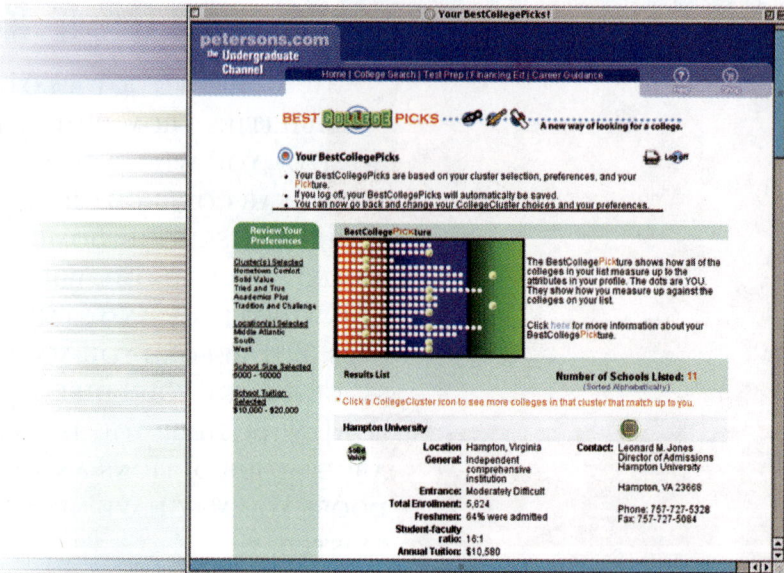

1 FIRST, A LOOK AT YOURSELF

Deciding what to do with your life is a lot like flying. Just look at the many ways you can fly and the many directions your life can take.

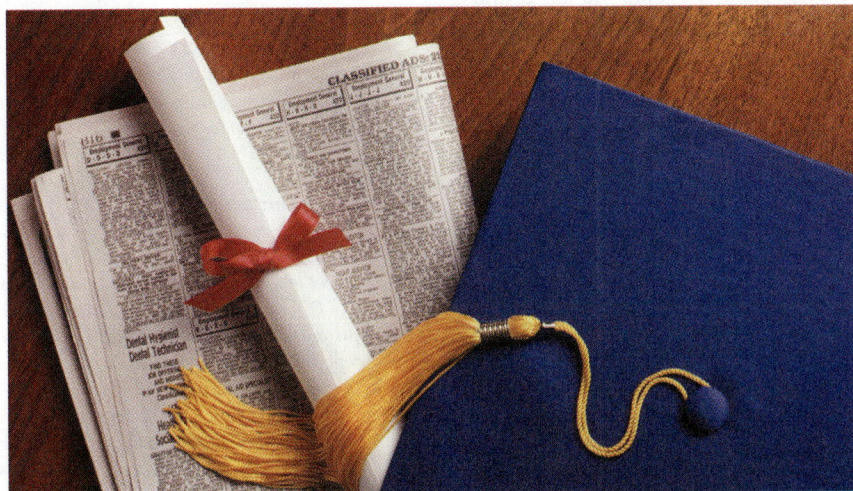

A teacher once asked her students to bring something to class that flies. Students brought kites, balloons, and models of airplanes, blimps, hot-air balloons, helicopters, spaceships, gliders, and seaplanes. But when class began, the teacher explained that the lesson was about career planning, not flying.

She was making the point that your plans for life after high school can take many forms. Some people take direct flights via jets. Others are carried along by circumstances. How you will make the journey is an individual matter. That's why it's important to know who you are and what you want before taking off.

You may not choose your life's career by reading *Get A Jump (GAJ)*, but you'll learn how to become part of the decision-making process and find resources that can help you plan your future.

Ready to fly?

Just having a high school diploma is not enough for many occupations. But, surprise, surprise, neither is a college degree. Different kinds of work require different kinds of training. Knowing how to operate a particular type of equipment, for instance, takes special skills and work experience that you might not learn in college. Employers always want to hire the best-qualified people available, but this does not mean that they always choose those applicants who have the most education. The type of education and training you have is just as important as how much. Right now, you're at the point in your life where you can choose how much and what kind of education and training you want to get.

If you have a definite career goal in mind, like being a doctor, you probably already know what it will take in terms of education. You're looking at about four years of college, then four years of medical school, and, in most states, one year of residency.

EDUCATIONAL ATTAINMENT
Highest level of education attained by persons 25 years and older

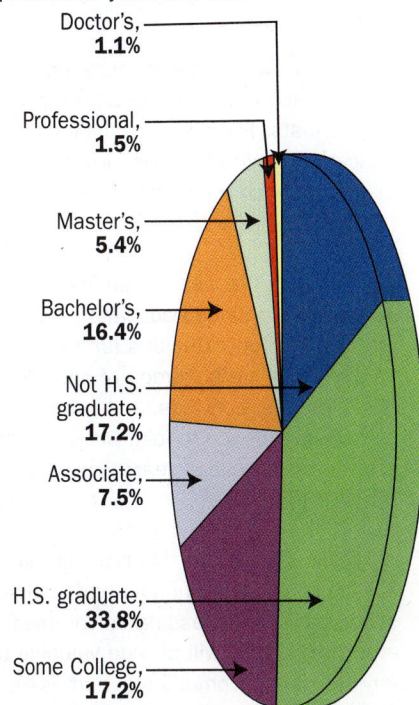

- Doctor's, **1.1%**
- Professional, **1.5%**
- Master's, **5.4%**
- Bachelor's, **16.4%**
- Not H.S. graduate, **17.2%**
- Associate, **7.5%**
- H.S. graduate, **33.8%**
- Some College, **17.2%**

Source: Digest of Educational Statistics, U.S. Department of Commerce, Bureau of the Census, Current Population Survey

Cosmetologists, on the other hand, complete a state-approved training program that ranges from eight to eighteen months.

But for most of you, deciding what to do after high school is not so easy. Perhaps you haven't chosen a field of work yet. You might just know for certain that you want a job that will give you status and a big paycheck. Or maybe you know what you want to do, but you're not sure what kind of education you'll need. For instance, you may love fixing cars, and the idea of being an auto mechanic sounds great. But you need to decide whether to learn on the job, attend a vocational school, seek an apprenticeship, or pursue a combination of these options.

THE TOP 10 REASONS TO CONTINUE YOUR EDUCATION

Continuing your education after high school is one choice that can give you a good start no matter what your final career decision is. There are many good reasons to do so. If you think college is not for you at all, take a look at this list. It might change your mind.

10 **Fullfill a dream—or begin one.** Some people hope to become teachers or scientists. For many, continuing their education provides the opportunity to make that wish a reality for one's self or family.

9 **Have fun.** Classes are an important part of continued education, but there are plenty of opportunities for some great times. There are hundreds of sports, clubs, groups, activities, and associations just waiting for you to join. Many people say that their college years were the best years of their lives.

8 **Make connections that can link you to future jobs.** The friends, professors, supervisors, and classmates you meet after high school will provide valuable ties for future jobs, committees, and associations within the community.

7 **Become part of a cultural stew.** As you have probably already figured out, not everyone is like you. Nor should they be. Being in college is a good way to expose yourself to many types of people from various backgrounds and geographic locations, with different viewpoints and opinions. You may discover that you like people and things you never knew existed.

6 **Meet new people.** By furthering your education, you will widen your circle of friends and, chances are, form meaningful lifelong relationships.

5 **Do what you love doing and get paid for it.** Have you ever taken a test during which everything clicked or played a video game and caught on immediately? This is what happens when you combine education and training with the right job. Work becomes more like play, which is far more satisfying and rewarding than just going through the motions.

4 **Exercise your mind.** Just as physical exercise keeps your body in shape, mental exercise keeps your mind free of cobwebs. No matter what your area of interest, education holds the key to the most interesting and challenging information you can imagine. Explore your outer limits and become a lifelong learner.

3 **Earn a higher income.** Although money isn't everything, it is necessary for survival. A good education prepares you to become a solid member of society. (See the chart, "Increase Your Earning Power.")

2 **Learn critical-thinking and analytical skills.** More than any other skill, education teaches you to think. Furthering your learning will help you to think critically, organize and analyze information, and write clearly.

1 **You won't get left behind.** In the next decade, you will need to be prepared to change jobs and continually learn new skills in order to keep up with changes in industry, communications, and technology. Education and training will give you a solid background.

INCREASE YOUR EARNING POWER

PEOPLE WITH MORE EDUCATION TEND TO EARN MORE MONEY. LOOK AT THE AVERAGE YEARLY EARNINGS OF WORKERS OVER THE AGE OF 25 BY EDUCATION LEVEL.

Professional Degree	$71,700
Doctoral Degree	$62,400
Master's Degree	$50,000
Bachelor's Degree	$40,100
Associate Degree	$31,700
Some College	$30,400
High School Diploma	$26,000
Less Than High School Diploma	$19,700

Source: Bureau of Labor Statistics

Breaking Down the Barriers to Continuing Your Education

Some of you may say, "Forget the reasons why I should continue my education. I can't because (fill in the blank)." Let's see if your objections stand up to this list.

You say:
Nobody in my family has ever gone to college.

GAJ says:
You can be the first! It's a little scary and not always easy, but just think how great you'll feel being the first person in your family to receive a degree, diploma, or certificate.

You say:
My grades are not good enough.

GAJ says:
Don't let less-than-perfect grades stand in your way. Different institutions have different requirements, including what grades they accept. Schools also evaluate you for admission as a whole person, such as participation in extracurricular activities; your talents, such as academics and athletics; and your employment and volunteer history. There are also classes that you can take to improve your skills in various subject areas. Get a tutor now or form a study group in high school to improve your grades as much as possible. Talk to your guidance counselor about what the appropriate high school curriculum for you is so you'll have more options when making decisions about continuing your education.

You say:
I can't afford it.

GAJ says:
Many families cannot afford to pay education costs completely out of pocket. That's why there are so many opportunities for financial aid, scholarships, grants, and work-study programs. Federal, state, school-sponsored, private, and career-specific financial aid resources are available to students who take the time to look. Talk to a guidance counselor, go to the library, and look on the Internet. Read the Financial Aid Dollars and Sense section of GAJ for more information about how to finance your continued education. Be creative and persistent. It can happen for you.

You say:
I don't know how to apply or where I want to go.

GAJ says:
Fortunately, there are resources to help you decide which institution to select. Talk to friends, family members, neighbors, your guidance counselor, pastor, coach, or librarian. Take

a look at the appendix at the back of GAJ for a guide to two-year and four-year colleges as well as vocational and technical schools in your state.

You say:

I think it may be too difficult for me.

GAJ says:

Think back to something you have done in your life that seemed too difficult in the beginning. Didn't you find that once you began, put your mind to it, and stuck with it that you succeeded? You can do almost anything if you set your mind to it and are willing to work for it.

You say:

I'm not sure I'll fit in.

GAJ says:

One of the best things about furthering your education is the chance to meet new people and be part of new experiences in new surroundings. Colleges and other continuing education options attract a wide variety of students from many different backgrounds. Chances are you won't have any problem finding someone else with interests that are similar to yours. Because schools differ in size, location, student body, and lifestyle, you'll surely find one that meets your needs. Advance visits and interviews can help you determine which school is right for you.

You say:

I don't even know what I want to do with my life.

GAJ says:

Many students don't know this about themselves until they get to experience some of the possibilities. Take the self-assessment on page 8 to help you determine what your interests and talents are. Read "How to Choose a Major" on page 101 for a listing of the most popular college majors and their related careers.

You say:

There is no way I can pursue my education full-time.

GAJ says:

Part-time students are becoming the norm. In fact, a recent study determined that 43 percent of undergraduate students attend school part-time. Most schools offer evening and weekend classes, and many offer work-study opportunities to help students pay for their education. Also, some employers will pay or reimburse you if you are working and want to further your education. If you are enrolled part-time, it takes longer to graduate. But if full-time enrollment is not an option for you, don't give up the opportunity to continue your education. There are many nontraditional ways to achieve your goals.

CHOOSING A CAREER YOU'LL BE HAPPY WITH

Did you know that of the estimated 15 million people searching for employment in the American job market, approximately 12 million are looking for a new occupation or a different employer? That's an awful lot of people who aren't happy with their jobs. Hopefully, you won't be one of them if you take some time to consider what it is you really want to do now, while you're still in school. Is there a particular type of job you've always dreamed of doing? Or perhaps you're one of the many high school students who say:

"I Kind of Know What I Want, But I'm Not Really Sure."

A good way to gather information about potential occupations is by talking with people who have achieved goals that are similar to yours. Talk to teachers, neighbors, and adult friends about their work experiences. The formal name for that activity is an "informational interview." You're interviewing them about the work they do—not to get a job from them but to gather information about their jobs.

If you don't have any contacts in a field that sparks your interest, do some poking around in the workplace. For instance, if you're interested in a career in nursing, you could visit a hospital, doctor's office, or nursing home. Most people love to talk about themselves, so don't be afraid to ask if they'll chat with you about their profession. Offering to volunteer your services can be the best way to know whether you'll be happy doing that type of work.

"I Haven't a Clue about What I Want to Do."

If you're completely unsure about what kind of work you'd like to do, contact a career counselor who can help you explore your options and possibly administer some interest and aptitude tests. You also might think about contacting a college career planning and placement office, a vocational school placement office, the counseling services of community agencies, or a private counseling service, which may charge you a fee. Many high schools offer job-shadowing programs, where students actually shadow someone in a particular occupation for an entire day or more. Don't forget that as a high school student, your best resource is your high school guidance counselor. Take a look at the list of the fastest-growing occupations on page 9 to get a sampling of the careers with the largest projected job growth in the coming years.

ON THE HUNT FOR INFORMATION

Regardless of how unsure you may be about what you want to do after high school, here's a list of things you can do to get the information you need to head in the right direction. Many people start off thinking they want one career and end up doing something completely different. But this is a good place to begin:

- Investigate careers both in and out of school. Participate in mentoring, job shadowing, and career day opportunities whenever possible.
- Get some on-the-job experience in a field that interests you.
- Research two-year and four-year colleges, vocational and technical schools, and apprenticeship programs.
- Participate in school and state career development activities.
- Prepare for and take aptitude and college entrance tests.

Here are a few Web sites where you can receive valuable direction by completing a career interest questionnaire or by reading about various occupations:

(Continued on page 10)

WHAT WILL WE DO FOR WORK?

BY TOM PETERS

I BELIEVE THAT 90% OF WHITE-COLLAR JOBS IN the U.S. will be either destroyed or altered beyond recognition in the next 10 to 15 years. That's a catastrophic prediction, given that 90% of us are engaged in white-collar work of one sort or another. Even most manufacturing jobs these days are connected to such white-collar services as finance, human resources and engineering.

I talked to an old London dockhand some time back. He allowed as how in 1970 it took 108 guys about five days to unload a timber ship. Then came containerization. The comparable task today takes eight folks one day. That is, a 98.5% reduction in man-days, from 540 total to just eight.

This time the productivity tool kit aims, belatedly, to reconstruct—make that deconstruct—the white-collar world. In fact, I see a five-sided pincer movement that will bring to fruition my apparently bizarre "90% in 10 years" prognostication.

FIRST The destructive nature of the current flavor of competition, dotcoms. Sure, most will fail. But the survivors will exert enormous pressure—fast!—on the Big Guys. When an Amazon or a Charles Schwab moves into your neighborhood, you've got moments to react. Or take king entrepreneur Jim Clark of Netscape fame. His venture Healtheon/WebMD intends to squeeze hundreds of billions of dollars of waste out of the health-care system. These new firms aim to create nothing less than havoc in the theaters in which they operate.

SECOND Enterprise software. It's a jargony name for the tools that will hook up every aspect of a business's innards—personnel, production, sales, accounting—and then hook up all that hooked-up stuff to the rest of the "family" of suppliers and the suppliers' suppliers and wholesalers and retailers and end users.

They are your nightmare, these "white-collar robots." The complex products from German software giant SAP will do to your company's innards exactly what forklifts and robots and containerization did to the blue-collar world circa 1960. Installing these tools is not easy. The technical part is harrowing; the politics are horrendous. When the blue-collar robots arrived, the unions raised hell. This time it's management bureaucrats who are turning Luddite. Why? These tools threaten their cozy baronies, carefully crafted over several generations.

But the robots did come. And they triumphed.

THIRD Outsourcing. M.I.T.'s No. 1 computer guru,

Drastic change is afoot. You'll have to be flexible and upgradable, but you may actually enjoy what you're doing

---

Consultant Tom Peters published a series of books on reinventing work, including The Brand You 50 *and* The Project 50

Michael Dertouzos, said India could easily boost its GDP by a trillion dollars in the next few years performing backroom white-collar tasks for Western companies. He guessed that 50 million jobs from the white-collar West could go south to India, whose population hit 1 billion this year. The average annual salary for each of those 50 million new Indian workers: $20,000.

FOURTH The Web. Ford, GM and DaimlerChrysler announce a rare hookup. They will link all their tens of thousands of suppliers into a single, Internet-based network. This entity will encompass $250 billion annually of suppliers' products (and perhaps an additional $500 billion of those suppliers' suppliers' products). In short, every penny of waste will be wrung from the mammoth procurement system. The order cycle will speed up dramatically. Medibuy aims for the same hat trick in medical supplies, DigitalThink in training, CarStation in the auto-body-shop world. This is the white-hot world of B2B (business to business) electronic commerce, which will soon encompass trillions upon trillions of dollars in transactions.

FIFTH Time compression. It took 37 years for the radio to get to 50 million homes. The Web got there in four. Hence my belief that while it took about a century to revolutionize blue-collar job practices, this brave new white-collar regime will be mostly installed in a tenth of that time—10 years.

Each of these five forces is fact, not supposition. Each influences the others multiplicatively. Therefore my unwillingness to back off my predictions about the power of the white-collar tsunami bearing down on us. Unsettling madness is afoot. Especially if I'm a 48-year-old white-collar staff member or middle manager entombed in a corporate tower in Manhattan or Miami or Milan.

Yet these forces are liberating. Blue-collar robots took the grunt work out of factory and warehouse and dockside. The same will happen to white-collar work. Just as workin' the line at U.S. Steel was no walk in the park in 1946, passing papers in the tower is no great joy. My dad did it for 41 years at the Baltimore Gas & Electric Co. He was, sad to say, a white-collar indentured servant.

The world is going through more fundamental change than it has in hundreds, perhaps thousands of years. The head economist at Sandia National Laboratories, Arnold Baker, said it's the "biggest change since the cavemen began bartering." Do you want to be a player, a full-scale participant who embraces change? Here is the opportunity to participate in the lovely, messy playground called "Let's reinvent the world."

Here's a new role model I call Icon Woman:
> She is turned on by her work!
> The work matters!
> The work is cool!
> She is "in your face"!
> She is an adventurer!
> She is the CEO of her life!
> She is not God. She is not the Bionic Woman. She is determined to make a difference! (Dilbert would be appalled, no doubt.)

My Icon Woman, of course, embraces and exploits the Web.
> She submits her résumé on the Web and keeps it perpetually active there.
> She is recruited and negotiates and is hired on the Web.
> She is trained on the Web.
> She creates and conducts scintillating projects on the Web via a far-flung "virtual" stable of teammates (most of whom she's never met).
> She manages her career and reputation-building efforts on the Web. And she has a fab personal website!

But what—exactly?—will she actually do?

Circa 2010. She will be at home. Working—for the next several months—for Ford on a fiendishly difficult engineering problem. She won't be on Ford's payroll, though she will be drawing full benefits, even as a contractor. (During President Hillary Rodham's second term, health care, pensions and retraining will no longer be tied to a company but to the individual.) Her 79-member project team, only one of whom she's met face-to-face (she considers face-to-face a quaint idea that her mom suffered), comes from 14 nations. Her fully wired home is her castle. After half a dozen virtual meetings this morning, she'll take a so-called RETRB (ReTRaining Break) and attend a virtual class in engineering (conducted from God knows where) as part of her virtual/online master's degree program.

She is deeply committed to her self-designed, do-it-from-anywhere-with-anybody "career" path. She is relieved, by the white-collar robots, of 95% of the drudge work ... and is adding value by being on the tippy top of her intellectual game. Her only security is her personal commitment to constant growth and her global (virtual) rep for great work.

"Get a grip, Peters," you retort. Is this "be wild and crazy and Webby and CEO of your own life" picture anything other than New Age/new economy/Palo Alto-consultantspeak b.s.?

I think it is relevant and real rather than wild and crazy—on at least two important scores.

One is that though my "house" is in Vermont, I've hung my professional shingle in Palo Alto since 1981. All hell is breaking loose "out there/here." These folks may sound weird, but they may also be redefining the world. And speaking as a 57-year-old, "they" don't look or eat or taste or smell—or work—much like Frank Peters or George Babbitt or Dilbert.

Two is back to the future! I constantly remind my middle-aged seminar participants that George Babbitt and Dilbert are not the quintessential Americans. Who are? Ben Franklin (the father of self-help literature). Ralph Waldo Emerson (self-reliance was his shtick, recall). Walt Whitman. And yes, motivational guru Tony Robbins. And yes, Donald Trump. And ... Bentonville, Arkansas' Sam Walton ... and Bill Gates.

Hero Jim Clark, mentioned above, is no charmer, as revealed by Michael Lewis in *The New New Thing*. In fact, to my reading, he comes off as about as delectable as Donald Trump. But he's pure American bravado, a bravado that was lost in the Babbitt-Dilbert-Big Bureaucracy-Cubicle Slave decades.

WHAT IF? Maybe the wild new-economy America is the old America. Truer to ourselves. We came here to break free, to make our records in our awkward ways, as did my German grandfather Jacob Ebert Peters. He arrived in the 1880s and was a wildly successful Baltimore contractor 30 years later. Then he lost it all in the Great Depression. How quintessentially American.

Like Grandpa, I am facing extinction, only by this new set of powerful forces. I make most of my living giving live seminars and training programs and as a management consultant. It's all gravitating to the Web—gravitating, heck. It's moving at the speed of light. I am scrambling to reinvent myself, to not just "cope" but to exploit the new communication and connection media. Hey, there are young management gurus hot on my trail. Hot = Web speed.

I'm completely fed up with Dilbert. He's funny. He's unerringly on the money. But he's a hapless victim too. Damned if I'm going to be.

In any event, it's going to be one hell of an interesting ride. ∎

SELF-ASSESSMENT INVENTORY

In addition to looking to outside sources for information, there's another rich source of data: yourself. Knowing what you want to do begins with knowing yourself—the real you. That's because the better you understand your own wants and needs, the better you will be able to make decisions about your career goals and dreams. This self-assessment inventory can help.

Who do you admire most, and why?

What is your greatest strength?

What is your greatest talent?

What skills do you already have?

DESCRIBE HOW YOU CURRENTLY USE THESE SKILLS IN YOUR LIFE.

Athletic ability

Mechanical ability

Ability to work with numbers

Leadership skills

Teaching skills

Artistic skills

Analytical skills

Check the areas that most interest you.

○ Providing a practical service for people

○ Self-expression in music, art, literature, or nature

○ Organizing and record keeping

○ Meeting people and supervising others

○ Helping others in need, either mentally, spiritually, or physically

○ Solving practical problems

○ Working in forestry, farming, or fishing

○ Working with machines and tools

○ Taking care of animals

○ Physical work out of doors

○ Protecting the public via law enforcement or fire fighting

○ Medical, scientific, or mathematical work

○ Selling, advertising, or promoting

WHAT GIVES YOU SATISFACTION?

Answer the following questions True (T) or False (F).

T F I get satisfaction not from personal accomplishment, but from helping others.

T F I'd like to have a job in which I can use my imagination and be inventive.

T F In my life, money will be placed ahead of job security and personal interests.

T F It is my ambition to have a direct impact on other people's lives.

T F I am not a risk-taker and would prefer a career that offers little risk.

T F I enjoy working with people rather than by myself.

T F I would not be happy doing the same thing all the time.

WHAT MATTERS THE MOST TO YOU?

Rate the items on the list below from 1 to 10, with 10 being extremely important and 1 being not at all important.

___ Good health

___ Justice

___ Marriage/family

___ Faith

___ Fame

___ Beauty

___ Safety

___ Friendship

___ Respect

___ Accomplishment

___ Seeing the world

___ Love

___ Fun

___ Power

___ Individualism

___ Charity

___ Honor

___ Intelligence

___ Wealth

What would you do if you were in a blizzard survival situation? Check the one that would be your most likely role.

○ The leader

○ The one who explains the situation to the others

○ The one who keeps morale up

○ The one who invents a way to keep warm and melt snow for water

○ The one who listens to instructions and keeps the supplies organized

○ The one who positions sticks and rocks to signal SOS

LOOKING AHEAD AND LOOKING BACK

What are your goals for the next five years?

Where would you like to be in ten years?

What has been your favorite course, and why?

What was your least favorite course, and why?

Who was your favorite teacher, and why?

What are your hobbies?

What are your extracurricular activities?

What jobs have you held?

What volunteer work, if any, have you performed?

Have you ever shadowed a professional for a day? If so, what did you learn?

Do you have a mentor? If so, who? What have you learned from this person?

Do you want to stay close to home, or would you prefer to travel to another city after high school?

What are your career goals?

MY INTERESTS, SKILLS, AND KNOWLEDGE SUPPORTING MY CAREER GOALS ARE:

To fulfill my career goals, I will need additional skills and knowledge in:

I will obtain the additional skills and knowledge by taking part in the following educational activities:

I will need a degree, certification, and/or specialized training in:

When I look in the classified ads of the newspaper, the following job descriptions sound attractive to me:

WHAT WILL YOU NEED TO GET WHERE YOU'RE GOING?

The information I have given indicates that I will be selecting courses that are primarily:

○ College path (Four-year or two-year education that offers liberal arts courses combined with courses in your area of interest.)

○ Vocational path (One or more years of education that includes hands-on training for a specific job.)

○ Combination of the two

What are your immediate plans after high school?

AFTER HIGH SCHOOL, I PLAN TO:

○ work full-time
○ work part-time and attend school
○ attend college full-time
○ attend technical college
○ enter the military

MY PERFECT JOB WOULD BE ...

Let your imagination run wild. You can have any job you want. What's it like? Start by describing to yourself the following job conditions:

Work conditions: What hours are you willing to work? Do you feel most satisfied in an environment that is indoors/outdoors, var-ied/regular, noisy/quiet, or casual/traditional?

Duties: What duties do you feel comfortable carrying out? Do you want to be a leader, or do you perform best as a team player?

People: Do you want to work with other people or more independently? How much people contact do you want/need?

Education: How much special training or education is required? How much education are you willing to seek? Can you build upon the education or experience you have to date? Will you need to gain new education or experience?

Benefits: What salary and benefits do you expect? Are you willing to travel?

Disadvantages: There are disadvantages with almost any job. Can you imagine what the disadvantages may be? Can you confirm or disprove these beliefs by talking to someone or researching the industry or job further? If these disadvantages really exist, can you live with them?

Personal qualities: What qualities do you want in the employer you ultimately choose? What are the most important qualities that you want in a supervisor? In your coworkers?

Look over your responses to this assessment. Do you see recurring themes in your answers that start to show you what kind of career you might like? If not, there are many more places to get information to decide where your interests lie. You can go to your guidance counselor for advice. You can take the Campbell (TM) Interest and Skills Inventory, the Strong Interest Inventory, the Self-Directed Search, or other assessment tests that your guidance counselor recommends.

FASTEST-GROWING OCCUPATIONS

WANT TO HAVE A CAREER THAT'S GOING PLACES? CHECK OUT THIS CHART TO SEE WHICH OCCUPATIONS ARE GROWING THE FASTEST AND WHAT TYPE OF TRAINING YOU'LL NEED TO GET THE JOB.

OCCUPATION	EXPECTED JOB OPENINGS	MOST SIGNIFICANT SOURCE OF TRAINING
Computer engineers	323,000	Bachelor's degree
Computer support specialists	439,000	Associate degree
Systems analysts	577,000	Bachelor's degree
Database administrators	67,000	Bachelor's degree
Desktop publishing specialists	19,000	Long-term on-the-job training
Paralegals and legal assistants	84,000	Associate degree
Medical assistants	146,000	Moderate-term on-the-job training
Personal care and home health aides	433,000	Short-term on-the-job training
Social and human service assistants	141,000	Moderate-term on-the-job training
Physician's assistants	32,000	Bachelor's degree
Data processing equipment	37,000	Postsecondary vocational repairers training
Residential counselors	88,000	Bachelor's degree
Electronic semiconductor processors	29,000	Moderate-term on-the-job training
Engineering, natural science, and computer and information systems managers	142,000	Work and experience, plus degree
Physical therapy assistants and aides	36,000	Associate degree
Medical records and health information technicians	41,000	Associate degree
Respiratory therapists	37,000	Associate degree
Surgical technologists	23,000	Postsecondary vocational training
Dental assistants	97,000	Moderate-term on-the-job training
Securities, commodities, and financial services sales agents	124,000	Bachelor's degree
Dental hygienists	58,000	Associate degree
Occupational therapy assistants and aids	7,000	Associate degree
Speech-language pathologists and audiologists	40,000	Master's degree
Cardiovascular technologists and technicians	8,000	Associate degree
Correctional officers	148,000	Long-term on-the-job training
Social workers	218,000	Bachelor's degree
Biological scientists	28,000	Doctoral degree
Ambulance drivers and attendants, except EMTs	7,000	Short-term on-the-job training
Bill and account collectors	110,000	Short-term on-the-job training
Physical therapists	41,000	Master's degree

Source: Bureau of Labor Statistics, Occupational Outlook Handbook

Bryant College —
Nothing like it in the world!

A superior education. A lifelong network of friends. A rewarding career. An unforgettable experience. All at Bryant College.

For more than 130 years, Bryant has provided the education and skills required to begin and grow in your career. Our graduates enter fields like financial services, communications, computer information systems, marketing, accounting, psychology, and management.

Our computer resources are among the best available in colleges today. And special facilities like The John H. Chafee Center for International Business and the Verizon Telecommunications Center bring leading businesses into direct contact with our students, and ensure that Bryant is on the cutting edge of industry trends.

Located in scenic New England, Bryant is close to Providence, Boston, Hartford, and Worcester. Campus life is active with more than 60 student organizations and plenty of varsity and intramural sports. With great housing options, there's good reason that more than 80 percent of our students choose to live on campus.

Bryant College. Respected academics. Dynamic environment. Graduates in demand. Reply now to receive an application and viewbook. When you look at Bryant you'll see—nothing like it in the world.

Academic Programs

Bachelor of Science in Business Administration
Accounting	Accounting Information Systems
Applied Actuarial Mathematics	Computer Information Systems
Finance	Financial Services
Management	Marketing

Bachelor of Arts in Liberal Studies
Communication	Economics	English
History	International Studies	

Bachelor of Science in Information Technology

Bachelor of Arts in Communication

Bachelor of Arts in Psychology

Minors:
Applied Actuarial Mathematics, Applied Statistics, Biotechnology, Communication, Computer Information Systems, Economics, English, Environmental Science, Finance, History, International Business, Legal Studies, Political Science, Psychology, Sociology, Women's Studies

1150 Douglas Pike
Smithfield, RI 02917-1285
Admission: (800) 622-7001 or (401) 232-6100
Financial Aid: (800) 248-4036 or (401) 232-6020
Fax: (401) 232-6741
E-Mail: admissions@bryant.edu
Web site: www.bryant.edu

Peterson's
www.petersons.com
On Peterson's career channel, you can take a variety of career assessments, read helpful articles about the world of work, and search for undergraduate academic and career-oriented degree and certificate programs.

OccupationalOutlook Handbook
www.bls.gov/ocohome.htm
The Bureau of Labor Statistics, an agency within the U.S. Department of Labor, produces this Web site, which offers more information than you'll ever need about a specific career. The site also includes help with writing your resume, interviewing, and knowing which jobs are hot and which are not.

Mapping Your Future
www.mapping-your-future.org
On this site, you can find out how to choose a career and how to reach your career goals. You can also pick up useful tips on job hunting, resume writing, and job interviewing techniques. This site also provides a ten-step plan for determining and achieving your career goals.

University of Waterloo-Career Services
www.careerservices.uwaterloo.ca/manual-home.html
This site provides a thorough online career interest survey, and you can use strategies to get the job that's right for you.

Motivational Appraisal of Personal Potential
www.assessment.com
Features a free 71-question career assessment that analyzes your motivation and points you to the ten best careers for you.

Monster.com
www.monster.com
Includes information about thousands of job and career fairs, advice on resumes, and much more.■

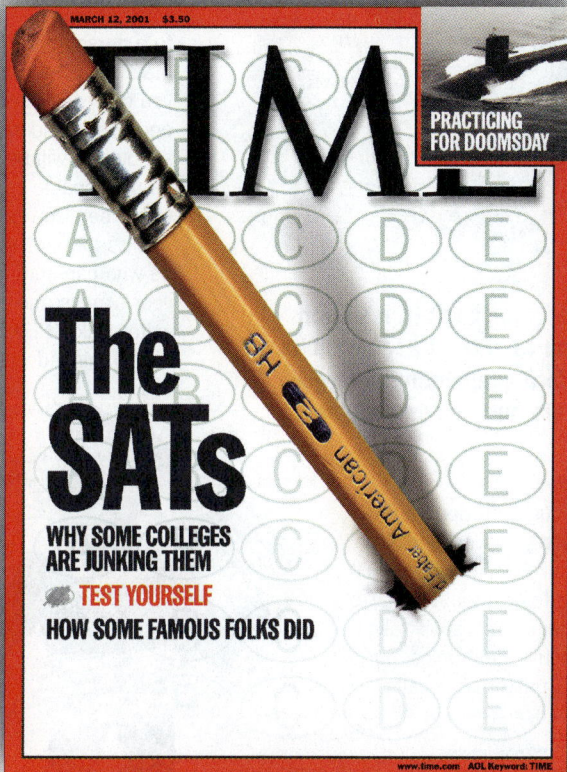

what will be the 10 hottest jobs?

By Julie Rawe

Looking for a career change? A decade ago, who would have guessed that Web designer would be one of the hottest jobs of 2000? Here are some clues

1 TISSUE ENGINEERS

With man-made skin already on the market and artificial cartilage not far behind, 25 years from now scientists expect to be pulling a pancreas out of a Petri dish. Or trying, anyway. Researchers have successfully grown new intestines and bladders inside animals' abdominal cavities, and work has begun on building liver, heart and kidney tissue.

2 GENE PROGRAMMERS

Digital genome maps will allow lab technicians to create customized prescriptions, altering individual genes by rewriting lines of computer code. After scanning your DNA for defects, doctors will use gene therapy and "smart" molecules to prevent a variety of diseases, including certain cancers.

3 PHARMERS

New-age Old MacDonalds will raise crops and livestock that have been genetically engineered to produce therapeutic proteins. Works in progress include a vaccine-carrying tomato and drug-laden milk from cows, sheep and goats.

4 FRANKENFOOD MONITORS

Not sure what's for dinner? With a little genetic tinkering, fast-growing fish and freeze-resistant fruits will help feed an overpopulated planet, but such hybrids could unwittingly wipe out the food chain. Eco-scouts will be on the lookout for so-called Trojan gene effects, and bounty hunters will help the USDA eliminate transgenic species that get out of hand.

5 DATA MINERS

When Ask Jeeves just won't cut it, research gurus will be on hand to extract useful tidbits from mountains of data, pinpointing behavior patterns for marketers and epidemiologists alike.

6 HOT-LINE HANDYMEN

Still daunted by the thought of reprogramming your VCR, let alone your newfangled DVD? Just wait until your 3-D holographic TV won't power up or your talking toaster starts mouthing off. Remote diagnostics will take care of most of your home electronics, but a few repairmen will still make house calls ...via video phone.

7 VIRTUAL-REALITY ACTORS

Pay-per-view will become pay-per-play, allowing these pros to interact with you in cyberspace dramas. Scriptwriters will also be in high demand, as mouse potatoes clamor for new story lines to escape from their droned-out existence.

8 NARROWCASTERS

Today's broadcasting industry will become increasingly personalized, working with advertisers to create content (read: product placement) just for you. Ambient commercials will also hijack your attention by using tastes and smells, with the ultimate goal of beaming buy-me messages directly into your brain.

9 TURING TESTERS

Computer engineers will continue to measure their efforts to mimic human intelligence, as British mathematician Alan Turing suggested 50 years ago, by asking you whether you're talking to a person or a machine. By the time you can't tell the difference, these human simulators will be used as unflappable customer service reps as well as Internet attaches who can summarize your e-mails and even write back: "Hi, Mom, sorry I missed your call..."

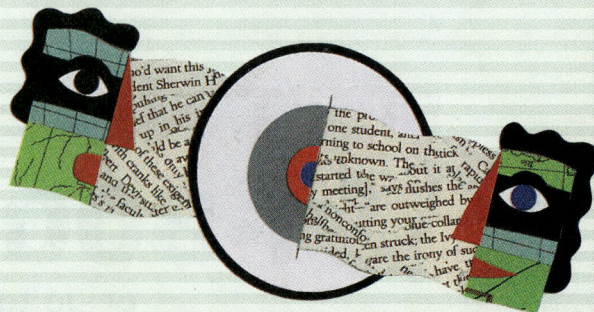

10 KNOWLEDGE ENGINEERS

Artificial-intelligence brokers will translate your expertise into software, then downsize you.

Illustrations for TIME by David McLimans

...and what jobs will disappear?

1 STOCKBROKERS, AUTO DEALERS, MAIL CARRIERS, INSURANCE AND REAL ESTATE AGENTS

The Internet will eradicate middlemen by the millions, with a hardy few remaining to service the clueless. You'll cut us a deal, right, HAL?

2 TEACHERS

Distance learning is becoming more popular, and through the miracle of online classes and electronic grading, today's faculty lounge could become tomorrow's virtual help desk. Though a complete conversion is unlikely, outsourcing our education system might cost less than installing all those metal detectors.

3 PRINTERS

President Oprah may use her book club to rescue the printing press from extinction when newspapers and magazines make the switch to digital paper. Xerox and other visionaries are racing to produce a material that's as flexible as regular paper and as versatile as a computer screen, with the end result keeping news junkies happy, not to mention all those trees.

4 STENOGRAPHERS

Sophisticated voice-recognition software will replace court reporters and lots of secretaries and executive assistants. Note to self: don't ditch the assistant just yet—technology may cover the grunt work, but who'll cover for you when that report isn't ready or get blamed for the snafu?

5 CEOS

Top-down decision making will be too cumbersome, and golden parachutes too obscene, for the blistering 24-hour business day. A global team of quick-thinking experts will carry companies through the Internet age and beyond.

6 ORTHODONTISTS

No more metal mouth, thanks to 3-D simulation programs that will crank out a series of disposable, clear-plastic "aligners" to shift your teeth into position. Already in clinical trials, this technology is geared for adults, so all you gap-toothed prepubes will have something to look forward to.

7 PRISON GUARDS

Microscopic implants will restrain convicts from engaging in criminal activity. The sensors will require lots of fine tuning, though—we wouldn't want an aggressive telemarketer getting zapped, would we?

8 TRUCKERS

Interstates will have "smart" lanes enabling computer-driven vehicles to travel bumper to bumper at high speeds. Suburbia will decongest by using bottleneck sensors in cars to suggest alternate routes, and while you can kiss those meter maids goodbye, expect tickets to appear on your virtual dash.

9 HOUSEKEEPERS

If fridges today can decide to buy you more milk (online), then self-motivated vacuums don't sound so far afield. Perhaps self-cleaning homes will use a central vacuuming system or dust-eating nanobots. Either way, you can bet your retirement community there are people working on it.

10 FATHERS

Between in-vitro fertilization and cloning, dads could become dinosaurs. Moms, too, with the possibility looming of an artificial womb. Did somebody say George Orwell?

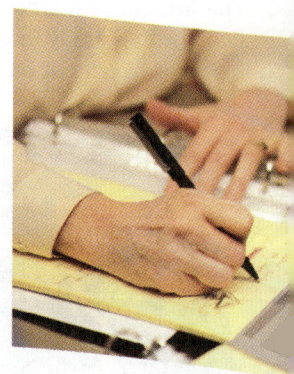

THE FIRST STEPS TO A CAREER

Don't be too surprised when your summer job turns into your career.

The word "career" has a scary sound to it when you're still in high school. Careers are for college graduates or those who have been in the workplace for years. But unless you grew up knowing for sure that you wanted to fly airplanes or be a marine biologist, what will you do? You'll be happy to know that interests you have now can very possibly lead to a college major or into a career. Like that job at a clothing store could lead to a career designing clothes. Perhaps those hours you spend chasing Laura Croft, Tomb Raider will lead to a career creating video games.

Maybe you baby-sit and love being around kids, so teaching becomes an obvious choice. Or cars fascinate you and you find out you want to fix them for a living.

This section will show you how you can begin exploring your interests—sort of like getting into a swimming pool starting with your big toe, rather than plunging in. School-to-work classes in which you attend high school part-time and work part-time, summer jobs, and volunteering are all ways you can test various career paths to decide if you like them.

The School-to-Work Path

Whether you go to college right after high school and then to the workplace or start working immediately, you're going to find that employers want more than just order takers. People who do well can solve problems, think about ideas in a critical way, work well in teams, and constantly learn on the job. So, how do you learn those skills?

In order to help students prepare for the workplace, the School-to-Work approach to learning was designed. It is based on the realization that students learn best by doing, by relating what they learn in school to what they experience in the workplace, and by having an adult mentor to help them master skills. Developed with the input of business, education, labor, and community-based organizations that have a strong interest in how students prepare for careers, the School-to-Work system contains three fundamental elements: school-based learning, work-based

learning, and activities that connect the two.

School-based learning works this way:

- ☀ Students learn how academic subjects relate to the workplace.

- ☀ Teachers work together with employers to develop broad-based curricula that help students understand what skills they will need in the workplace.

From the Guidance Office

Q: What if going to college is not for me?

A: When adults ask kids what they want to do as a career, kids feel pressured. They think adults want them to identify with one single career. But there are more than 40,000 job titles a person can hold. We tell kids to pick a path first. When you exit high school, there are three paths you can take. One is to the workplace. One leads to the military as a career or as a stepping stone. The third leads to more education— a professional degree, a four-year degree, or a two-year degree. They have to determine which path they'll take.

One of the main selling points about getting career education in high school is that nearly every employer wants you to have some experience before you are hired. In career tech, students are in a workplace environment and can list their time as work experience, and they'll have previous employers who can vouch for them.

Lenore Lemanski
Counselor, Technology Center
Tuscola ISD
Caro, Michigan

- Teachers work in teams to blend their usually separate disciplines and to create projects that are relevant to work and life in the real world.

Work-based learning works this way:

- Employers provide experiences for students to develop skills that are transferable (not just used for one job).

- Students have opportunities to study complex subject matter.

- Students get vital workplace skills in a hands-on, real-life environment.

- Students learn how to work in teams, solve problems, and meet employers' expectations.

Connecting activities work like this:

- School and business staff work together to provide program coordination and administration and to integrate school and work. For example, you could get help with career counseling and college placement.

What You'll Do in a School-to-Work Program

- Learn about job possibilities by shadowing existing workers in different departments and discussing work and life with adult mentors.

- Experience the workplace environment firsthand through volunteer work, internships, and paid work experiences.

- Apply academics to real tasks performed in the workplace and participate as productive employees.

- Acquire the skills necessary for successful careers.

- Formulate goals and plans for a future you probably never dreamed of.

THE NEED FOR VOCATIONAL/ CAREER EDUCATION

- Vocational/career education prepares students for 80 percent of the occupations that the U.S. Bureau of Labor Statistics predicts will account for the largest number of new jobs during the next decade.

- The fastest-growing occupations include technicians, health-care workers, skilled trade workers, retail workers, paralegals, and secretaries. You can become proficient in these occupations through career education.

- Eighty percent of all U.S. jobs don't require a college diploma but do demand skills attainable through career education.

Source: Ohio Department of Education.

Today's high-skill job market demands that when you graduate, you'll have advanced academic knowledge, up-to-date workplace skills, and training. The School-to-Work program prepares you for college, careers, and citizenship.

For more information about the School-to-Work program, ask a teacher or guidance counselor to contact a state School-to-Work Regional Coordinator or the School-to-Work Learning and Information Center at 800-251-7236 (toll-free).

THE VOCATIONAL/CAREER EDUCATION PATH

If you're looking for a more real-world education, add yourself to the nearly 11 million youths and adults who are getting a taste of the workplace through vocational and career education programs offered in high schools across the nation. These programs are designed to help you develop competency in the skills you'll need in the workplace as well as in school. (See "The Need for Vocational/ Career Education.")

What makes this kind of program different is that you learn in the classroom and in the "real world" of the workplace. Not only do you learn the academics in school, but you also get hands-on training by job shadowing, working under a mentor, and actually performing a job outside of school. Your interests and talents are usually taken into consideration, and you can choose from a variety of traditional, high-tech, and service industry training programs. Take a look at the following categories and see what peaks

your interest.

Agricultural education. These programs prepare students for careers in agricultural production, animal production and care, agribusiness, agricultural and industrial mechanics, environmental management, farming, horticulture and landscaping, food processing, and natural resource management.

Business education. Students prepare for careers in accounting and finance and computer and data processing as well as administrative/secretarial and management/supervisory positions in professional environments (banking, insurance, law, public service).

Family and consumer sciences. These programs prepare students for careers in child care, food management and production, clothing and interiors, and hospitality and facility care. Core elements include personal development, family life and planning, resource management, and nutrition and wellness.

Trade and industrial and health occupations. Students prepare for careers in such fields as auto mechanics, the construction trades, cosmetology, electronics, graphics, public safety, and welding. Health occupations programs offer vocational training for careers in dental and medical assisting, practical nursing, home health care, and medical office assisting.

Marketing education. These programs prepare individuals for careers in sales, retail, advertising, food and restaurant marketing, and hotel management.

There are many vocational/career education programs available; the kinds listed above represent only a few of the possibilities. To find a program that suits your interests and that is located near you, refer to the listing of schools in the appendix of this book. Or, you can get more information about vocational education programs by calling 202-205-5451 or e-mailing the U.S. Department of Education, Office of Vocational and Adult Education via its Web site, www.ed.gov/offices/OVAE.

THE TECH-PREP PATH

An even more advanced preparation for the workplace and/or an associate degree from a college is called tech prep. It's an educational path that combines college-prep and vocational/technical courses of study.

(Continued on page 19)

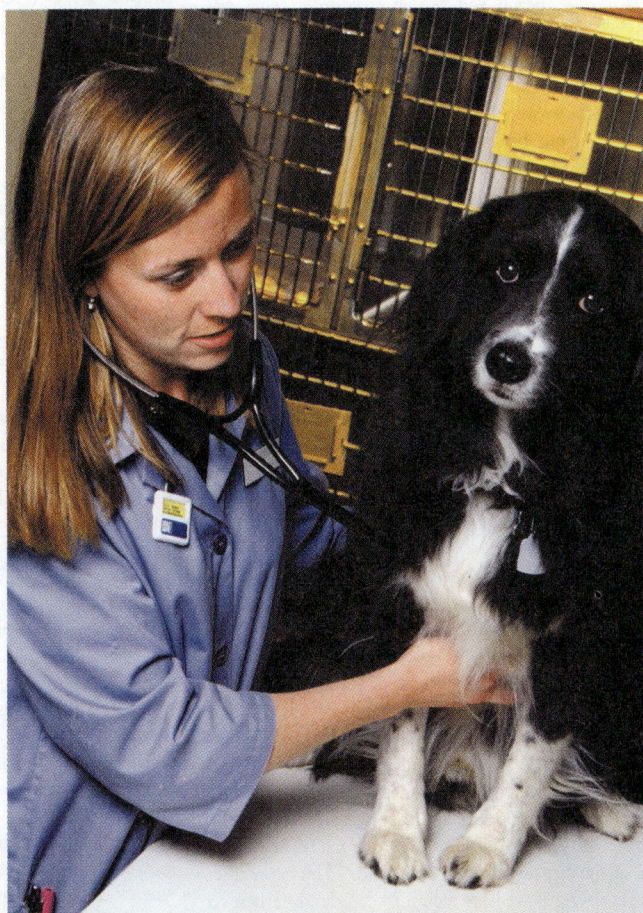

NO TIME FOR FUN

Students used to kick back when summer came. Now they're too busy beefing up their résumés.

By NADYA LABI

Once upon a time, in the land of the silver screen, summer was reserved for hanging out and making out—preferably at the beach and not in that order. That was how Gidget found her Moondoggie, how Frankie and Annette learned beach-blanket bingo and how *Grease's* Danny met a girl crazy for him. Sure, those were movies, but when Danny waxed poetic about his nights of summer loving, nobody thought, "What a slacker!"

Compare Moondoggie to Lovelle Menzie, who just completed his junior year at Morehouse College in Atlanta. As a summer intern at New York City's Chase Manhattan Bank, he plans to fit right into the city that never sleeps. "We've been told that if we are given a project at 10 a.m., it may require that we work straight through for 24 hours until it's done," says Menzie. What's more, he had to fight for those 100-hour workweeks. Wall Street internships are so prized that it's not uncommon for students to steal application materials and journal articles from college libraries to keep competitors away. And no wonder: Wall Street interns can earn up to $700 weekly, and sometimes get bonuses of $2,000 to $3,000.

The lazy hazy days of summer now bear a distressing resemblance to the rest of the year—and the rest of your life. Students who once settled for stints as lifeguards, camp counselors or Gap greeters are scrambling for career-oriented summer jobs and high-profile internships, with an eye toward boosting credentials for college admissions officers or prospective employers. These are students with enough memory of corporate downsizing to know that the job market can be ruthless, and they're dazzled enough by tales of 24-year-old Internet millionaires to realize that the fast track runs year-round. "The job market is as strong as we have seen it in decades, but there's a signal pressure—a race to be more qualified than the next person," says Philo Hutcheson, a professor of education at Georgia State University.

More than 80% of new college graduates interned at least once in their university career, according to Samer Hamadeh, co-author of *The Internship Bible*. He estimates that the number of interns has doubled in the past decade. *Peterson's Summer Opportunities for Kids & Teenagers* contains 1,800 entries this year—internships, specialized camps and summer-abroad programs—nearly twice the 1995 number. Summer-school enrollment is on the rise, as are prep courses for the SATs; the Princeton Review got so many tutoring requests in the ritzy Hamptons this year that it had to rent a summer house to accommodate all the tutors. "It's getting pretty grim out there," says Dave Berry, president of College Prep Services, Inc. "Colleges want to see that high school students aren't sitting around watching *Seinfeld* reruns all summer."

Comic relief seems to be the last thing on the mind of teens like Michael Teng, who graduated from high school in Palo Alto, Calif., and worked 40 hours a week as a computer programmer. "If you are a student who is anticipating applying to selective colleges," he says, "it really isn't acceptable to do nothing." Tony Bialorucki, 18, of Toledo, Ohio, was a caddy before trading in his golf clubs for a toolbox to help build an orphanage in Guatemala. "I didn't want to work in a mall or a restaurant," he says. "That's kind of worthless."

Some adults lament the growing intensity of kids' summertime pursuits. "I like the era of America when kids had summer off," says Frank Farley, a psychologist at Temple University in Philadelphia. "They could stare at the clouds, run, jump, explore, do the roller coasters and Ferris wheels, fall in love, backpack, hang out." Creativity, he argues—that intangible, untestable good—is enhanced by allowing adolescents to pursue their own interests.

But it doesn't much impress a corporate recruiter. Companies can save on recruitment costs by trying out potential employees over a 10-week summer period. At the investment firm Lehman Brothers, half the college students who intern after junior year become permanent employees. Says Jim Roper, a recruiter there: "They get a look at us, we get a look at them, and it works out pretty well."

That wasn't the kind of sightseeing Amanda Sandoval had in mind for her fling in New York City. A student at the University of Denver, she had planned on trips to Central Park, classes at New York University and lots of good books for her "last summer to hang out, be a kid." But after guidance counselors warned her that she had better shape up her résumé, Sandoval made a last-minute search for a job, sending off applications to the parks and recreation department, the U.N. and even the sanitation department. No luck so far, but she could always try Rockaway Beach. We checked—there's an opening for a lifeguard. ∎

During the two-year course, the focus is on blending academic and vocational/technical competencies. When you graduate from high school, you'll be able to jump right into the workforce or get an associate degree. But if you want to follow this path, you've got to plan for it starting in the ninth grade.

You can find out more about this career path by turning to the appendix at the end of this book.

USING THE SUMMER TO YOUR ADVANTAGE

When you're sitting in class, a summer with nothing to do might seem appealing. But after you've listened to all of your CDs, aced all of your video games, hung out at the same old mall, and talked to your friends on the phone about being bored, what's left? How about windsurfing on a cool, clear New England lake? Horseback riding along breathtaking mountain trails? Parlez en français in Paris? Trekking through spectacular canyon lands or living with a family in Costa Rica, Spain, Switzerland, or Japan? Exploring college majors or possible careers? Help out on an archeological dig or community-service project? Along the way, you'll meet some wonderful people and maybe even make a couple of lifelong friends.

Interested? Get ready to pack your bags and join the 1 million kids and teens who will be having the summer of a lifetime at thousands of terrific camps, academic programs, sports clinics, arts workshops, internships, volunteer opportunities, and travel adventures throughout North America and abroad.

Oh, you don't have the money, you say? Not to worry. There are programs to meet every budget, from $50 workshops to $4,500 world treks and sessions that vary in length from just a couple of days to a couple of months.

For a list of summer opportunities, take a look at the appendix in this book. You can also find out about summer opportunities by visiting www.petersons.com.

FLIP BURGERS AND LEARN ABOUT LIFE

A lot of teenagers who are anxious to earn extra cash spend their summers in retail or food service since those jobs are plentiful. If you're flipping burgers or helping customers find a special outfit, you might think the only thing you're getting out of the job is a paycheck. Think again. You will be amazed to discover that you have gained far more.

Being employed in these fields will teach you how to get along with demanding (and sometimes downright unpleasant) customers, how to work on a team, and how to handle money and order supplies. Not only do summer jobs teach you life skills, they offer ways to explore potential careers. What's more, when you apply to college or for a full-time job after high school graduation, the experience will look good on your application.

Sometimes, summer jobs become the very thing you want to do later in life. Before committing to a college major, summer jobs give you the opportunity to try out many directions. Students who think they want to be engineers, lawyers, or doctors might spend the summer shadowing an engineer, being a gofer in a legal firm, or volunteering in a hospital.

However, rather than grab the first job that comes along, find out where your interests are and build on what is natural for you. Activities you take for granted provide clues to what you are good at. What about that bookcase you built? Or those kids you love to baby-sit? Same thing with that big party you arranged. The environments you prefer provide other hints, too. Perhaps you feel best in the middle of a cluttered garage or surrounded by people. That suggests certain types of jobs.

Getting a summer job while in high school is the first step in a long line of work experiences to come. And the more experience you have, the better you'll be at getting jobs all your life.

To search for summer jobs on the Internet, visit www.petersons.com, click on the Summer Opportunities button, and follow the links to the Summer Jobs homepage.

EXPLORE VOLUNTEER AND COMMUNITY SERVICE

You've probably heard the saying that money isn't everything. Well, it's true, especially when it comes to volunteering and community service. There are a number of benefits you'll get that don't add up in dollars and cents but do add up to open doors in your future.

Community service looks good on a college application. Admissions staff members look for applicants who have volunteered and done community service in addition to grades. You could have gotten top grades, but if that's all that's on your application, you won't come across as a well-rounded person.

Community service lets you try out careers. How will you know you'll like a certain type of work if you haven't seen it done? For instance, you might think you want to work in the health-care field. Volunteering in a hospital will let you know if this is really what you want to do.

Community service is an American tradition. You'll be able to meet some of your own community's needs and join with all of the people who have contributed their talents to our country. No matter what your talents, there are unlimited ways for you to serve your community. Take a look at your interests, and then see how they can be applied to help others.

Here are some ideas to get you started:

- *Do you like kids?* Volunteer at your local parks and recreation department, for a Little League team, or as a big brother or sister.

- *Planning a career in health care?* Volunteer at a blood bank, clinic, hospital, retirement home, or hospice. There are also several organizations that raise money for disease research.

- *Interested in the environment?* Volunteer to assist in a recycling program. Create a beautification program for your school or community. Plant trees and flowers or design a community garden.

- *Just say no.* Help others stay off drugs and alcohol by volunteering at a crisis center, hotline, or prevention program. Help educate younger kids about the dangers of drug abuse.

- *Lend a hand.* Collect money, food, or clothing for the homeless. Food banks, homeless shelters, and charitable organizations need your help.

- *Is art your talent?* Share your knowledge and skills with youngsters, the elderly, or local arts organizations that depend on volunteers to help present their plays, recitals, and exhibitions.

- *Help fight crime* by forming a neighborhood watch or organizing a group to clean up graffiti.

- *Your church or synagogue may have projects that need youth volunteers.* The United Way, your local politician's office, civic groups, and special interest organizations also provide exceptional opportunities to serve your community. Ask your principal, teachers, or counselors for additional ideas.

For more information on joining in the spirit of youth volunteerism, write to the Consumer Information Center, CIC-00A, P.O. Box 100, Pueblo, Colorado 81002, and request the Catch the Spirit booklet, or call 719-948-3334. ■

PART 2

A MATTER OF PLANNING

SOME PEOPLE WAKE UP AT AGE THREE AND ANNOUNCE THAT THEY WANT TO BE DOCTORS, TEACHERS, OR MARINE BIOLOGISTS— AND THEY DO IT.

THE ROAD TO MORE EDUCATION

THEY'RE THE EXCEPTIONS. MANY HIGH SCHOOL STUDENTS DON'T HAVE A CLUE ABOUT WHAT THEY WANT TO BE. THEY DREAD THE QUESTION, "SO, WHAT ARE YOU DOING AFTER GRADUATING FROM HIGH SCHOOL?" UNFORTUNATELY, SOME OF THOSE SAME PEOPLE ALSO END UP IN CAREERS THAT DON'T SATISFY THEM.

YOU DON'T HAVE TO PLAN THE REST OF YOUR LIFE DOWN TO THE LAST DETAIL, BUT YOU CAN START TO TAKE SOME GENERAL STEPS TOWARD YOUR FUTURE AND LAY THE GROUNDWORK. THEN, WHEN YOU DO DECIDE WHAT YOU WANT TO DO, YOU'LL BE ABLE TO SEIZE HOLD OF YOUR DREAM AND GO WITH IT.

3 PLANNING YOUR EDUCATION IN HIGH SCHOOL

Some people are planners. They make a plan, and they follow it.
Then there are the non-planners.

Non-planners see the words "plan" and "future" and say, "Yeah, yeah, I know." Meanwhile they're running out the door for an appointment they were supposed to be at five minutes ago.

Unfortunately, when it comes time to really do something about those goals and future hopes, the non-planners often discover that much of what should have been done wasn't done—which is not good when they're planning their future after high school. What about those classes they should have taken? What about those jobs they should have volunteered for? What about that scholarship they could have had if only they'd found out about it sooner?

But there is hope for poor planners. Now that you've thought about yourself and the direction you might want to go after graduating, you can use this section to help you plan what you should be doing while still in high school and when you should be doing it.

Regardless of what type of education you're planning on after high school, here's a plan to help you get there.

YOUR EDUCATION TIMELINE

Use this timeline to help you make sure you're accomplishing everything you need to accomplish on time.

Ninth Grade

- As soon as you can, meet with your counselor to begin talking about colleges and careers.

- Make sure you are enrolled in the appropriate college-preparatory or tech-prep courses.

- Get off to a good start with your grades. The grades you earn in ninth grade will be included in your final high school GPA and class rank.

- College might seem a long way off now, but grades really do count toward college admission and scholarships.

- Explore your interests and possible careers. Take advantage of career day opportunities.

- Get involved in extracurricular activities (both school and non-school-sponsored).

- Talk to your parents about planning for college expenses. Continue or begin a savings plan for college.

- Look at the college information available in your counselor's office and library. Use the Internet to check out college Web sites. Visit Peterson's at www.petersons.com to start a list of colleges that might interest you.

- Tour a nearby college, if possible. Visit relatives or friends who live on or near a college campus. Check out the dorms, go to the library or student center, and get a feel for college life.

- Investigate summer enrichment programs. Visit www.petersons.com for some neat ideas about summer opportunities.

Tenth Grade

Fall

- In October, take the Preliminary SAT/National Merit Scholarship Qualifying Test (PSAT/NMSQT) for practice. When you fill out your test sheet, check the box that releases your name to colleges so you can start receiving brochures from them.

- Ask your guidance counselor about the American College Testing program's PLAN (Pre-ACT) assessment program, which helps determine your study habits and academic progress and interests. This test will prepare you for the ACT Assessment next year.

- Take geometry if you have not already done so. Take biology and a second year of a foreign language.

Parent Perspective

Q: When should parents and their children start thinking about preparing for college?

A: The discussion needs to start in middle school. If parents don't expose their children to these concepts at that time, then it can be too late in the game. Children need to take the right courses in high school. Many kids here end up going to junior colleges because they don't meet the minimum requirements when they graduate. Many universities and private colleges don't count some of the classes kids take in high school. You can't wait until the child is 18 and then say, "Maybe we should do something about getting into college."

Kevin Carr
Parent
Oak Park, California

and careers that you think you might like.

- Begin zeroing in on the type of college you would prefer (two-year or four-year, small or large, rural or urban). To get an idea of what's available, take a look at college profiles on Petersons.com or read books about college.

- Become familiar with general college entrance requirements.

- Participate in your school's or state's career development activities.

- Visit Petersons.com for advice on test taking and general college entrance requirements.

Admissions Advice

Q: Other than grades and test scores, what are the most important qualities that you look for in students?

A: We consider the types of classes students have taken. A grade of a B in an honors class is competitive to an A in a regular course. We seek not only academically talented students but those who are well rounded. They need to submit their interests and activities, letters of recommendation, and writing samples in addition to their test scores. We look for someone that's involved in his or her community and high school, someone that holds leadership positions and has a balance of activities outside of academics. This gives us a look at that person as a whole.

Cheyenna Smith
Admission Counselor
University of Houston
Houston, Texas

Winter

- Discuss your PSAT score with your counselor.

- The people who read college applications aren't looking just for grades. Get involved in activities outside the classroom. Work toward leadership positions in the activities that you like best. Become involved in community service and other volunteer activities.

- Read, read, read. Read as many books as possible from a comprehensive reading list, like the one on page 28.

- Read the newspaper every day to learn about current affairs.

- Work on your writing skills—you'll need them no matter what you do.

- Find a teacher or another adult who will advise and encourage you to write well.

Spring

- Keep your grades up so you can have the highest GPA and class rank possible.

- Ask your counselor about postsecondary enrollment options and Advanced Placement (AP) courses.

- Continue to explore your interests

Parent Perspective

Q: How involved should parents get in the selection of a college for their children?

A: Parents are getting more involved than ever before in supporting their children in the college process. This phenomenon is due to two factors:

This generation of parents has been much more involved with their children in dealing with the outside world than were their parents.

The investment made by today's parents is much more than that made by parents 20 or 30 years ago. As parents focus on the cost of this big-ticket item, there's interest to be more involved, to get the proper return.

Parents certainly should be involved in the college selection and application process. Studies clearly indicate that parental support in this process and throughout the college years can make a big difference in the success of a student. But this process also should be a learning opportunity in decision making for students. In that regard, parents shouldn't direct the student but provide input and the framework to assist their students.

Parents should not feel uncomfortable making suggestions to help their children through the thought and selection process—especially when it comes to identifying schools that their pocketbooks can accommodate. However, the child must be comfortable with the final decision and must have ultimate responsibility for the selection of the school. When students have made the final decision, it can help in their level of commitment because they've invested in it. They have a responsibility to do well and complete their academics at that location.

Richard Flaherty
President
College Parents of America
www.collegeparents.org

- If you are interested in attending a military academy such as West Point or Annapolis, now is the time to start planning and getting information.

- Write to colleges and ask for their academic requirements for admission.

- Visit a few more college campuses. Read all of the mail you receive from colleges. You may see something you like.

- Attend college fairs.

- Keep putting money away for college. Get a summer job.

- Consider taking SAT II Subject Tests in the courses you took this year while the material is still fresh in your mind. These tests are offered in May and June.

Eleventh Grade

Fall

- Meet with your counselor to review the courses you've taken, and see what you still need to take.

- Check your class rank. Even if your grades haven't been that good so far, it's never too late to improve. Colleges like to see an upward trend.

- If you didn't do so in tenth grade, sign up for and take the PSAT/NMSQT. In addition to National Merit Scholarships, this is the qualifying test for the National Scholarship Service and Fund for Negro Students and the National Hispanic Scholar Recognition Program.

- Make sure that you have a social security number.

- Take a long, hard look at why you want to continue your education after high school so you will be able to choose the best college or university for your needs.

- Make a list of colleges that meet your most important criteria (size, location, distance from home, majors, academic rigor, housing, and cost). Weigh each of the factors according to their importance to you.

- Continue visiting college fairs. You may be able to narrow your choices or add a college to your list.

- Speak to college representatives who visit your high school.

- If you want to participate in Division I or Division II sports in college, start the certification process. Check with your counselor to make sure you are taking a core curriculum that meets NCAA requirements.

- If you are interested in one of the military academies, talk to your guidance counselor about starting the application process now.

Winter

- Collect information about college application procedures, entrance requirements, tuition and fees, room and board costs, student activities, course offerings, faculty composition, accreditation, and financial aid. The Internet is a good way to visit colleges and obtain this information. Begin comparing the schools by the factors that you consider to be most important.

- Discuss your PSAT score with your counselor.

- Begin narrowing down your college choices. Find out if the colleges you are interested in require the SAT I, ACT Assessment, or SAT II Subject Tests for admission.

- Register for the SAT I and additional SAT II Subject Tests, which are offered several times during the winter and spring of your junior year (see the "Tackling the Tests" section for a schedule). You can take them again in the fall of your senior year if you are unhappy with your scores.

- Register for the ACT Assessment, which is usually taken in April or June. You can take it again late in your junior year or in the fall of your senior year, if necessary.

- Begin preparing for the tests

SUGGESTED COURSES

COLLEGE-PREPARATORY CURRICULUM

English. Four units, with emphasis on composition (English 9, 10, 11, 12)

Mathematics. Three units (algebra I, algebra II, geometry) are essential. Trigonometry, precalculus, calculus, and computer science are recommended for some fields of study.

Social Science. Three units (American history, world history, government/economics)

Science. Four units (earth science, biology, chemistry, physics)

Foreign Language. Three units (at least 2 years in the same language)

Fine Arts. One to 2 units

Other. Keyboarding, computer applications, computer science I, computer science II, physical education, health

COLLEGE-PREPARATORY CURRICULUM COMBINED WITH A CAREER EDUCATION OR VOCATIONAL PROGRAM

English. Four units

Mathematics. Three units (algebra I, algebra II, geometry)

Social Science. Three units (American history, world history, government/economics)

Science. Two units (earth science, biology)

Foreign Language. Three units (at least 2 years in the same language)

Fine Arts. One to 2 units

Other. Keyboarding, computer applications, physical education, and health and half-days at the Career Center during junior and senior year.

you've decided to take.

- Have a discussion with your parents about the colleges in which you are interested. Examine financial resources, and gather information about financial aid. Visit Petersons.com for a step-by-step explanation of the financial aid process.

- Set up a filing system with individual folders for each college's correspondence and printed materials.

Spring

- Meet with your counselor to review senior-year course selection and graduation requirements.

- Discuss ACT Assessment/SAT I scores with your counselor. Register to take the ACT Assessment and/or SAT I again if you'd like to try to increase your score.

- Discuss the college essay with your guidance counselor or English teacher. Visit Petersons. com for articles on writing college essays.

- Stay involved with your extracurricular activities. Colleges look for consistency and depth in activities.

- Consider whom you will ask to write your recommendations. Think about asking teachers who know you well and who will write positive letters about you. Letters from a coach, activity leader, or an adult who knows you well outside of school (e.g., volunteer work contact) are also valuable.

- Inquire about personal interviews at your favorite colleges. Call or write for early summer appointments. Make necessary travel arrangements.

- See your counselor to apply for on-campus summer programs for high school students. Apply for a summer job. Be prepared to pay for college application, financial aid, and testing fees in the fall.

- Request applications from schools you're interested in by mail or via the Internet.

Summer

- Visit the campuses of your top-five college choices.

- After each college interview, send a thank-you letter to the interviewer.

- Talk to people you know who have attended the colleges in which you are interested.

- Continue to read books, magazines, and newspapers.

- Practice filling out college applications, and then type the final application forms or apply on line through the Web sites of the colleges in which you're interested.

- Volunteer in your community.

- Compose rough drafts of your college essays. Have a teacher read and discuss them with you. Polish them, and prepare final drafts. Proofread your final essays at least three times.

- Develop a financial aid application plan, including a list of the aid sources, requirements for each application, and a timetable for meeting the filing deadlines.

Twelfth Grade

Fall

- Continue to take a full course load of college-prep courses.

- Keep working on your grades. Make sure you have taken the courses necessary to graduate in the spring.

- Continue to participate in extracurricular and volunteer activities. Demonstrate initiative, creativity, commitment, and leadership in each.

- To male students: you must register for selective service on your eighteenth birthday to be eligible for federal and state financial aid.

- Talk to counselors, teachers, and parents about your final college choices.

- Make a calendar showing application deadlines for admission, financial aid, and scholarships.
- Check resource books, computer programs, and your guidance office for information on scholarships and grants. Ask colleges about scholarships for which you may qualify. Check out Petersons.com for information on scholarships.
- Give recommendation forms to the teachers you have chosen, along with stamped, self-addressed envelopes so your teachers can send them directly to the colleges. Be sure to fill out your name, address, and school name on the top of the form. Talk to your recommendation writers about your goals and ambitions.
- Give School Report forms to your high school's guidance office. Fill in your name, address, and any other required information on top. Verify with your guidance counselor the schools to which transcripts, test scores, and letters are to be sent. Give your counselor any necessary forms at least two weeks before they are due or whenever your counselor's deadline is, whichever is earlier.
- Register for and take the ACT Assessment, SAT I, or SAT II Subject Tests, as necessary.
- Be sure you have requested (either by mail or on line) that your test scores be sent to the colleges of your choice.
- Mail or send electronically any college applications for early decision admission by November 1.
- If possible, visit colleges while classes are in session.
- If you plan to apply for an ROTC scholarship, remember that your application is due by December 1.
- Print extra copies or make photocopies of every application you send.

Winter

- Attend whatever college-preparatory nights are held at your school or by local organizations.
- Send midyear grade reports to colleges. Continue to focus on your schoolwork!
- Fill out the Free Application for Federal Student Aid (FAFSA) and, if necessary, the Financial Aid Profile (FAP). These forms can be obtained from your guidance counselor or at www.ed.gov/offices/OPE/express.html to download the forms or to file electronically. These forms may not be processed before January 1, so don't send it before then.
- Mail or send electronically any remaining applications and financial aid forms before winter break. Make sure you apply to at least one college that you know you can afford and where you know you will be accepted.
- Follow up to make sure that the colleges have received all application information, including recommendations and test scores.
- Meet with your counselor to verify that all applicable forms are in order and have been sent out to colleges.

Spring

- Watch your mail between March 1 and April 1 for acceptance notifications from colleges.
- Watch your mail for notification of financial aid awards between April 1 and May 1.
- Compare the financial aid packages from the colleges and universities that have accepted you.
- Make your final choice, and notify all schools of your intent by May 1. If possible, do not decide without making at least one campus visit. Send your nonrefundable deposit to your chosen school by May 1 as well.

- Request that your guidance counselor send a final transcript to the college in June.
- Be sure that you have received a FAFSA acknowledgment.
- If you applied for a Pell Grant (on the FAFSA), you will receive a Student Aid Report (SAR) statement. Review this Pell notice, and forward it to the college you plan to attend. Make a copy for your records.
- Complete follow-up paperwork for the college of your choice (scheduling, orientation session, housing arrangements, and other necessary forms).

Summer

- If applicable, apply for a Stafford Loan (formerly Guaranteed Student Loan) through a lender. Allow eight weeks for processing.
- Receive the orientation schedule from your college.
- Get residence hall assignment from your college.
- Obtain course scheduling and cost information from your college.
- Congratulations! You are about to begin the greatest adventure of your life. Good luck.

CLASSES TO TAKE IF YOU'RE GOING TO COLLEGE

Did you know that classes you take as early as the ninth grade will help you get into college? Make sure you take at least the minimum high school curriculum requirements necessary for college admission. Even if you don't plan to enter college immediately, take the most demanding courses you can handle.

Review the list of suggested courses on page 26. Some courses, categories, and names might vary from state to state, but the following may be used as a guideline. Talk with your guidance

(Continued on page 30)

SUGGESTED READING LIST FOR GRADES 9 THROUGH 12

Instead of flipping on the TV or putting on those headphones, how about picking up a book instead? Reading not only will take you to wonderful, unexplored worlds in your imagination, but there are practical reasons as well. Reading gives you a more well-rounded background. College admissions and future employers pick up on that. And you'll be able to answer the questions, "Did you read that book? What did you think of it?" How many of the books on this list have you read?

ADAMS, RICHARD
Watership Down

AESOP
Fables

AGEE, JAMES
A Death in the Family

ANDERSON, SHERWOOD
Winesburg, Ohio

ANONYMOUS
Go Ask Alice

ASIMOV, ISAAC
Short Stories

AUSTEN, JANE
Emma
Northanger Abbey
Pride and Prejudice
Sense and Sensibility

BALDWIN, JAMES
Go Tell It on the Mountain

BALZAC, HONORE DE
Pere Goriot

BECKETT, SAMUEL
Waiting for Godot

BOLT, ROBERT
A Man for All Seasons

BRONTË, CHARLOTTE
Jane Eyre

BRONTË, EMILY
Wuthering Heights

BROOKS, GWENDOLYN
In the Mecca
Riot

BROWNING, ROBERT
Poems

BUCK, PEARL
The Good Earth

BUTLER, SAMUEL
The Way of All Flesh

CAMUS, ALBERT
The Plague
The Stranger

CATHER, WILLA
Death Comes for the Archbishop
My Antonia

CERVANTES, MIGUEL
Don Quixote

CHAUCER, GEOFFREY
The Canterbury Tales

CHEKHOV, ANTON
The Cherry Orchard

CHOPIN, KATE
The Awakening

COLLINS, WILKIE
The Moonstone

CONRAD, JOSEPH
Heart of Darkness
Lord Jim
The Secret Sharer
Victory

CRANE, STEPHEN
The Red Badge of Courage

DANTE
The Divine Comedy

DEFOE, DANIEL
Moll Flanders

DICKENS, CHARLES
Bleak House
David Copperfield
Great Expectations
Hard Times
Oliver Twist
A Tale of Two Cities

DICKINSON, EMILY
Poems

DINESEN, ISAK
Out of Africa

DOSTOEVSKI, FYODOR
The Brothers Karamazov
Crime and Punishment

DOUGLAS, FREDERICK
The Life of Frederick Douglas

DREISER, THEODORE
An American Tragedy
Sister Carrie

EARLY, GERALD
Tuxedo Junction

ELIOT, GEORGE
Adam Bede
Middlemarch
The Mill on the Floss
Silas Marner

ELIOT, T. S.
Murder in the Cathedral

ELLISON, RALPH
Invisible Man

EMERSON, RALPH WALDO
Essays

FAULKNER, WILLIAM
Absalom, Absalom!
As I Lay Dying
Intruder in the Dust
Light in August
The Sound and the Fury

FIELDING, HENRY
Joseph Andrews
Tom Jones

FITZGERALD, F. SCOTT
The Great Gatsby
Tender Is the Night

FLAUBERT, GUSTAVE
Madame Bovary

FORSTER, E. M.
A Passage to India
A Room with a View

FRANKLIN, BENJAMIN
The Autobiography of Benjamin Franklin

GALSWORTHY, JOHN
The Forsyte Saga

GOLDING, WILLIAM
Lord of the Flies

GOLDSMITH, OLIVER
She Stoops to Conquer

GRAVES, ROBERT
I, Claudius

GREENE, GRAHAM
The Heart of the Matter
The Power and the Glory

HAMILTON, EDITH
Mythology

HARDY, THOMAS
Far From the Madding Crowd
Jude the Obscure
The Mayor of Casterbridge
The Return of the Native
Tess of the D'Urbervilles

HAWTHORNE, NATHANIEL
The House of the Seven Gables
The Scarlet Letter

HEMINGWAY, ERNEST
A Farewell to Arms
For Whom the Bell Tolls
The Sun Also Rises

HENRY, O.
Stories

HERSEY, JOHN
A Single Pebble

HESSE, HERMANN
Demian
Siddhartha
Steppenwolf

HOMER
The Iliad
The Odyssey

HUGHES, LANGSTON
Poems
The Big Sea

HUGO, VICTOR
Les Misérables

HUXLEY, ALDOUS
Brave New World

IBSEN, HENRIK
A Doll's House
An Enemy of the People
Ghosts
Hedda Gabler
The Master Builder
The Wild Duck

JAMES, HENRY
The American
Daisy Miller
Portrait of a Lady
The Turn of the Screw

JOYCE, JAMES
Dubliners
*A Portrait of the Artist as a
    Young Man*

KAFKA, FRANZ
The Castle
The Metamorphosis
The Trial

KEATS, JOHN
Poems

KEROUAC, JACK
On the Road

KOESTLER, ARTHUR
Darkness at Noon

LAWRENCE, JEROME, AND ROBERT
E. LEE
Inherit the Wind

LEWIS, SINCLAIR
Arrowsmith
Babbitt
Main Street

LLEWELLYN, RICHARD
*How Green Was My
    Valley*

MACHIAVELLI
The Prince

MACLEISH, ARCHIBALD
J.B.

MANN, THOMAS
Buddenbrooks
The Magic Mountain

MARLOWE, CHRISTOPHER
Dr. Faustus

MAUGHAM, SOMERSET
Of Human Bondage

MCCULLERS, CARSON
The Heart Is a Lonely Hunter

MELVILLE, HERMAN
Billy Budd
Moby-Dick
Typee

MILLER, ARTHUR
The Crucible
Death of a Salesman

MONSARRAT, NICHOLAS
The Cruel Sea

NAYLOR, GLORIA
Bailey's Cafe
*The Women of Brewster
    Place*

O'NEILL, EUGENE
The Emperor Jones
Long Day's Journey Into Night
Mourning Becomes Electra

ORWELL, GEORGE
Animal Farm
1984

PASTERNAK, BORIS
Doctor Zhivago

POE, EDGAR ALLAN
Short Stories

REMARQUE, ERICH
All Quiet on the Western Front

ROLVAAG, O. E.
Giants in the Earth

ROSTAND, EDMOND
Cyrano de Bergerac

SALINGER, J. D.
The Catcher in the Rye

SANDBURG, CARL
*Abraham Lincoln:
    The Prairie Years*
*Abraham Lincoln: The War
    Years*

SAROYAN, WILLIAM
The Human Comedy
SAYERS, DOROTHY
The Nine Tailors

SHAKESPEARE, WILLIAM
Plays and Sonnets

SHAW, GEORGE BERNARD
Arms and the Man
Major Barbara
Pygmalion
Saint Joan

SHERIDAN, RICHARD B.
The School for Scandal

SHUTE, NEVIL
On the Beach

SINCLAIR, UPTON
The Jungle

SOPHOCLES
Antigone
Oedipus Rex

STEINBECK, JOHN
East of Eden
The Grapes of Wrath
Of Mice and Men

STOWE, HARRIET BEECHER
Uncle Tom's Cabin

SWIFT, JONATHAN
Gulliver's Travels

THACKERAY, WILLIAM M.
Vanity Fair

THOREAU, HENRY DAVID
Walden

TOLSTOY, LEO
Anna Karenina
War and Peace

TROLLOPE, ANTHONY
Barchester Towers

TURGENEV, IVAN
Fathers and Sons

TWAIN, MARK
Pudd'nhead Wilson

UPDIKE, JOHN
Rabbit, Run

VERGIL
The Aeneid

VOLTAIRE
Candide

WALKER, ALICE
The Color Purple
Meridian

WARREN, ROBERT PENN
All the King's Men

WAUGH, EVELYN
Brideshead Revisited
A Handful of Dust

WHARTON, EDITH
The Age of Innocence

WHITE, T. H.
The Once and Future King
The Sword in the Stone

WILDE, OSCAR
*The Importance of Being
    Earnest*
The Picture of Dorian Gray

WILDER, THORNTON
Our Town

WILLIAMS, TENNESSEE
The Glass Menagerie
A Streetcar Named Desire

WOLFE, THOMAS
Look Homeward, Angel

WOOLF, VIRGINIA
Mrs. Dalloway
To the Lighthouse

WOUK, HERMAN
The Caine Mutiny

WRIGHT, RICHARD
Black Boy
Native Sun

*Source: The National Endowment for
the Humanities.*
*For more book recommendations, see
what college professors suggest in
Arco's Reading Lists for College-Bound
Students, available at your local bookstore.*

counselor to select the curriculum that best meets your needs and skills.

Of course, learning also occurs outside of school. While outside activities will not make up for poor academic performance, skills learned from jobs, extracurricular activities, and volunteer opportunities will help you become a well-rounded student and will strengthen your college or job application.

Getting a Head Start on College Courses

You can take college courses while still in high school so that when you're in college, you'll be ahead of everyone else. The formal name is postsecondary enrollment. What it means is that some students can take college courses and receive both high school and college credit for the courses taken. It's like a two-for-one deal!

Postsecondary enrollment is designed to provide an opportunity for qualified high school students to experience more advanced academic work. Participation in a postsecondary enrollment program is not intended to replace courses available in high school but to enhance the educational opportunities available to students while in high school. There are two options for postsecondary enrollment:

Option A: Qualified high school juniors and seniors take courses for college credit. Students enrolled under Option A must pay for all books, supplies, tuition, and associated fees.

Option B: Qualified high school juniors and seniors take courses for high school and college credit. For students enrolled under this option, the local school district covers the related costs, provided that the student completes the selected courses. Otherwise, the student and parent will be assessed the costs.

Certain preestablished conditions must be met for enrollment, so check with your high school counselor for more information. ■

TACKLING THE TESTS

Unless you've been on another planet for the last two or three years, you've probably heard older high school students buzzing about the alphabet soup list of college entrance exams—SAT, ACT, and PSAT.

Some of the students who are getting ready to take one of these tests look like they're in various shades of hysteria. Others have been studying for months on end, so when they open their mouths, out pops the definition for "meretricious" or the answer to "What is the ratio of 3 pounds to 6 ounces?" Well, the talk that you've heard about the tests is partly true. They are a big deal and can be crucial to your academic plans. On the other hand, you don't have to walk in cold. Remember that word "planning"? It's a whole lot nicer than the word "panic." Preparing for the tests takes a lot of planning and time, but if you're reading this section, you're already ahead of the game.

A FEW FACTS ABOUT THE MAJOR TESTS

The major standardized tests students take in high school are the PSAT, SAT I, and ACT Assessment. Colleges across the country use them to get a sense of a student's readiness to enter their ivy-covered halls. These tests, or "boards" as they are sometimes called, have become notorious because of how important they can be. There is a mystique that surrounds them. People talk about the "magic number" that will get you into the school of your dreams.

Beware! There is a lot of misinformation out there. First and foremost, these are not intelligence tests; they are reasoning tests designed to evaluate the way you think. These tests assess the basic knowledge and skills you have gained through your classes in school, and they also gauge the knowledge you have gained through outside experience. The material on these tests is not curriculum-based, but the tests do emphasize those academic experiences that educational institutions feel are good indicators of your probable success in college.

ANSWERING YOUR QUESTIONS

Before you go any further, students who have gone through this process have already asked a lot of questions about the standardized tests. Here are answers to some commonly asked questions.

What Is the ACT Assessment?

The ACT Assessment is a standardized college entrance examination that measures knowledge and skills in English, mathematics, reading, and science reasoning and the application of these skills to future academic tasks. The ACT Assessment consists of four multiple-choice tests.

Test 1: English

- 75 questions, 45 minutes
- Punctuation
- Grammar and usage
- Sentence structure
- Strategy
- Organization
- Style

Test 2: Mathematics

- 60 questions, 60 minutes
- Pre-algebra
- Elementary algebra
- Intermediate algebra
- Coordinate geometry
- Plane geometry
- Trigonometry

Test 3: Reading

- 40 questions, 35 minutes
- Prose fiction
- Humanities
- Social studies
- Natural sciences

(Continued on page 33)

An Excuse to Mention My 1480 SAT Score

By JOEL STEIN

I had always heard that your 20s are your most fertile creative time; few people have accomplished anything great after 30—not Einstein, not Newton, not Linda Lovelace. Now I know it's true. At the age of 29, I have tabled all ambitions to write a novel, play or episode of *JAG*. Even my planned autobiography, *A Mildly Amusing Work of Limited Intellect*, has been set aside.

To verify my deterioration, I signed up to take the SATs again so I could objectively compare my current self with my old, quite impressive, high school self, who got a score of 1480. Anyone can sign up online, as long as he can come up with creative answers like "24th grade." I vowed to beat my 1480 without any preparation whatsoever, unless you consider that the SATs are designed to measure your preparedness for college and I had four years under my belt. But I wouldn't do any extra studying to beat my original score, which I should mention was a 1480.

I showed up at Xavier High School 15 minutes early on Saturday morning, which meant lots of time to be stared at by 17-year-olds. I felt creepy, like some intellectual pedophile. Actually, I felt like a real pedophile, but I tried to make myself feel better with the intellectual part.

Eventually I was ushered into a small room, where I was not only older than all the other test takers but also older than the teacher monitoring the test. A large carving of Jesus hung above the blackboard, and a copy of TIME magazine, in which I'm pretty sure I mentioned masturbating, lay on a desk. I was sure I was going to hell.

As I had hoped, I breezed through the verbal section, in which the hardest vocabulary word was "megalomania," which I had no trouble whatsoever defining. And the math section, which I had feared, didn't have any

tangents or cosines and gave you all the geometry formulas you needed. I never even had to go to my third No. 2 pencil. I felt far more confident than the first time around, when I actually got a 1480.

> "To verify my deterioration, I signed up to take the SATs again so I could objectively compare my current self with my old, quite impressive, high school self, who got a score of 1480."

For the next three weeks, I bragged about how well I did, weakly hiding behind the first-person plural and pop sociology. "It turns out we are so much smarter than we were in high school," I'd say. "Not only our vocabulary but also our reasoning skills have developed exponentially." With everyone I talked to, I seemed to strike some hidden nerve, revealing that not only do most people harbor a secret desire to retake the SATs but they also dislike being around me.

Then I got my scores back. I did indeed land a perfect 800 in verbal, but I got a 650 in math, for a total of 1450. Worse yet, the College Board rigged the system in 1995, so my score would have been worth only 1430 in 1988. My brain had deteriorated nearly 5%, which is all you really use of your brain anyway. So really, more like 100%. You can see why I struggled on the math section.

At 17, certain I had blown my SATs, I kept quiet about my test performance until I got my scores back. So while my brave experiment did confirm that now I am indeed dumber, it also revealed that I am much cockier. And that, I have learned in my brief working career, is a far more important predictor of success than intelligence. ∎

Test 4: Science Reasoning

- 40 questions, 35 minutes
- Biology
- Physical science
- Chemistry
- Physics

Each section is scored from 1 to 36 and is scaled for slight variations in difficulty. Students are not penalized for incorrect responses. The composite score is the average of the four scaled scores.

To prepare for the ACT Assessment, ask your guidance counselor for a free guidebook called Preparing for the ACT Assessment. Besides providing general test-preparation information and additional test-taking strategies, this guidebook describes the content and format of the four ACT Assessment subject area tests, summarizes test administration procedures followed at ACT Assessment test centers, and includes a practice test.

What Is the PLAN?

The PLAN is an instrument designed for sophomores to help guide them in their postsecondary planning. The test measures the same academic skills as the ACT Assessment (English, mathematics, reading, and science reasoning) but measures them at the tenth-grade level. The PLAN includes an interest inventory, a study-skills assessment, an educational/occupational planning section, and a student-needs profile. The PLAN also provides the student with an estimated ACT composite score range. Students can use the skills diagnosis section to focus on academic weaknesses that need attention before taking the ACT.

Achievement tests

- 120 questions, 1 hour 55 minutes
- Writing skills test
- Mathematics test

- Reading test
- Science reasoning test

Nonacademic sections

- 120 items, 50 minutes
- Interest inventory
- High school course information
- Educational/occupational plans
- Needs assessment profile

What Is the SAT I?

The SAT I measures developed verbal and mathematical reasoning abilities as they relate to successful performance in college. It is intended to supplement the secondary school record and other information about the student in assessing readiness for college. There is one unscored, experimental section on the exam, which is used for equating and/or pretesting purposes, and can cover either the mathematics or verbal subject area.

Verbal Reasoning

- 78 questions, 75 minutes
- Analogies
- Sentence completions
- Critical reading passages

Mathematical Reasoning

- 60 questions, 75 minutes
- Student-produced responses

- Quantitative comparisons
- Regular math
- Experimental Section
- 30 minutes

Students receive one point for each correct response and lose a fraction of a point for each incorrect response (except for student-produced responses). These points are totaled to produce the raw scores, which are then scaled to equalize the scores for slight variations in difficulty for various editions of the test. Both the verbal scaled score range and the math scaled score range are from 200 to 800. The total scaled score range is from 400 to 1600.

To prepare for the SAT I, check out www.GetA1600.com, a Web site with over 1,000 practice questions and tips. You should carefully review "Taking the SAT I: Reasoning Test" (you can get this pamphlet from your guidance counselor or through the College Board at www.collegeboard.com) and know the content of the test. Also, most libraries and bookstores stock a large selection of material about the SAT I and other standardized tests.

What Is the PSAT/NMSQT?

The Preliminary SAT/National Merit Scholarship Qualifying Test, better known as the PSAT/NMSQT, is a practice test for the SAT I. Many

RECOMMENDED TEST-TAKING DATES

SOPHOMORE YEAR	
October	PSAT/NMSQT and PLAN *For practice, planning, and preparation*
May–June	SAT II Subject Tests (if necessary)
JUNIOR YEAR	
October	PSAT/NMSQT *For the National Merit Scholarship Program and practice*
January–June	ACT and/or SAT I, SAT II Subject Tests (if necessary) *For college admission*
SENIOR YEAR	
October–December	ACT and/or SAT I, SAT II Subject Tests (if necessary) *For college admission*

students take the PSAT more than once because scores tend to increase with repetition and because it allows students to become more comfortable with taking standardized tests. During the junior year, the PSAT is also used as a qualifying test for the National Merit Scholarship Program and the National Scholarship Service and Fund for Negro Students. It is also used in designating students for the National Hispanic Scholar Recognition Program. The PSAT includes a writing skills section, which consists entirely of multiple-choice questions. This section does not appear on the SAT.

Verbal Reasoning

- Approximately 50 questions, two 25-minute sections
- Analogies
- Sentence completion
- Critical reading passages

Mathematical Reasoning

- 40 questions, two 25-minute sections
- Student-produced responses
- Quantitative comparisons
- Regular math

Writing Skills

- 39 questions, one 30-minute section
- Identifying sentence errors
- Improving sentences
- Improving paragraphs

Students receive a score in each content area (verbal, math, and writing). Each score ranges from 20 to 80 and is totaled with the others for the combined score. The total score ranges from 60 to 240.

Selection Index (used for National Merit Scholarship purposes)

- Verbal + Math + Writing
- Score Range: 60 to 240
- Mean Junior Score: 147

National Merit Scholarship Program

- Semifinalist Status: Selection
- Index of 201 to 222
- Commended Student: Selection Index of 199

Admissions Advice

Q: What can students who don't have the best of grades do to improve their chances of getting into the college of their choice?

A: We encourage students to take the SAT or ACT more than once and see how they do. There are options for students who may not meet the academic requirements because they've had to work or are gifted in other areas, such as art or athletics, or who perhaps have been through something tragic. We ask them to submit letters or recommendations, a personal statement, and any other documentation that might help support their cases. What were the factors that affected their grades? What else can they offer the university?

We often encourage students who still may not meet the requirements to start at a community college and then transfer. We'll look at their college credit vs. their high school credit. They can prove to us that they can handle a college curriculum.

Cheyenna Smith
Admission Counselor
University of Houston
Houston, Texas

AVERAGE TEST SCORES FOR COLLEGE-BOUND SENIORS IN 2000

SAT I Verbal	505
SAT I Math	514
SAT I Overall	1019
ACT English	20.5
ACT Math	20.7
ACT Reading	21.4
ACT Science Reasoning	21.0
ACT Composite	21.0

Should I Take the ACT or the SAT I?

It's not a bad idea to take both. This assures that you will have the test scores required for admission to all schools, because some colleges accept the results of one test and not the other. Some institutions use test results for proper placement of students in English and math courses.

You should take the ACT and SAT I during the spring of your junior year, if not earlier. This enables you to retake the test in the fall of your senior year if you're not satisfied with your scores. Also, this makes it possible for institutions to receive all test scores before the end of January. Institutions generally consider the better score when determining admission and placement. Because most scholarship applications are processed between December and April of the senior year, your best score results can then be included in the application.

What Are the SAT II Subject Tests?

Subject Tests are required by some institutions for admission and/or placement in freshman-level courses. Each Subject Test measures one's knowledge of a specific subject and the ability to apply that knowledge. Students should check with each institution for its specific requirements. In general, students are required to take three Subject Tests (one English, one mathematics, and one of their choice).

Subject Tests are given in the following areas: writing, literature, U.S. history, world history, mathematics level IC, mathematics level IIC, biology E/M, chemistry, physics, French–reading only, French with listening, German–reading only, German with listening, Spanish–reading only, Spanish with listening, Italian–reading only, modern Hebrew–reading only, Latin–reading only, Chinese with listening, Japanese with listening, Korean with listening, and English language proficiency. These tests are 1 hour long and are primarily multiple-choice tests. Three SAT II Subject Tests may be taken on one test date.

Scored like the SAT I, students gain a point for each correct answer and lose a fraction of a point for each incorrect answer. The raw scores are then converted to scaled scores that range from 200 to 800.

What Is the TOEFL Test?

The Test of English as a Foreign Language (TOEFL) is designed to help assess a student's grasp of English if it is not the student's first language. Performance on the TOEFL Test may help interpret scores on the verbal section of the SAT I. The 3-hour test consists of four sections: listening comprehension, structure and written expression, reading comprehension, and a writing section. The test is given at more than 1,260 centers in 180 countries and is administered by Educational Testing Service (ETS). For further information, visit www.toefl.org.

What Other Tests Should I Know About?

The AP Program. This program allows high school students to try college-level work and build valuable skills and study habits in the process. Subject matter is explored in more depth in AP courses than in other high school classes. A qualifying score on an AP test—which varies from school to school—can earn you college credit or advanced placement. Getting qualifying grades on enough exams can even earn you a full year's credit and sophomore standing at more than 1,400 higher-education institutions. There are currently thirty-two AP courses in eighteen different subject areas, including art, biology, and computer science. Speak to your guidance counselor for information about your school's offerings.

College-Level Examination Program (CLEP). The CLEP enables students to earn college credit for what they already know, whether it was learned in school, through independent study, or through other experiences outside of the classroom. More than 2,800 colleges and universities now award credit for qualifying scores on one or more of the 34 CLEP exams. The exams, which are 90 minutes in length and are primarily multiple-choice, are administered at participating colleges and universities. For more information, check out the Web site at www.collegeboard.com/clep.

Armed Services Vocational Aptitude

WHAT DOES IT TAKE TO GET IN?

COLLEGE ADMISSION POLICY	CLASS RANK	AVERAGE ACT RANGE (1–36)	AVERAGE SAT RANGE (400–1600)
Highly selective	Top 10% of class, very strong academic record	27–31	1220–1380
Selective	Top 25% of class, strong academic record	22–27	1150–1230
Traditional	Top 50% of class, good academic record	20–23	950–1070
Liberal	Many accepted from lower half of class	18–21	870–990
Open	All accepted to limit of capacity	17–20	830–950

Battery (ASVAB). ASVAB is a career exploration program consisting of a multi-aptitude test battery that helps students explore their interests, abilities, and personal preferences. A career exploration workbook gives students information about the world of work, and a career information resource book helps students match their personal characteristics to the working world. Finally, an occupational outlook handbook describes in detail approximately 250 civilian and military occupations. Students can use ASVAB scores for military enlistment up to two years after they take the test. A student can take the ASVAB as a sophomore, junior, or senior, but students cannot use their sophomore scores to enter the armed forces. Ask your guidance counselor or your local recruiting office for more information. Also, see section 10 of *GAJ*, "Other Options After High School."

General Educational Development (GED) Test. If you have not completed your high school education, you may earn an equivalence by taking the GED test, sponsored by your state Department of Education. However, taking the GED test is not a legitimate reason for dropping out of school. In fact, it is more difficult to get into the armed services with only a GED, and some employees have difficulty getting promoted without a high school diploma.

You're eligible to take the GED if you are not enrolled in high school, have not yet graduated from high school, are at least 16 years old, and meet your local requirements regarding age, residency, and length of time since leaving school.

There are five sections to the GED test, covering writing skills, social studies, science, interpreting literature and the arts, and mathematics. Part II of the Writing Skills Test requires writing an essay. The GED costs an average of $35 but can vary from state to state, and the application fee may be waived under certain circumstances. You should

contact your local GED office to arrange to take the exam. Call 800-62-MYGED to find your local GED office and for more information.

What Can I Do to Prepare for These Tests?

Know what to expect. Get familiar with how the tests are structured, how much time is allowed, and the directions for each type of question. Get plenty of rest the night before the test and eat breakfast that morning.

There are a variety of products, from books to software to videos, available to help you prepare for most standard tests. Find the learning style that suits you best. As for which products to buy, there are two major categories—those created by the test makers and those created by private companies. The best approach is to talk to someone who has been through the process and find out which product or products he or she recommends.

Some students report significant increases in scores after participating in coaching programs. Longer-term programs (40 hours) seem to raise scores more than short-term programs (20 hours), but beyond 40 hours, score gains are minor. Math scores appear to benefit more from coaching than verbal scores.

Preparation Resources

There are a variety of ways to prepare for standardized tests—find a method that fits your schedule and your budget. But you should definitely prepare. Far too many students walk into these tests cold, either because they find standardized tests frightening or annoying or they just haven't found the time to study. The key is that these exams are standardized. That means these tests are largely the same from administration to administration; they always test the same concepts. They have to, or else you couldn't compare the scores of people who took the tests on different dates. The numbers or words may change, but the underlying content doesn't.

So how do you prepare? At the very least, you should review relevant material, such as math formulas and commonly tested vocabulary words, and know the directions for each question type or test section. You should take at least one practice test and review your mistakes so you don't make them again on test day. Beyond that, you know best how much preparation you need. Visit www.petersons.com for resources on a variety of standardized tests. You'll also find lots of material in libraries or bookstores to help you: books and software from the test makers and from other publishers or live courses that range from national test-preparation companies to teachers at your high school who offer classes. ■

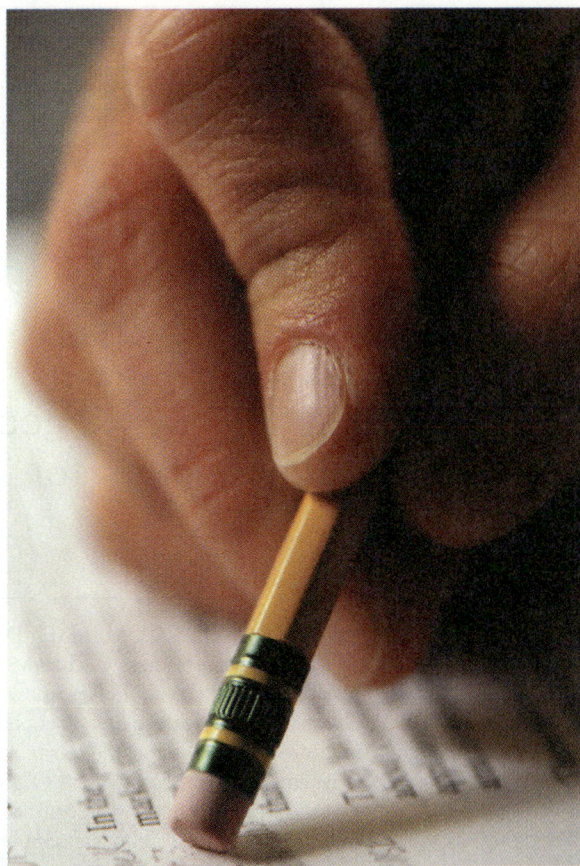

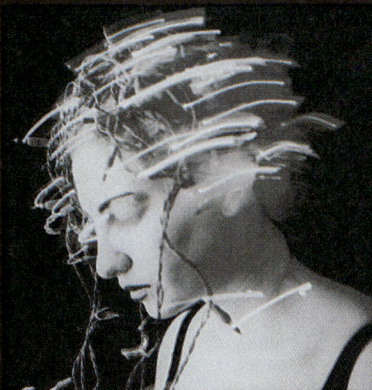

SHOULD SATs

A growing number of colleges are spurning a test that has measured and mortified Americans for 75 years. But what are the alternatives?

By JOHN CLOUD

TIME ASKED FAMOUS AND ACCOMPLISHED PEOPLE to tell us their SAT scores. Most of them declined—which is a little strange, since the big bad test couldn't possibly hurt Alan Greenspan or Oprah Winfrey. But the SAT occupies a central place in the American psyche, lying at the terrifying intersection of ability, class and pride. As TV's Conan O'Brien put it, "It has taken 20 years to forget the trauma of that damned test, and looking up my scores would be like going back to Vietnam."

The test's prominence ensures that shouting matches will erupt over it regularly. Usually one side says the SAT should die because it's racist; the other says it should flourish because it maintains standards. Their arguments are important but had started to seem pointless, since the number of SAT takers has increased virtually every year since Pearl Harbor.

Then, in a Feb. 18 speech to his fellow college presidents, the psychologist who runs the University of California suggested something radical: Scrap the thing. Richard Atkinson says the test hurls kids into months of practicing word games and math riddles at the expense of studying chemistry or poetry. He wants to make SAT scores an optional part of the application for all 90,000 kids who want to go to U.C. each year. "The SATs have acquired a mystique that's clearly not warranted," he proclaims. "Who knows what they measure?" Those of us who wanted to stick a No. 2 pencil in our eye while puzzling the meaning of "mendacious" gave a cheer.

U.C.'s faculty and regents started what will be a long, fiery debate over his proposal. Since Atkinson began attacking the test, college administrators across the U.S. have reopened old fights about the SAT

HOW THEY SCORED ON THE TEST:

Here's how some famous folks told us they did on their SATs. A perfect score is 1600, based on 800 math and 800 verbal.

PAUL WELLSTONE
SENATOR
UNDER 800
Combined! Yet he went on to become a Phi Beta Kappa at the University of North Carolina

JENNIFER LOPEZ
ACTRESS
"nail polish"
What she said she got on her SATs, as reported in the New York Post

STEPHEN KING
AUTHOR
1300s
"People don't like SATs these da[ys] because everyone's got the idea tha[t] tests are, like, unfair, dude."

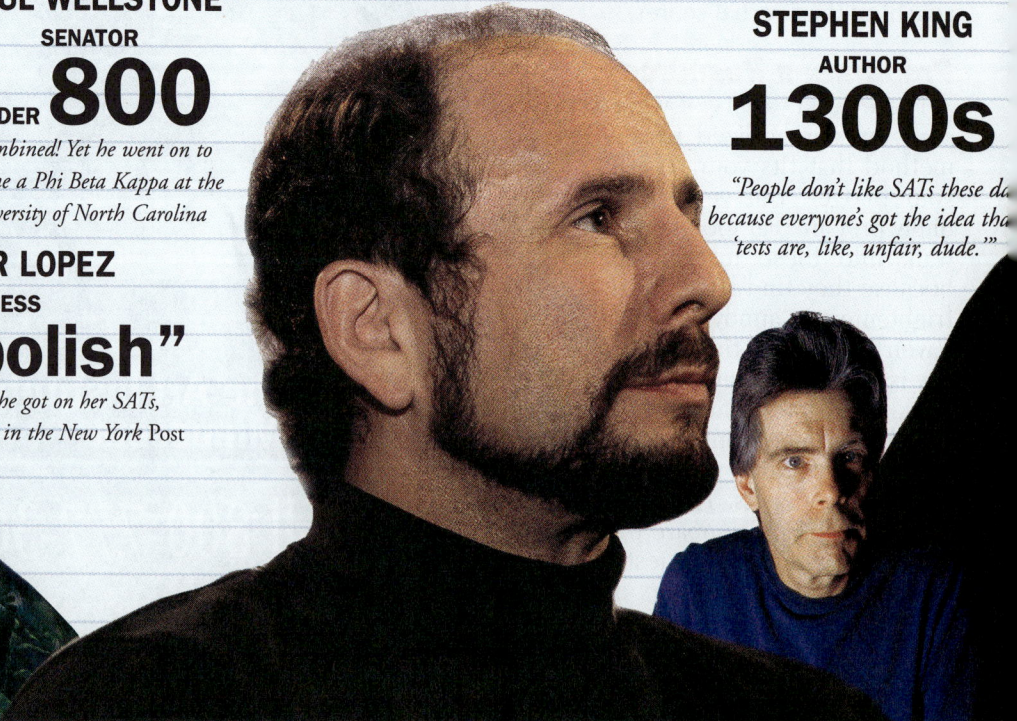

Left to right: Steve Finn—Alpha/Globe Photos; Najlah Feanny—SABA; Brian Smith—Corbis Outline; Robert Foothorap; Claudio Vazquez—Corbis Outline; Andrew Eccles—ABC; Cynthia Johnson for TIME

MATTER?

BEN STEIN
GAME-SHOW HOST
1573

"The people I know who are successful, hardworking, responsible people, by and large, were people who did well on their SATs."

MEREDITH VIEIRA
TALK-SHOW HOST
1300s

"I got 5's on my APs. Big deal! I still didn't get into Harvard."

AMY TAN
AUTHOR
1100s

"I was told I should become a doctor because the only thing I'd have to write is prescriptions."

GEORGE W. BUSH
PRESIDENT
1206

and started new ones. President John Peters of Northern Illinois University says the reaction of the hundreds of college officials to the speech was "extremely positive." The Georgia board of regents is reviewing admissions criteria, as are the University of Texas and the College of Wooster in Ohio.

Most universities have no immediate plans to stop asking for SAT scores. But at those schools that were having second thoughts about the test, Atkinson's stance will embolden anti- SAT forces. "It's gutsy," says Florida International University admissions chief Carmen Brown, "and a lot of other places will follow." The College Board, which oversees the SAT, was worried enough after the speech to e-mail colleges a defense of its test.

The board had plenty of reasons to worry before then. The California rumblings come at a precarious time for the SAT. To be sure, it remains a key part of the college-application process. Last year 44% of the kids who graduated from high school took it, up from 41% in 1995. In all, more than 2 million students took the SAT in 2000. The second biggest admissions test, the ACT, had 1.8 million takers last year. Published by an Iowa testing company, the ACT started in 1959 as a rival to the SAT and focuses more on subject matter than general reasoning. But the ACT never developed the SAT's aura of quality and rigor. Whenever a college suggests dropping its SAT requirement, traditionalists on campus inevitably say doing so would lower standards.

Over the past few years, however, the test's defenders have started to lose ground. About 280 of the nation's 2,083 four-year colleges and universities make the SAT optional for some or all applicants; a handful of prestigious colleges, including Franklin and Marshall and Mount Holyoke, have joined their ranks since the early '90s and say they aren't admitting idiots as a result. Hamilton College is considering making the SAT optional. Countless other schools have de-emphasized the SAT in more subtle ways—continuing to ask for scores but weighing other factors more heavily.

Granted many of the SAT-optional schools sit on utopian campuses in liberal New England villages. But it's getting hard to find an admissions officer anywhere who says an SAT score alone tells you anything important. Deans at prestigious, traditional bastions such as Vanderbilt support the SAT, but some of the test's assumed proponents aren't guarding it against the barbarians. Even conservatives at the *Weekly Standard* have written about how the SAT has "shaped—and misshaped—modern American life."

But if we drop the SAT, by what means should we allot membership in the nation's élite? Of course, plenty of people make movies and play in the major leagues and run companies and write for magazines without high SATs. But good scores sure don't hurt. Besides, don't they measure something valuable—something beyond the diligence it takes to memorize the details of the Franco-Prussian War for a history exam? Much of the debate over the SAT boils down to this: Assuming we can measure innate intelligence, do we want a society that rewards genes? Are we afraid of what kind of society that might be? Or should we instead reward only the achievements of a life—what we do with our gifts, not what we start with?

To answer these questions, you have to understand both how the SAT rose to prominence and how it has fallen into turmoil. Appropriately, the story begins in California. In the two decades after World War II, the College Board struggled to build the reputation of the SAT, which was first used experimentally in 1926. The board desperately wanted the University of California, then the biggest university in the nation, to fully adopt the test. In 1962, as Nicholas Lemann says in his brilliant history, *The Big Test*, an SAT honcho wrote to his colleagues of the dire consequences if U.C. decided to end its then limited use of the test: "If they drop the SAT, we will lose a great deal more than the revenue; we will suffer a damaging blow to our prestige."

In 1967, its confidence in the value of high school transcripts eroded, U.C. finally started requiring SAT scores from all applicants. From that point, the test grew into a national juggernaut. Within a matter of years, as college attendance skyrocketed, many admissions offices were relying heavily on the standardized SAT scores to help winnow piles of applications.

By the 1970s, when the inevitable backlash began, two arguments emerged. The one that drew more media attention charged that the test was inherently biased against blacks and Latinos, who to this day score worse on average than whites. The other was that SAT scores measure only the ability to take the SAT—a skill that, depending on your ability to pay, you could pick up in a coaching class (a growth industry that in 1999 alone raked in $400 million). Aside from that class inequality, the test's failure to measure anything meaningful also meant that kids were spending a lot of time fretting over pedagogical phantoms at the expense of real learning.

The College Board says the average SAT taker spends only 11 hours preparing—and that coaching on average adds fewer than 40 points to a score. But test prep has become a big part of teen culture in most suburbs. Even the College Board sells its own test-prep material. The Princeton Review's $799-to-$899 SAT classes typically meet weekly for six weeks, and students are expected to practice analogies and memorize vocabulary at home. "There has been a kind of testing mania that's hit us at all levels," says Sylvia Manning, a chancellor of the University of Illinois. It begins as early as middle school, when kids prepare for the Preliminary SAT, whose results are used by some colleges to identify potential matriculants when they are only in 10th grade. By senior year, "kids live and die by what they score on that three-hour test," says Ray Brown, dean of

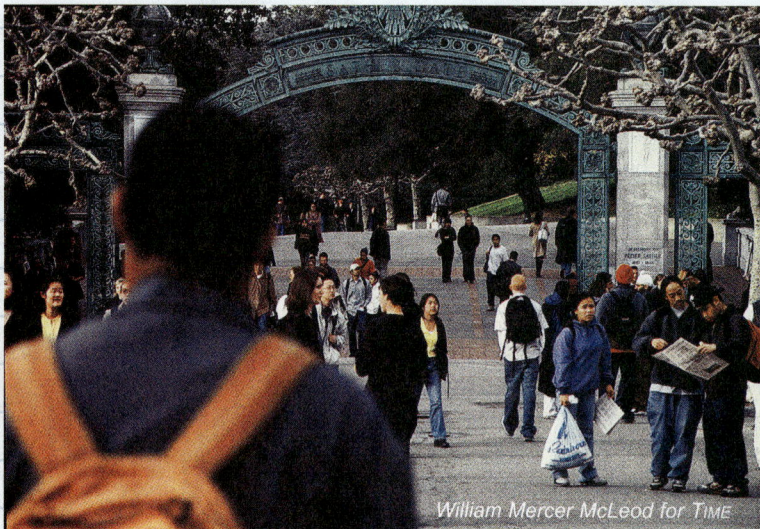

WHERE THEY'RE GOING

Defenders say campuses like U.C.'s élite Berkeley need SATs to maintain standards

AL GORE
EX-VICE PRESIDENT
1335

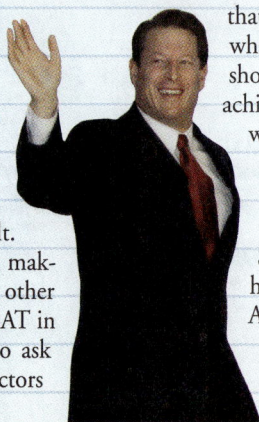

admissions at Texas Christian University. "Or at least they think so."

In fact, most admissions officers—both at élite colleges and giant state schools—say they work hard not to put too much emphasis on SATs. They know, says Florida State admissions chief John Barnhill, that "the SAT doesn't measure heart." Although his office generally rejects applicants who score below 900, he remembers a student who was admitted with a 720—but who had a 3.9 GPA. "We have space for students like that, provided they are in the special support program," he says. "I like the SAT, but I don't love it. I wish I could find something that was a more fair and accurate measure."

The racial gap in test scores is one of the most vexing problems in social science, in part because it opens the door to the whole creepy notion of eugenics. Eugenicists believe that the human species would advance more quickly if it discouraged reproduction among groups deemed unfit—say, those that score poorly on aptitude tests. It's worth noting that the SAT was designed by a psychology professor who became a leading member of the eugenics movement before denouncing it later in life.

The racial gap has fluctuated in size but never really declined. Today even blacks whose parents have the same level of education and income as a comparable sample of whites score about 120 points lower on average. Anti-testers often explain the gap by saying most of the test writers are white and import cultural biases into the SAT. But the College Board says SAT questions are always previewed by a large sample of test takers, and any questions that generate racial disparities are tossed out before they appear on SATs that count. "The SAT is probably the most thoroughly researched test in history," says College Board president Gaston Caperton. He attributes the test-score gap to the "different educational opportunities these students have had." Says Donald Stewart, one of Caperton's predecessors and the first African American to hold the job: "Poor kids are getting a lousy education. It's as simple as that."

Not really. Poor kids going to dismal schools doesn't explain why rich black kids score worse on average than white kids. Stanford psychologist Claude Steele has a theory that might explain it. His research shows that

even high-achieving African-American pupils may be distracted by a fear that they will confirm the stereotype that blacks don't do well on intelligence tests. Steele has tested his theory by giving an exam to two mixed-race groups of students. One group was told that the exam was a simple problem-solving exercise; the other was told that their scores would show how smart they were. The white kids scored about the same no matter what they were told. The black kids who thought they were taking an intelligence test performed considerably

worse than those told the test was no big deal.

That raises the question of whether we should try to test intelligence at all. Lemann, who wrote the history of the SAT, answers no. "You want to measure people on something they've done, not on supposedly innate abilities," he says. "I don't trust the whole idea of innateness." Fine, but what about those cool kids who would rather write concertos or build rockets than cram for a quiz on Grover Cleveland's second term? What about the bright rural Arkansas kid whose school is so screwed up that her grades mean nothing? Lemann says those students could still submit their perfect 1600 SAT score, since the test would simply be optional—although in his perfect world, the SAT would be replaced by other standardized tests that draw from nationally standardized course material.

But at some point such questions fly too high above the SAT, since almost no one seriously argues any longer that it's an intelligence test. Not even its sponsors. The College Board stopped referring to it as the Scholastic Aptitude Test

BILL BRADLEY

RHODES SCHOLAR

485

VERBAL

in 1994. For a while, the board redundantly called it an "assessment test." Now it just says the name is SAT and is unwilling to give the test much of an identity beyond that. President Kurt Landgraf of the Educational Testing Service, the company that designs the SAT under contract from the College Board, says it "is a relatively good predictor of how students will do in their first year of college." But he has a profoundly limited view of the nature of the test: "It's a measure of a student's ability to answer questions at a given place and time"— the kind of sentence you might find on an SAT to define the term tautology.

Research from colleges that have dropped the SAT requirement reinforces the notion that the test measures little. Bowdoin College, which started the SAT-optional movement in 1969, often studies how well its admissions officers predict college performance without SATs. It has repeatedly found that its rating—a numerical value assigned each applicant on the basis of GPA, essays and other factors— correlates very highly with the student's GPA at Bowdoin. Factoring in SAT scores improves that correlation only slightly. The College Board says that, across many colleges, SAT scores improve the correlation between admissions predictions and GPA realities by 10%.

And 10% means a lot on big campuses that can't afford to spend hours getting to know applicants. Even at Bowdoin, hero of the anti-testing crowd, head of admissions Richard Steele has mixed feelings about other schools' eliminating the SAT requirement. "I'm not one who would recommend this for everyone," he says, noting that Bowdoin is now "highly encouraging" one growing group of hard-to-evaluate applicants, home schoolers, to submit their SATs. "It works for us because we're only dealing with 5,000 applications, vs. 20,000 at the big schools."

Lafayette College, a small liberal-arts and engineering school in Pennsylvania, started a five-year experiment with making SATs optional in 1995. And Lafayette officials found that the test, combined with other measures, correlated better with their students' performance than other measures alone. In addition, admissions officers found themselves lost amid the inflated grades and unranked classes that became common in 1990s secondary education. "We felt the SAT gave us one more consistent, nationally recognized standard," says Barry McCarty, a Lafayette dean. When the college went back to using the test last year,

something unexpected happened: its applications surged 14%, and the school enrolled its strongest class in years. Though McCarty credits a flush economy and campus improvements for the increase, he raised another interesting possibility: "I do think students were more interested because of the perception of quality that's attached to [the SAT]."

Surprisingly, just as some U.S. schools are dumping the SAT because they consider it unfair, the British have discovered its potential value in elevating smart kids at poor schools. A study released in February shows that kids in state-run schools who did well on the SAT are falling through the cracks of the current British testing system, which rewards those who have mastered specific subjects rather than general skills. Britain's education czar said he thinks SATs could be compulsory there in a few years.

Admissions officers will always use hard-and-fast numbers to make decisions. But which numbers? U.C.'s Atkinson says California might develop its own test. Until it does, he suggests using scores on the SAT IIs, exams written by the same folks as the original SAT but focused on specific subject matter. "Once you start testing kids on what they learned in science or social studies, then high schools can start improving how they teach these things," says Michael Kirst, a Stanford education professor.

But SAT IIs (their name too was sanitized of meaning—they used to be Achievement Tests) have also spawned prep courses and racial score gaps. SAT II prep is actually more expensive than SAT I coaching, because most students take three separate SAT II exams, chosen from 22 subject areas. "[The SAT II] doesn't begin to approach a kind of equity solution," says University of Chicago dean Ted O'Neill.

College officials who de-emphasize the SAT usually focus more on evaluating the

SCOTT MC NEALY

CEO, SUN MICROSYSTEMS

1420

Louis Psihoyos—Matrix

high schools that students come from. "If we don't have SAT any longer, we'll have to weigh more heavily on what's left—the students' GPA, their curriculum of college-prep courses and other things," says Rae Lee Siporin, admissions director of UCLA, which receives more

Genaro Molina—Los Angeles Times

WHY THEY'RE SUING Some students allege that the U.C. admissions office favors wealthy students

applications each year—about 40,000—than any other U.S. college. But those measures can amplify the inequalities among high schools even more than the SAT. As Duke University admissions director Christoph Guttentag notes, "The students in school districts with more resources will be more equipped."

Take Advanced Placement classes, the top-level high school courses sponsored by the College Board. APs can help kids earn college credit early, but many high schools can't afford the superqualified teachers and advanced books required for AP classrooms. A California study found that the availability of AP offerings in a school decreases as the percentage of minority and low-income students increases. In 1999, the A.C.L.U. sued the state of California, accusing U.C. schools of favoring applicants who have taken APs. Rasheda Daniel, a plaintiff, says she and her classmates didn't have an equal chance of getting into U.C. "When you look at a lot of high schools, there are gross disparities across class lines," she says. "It's not fair."

Daniel's contention is right and explains why no

admissions scheme can be totally equitable. Some reformers say Florida and Texas come closest. By law, the public universities in those states must offer admission to all who graduate in the top 20% (Florida) or 10% (Texas) of their class, no matter how poor their high school. Public universities in both states still use SATs, however—Florida to sort out which kids will go to the larger, more presitigious colleges, Texas to decide who needs retention programs.

Of course, Florida and Texas lawmakers weren't attacking the SAT itself. They wanted to maintain diverse campuses even though affirmative action had been banned in their states. Conservatives suspect U.C.'s Atkinson has the same motive. Those who favor affirmative action have long wanted to ignore SAT scores, says Ward Connerly, a U.C. regent and anti-affirmative-action activist. (Atkinson has said he wasn't motivated by race.) Connerly believes moving away from standard measures like the SAT will mean colleges lose their fundamental goal of academic excellence. "Looking at a student's potential and the adversity they've overcome—what I call the Academic Misery Index—has the potential of totally reforming college," he says, turning campuses into institutions that value diversity and community service over learning.

High schools are changing too. Baby boomer parents have started movements against homework, stringent graduation requirements, class rankings; it's as though they believe their children should never have to suffer the indignity of being evaluated. Pity those kids when they get their first job. Earlier this year Laila Kouri, 16, reflected on the SAT as she sat through an expensive coaching class in ritzy Westport, Conn. "I know people who blow off classes, are failing school and walk into the SAT and get a 1200 the first time," she sighed. "How can this be a fair test?" Well, as Kouri has learned, no one ever said life's tests were fair. ■

—*Reported by Matt Baron/Chicago, Leslie Everton Brice/Atlanta, Daren Fonda, Andrew Goldstein, Jodie Morse, Desa Philadelphia and Rebecca Winters/New York, Marc Hequet/St. Paul, Kathie Klarreich/Miami, and Jeff Ressner/Los Angeles*

5 CHOOSING A COLLEGE

Now that you have examined your interests, talents, wants, and needs in great detail, you can begin to investigate some of the colleges that interest you.

THE BIG PICTURE

Each college offers its own advantages, but only a handful will be perfect matches for you. To help narrow your choices to a manageable number, let's look at the big picture first. Decide which of the following college characteristics are most important to you.

Academic Program

University. Usually has a liberal arts college as well as several other specialized colleges, such as business, engineering, education, agriculture, law, and medicine. Each of these individual colleges may have its own set of entrance requirements.

Four-year college. An institution of higher learning that offers a curriculum leading to a four-year Bachelor of Arts or Bachelor of Science degree.

Two-year college. Also known as a community college, technical college, or university regional campus, it offers associate degree programs that serve as the first two years of a bachelor's degree and/or provide skills needed for entry into technical career fields.

Vocational/trade school. Offers career-oriented programs that may last from a few months to a couple of years. These schools, which are often proprietary (for-profit) institutions, generally do not offer transfer programs or programs parallel to those of four-year colleges.

Affiliation

- Public
- Private, independent
- Private, church affiliated
- Proprietary

Size

- Very small (fewer than 1,000 students)
- Small (1,000–3,999 students)
- Medium (4,000–8,999 students)
- Large (9,000–19,999 students)
- Very large (more than 20,000 students)

Community

- Rural
- Small town
- Suburban
- Urban

Location

- In your hometown
- Less than 3 hours from home
- More than 3 hours from home

Housing

- Dorm
- Off-campus apartment
- Home
- Facilities and services for students with disabilities

Student body

- All male
- All female

- ⏲ Coed
- ⏲ Minority representation
- ⏲ Primarily one religious denomination
- ⏲ Primarily full-time students
- ⏲ Primarily part-time students
- ⏲ Primarily commuter students
- ⏲ Primarily residential students

Admissions

Highly selective. Students rank in the top 10 percent of the class and have a very strong academic record.

Selective. Students rank in the top 25 percent of the class and have a strong academic record.

Traditional. Students rank in the top 50 percent of the class and have a good academic record.

Liberal. Many students are accepted from the lower half of the class.

Open. All students are accepted to limit of capacity.

Academic Environment

- ⏲ Majors offered
- ⏲ Student-faculty ratio
- ⏲ Faculty teaching reputation
- ⏲ Instruction by professors versus teaching assistants
- ⏲ Facilities (such as classrooms and labs)
- ⏲ Libraries
- ⏲ Independent study available
- ⏲ International study available
- ⏲ Internships available

Cost

Colleges vary greatly in cost. Don't automatically pass over an institution that appears to be too expensive. You may be able to receive financial aid that will make your education affordable.

When estimating cost, remember tuition and fees, room and board, miscellaneous personal expenses, and transportation costs.

Financial Aid

- ⏲ Scholarships
- ⏲ Grants
- ⏲ Loans
- ⏲ Work-study program
- ⏲ Part-time or full-time jobs

Support Services

- ⏲ Academic counseling
- ⏲ Career/placement counseling
- ⏲ Personal counseling
- ⏲ Student health facilities

Activities/Social Clubs

- ⏲ Clubs, organizations
- ⏲ Greek life
- ⏲ Athletics, intramurals
- ⏲ Other

Athletics

- ⏲ Division I, II, or III
- ⏲ Sports offered
- ⏲ Scholarships available

Specialized Programs

- ⏲ Gifted student services
- ⏲ Services for students with disabilities or special needs

BestCollegePicks: A Brand-New Way to Pick a College

Some students have the decision about where to go to college locked in. Others take the first college that comes along. Most likely, you're in between those two extremes. You know that choosing a college is a big decision and that college costs a lot of money. You're just unsure of how to begin the whole process.

But ask yourself this: If you were to buy an expensive car, wouldn't you want to compare notes with satisfied customers to find out what they thought about the car? We're talking about a really expensive car, not just some clunker. You'd probably reach for a consumer's guide because that would give you impartial information about the car—not someone's opinion about it, but how it actually performed.

Well, you're choosing a college at the right time because now you do have a guide that lets you compare colleges based on what consumers say

about them—the college graduates. So why not talk to them and find out if what they are doing with their college education matches what you want to do?

Impractical you say? Kind of scary to call graduates? You're right. Calling college graduates is intimidating. But you don't have to because Peterson's has a Web-based tool called BestCollegePicks that has, in effect, talked to the college graduates for you. BestCollegePicks is a way for you to evaluate colleges using truly objective information. With BestCollege Picks, you will be able to say, "This is what I want to do with my college education. This is how I want my college to be." You'll get a list of colleges whose graduates most closely fit your goals, aspirations, and values and whose size, location, and kind of institution best match what you're interested in.

College guides, brochures, Web sites, and the lists that rank colleges are necessary sources of information for applicants, but they only provide part of the picture. They give data about incoming students such as GPAs and required test scores. This information is useful, but those facts are similar to finding out what materials go into the production of a car, not the results from driving it. BestCollegePicks looks at the driving record of a college.

You'll find BestCollegePicks is easy to use. The tool first pinpoints your skills, abilities, goals, and personal preferences with a comprehensive survey. Then, BestCollegePicks matches what you say you want with what graduates say they've gotten from a wide range of colleges and universities. You can take the survey more than once, each time setting different goals. Say you are not sure if you want to go into law or business. You can take the survey twice—once for law and once for business—by signing in under a different name each time. When you get the list of schools, you can compare them to see which schools overlap. If you choose to attend one of those schools, you'll know that either way, a high percent-

age of graduates from that school have been successful in business or law.

The benefits of BestCollegePicks are enormous. You will be led to lesser-known schools you might never have thought of whose graduates match your future plans. And the vague ideas that you have about what you want out of college will take shape. You can get to BestCollege Picks by going to www.bestcollege picks.com.

SHOULD YOU HEAD FOR THE IVY LEAGUES?

Determining whether to apply to one of the eight Ivy League schools is something you should think long and hard about. Sure, it can't hurt to toss your application into the ring if you can afford the application fee and the time you'll spend writing the essays. But if you want to figure out if you'd be a legitimate candidate for acceptance at one of these top-tier schools, you should understand the type of student that they look for and how you compare, says John Machulsky, a guidance counselor at Lawrenceville High School in New Jersey. Take a look at these statistics:

- Only 30 percent or fewer applicants are accepted at these highly competitive colleges each year.

- Most Ivy League students have placed in the top 10 percent of their class and have SAT I scores in the 700 levels for math and

Student Counsel

Q: What made you choose to apply to an Ivy League school?

A: My mother recommended that I apply to Princeton. She said, "Why not just try? What do you have to lose? All they can tell you is no." I was afraid of being rejected. I wasn't a straight-A student, and I thought they weren't going to want me, they get thousands of applications. Through the whole college process I had a whole lot of self-doubt. Looking back, I realize that you won't know if you don't try. Take the chance and fill out the application. If you don't get in, it doesn't mean you're less intelligent. It just wasn't the correct fit.
Zoelene Hill, College Freshman
Princeton University
High School: Stuart County Day School of the Sacred Heart
Princeton, New Jersey

verbal each or ACT scores of 29 or higher.

- Because Ivy League schools are so selective, they want a diverse student population. That means they want students that represent not only the fifty states but also a wide selection of other countries.

Lirio Jimenez, a guidance counselor at New Brunswick High School in New Jersey, says that being accepted by an Ivy League school is a process that starts early in the ninth grade. You should select demanding courses and maintain good grades in those courses throughout all four years of high school. Get involved in extracurricular activities as well, and, of course, do well on your standardized tests. When it comes time to apply for college, select at least three schools: one ideal, one possible, and one shoe-in. Your ideal can be an Ivy League if you wish.

GAJ certainly doesn't want to discourage you from applying to one of these prestigious schools. We're in your corner and want to see you get the best education possible. However, students are sometimes more concerned about getting accepted than

with taking a hard look at what a school has to offer them. Often, a university or college that is less competitive than an Ivy League may have exactly what you need to succeed in the future. Keep that in mind as you select the colleges that would offer you what you need.

CAMPUS VISITS

You've heard the old saying, "A picture is worth a thousand words." Well, a campus visit is worth a thousand brochures. Nothing beats walking around a campus to get a feel for it. Some students report that all they needed to know that they loved or hated a campus was to drive through it. Then there is the true story of the guy who applied to a school because it had a prestigious name. Got accepted. Didn't visit, and when he arrived to move into the dorms, discovered to his horror it was an all-male school. A visit would have taken care of that problem.

The best time to experience the college environment is during the spring of your junior year or the fall of your senior year. Although you may

From the Guidance Office

Q: What are the advantages of a community or junior college?

A: Many students aren't ready to be outside the supervision of Mom and Dad. Junior colleges are a good option, but junior colleges should be a choice rather than the only option for kids who end up not achieving well enough to go to a four-year college. Two years of general education is a positive decision rather than having a student say that he or she just doesn't want to work so hard or that they're resigned to only being able to get into a junior college. I tell students not to close the doors on themselves. Take the more challenging courses in junior college. Attempt to get the grades that will earn them the opportunity to transfer to a four-year college. At the junior college, they can take the foreign languages or advanced math classes they were not able to complete in high school.
Randy McLelland
Counselor
Oak Park High School
Oak Park, California

have more time to make college visits during your summer off, your observations will be more accurate when you can see the campus in full swing. Open houses are a good idea and provide you with opportunities to talk to students, faculty members, and administrators. Write or call in advance to take student-conducted campus tours. If possible, stay overnight in a dorm to see what living at the college is really like.

Bring your transcript so that you are prepared to interview with admission officers. Take this opportunity to ask questions about financial aid and other services that are available to students. You can get a good snapshot of campus life by reading a copy of the student newspaper. The final goal of the campus visit is to study the school's personality and decide if it matches yours. Your parents should be involved with the campus visits so that you can share your impressions. Here are some additional campus visit tips:

- Read campus literature prior to the visit.
- Ask for directions, and allow ample travel time.
- Make a list of questions before the visit.
- Dress in neat, clean, casual clothes and shoes.
- Ask to meet one-on-one with a current student.
- Ask to meet personally with a professor in your area of interest.
- Ask to meet a coach or athlete in your area of interest.
- Offer a firm handshake.
- Use good posture.
- Listen, and take notes.
- Speak clearly, and maintain eye contact with people you meet.
- Don't interrupt.
- Be honest, direct, and polite.
- Be aware of factual information so that you can ask questions of comparison and evaluation.
- Be prepared to answer questions about yourself. Practice a mock interview with someone.
- Don't be shy about explaining your background and why you are interested in the school.
- Ask questions about the background and experiences of the people you meet.
- Convey your interest in getting involved in campus life.
- Be positive and energetic.
- Don't feel as though you have to talk the whole time or carry the conversation yourself.
- Relax, and enjoy yourself.
- Thank those you meet, and send thank-you notes when appropriate.

After you have made your college visits, use the "College Comparison Worksheet" on page 50 to rank the schools in which you're interested. This will help you decide not only which ones to apply to, but also which one to attend once you receive your acceptance letters.

THE COLLEGE INTERVIEW

Not all schools require or offer an interview. However, if you are offered an interview, use this one-on-one time to evaluate the college in detail and to sell yourself to the admission officer. The following list of questions can help you collect the information you may need to know.

- How many students apply each year? How many are accepted?
- What are the average GPA and average ACT or SAT I score(s) for those accepted?
- How many students in last year's freshman class returned for their sophomore year?
- What is the school's procedure for credit for Advanced Placement high school courses?
- As a freshman, will I be taught by professors or teaching assistants?
- How many students are there per teacher?
- When is it necessary to declare a major?
- Is it possible to have a double major or to declare a major and a minor?
- What are the requirements?
- How does the advising system work?
- Does this college offer overseas study, cooperative programs, or academic honors programs?
- What is the likelihood, due to overcrowding, of getting closed out of the courses I need?
- What technology is available?
- How well equipped are the libraries and laboratories?
- Are internships available?
- How effective is the job placement service of the school?
- What is the average class size in my area of interest?
- Have any professors in my area of interest recently won any honors or awards?
- What teaching methods are used in my area of interest (lecture, group discussion, fieldwork)?
- How many students graduate in four years in my area of interest?
- What are the special requirement for graduation in my area of interest?
- What is the student body like? Age? Sex? Race? Geographic origin?
- What percentage of students live in dormitories? Off-campus housing?
- What percentage of students go home for the weekend?
- What are some of the regulations that apply to living in a dormitory?

- ⏱ What are the security precautions taken on campus and in the dorms?
- ⏱ Is the surrounding community safe?
- ⏱ Are there problems with drug and alcohol abuse on campus?
- ⏱ Are there dorms available that are free of any use of drugs and alcohol?
- ⏱ Do faculty members and students mix on an informal basis?
- ⏱ How important are the arts to student life?
- ⏱ What facilities are available for cultural events?
- ⏱ How important are sports to student life?
- ⏱ What facilities are available for sporting events?
- ⏱ What percentage of the student body belongs to a sorority/fraternity?
- ⏱ What is the relationship between those who belong to the Greek system and those who don't?
- ⏱ Are students involved in the decision-making process at the college? Do they sit on major committees?
- ⏱ What other activities can students get involved in?
- ⏱ What percentage of students receive financial aid based on need?
- ⏱ What percentage of students receive scholarships based on academic ability?
- ⏱ What percentage of a typical financial aid offer is in the form of a loan?
- ⏱ If my family demonstrates financial need on the FAFSA (and FAF, if applicable), what percentage of the established need is generally awarded?
- ⏱ How much did the college increase the cost of room, board, tuition, and fees from last year?
- ⏱ Do opportunities for financial aid, scholarships, or work-study increase each year?

WRITING TO A COLLEGE FOR INFORMATION

IF NEITHER YOU NOR YOUR GUIDANCE COUNSELOR HAS AN APPLICATION FOR A COLLEGE THAT YOU ARE INTERESTED IN, WRITE A BRIEF LETTER TO THE COLLEGE ADMISSIONS OFFICE TO REQUEST AN APPLICATION.

Date

Your Name
Street Address
City, State, Zip

Office of Admission
Name of College
Street Address
City, State, Zip

To Whom It May Concern:

I am a *(freshman, sophomore, junior, senior)* at *(name of your school)* and plan to graduate in *(month) (year)*.

Please send me the following information about your college: a general information brochure, program descriptions, an admission application, financial aid information, and any other information that might be helpful. I am considering _____ as my major field of study *(optional, if you know your major)*.

I am interested in visiting your campus, taking a campus tour, and meeting with an admission counselor and a financial aid officer. I would also like to meet with an adviser or professor in the *(your preferred field of study)* department, if possible *(optional, if you know your major)*. I will contact you in a week to set up a time that is convenient.

If you would like to contact me directly, I can be reached at *(your phone number with area code)*. Thank you.

Sincerely,

(Signature)

Name

COLLEGE COMPARISON WORKSHEET

FILL IN YOUR TOP FIVE SELECTION CRITERIA AND ANY OTHERS THAT MAY BE OF IMPORTANCE TO YOU. ONCE YOU NARROW YOUR SEARCH OF COLLEGES TO FIVE, FILL IN THE COLLEGES ACROSS THE TOP ROW. USING A SCALE OF 1 TO 5, WHERE 1 IS POOR AND 5 IS EXCELLENT, RATE EACH COLLEGE BY YOUR CRITERIA. TOTAL EACH COLUMN TO SEE WHICH COLLEGE RATES THE HIGHEST BASED UPON YOUR CRITERIA.

Selection Criteria	College 1	College 2	College 3	College 4	College 5
1.					
2.					
3.					
4.					
5.					
Other Criteria					
6.					
7.					
8.					
9.					
10.					
TOTAL					

Sample criteria: (Use this list as a starting point—there may be other criteria important to you not listed here.) Arts facilities, athletic facilities, audiovisual center, campus setting, class size, classrooms/lecture halls, computer labs, dining hall, dorms, financial aid, fraternity/sorority houses, majors offered, religious facilities, professor profiles, student-professor ratio, student profile, student union, surrounding community.

⏱ When is the application deadline?

⏱ When does the school notify you of the admission decision?

⏱ If there is a deposit required, is it refundable?

Keep in mind that you don't need to ask all these questions—in fact, some of them may have already been answered for you in the catalog, on the Web site, or in the interview. Ask only the questions for which you still need answers.

ONLINE HELP

To help you find two-year and four-year colleges or universities in your specific region, take a look at the appendix in the back of this magazine for a table of schools in each state of your region. Then check out the following online resources for additional information on college selection, scholarships, student information, and much more.

BestCollegePicks. Find out from graduates of a college or university if what they're doing with their degrees matches up with what you want to accomplish in college. Visit www.bestcollegepicks.com to pair your hopes and dreams with the realities of the graduates of a college or university you're considering.

Peterson's Undergraduate Channel. Petersons.com provides information and tools that will help you prepare, search, and pay for college. You can find the schools that BestCollege Picks matched you to in order to view in-depth profiles or do a side-by-side comparison of selected colleges. Or you can search for a school by name or location. In addition to college search and selection tools, the undergraduate channel on Petersons.com also offers tips on financial aid, test preparation, and online applications.

College Board Online. This Web site offers advice on how to prepare and pay for college. You can also order resource materials that help you with the AP and SAT exams. Visit www.collegeboard.com.

ETS Net. This site is brought to you by the Educational Testing Service, the folks who prepare the SAT I. Visit www.ets.org.

The National Association for College Admission Counseling. This home page offers information for professionals, students, and parents. The Internet address is www.nacac.com.

U.S. Department of Education. This federal agency's National Center for Education Statistics produces reports on every level of education, from elementary to postgraduate. Dozens are available for downloading. You can hook up with these and other links at www.ed.gov. ∎

6 APPLYING TO COLLEGE

The big moment has arrived. It's time to make some decisions about where you want to apply.

Once that list is finalized, the worst part is filling out all the forms accurately and getting them in by the deadlines. Because requirements differ, you should check with all the colleges that you are interested in attending to find out what the specific requirements are at those schools.

WHAT SCHOOLS LOOK FOR IN PROSPECTIVE STUDENTS

As if you were sizing up the other team to plan your game strategy, understand what admissions committees want from you as you assemble all the pieces of your application.

Academic record: Admission representatives look at the breadth (how many), diversity (which ones), and difficulty (how challenging) of the courses on your transcript.

Grades: You should show consistency in your ability to work to your potential. If your grades are not initially good, colleges look to see that significant improvement has been made. Some colleges have minimum grade point averages that they are willing to accept.

Class rank: Colleges consider the academic standing of a student in relation to the other members of his or her class. Are you in the top 25 percent of your class? Top half? Ask your counselor for your class rank.

Standardized test scores: Colleges look at test scores in terms of ranges. If your scores aren't high but you did well academically in high school, you shouldn't be discouraged. There is no set formula

(Continued on page 54)

The committee gathers to vote on applicants—many without SATs

NO TEST SCORES REQUIRED

MOUNT HOLYOKE has made the SAT optional.
An inside look at how the experiment is working

By Jodie Morse

Should we give a spot to Susan? That's the question before a roomful of admissions officers at Mount Holyoke College. Susan, who has top grades and gushing recommendations, could surely prosper here. But what more, they wonder, would she bring to this cozy all-women's college in South Hadley, Mass.? Giulietta Aquino, Susan's advocate on the six-member committee, ticks off a few of her accomplishments. She is a decorated horseback rider aiming for the Olympics who commutes three hours a day between her home, school and horse barn but still finds time to tutor immigrant children and work as a physician's scribe in an E.R.

But the committee is still not sold. Though Susan intends to study literature, dean of admissions Diane Anci is worried because her transcript is "thin" in science credits and notes that she has progressed in math no further than pre-calculus. "Let's have a dramatic reading from her essay," says Anci. Susan's meditation on the ferryboats she rides across Puget Sound each morning to her Seattle school elicits approving chuckles from the jury. Anci is convinced. Moments later, the committee votes to rate Susan a 3 on a descending scale of 1 to 9—high enough to earn her one of 300 remaining seats in the class of 2005.

Conspicuously absent from the determination of Susan's fate is any mention of her SATs. That's because, in the parlance of Mount Holyoke's admissions officers, Susan is a "score blocker." In the summer of 2000, Mount Holyoke announced that for a five-year trial period, it would give applicants the option of withholding their test scores, allowing the college to test the effectiveness of the SAT as a predictor of college success. Last fall applications rose 10%, with 1 in 6 scores withheld. Now it's crunch time for the school's admissions officers, who have holed up in an unassuming white clapboard house on campus to carry out the new policy. For two weeks, Mount Holyoke allowed TIME to sit in on its selection process, provided we did not use the real names of the applicants under discussion.

Like many highly selective small colleges, 164-year-old Mount Holyoke has traditionally required rigorous entrance exams. In recent years, however, the college has been relying less and less on tests, assuring applicants that other factors were more important. Still, students continued to obsess over scores. Four years ago, in an effort to ease some of that stress, Mount Holyoke cut back on the number of tests it required, making the more subject-specific SAT IIs optional. But the admissions staff continued to hear

SAT horror stories—about applicants spending $845 an hour on test prep, for example. So the college went a step further and conducted an informal study of the SAT's role in its admissions. It showed that the scores bore little relation to how well the students performed once they were on campus. A second analysis found that the SAT accounted at most for just 10% of each admissions decision. Says Jane Brown, the school's vice president for enrollment and college relations: "We concluded that the SAT was just a blunt instrument which doesn't help us cut to the core of who a student is."

To probe for this essence, officers now pore over transcripts, parse teacher recommendations and consult regularly with high school guidance counselors. Then they gather for closed-door deliberations that range from the celebratory (a budding feminist poet is crowned "the next Anne Sexton") to the snippy ("Her thank-you note to her interviewer looks like a third-grader wrote it"). Rarely, if ever, do these discussions touch on SATs, even for students who turn in 800s. The committee does dwell, however, on other scores, like those on Advanced Placement exams, SAT IIs if students submit them and even state tests like New York's Regents Exams. For students who shield their SATs, these secondary scores inevitably take on more weight. The committee, for example, is divided over one straight-A applicant. Then assistant director Debbie McCain Wesley men-

SENIOR Bernhardt blocked her scores

Scott Houston for TIME

tions that the student took just two AP courses out of 15 offered by her school—and scored 1 out of 5 on her AP test in U.S. history. "A 1 on an AP is really just showing up," argues her colleague Sara Schick. "I can't get past that score." Neither can the rest of the room. The girl is rated a 5, all but assuring her rejection.

The success of SAT blockers often turns on more subjective measures, such as a student's writing style—Mount Holyoke requires three essays and one graded writing sample—or her poise during an interview. The committee happily devours one student's account of her German ancestry, titled "Ode to Sauerkraut" but spends 20 minutes agonizing over an otherwise stellar applicant who wrote a "young" essay on the inspirational aspects of *Charlotte's Web*. Despite her banal musings, she is admitted. But the panel is far less forgiving of an applicant whose interview was "enjoyable but not terribly deep." Her faux pas? She confided her aspirations to study fashion design, a major the college does not offer.

Mount Holyoke has high hopes that its future applicants will devote the hours they once spent fretting over word analogies to worthier pursuits like community service or starring in school plays. Best of all, says Jane Brown, "we also think we'll see high-scoring students who don't submit scores simply on principle." Lis Bernhardt, a senior at Fairfield High School in Fairfield, Conn., was concerned more with pragmatism than principle. She spent months "consumed" by the SATs, investing countless hours—and more than $1,000—in tutoring to lift her scores. Then she toured Mount Holyoke, loved the campus and heard about its new SAT-optional stance. She submitted an early-decision application and received a thick acceptance letter in January. Says Lis: "It just appealed to me that they wanted to look at me as a person, the whole package." So she let them see it all—minus her SATs. ∎

Here Comes the Lego Test

Can't remember the last time your boss asked you to find the volume of a cylinder? Most of the skills and knowledge we use in our jobs are very different from those tested by traditional college-entrance exams, and those of us who score poorly on those tests will probably do just fine in the work world. So Deborah Bial, a doctoral student in education at Harvard, has developed a three-hour exam that uses group activities, personal interviews and even Lego blocks to identify kids with potential that might be missed by a test like the SAT. "Students

who succeed in college can overcome obstacles," says Bial, whose research is funded by a $1.9 million grant from the Andrew W. Mellon Foundation. "A standard paper-and-pencil test doesn't tell you much about these skills."

Bial's exam, the Bial-Dale College Adaptability Index, has been nicknamed the Lego Test for a 10-minute portion that asks small groups of students to reproduce a relatively complicated Lego robot. One at a time, students are allowed to go and look at the structure, which is placed in another room, but they can't take notes. In another tested activity, students lead a group discussion on a topic drawn from an envelope. In both cases, observers are watching to see who takes

initiative, who collaborates well and who is persistent.

Nine colleges are participating in a trial of Bial's test, which was first given to 400 students in New York City in October 1999. James Sumner, dean of admissions at 1,400-pupil Grinnell College in Iowa, is hoping a test like Bial's will help identify strong minority candidates the college might miss in its traditional SAT-and-ACT-based selection process. This year Grinnell accepted two minority students who participated in the Bial-Dale test. The next step for the research is to track whether the participants stay in school and how much they contribute to the campus environment. If the test does predict with any accuracy a student's persistence or adaptability in college, Bial hopes it will eventually become a standard that colleges use

along with high school grades and SAT or ACT scores.

Research on another alternative exam, this one written by Robert Sternberg, a psychologist at Yale, asks students to perform tasks reflecting their creativity and practicality. In one section, students write the caption for a cartoon or design the logo for a company. In another, they are asked how they would handle requesting a letter of recommendation from a teacher or sharing rent payments on an apartment. The test, given to 1,400 students this year, is being paid for by the College Board, the people behind the SAT. Even they realize, it seems, that some folks can succeed without knowing how to find the volume of a cylinder.

—By Rebecca Winters

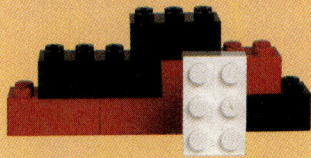

for admission. Even at the most competitive schools, some students' test scores are lower than you would think.

Out-of-class activities: Colleges look for depth of involvement (variety and how long you participated), initiative (leadership), and creativity demonstrated in activities, service, or work.

Recommendations: Most colleges require a recommendation from your high school guidance counselor. Some ask for references from teachers or other adults. If your counselor or teachers don't know you well, you should put together a student resume, or brag sheet, that outlines what you have done during your four years of high school. In this section, you'll find a worksheet that will help you put together your resume.

College interview: Required by most colleges with highly selective procedures. For further information, see "The College Interview" in the previous section.

ADMISSION PROCEDURES

Your first task in applying is to get application forms. That's easy. You can get them from your high school's guidance department, at college fairs, or by calling or writing to colleges and requesting applications. (See "Writing to a College for Information" in the previous section.) The trend, however, is leaning toward online applications, which you can do at the school's Web site. Admission information can also be gathered from college representatives, catalogs, Web sites, and directories; alumni or students attending the college; and campus visits. Take a look at "Dos and Don'ts for Filling out an Application" on page 57 for some guidelines.

Which Admissions Option is Best for You?

One of the first questions you will be asked on applications for four-year colleges and universities is which admission option you want. What they're talking about is whether you want to apply early action, early decision, etc.

If you're going to a two-year college, this doesn't apply to you. Two-year colleges usually have an "open-door" admission policy, which means that high school graduates may enroll as long as space is available. Sometimes vo-tech schools are somewhat selective, and competition for admission may be fairly intense for programs that are highly specialized.

Four-year institutions generally offer the following admissions options:

Early admission: A student of superior ability is admitted into college courses and programs before completing high school.

Early decision: A student declares

a first-choice college, requests that the college decide on acceptance early (between November and January), and agrees to enroll if accepted. Students with a strong high school record who are sure they want to attend a certain school should consider early decision admission. (See "More on Early Decision," on the next page.)

Early action: Similar to early decision, but if a student is accepted, he or she has until the regular admission deadline to decide whether or not to attend.

Early evaluation: A student can apply under early evaluation to find out if the chance of acceptance is good, fair, or poor. Applications are due before the regular admission deadline, and the student is given an opinion between January and March.

Regular admission: This is the most common option offered to students. A deadline is set when all applications must be received, and all notifications are sent out at the same time.

Rolling admission: The college accepts students who meet the academic requirements on a first-come, first-served basis until it fills its freshman class. No strict application deadline is specified. Applications are reviewed and decisions are made immediately (usually within two to three weeks). This method is commonly used at large state universities, so students should apply early for the best chance of acceptance.

Open admission: Virtually all high school graduates are admitted, regardless of academic qualifications.

Deferred admission: An accepted student is allowed to postpone enrollment for a year.

More on Early Decision

Early decision is a legally binding agreement between you and the college. If the college accepts you, you pay a deposit within a short period of time and sign an agreement stating that you will not apply to other colleges. To keep students from backing out, some colleges mandate that applicants' high school counselors cannot send transcripts to other institutions.

In many ways, early decision is a win-win for both students and colleges. Students can relax and enjoy their senior year of high school without waiting to see if other colleges

Student Counsel

Q: What made you want to apply to college early decision?

A: I visited lots of schools in Pennsylvania, but the minute I walked on the campus at Gettysburg, I knew I wanted to come here. I liked the way the campus was set up. It was small, and everything was together. The student-teacher ratio was low, and it had a good political science program. It had everything that I wanted.

But if you want to go early decision you have to visit the schools to be able to compare and contrast the different campuses. Many of the schools will have the same things, like small class size, but the way you feel about the campus is the largest factor because that's where you will be living. I visited Gettysburg four times, so when I went early decision, I was confident about it. I realized it was a huge step and knew I had to be sure. But after visiting here so many times, I knew I'd be unhappy anywhere else.

Kelly Keegan, College Freshman
Gettysburg College
Gettysburg, Pennsylvania
West Islip High School
West Islip, New York

have accepted them. And colleges know early in the year who is enrolled and can start planning the coming year.

When Is Early Decision the Right Decision?

For good and bad reasons, early decision is a growing trend, so why not just do it? Early decision is an excellent idea that comes with a warning. It's not a good idea unless you have done a thorough college search and know without a shred of doubt that this is the college for you. Don't go for early decision unless you've spent time on the campus, in classes and dorms, and you have a true sense of the academic and social climate of that college.

Early decision can get sticky if you change your mind. Parents of students who have signed agreements and then want to apply elsewhere get angry at high school counselors, saying they've taken away their rights to choose among colleges. They try to force them to send out transcripts even though their children have committed to one college. To guard against this scenario, some colleges ask parents and students to sign a statement signifying their understanding that early decision is a binding plan. Even some high schools now have their own form for students and parents to sign acknowledging that they completely realize the nature of an early decision agreement.

The Financial Reason Against Early Decision

Another common argument against early decision is that if an institution has you locked in, there's no incentive to offer applicants the best financial packages. The consensus seems to be that if you're looking to play the financial game, don't apply for early decision.

However, some folks argue that the best financial aid offers are usually made to attractive applicants. Generally, if a student receives an early decision offer, they fall into that category and so would get "the sweetest" financial aid anyway. That doesn't

mean that there aren't colleges out there using financial incentives to get students to enroll. A strong candidate who applies to six or eight schools and gets admitted to them all will look at how much money the colleges throw his or her way before making a decision.

Before You Decide...

If you're thinking about applying for early decision at a college, ask yourself these questions first. You'll be glad you did.

- ⏱ Why am I applying early decision?

- ⏱ Have I thoroughly researched several colleges and know what my options are?

- ⏱ Do I know why I'm going to college and what I want to accomplish there?

- ⏱ Have I visited several schools, spent time in classes, stayed overnight, and talked to professors?

- ⏱ Do the courses that the college offers match my goals?

- ⏱ Am I absolutely convinced that one college clearly stands out above all others?

WHAT DO YOU NEED IN ORDER TO APPLY?

Freshman applications can be filed any time after you have completed your junior year of high school. Colleges strongly recommend that students apply by April (at the latest) of their senior year in order to be considered for acceptance, scholarships, financial aid, and housing. College requirements may vary, so always read and comply with specific requirements. In general, admission officers are interested in the following basic materials:

➢ A completed and signed application and any required application fee.

➢ An official copy of your high school transcript, including your class ranking and grade point average. The transcript must include all work completed as of the date the application is submitted. Check with your guidance counselor for questions about these items. If you apply on line,

DO'S AND DON'TS FOR FILLING OUT AN APPLICATION

ONE OF THE MOST INTIMIDATING STEPS OF APPLYING FOR ADMISSION TO COLLEGE IS FILLING OUT ALL THE FORMS. THIS LIST OF DOS AND DON'TS WILL HELP YOU PUT YOUR BEST FOOT FORWARD ON YOUR COLLEGE APPLICATIONS.

DO

- Read applications and directions carefully.
- Make sure that everything that is supposed to be included is enclosed.
- Fill out your own applications. Type the information yourself to avoid crucial mistakes.
- Start with the simple applications and then progress to the more complex ones.
- Make copies of applications, and practice filling one out before you complete the original.
- Type or neatly print your answers, and then proofread the applications and essays several times for accuracy. Also ask someone else to proofread it for you.
- If asked, describe how you can make a contribution to the schools to which you apply.
- Be truthful, and do not exaggerate your accomplishments.
- Keep a copy of all forms you submit to colleges.
- Be thorough and on time.

DON'T

- Use correction fluid. If you type your application, use a correctable typewriter or the liftoff strips to correct mistakes. Better yet, fill out your application online.
- Write in script. If you don't have access to a computer or typewriter, print neatly.
- Leave blank spaces. Missing information may cause your application to be sent back or delayed while admission officers wait for complete information.
- Be unclear. If the question calls for a specific answer, don't try to dodge it by being vague.

you must inform your guidance counselor and request that he or she send your transcript to the schools you're applying to. Your application will not be processed without a transcript.

- An official record of your ACT or SAT I scores.
- Other items that may be required include letters of recommendation, an essay, the secondary school report form and midyear school report (sent in by your guidance counselor after you fill out a portion of the form), and

any financial aid forms required by the college.

Use the "College Application Checklist" in this section to make sure you have everything you need before you send off that application.

MORE MUMBO JUMBO

Besides confusing terms like deferred admission, early decision, and early evaluation discussed previously in this section, you'll most likely stumble upon some additional terms that might bamboozle you. Here, we explain a few more:

Academic Calendar

Traditional semesters: Two equal periods of time during a school year.

Early semester: Two equal periods of time during a school year. The first semester is completed before Christmas.

Trimester: Calendar year divided into three equal periods of time. The third trimester replaces summer school.

Quarter: Four equal periods of time during a school year.

4-1-4: Two equal terms of about four months separated by a one-month term.

Accreditation

Accreditation is recognition of a college or university by a regional or national organization, which indicates that the institution has met its objectives and is maintaining prescribed educational standards. Colleges may be accredited by one of six regional associations of schools and colleges and by any one of many national specialized accrediting bodies.

Specialized accreditation of individual programs is granted by national professional organizations. This is intended to ensure that specific programs meet or exceed minimum requirements established by the professional organization. States may require that students in some professions that grant licenses graduate from an accredited program as one qualification for licensure.

Accreditation is somewhat like receiving a pass/fail grade. It doesn't differentiate colleges and universities that excel from those that meet minimum requirements. Accreditation applies to all programs within an institution, but it does not mean that all programs are of equal quality within an institution. Accreditation does not guarantee transfer recognition by other colleges. Transfer decisions are made by individual institutions.

Affiliation

Not-for-profit colleges are classified into one of the following cate-

CREATING YOUR STUDENT RESUME

At the beginning of this section, we described how a student resume can help your guidance counselors and teachers write their letters of recommendation for you and for college admissions counselors to see who you are "at a glance." Take the time now to write your own resume, or brag sheet. You can use this sample student resume as a template to create one for yourself. Be sure to keep your resume to one page, be truthful, and don't be afraid to toot your own horn.

Name
Street Address
City, State, Zip
Phone
E-mail, if applicable

High School	Name
	Address
	City, State, Zip
Graduation Date	Month, Year
Current GPA	3.5
Current Class Rank	Top 25 percent
Test Scores	SAT I: May 2001
	V-600; M-540
	ACT: April 2001
	Composite-22; English-22; Math-21;
	Reading-22; Science Reasoning-24
Academic Honors	National Honor Society, April 2000
	Honor Roll, 1998–2001
Athletics	Soccer, October 1998–present
	Most Valuable Player–2000
Activities	Student Government, September 1998–present
	Secretary, 2000–2001
	Volunteer, spring 1997–present
	Children's Hospital, Philadelphia, PA
	5 hours per week
Part-Time Work	Sales Clerk, May 1998–present
	Philadelphia Zoo gift shop
	Cashier/Sales, July 1997–May 1998
	Petsmart
Major Goals	To major in biology or zoology
	(optional, if you know your major)
Interests	Sports, reading, animals

gories: state-assisted, private/independent, or private/church-supported. The institution's affiliation does not guarantee the quality or nature of the institution, and it may or may not have an effect on the religious life of students.

State-assisted colleges and universities and private/independent colleges do not have requirements related to the religious activity of their students. The influence of religion varies among private/church-supported colleges. At some, religious services or study are encouraged or required; at others, religious affiliation is less apparent.

Articulation Agreement

Articulation agreements facilitate the transfer of students and credits among state-assisted institutions of higher education by establishing transfer procedures and equitable treatment of all students in the system.

One type of articulation agreement links two or more colleges so that students can continue to make progress toward their degree, even if they must attend different schools at different times. For example, some states' community colleges have agreements with their universities that permit gradu-

---

From the Guidance Office

Q: Why are essays so important to the college application?

A: Students focus more on grades than anything else. They think grades are the be-all and end-all and that an SAT score will get them in. For most selective schools, that's just one piece of the pie. Many of the schools in the upper 20 percent of competitive schools consider the essay more heavily. Essays show whether the student is a thinker, creative, and analytical. They're looking for the type of personality that can shine rather than one that simply can spit out names and dates. When everyone has high SATs in a pool of applicants, the essay is what makes one student stand out over another.

Patsy Lovelady
Counselor
MacArthur High School
San Antonio, Texas

ates of college parallel programs to transfer with junior standing.

A second type of articulation agreement links secondary (high school) and postsecondary institutions to allow students to gain college credit for relevant vocational courses. This type of agreement saves students time and tuition in the pursuit of higher learning.

Because articulation agreements vary from school to school and from program to program, it is recommended that students check with their home institution and the institution they are interested in attending in order to fully understand the options available to them and each institution's specific requirements.

Cross-Registration

Cross-registration is a cooperative arrangement offered by many colleges and universities for the purpose of increasing the number and types of courses offered at any one institution. This arrangement allows students to cross-register for one or more courses at any participating host institution. While specific cross-registration program requirements may vary, typically a student can cross-register without having to pay the host institution additional tuition.

If your college participates in cross-registration, check with your home institution concerning any additional tuition costs and request a cross-registration form. Check with your adviser and registrar at your home institution to make sure that the course you plan to take is approved, and then contact the host institution for cross-registration instructions. Make sure that there is space available in the course you want to take at the host institution, as some host institutions give their own students registration priority.

To participate in cross-registration, you may need to be a full-time student (some programs allow part-time student participation) in good academic and financial standing at your home institution. Check with both colleges well in advance for all of the specific requirements.

WRITING THE APPLICATION ESSAY

Application essays show how you think and how you write. They also reveal additional information about you that is not in your other application material. Not all colleges require essays, and those that do often have a preferred topic. Make sure you write about the topic that is specified and keep to the length of pages or words. If the essay asks for 300 words, don't submit 50 or 500.

Some examples of essay topics include:

Tell us about yourself. Describe your personality and a special accomplishment. Illustrate the unique aspects of who you are, what you do, and what you want out of life. Share an experience that made an impact on you, or write about something you have learned from your parents.

Tell us about an academic or extracurricular interest or idea. Show how a book, experience, quotation, or idea reflects or shapes your outlook and aspirations.

Tell us why you want to come to our college. Explain why your goals and interests match the programs and offerings of that particular school. This question requires some research about the school. Be specific.

Show us an imaginative side of your personality. This question demands originality but is a great opportunity to show off your skills as a writer. Start writing down your thoughts and impressions well before the essay is due. Think about how you have changed over the years so that if and when it comes time to write about yourself,

you will have plenty of information. Write about something that means a lot to you, and support your thoughts with reasons and examples. Then explain why you care about your topic.

The essay should not be a summary of your high school career. Describe yourself as others see you, and use a natural, conversational style. Use an experience to set the scene in which you will illustrate something about yourself. For example, you might discuss how having a disabled relative helped you to appreciate life's simple pleasures. Or you may use your athletic experiences to tell how you learned the value of teamwork. The essay is your chance to tell something positive or enriching about yourself, so highlight an experience that will make the reader interested in you.

Outline in the essay what you have to offer the college. Explain why you want to attend the institution and how your abilities and goals match the strengths and offerings at the university. Write, rewrite, and edit. Do not

COLLEGE APPLICATION CHECKLIST

Keep track of your applications by inserting a check mark or the completion date in the appropriate column and row.

	College 1	College 2	College 3	College 4
Campus visit				
Campus interview				
Letters of recommendation				
NAME:				
Date requested				
Follow-up				
NAME:				
Date requested				
Follow-up				
NAME:				
Date requested				
Follow-up				
Counselor recommendation form to counselor				
Secondary school report form to counselor				
Test scores requested				
Transcripts sent				
Application completed				
Essay completed				
All signatures collected				
Financial aid forms enclosed				
Application fee enclosed				
Postage affixed/copies made/return address on envelope				
Letters of acceptance/denial/wait list received				
Colleges notified of intent				
Tuition deposit sent				
Housing and other forms submitted to chosen college				
Orientation scheduled				

try to dash off an essay in one sitting. The essay will improve with time and thought. Proofread and concentrate on spelling, punctuation, and content. Have someone else take a look at your essay. Make copies and save them after mailing the original.

Admission officers look for the person inside the essay. They seek students with a breadth of knowledge and experiences, someone with depth and perspective. Inner strength and commitment are admired, too. Not everyone is a winner all the time. The essay is a tool you can use to develop your competitive edge. Your essay should explain why you should be admitted over other applicants.

As a final word, write the essay from the heart. It should have life and not be contrived or one-dimensional. Avoid telling them what they want to hear; instead, be yourself.■

7 COLLEGE BOUND AND MORE—
FOR THOSE WITH SPECIAL NEEDS AND TALENTS

Athletes, minorities, artists/musicians, students with disabilities, homeschoolers, and distance learners—this section's for you.

Those who plan to attend college have a lot to think about. But some of you add a little more to the heap of things to consider because you have a few more needs to consider. Perhaps you're an athlete or student with a special talent—you'll want to find out how to use that talent to your advantage. If you're an African-American, Hispanic/Latino, or Native American student, you'll find many organizations that you can use for help and information. Students with disabilities have special needs they must accommodate, while homeschooled students and distance learners have other factors to think about. *GAJ* has assembled information for all of these groups in one place, including financial aid information that might apply to you.

ATHLETES GO TO COLLEGE

If you weren't a planner before, but you want to play sports while in college or go to college on an athletic scholarship, you'd better become a planner now. There are many regulations and conditions you need to know ahead of time so that you don't miss out on possible opportunities.

First, think about whether or not you have what it takes to play college sports. It's a tough question to ask, but it's a necessary one. In general, playing college sports requires the basic skills and natural ability, a solid knowledge of the sport, overall body strength, speed, and sound academics. Today's athletes are stronger and faster because of improved methods of training and conditioning. They

are coached in skills and techniques, and they begin training in their sport at an early age. Remember, your talents will be compared with those from across the U.S. and around the world.

Second, know the background. Most college athletic programs are regulated by the National Collegiate Athletic Association (NCAA), an organization that has established rules on eligibility, recruiting, and financial aid. The NCAA has three membership divisions: Division I, Division II, and Division III. Institutions are members of one or another division according to the size and scope of their athletic programs and whether they provide athletic scholarships.

If you are planning to enroll in college as a freshman and you wish to participate in Division I or Division II athletics, you must be certified by the NCAA Initial-Eligibility Clearinghouse. The Clearinghouse was established as a separate organization by the NCAA member institutions to ensure consistent interpretation of NCAA initial-eligibility requirements for all prospective student athletes at all member institutions.

You should start the certification process when you are a junior in high school. Check with your counselor to make sure you are taking a core curriculum that meets NCAA requirements. Also, register to take the ACT or SAT I as a junior. Submit your Student Release Form (available in your guidance counseling

ATHLETIC RESUME

Name

Address

High school address and phone number

Coach's name

Height/weight

Foot speed (by specific event)

Position played

Weight classification

GPA

Class rank

ACT or SAT I scores (or when you plan to take them)

Athletic records

All-state teams

Special awards

Off-season accomplishments

Weightlifting exercises

Vertical jumps

Pushups

Bench jumps

Shuttle run

Leadership characteristics

Former successful athletes from your high school

Outstanding capabilities

Citizenship

Alumni parents/relatives

Team schedule with dates and times

Videotape with jersey number identified

Newspaper clippings about you or your team

---

office) to the Clearinghouse by the beginning of your senior year.

Currently, in order to be eligible for practice, participation in regular season competition, and athletically related financial aid during the freshman year of college, a student must meet the following criteria:

Division I Requirements

- Graduate from high school
- Maintain a minimum 2.5 grade-point average in a core curriculum of at least thirteen academic courses. If you do not maintain this minimum GPA, please refer to Minimum SAT I and ACT Requirements.
- 4 units of English
- 2 units of social science
- 2 units of mathematics (must be 1 unit of algebra and 1 unit of geometry)
- 2 units of natural or physical science (including 1 laboratory science)
- 2 units of additional courses in the above areas and/or foreign-language or computer science
- 1 unit of an additional course in English, mathematics, or natural/physical science
- Receive a minimum score on the SAT I or the ACT:
  - SAT I—minimum combined score of 820 (verbal + math score)
  - ACT—minimum combined score of 68 (sum of the four scores)

Division II Requirements

- Graduate from high school
- Maintain a minimum 2.0 grade-point average in a core curriculum of at least thirteen academic courses:
- 3 units of English
- 2 units of social science
- 2 units of mathematics (algebra/geometry)
- 2 units of natural or physical science (including 1 laboratory science)
- 2 units of additional courses in the above areas and/or foreign language or computer science
- 2 units of additional courses in English, mathematics, or natural/physical science
- Receive a minimum score on the SAT I or the ACT:
  - SAT I—minimum combined score of 820 (verbal + math score)
  - ACT—minimum combined score of 68 (sum of the four scores)

Division III Requirements

In order to be eligible for practice, participation in regular season competition, and need-based or merit-based financial aid, an entering freshman must satisfy the following:

- The eligibility rules and requirements of the institution

⑦ The eligibility rules of the athletic-conference in which the institution holds membership

Initial Eligibility of Freshman Athletes for Division I and II

Students who plan to participate in NCAA Division I or II college sports must obtain the Student Release Form from their high school, complete it, and send it to the NCAA Clearinghouse. This form authorizes high schools to release student transcripts, including test scores, proof of grades, and other academic information, to the Clearinghouse. It also authorizes the Clearinghouse to release this information to the colleges that request it. The form and corresponding fee must be received before any documents will be processed. (Fee waivers are available for economically disadvantaged students. Check with your counselor for fee waiver information.)

Students must also make sure that the Clearinghouse receives ACT and/or SAT I score reports. Students can have score reports sent directly to the Clearinghouse by entering a specific code (9999) printed in the ACT and SAT I registration packets.

Once a year, high schools will send an updated Form 48-H, which lists each course offering that meets NCAA core course requirements. The Clearinghouse personnel will validate the form. Thereafter, the Clearinghouse will determine each student's initial eligibility.

Collegiate institutions will request information from the Clearinghouse on the initial eligibility of prospective student-athletes. The Clearinghouse will make a certification decision and report it directly to the institution.

Three Types of Eligibility Are Possible

1 Certification of eligibility for expense-paid campus visits.

2 Preliminary certification of eligibility to participate in college sports (appears likely to meet all NCAA requirements but not yet graduated).

3 Final certification granted when proof of graduation is received.

Additional information about the Clearinghouse can be found in the *Guide for the College-Bound Student-Athlete*, published by the NCAA. To get a copy of this guide, call 800-638-3731 (toll-free).

You can also visit the NCAA Web site at www.ncaa.org.

National Association of Intercollegiate Athletics (NAIA) Regulations

The National Association of Intercollegiate Athletics (NAIA) has different eligibility requirements for student athletes. To be eligible to participate in intercollegiate athletics as an incoming freshman, two of the following three requirements must be met:

1 Have a 2.0 (C) or higher cumulative final grade point average in high school.

2 Have a composite score of 18 or higher on the ACT or an 860 total score or higher on the SAT I on a single test administered on a national test date.

3 Have a top-half final class rank in his/her high school graduating class.

Student-athletes must also have on file at the college an official ACT or SAT I score report from the appropriate national testing center. Results reported on the student's high school transcript are not acceptable. Students must request that their test scores be forwarded to the college's admission office.

If you have additional questions about NAIA eligibility, write to:

NAIA
6120 South Yale Avenue
Suite 1450
Tulsa, Oklahoma 74136
Phone: 918-494-8828

Or visit their Web site at www. naia.org

What You Need to Know about Athletic Scholarships

Whether you're male or female or interested in baseball, basketball, crew, cross-country, fencing, field hockey, football, golf, gymnastics, lacrosse, sailing, skiing, soccer, softball, swimming and diving, tennis, track and field, volleyball, or wrestling, there may be scholarship dollars available for you. But, there's that word again—planning. You must plan ahead if you want to get your tuition paid for in return for your competitive abilities.

At the beginning of your junior year, ask your guidance counselor to help you make sure that you take the required number and mix of academic courses and to inform you of the SAT I and ACT score minimums that must be met to play college sports. Also ask your counselor about academic requirements, because you must be certified by the NCAA Initial-Eligibility Clearinghouse, and this process must be started by the end of your junior year.

But before you do all that, think. Do you want and need an athletic

TYPES OF ATHLETIC SCHOLARSHIPS

COLLEGES AND UNIVERSITIES OFFER TWO BASIC TYPES OF ATHLETIC SCHOLARSHIPS: THE INSTITUTIONAL GRANT, WHICH IS AN AGREEMENT BETWEEN THE ATHLETE AND THE COLLEGE, AND THE CONFERENCE GRANT, WHICH ALSO BINDS THE COLLEGE TO THE ATHLETE. THE DIFFERENCE IS THAT THE ATHLETE WHO SIGNS AN INSTITUTIONAL GRANT CAN CHANGE HIS OR HER MIND AND SIGN WITH ANOTHER TEAM. THE ATHLETE WHO SIGNS A CONFERENCE CONTRACT CANNOT RENEGOTIATE ANOTHER CONTRACT WITH A SCHOOL THAT HONORS CONFERENCE GRANTS. HERE ARE THE VARIOUS WAYS THAT A SCHOLARSHIP MAY BE OFFERED.

FULL FOUR-YEAR. Also known as full ride, these scholarships pay for room, board, tuition, and books. Due to the high cost of awarding scholarships, this type of grant is being discouraged by conferences around the country in favor of the one-year renewable contract or the partial scholarship.

FULL ONE-YEAR RENEWABLE CONTRACT. This type of scholarship, which has basically replaced the four-year grant, is automatically renewed at the end of each school year for four years if the conditions of the contract are met. The recruiter will probably tell you in good faith that the intent is to offer a four-year scholarship, but he is legally only allowed to offer you a one-year grant. You must ask the recruiter as well as other players what the record has been of renewing scholarships for athletes who comply athletically, academically, and socially. Remember—no athlete can receive more than a full scholarship.

ONE-YEAR TRIAL GRANT (FULL OR PARTIAL). A verbal agreement between you and the institution that at the end of the year, your renewal will be dependent upon your academic and athletic performance.

PARTIAL SCHOLARSHIP. The partial grant is any part of the total cost of college. You may be offered room and board but not tuition and books, or you may be offered just tuition. The possibility exists for you to negotiate to a full scholarship after you complete your freshman year.

WAIVER OF OUT-OF-STATE FEES. This award is for out-of-state students to attend the college or university at the same fee as an in-state student.

scholarship? Certainly, it is prestigious to receive an athletic scholarship, but some athletes compare having an athletic scholarship to having a job at which you are expected to perform. Meetings, training sessions, practices, games, and (don't forget) studying take away from social and leisure time. Also, with very few full-ride scholarships available, you will most likely receive a partial scholarship or a one-year renewable contract. If your scholarship is not renewed, you may be left scrambling for financial aid. So ask yourself if you are ready for the demands and roles associated with accepting an athletic scholarship.

If you decide that you want an athletic scholarship, you need to market yourself to beat the stiff competition. Think of yourself as a newly designed sports car, and you're selling the speed, look, and all those other goodies to a waiting public. The point is that you're going to have to sell, or market, your abilities to college recruiters. You're the product, and the college recruiter is the buyer. What makes you stand out from the rest?

College recruiters look for a combination of the following attributes when awarding athletic scholarships: academic excellence, a desire to win, self-motivation, ability to perform as a team player, willingness to help others, cooperation with coaching staff, attitude in practice, attitude in games/matches, toughness, strength, optimal height and weight, and excellence.

In order to successfully sell your skills to a college or university, you'll need to take three main steps: 1) locate the colleges and universities that offer scholarships in your sport, 2) contact the institution in a formal manner, and 3) follow up each lead.

Finding and Getting Athletic Scholarships

Ask your coach or assistant coaches for recommendations; learn about the conference or institution from newspaper or television coverage; ask your guidance counselor; review guidebooks, reference books (check out *Peterson's Sports Scholarships and College Athletics Programs*) and the Internet; ask alumni; or attend a tryout or campus visit. You can also call the NCAA to request a recruiting guide for your sport. These three steps can help you snag that scholarship.

1 **Contact the school formally.** Once you make a list of schools in which you are interested, get the name of the head coach and write a letter to the top twenty schools on your list. Then compile a factual resume of your athletic and academic accomplishments. (See the sample "Athletic Resume" included in this section.) Put together 10 to 15 minutes of video highlights of your athletic performance (with your jersey number noted), get letters of recommendation from your high school coach and your off-season coach, and include a season schedule.

2 **Ace the Interview.** When you meet a recruiter or coach, exhibit self-confidence with a firm handshake, by maintaining eye contact, and by making sure that you are well groomed. According to recruiters, the most effective attitude is quiet confidence, respect, sincerity, and enthusiasm.

3 **Ask Good Questions.** Don't be afraid to probe the recruiter by getting answers to the following questions: Do I qualify athletically and academically? If I am recruited, what would the parameters of the scholarship be? For what position am I being considered? It's okay to ask the recruiter to declare what level of interest he or she has in you.

4 **Follow Up.** Persistence pays off when it comes to seeking an athletic scholarship, and timing can be everything. There are four good times when a follow-up letter from your coach or a personal letter from you is extremely effective: prior to your senior season, during or just after the senior season, just prior to or after announced conference-affiliated signing dates or national association signing dates, and late summer, in case scholarship offers have been withdrawn or declined. *(Continued on page 66)*

Dividing Line ■ Jack E. White

WHY DROPPING THE SAT IS BAD FOR BLACKS

Until we ace the test, we can't say we're equal

If I had my way, the University of California would keep using the SAT until black students catch up with whites, Asians and immigrants from the Caribbean. It's a matter of ethnic pride. I'm as fed up with the tortuous theories experts have concocted to explain why our kids' scores are the lowest of any racial group as I am with the bigots who claim that proves they can't ever measure up. There's simply no excuse for black youngsters with college-educated parents to perform worse than white youths whose folks only finished high school. The only way to silence the critics is to close the black achievement gap, not to throw out the test because we're embarrassed by the results.

I can already hear my black and white liberal friends howling that I've bought into Ward Connerly's crusade against affirmative action. So be it. I'm less interested in what right-wingers like him think than I am in what we think, and frankly, I don't understand why so many of us continue to pour so much more energy into attacking the alleged biases of standardized tests than we invest in improving our children's scores. I suspect it's because we're afraid that the racists are right when they claim that our kids can't cut it intellectually, so why bother trying. That's nonsense, of course—an echo of the sense of inferiority that afflicted blacks during the bad old days of Jim Crow. But despite our growing affluence and our gains from the civil rights movement, a lot of African Americans seem to have been unable to put those nagging racial self-doubts behind them. In my opinion, such inner fears constitute the most difficult obstacle to our continued progress.

This doesn't mean that African Americans on the whole are suffering from a "cult of anti-intellectualism," as John McWhorter, a black professor at the University of California, Berkeley, claims in his book *Losing the Race: Self-Sabotage in Black America*. Despite all the fuss about some black teenagers' disparaging their more studious peers for "acting white," most of us, regardless of age or where we stand on the economic ladder, value high achievement as much as anyone. Our problem is not cultural. It's political and psychological. Too many of us have forgotten that we are still engaged in a struggle for racial redemption that involves, among other things, beating whites at their own game in the classroom as well as on the playing field. We've got to start hitting the books with the same passion and moral courage that we used to overcome slavery and segregation. Our honor demands it. And so does our history.

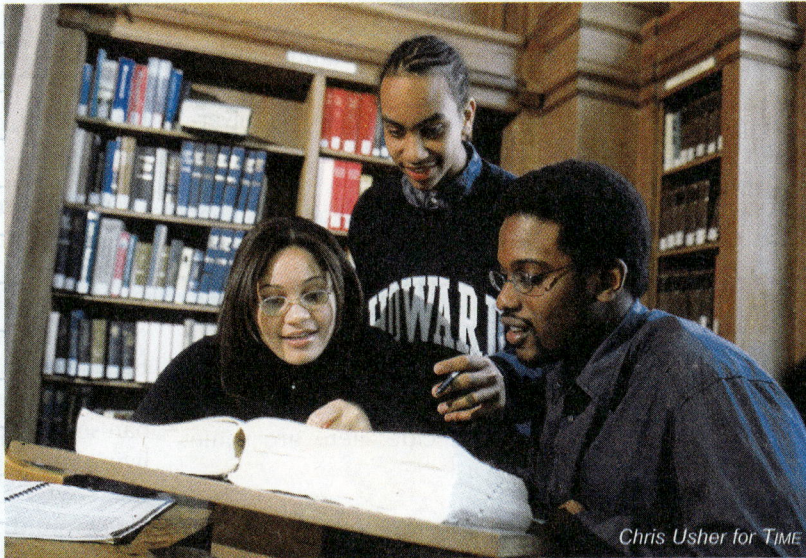

AT HOWARD UNIVERSITY: Academic standards are rising—and so are the SAT scores

Chris Usher for TIME

The sad truth is that as long as we're lagging behind academically, we can't call ourselves equal. Now that our civil rights are legally secure and many of us have become prosperous, we need to erase every last, lingering scintilla of doubt about black intellectual ability. It doesn't matter that such beliefs are totally specious and rooted in racism. They influence decision makers in colleges, the government and corporations. If the powers that be believe in their hearts that blacks aren't as smart as everyone else (as many of them do—even if they would never admit it), we will be patronized, not treated with respect.

That's one of the reasons why thoughtful blacks in higher education like H. Patrick Swygert, president of Howard University, aren't willing to jettison the SAT. He's adamantly opposed to "any abandonment of standardized tests that would carry with it the implication that we just can't meet the mark." He doesn't think the SAT by itself is an adequate measure of students' potential (nor do I). But it is an important indicator of how well prepared they are for demanding college work. As a consequence, Howard (where my dad taught for 40 years) has been raising its admissions standards. The average SAT score of incoming freshmen has gone up from about 900 to 1062 in the five years that Swygert has been president. Yet Howard is attracting more applicants than ever, welcoming 1,432 freshmen last year, the largest incoming class in decades. Swygert insists there's only one way to ensure that the opportunities created by the civil rights movement won't be slammed shut again: by meeting the same standards as everyone else. "We can't let those openings be constricted because we somehow either failed to make the cut or were viewed as being unable to make it," says he.

What I hear in those words is an appeal to black pride and determination as we fight to attain the elusive commodity that economist Glenn Loury once described as "equal respect in the eyes of one's fellow citizens." It's going to require, among other things, installing tougher classes, especially in math, sciences and literature, and making sure our kids take them; better teachers; changes in study habits; and above all else, a new burst of self-confidence. We've got to believe that even at their most bigoted, whites never came up with a test blacks couldn't ace, including the SAT. We've got to make second-class scholarship—and low test scores—as intolerable to us as second-class citizenship used to be. ■

To sum up, you know yourself better than anyone, so you must look at your skills—both athletic and academic—objectively. Evaluate the skills you need to improve, and keep the desire to improve alive in your heart. Develop your leadership skills, and keep striving for excellence with your individual achievements. Keep your mind open as to what school you want to attend, and keep plugging away, even when you are tired, sore, and unsure. After all, athletes are trained to be winners!

MINORITY STUDENTS GO TO COLLEGE

African-American, Hispanic/Latino, and Native-American high school students have a lot of doors into higher education opening for them. In fact, most colleges want to respond to the social and economic disadvantages of certain groups of Americans. They want to reflect the globalization of our economy. They want their student populations to look like the rest of America, which means people from many different backgrounds and ethnic groups. This isn't just talk either. You'll find that most colleges have at least one member of the admissions staff who specializes in recruiting minorities.

One of the reasons college admissions staff are recruiting minorities and want to accommodate their needs is because there are more minorities thinking of attending college—and graduating. Let's put some numbers to these statements. According to the Department of Education, in 1976, 16 percent of college students were minorities, compared to 27 percent in 1997. Much of the change can be attributed to rising numbers of Hispanic and Asian students. The proportion of Asian and Pacific Islander students rose from 2 percent to 6 percent, and the Hispanic proportion rose from 4 percent to 9 percent during that same time period. The proportion of black students fluctuated during most of the early part of the period before rising slightly to 11 percent in 1997, the last year for which data was collected on this subject.

GAJ has a lot of information in this section to help you make decisions about college and paying for college. Perhaps the most important information we can give you is that if you want to go to college, you can. There are a lot of organizations ready to assist you. So go for it. See the list of organizations in this section and check with the colleges in which you're interested to connect with the minority affairs office.

Should You Attend a Historically Black College or University?

Choosing which college to attend is usually a difficult decision for anyone to make, but when an African-American student is considering attending either a historically black college or university (HBCU) or a traditionally white university, a whole other set of family and cultural issues are raised.

There are many valid reasons that favor one or the other. Some are obvious differences. Parents and their children have to be honest with themselves and take a long, hard look at the needs of the student and how the campus environment can fulfill them. To help you decide, here are some questions to ask:

Do I know what's really important to me?

Look at the reasons why you want a degree and what you want to achieve with it. Is the choice to attend an HBCU yours or your family's? Do you have a particular field of study you want to pursue? Sometimes students can get so caught up in applying to a particular institution, they don't realize it doesn't even offer their major.

How will this campus fit my plans for the future?

There's no substitute for doing your homework about the campuses you're seriously considering. Know the reputation of those campuses in the community and among employers and the general population. Find out about graduation, retention, and placement rates.

Does this campus have the facilities and living conditions that suit my comfort level?

Finding a campus where you're comfortable is a big factor in choosing a college. What do you want in campus facilities and living conditions? For instance, if you currently attend a small private high school in a suburban setting, perhaps you wouldn't like living on a large urban campus with peers who don't mirror your kind of background.

What level of support will I get on campus?

Students considering institutions where few people are like them should look at the available support systems and organizations that will be available to them. Parents need to feel comfortable with the contact person on campus.

When all the factors that determine the choice of a college are laid out, the bottom line is which institution best meets your needs. For some African-American students, an HBCU is the best choice. For others, it's not. African-American students reflect many backgrounds, and there is no single decision that will be right for everyone.

Academic and Financial Resources for Minority Students

In addition to churches, sororities and fraternities, and college minority affairs offices, minority students can receive information and assistance from the following organizations:

ASPIRA

An association of community-based organizations that provide leadership, development, and educational services to Latino youths.

1444 Eye Street, NW, Suite 800
Washington, D.C. 20005
202-835-3600
www.aspira.org

INROADS

A national career-development organization that places and develops talented minority students (African American, Hispanic American, and Native American) in business and industry.

10 South Broadway, Suite 700
St. Louis, Missouri 63102
314-241-7488
www.inroadsinc.org

National Action Council for Minorities in Engineering (NACME)

An organization that aims to increase the number of minorities who earn bachelor's degrees in engineering by offering an Incentive Grants Program, Summer Engineering Employment Project, field services, and publications for parents and students.

The Empire State Building
350 Fifth Avenue, Suite 2212
New York, New York 10118-2299
212-279-2626
www.nacme.org

National Association for the Advancement of Colored People (NAACP)

The purpose of the NAACP is to improve the political, educational, social, and economic status of minority groups; to eliminate racial prejudice; to keep the public aware of the adverse effects of racial discrimination; and to take lawful action to secure its elimination, consistent with the efforts of the national organization.

4805 Mt. Hope Drive
Baltimore, Maryland 21205
410-358-8900
www.naacp.org

The National Urban League

The Education and Youth Services Department of the Urban League provides services for African Americans and economically disadvantaged people. These services include basic academic development, GED test preparation for youths and adults, after-school tutoring for children, parent training classes, scholarships, an annual tour of historically black colleges and universities, and summer employment for youths. Call individual Urban League offices in your state.

120 Wall Street
8th Floor
New York, New York 10005
212-558-5300 (national office)
www.nul.org

United Negro College Fund (UNCF)

The UNCF provides scholarships for undergraduates who attend one of forty private, historically black colleges. Students must be accepted first and then nominated by the college's financial aid director. Programs and services include summer learning programs, internships, precollege and mentoring programs, and international programs.

8260 Willow Oaks Corporate Drive
Fairfax, Virginia 22031
800-331-2244 (toll-free)
www.uncf.org

Scholarships for Minority Students

The following is just a sample of the many scholarships available to minority students.

Blackfeet Tribal Education Grants

Available to members of the Blackfeet Tribe. Up to $3,500 in awards.

P.O. Box 850
Browning, Montana 59417
406-338-7521

Bureau of Indian Affairs Office of Indian Education Programs

Available to undergraduates in a federally recognized tribe. Award amounts vary.

1849 C Street, NW, MS 3512-MIB
Washington, D.C. 20240
202-208-6123

Hispanic Scholarship Fund General Program

Limited to Hispanic students enrolled at a two- or four-year institution. Up to $2,000 in awards.

Scholarship Committee
Hispanic Scholarship Fund
One Sansome Street, Suite 1000
San Francisco, California 94104
415-445-9930

National Achievement Scholarship Corporation

Limited to African-American high school students who have taken the PSAT/NMSQT. Up to $2,000 in awards.

Achievement Program
1560 Sherman Avenue, Suite 200
Evanston, Illinois 60201
847-866-5100

National Association of Minority Engineering Program Administrators National Scholarship Fund

Limited to African-American, Hispanic, and Native-American/ Eskimo students with interest and potential for an undergraduate degree in engineering. Up to $30,000.

National Scholarship Selection Committee Chair
NAMEPA National Scholarship Foundation
1133 West Mores Boulevard
Suite 201
Winter Park, Florida 32789-3788
407-647-8839

Jackie Robinson Foundation Scholarship

For minority students accepted to a four-year college and with demonstrated academic achievement and financial need. Award up to $6,000. Visit the Web site at www. jackierobinson.org for more information.

Online Resources

Hispanic Association of Colleges and Universities
www.hacu.com

The American Indian Higher Education Consortium
www.aihec.org

Minority On-Line Information Service (MOLIS)
www.sciencewise.com/molis

Petersons.com has a listing of historically black colleges and universities plus articles of interest to minority students who are college bound.
www.petersons.com

Print Resources

The Big Book of Minority Opportunities, by Elizabeth Oaks, Ferguson Publishing, 1997

The Black Student's Guide to Scholarships, by Barry Beckham, Madison Books, 1999

The Minority and Women's Complete Scholarship Book, Sourcebooks Trade, 1998

Financial Aid for Hispanic Americans, by Gail Ann Schlacter et al, Reference Services Press, 1999

ARTISTS, MUSICIANS, DANCERS, AND ACTORS GO TO COLLEGE

For some high school students, there's no question that they will go to an institution that will take their love for music, art, or theater and develop it into a career. But how will you know if you have what it takes to go to a school where everyone there lives and breathes only one subject? This section can help you decide what's right for you.

What's the Best Way to Develop Your Talent?

Passion is the key element for which to look if you think you want to go to a specialized school or conservatory. However, not every student is cut out for such a concentrated focus at the undergraduate degree level.

If you're not absolutely sure you want to paint or play music for a living, it's probably more advantageous to attend a liberal arts university with a respected music, art, or theater department. Specialty schools accelerate the process of developing talent, as students are quickly immersed into the very heart of their skills. Such a focused environment is not the place

for the undecided student.

The Case for NOT Going to a Specialty School

A highly specialized degree might make it difficult to succeed in today's workplace. Whether you get your degree from a specialty school or university, you're still going to need a job after graduation. Those few stellar talents who are immediately snapped up by top orchestras, theaters, and galleries need not be concerned with a workplace that increasingly demands flexibility. For the majority, however, highly specialized skills can be a hindrance. A liberal arts education offers the well-rounded background that employers seek. You can specialize later, but getting a general education first might lay the best foundation for your particular talent.

You CAN Do Both.

Several avenues exist to mix and match a general education and specialty focus. One is to get a bachelor's degree in liberal arts and then to develop your talent in graduate school. For many areas, a master's is an entry-level degree. Another possibility is to attend a specialty school that has an agreement with a traditional university or college to offer joint degrees. Some students, for instance, combine a design and business degree.

Auditions and Portfolios

If you decide to study the arts, such as theater, music, or fine arts, you may be required to audition or show your portfolio to admissions personnel. The following tips will help you showcase your talents and skills when preparing for an audition or portfolio review.

Music Auditions

Freshmen who wish to pursue a degree in music, whether it is vocal or instrumental, typically must audition. If you're a singer, prepare at least two pieces in contrasting styles. One should be in a foreign language, if possible. Choose from operatic, show music, or art song repertories, and make sure you memorize each piece. If you're an instrumentalist or pianist, be prepared to play scales and arpeggios, at least one etude or technical study, and a solo work. Instrumental audition pieces need not be memorized. In either field, you may be required to do sight-reading.

When performing music that is sight-read, you should take time to look over the piece and make certain of the key and time signatures before proceeding with the audition. If you're a singer, you should bring a familiar accompanist to the audition.

"My advice is to ask for help from teachers, try to acquire audition information up front, and know more than is required for the audition," says one student. "It is also a good idea to select your audition time and date early."

"Try to perform your solo in front of as many people as you can as many times as possible," says another student. "You may also want to try to get involved in a high school performance."

Programs differ, so students are encouraged to call the college and ask for audition information. In general, music departments seek students who demonstrate technical competence and performance achievement.

A Music Professor Talks about Developing Your Music Talent.

- Work with a private or high school choir, orchestra, or band teacher to select solo materials. Selections from your state music contest list are recommended.

- Attend concerts of varying styles of music.

- Build a music library of jazz, non-Western, and classical music.

- Attend music camps and all-state programs.

- Talk to adults involved in the industry (professionals).

- Talk to a music professor about your interests. Take a music theory/history course.

- Get involved in community youth ensembles.

- Gain as much performance experience outside of high school as possible.

Admission to music programs varies in degree of competitiveness, so you should audition at a minimum of three colleges and a maximum of five to amplify your opportunity. The degree of competitiveness varies also by instrument, especially if a renowned musician teaches a certain instrument. Some colleges offer a second audition if you feel you did not audition to your potential. Ideally, you will be accepted into the music program of your choice, but keep in mind that it's possible to not be accepted. You must then make the decision to either pursue a music program at another college or consider another major at that college.

Dance Auditions

At many four-year colleges, an open class is held the day before auditions. A performance piece that combines improvisation, ballet, modern, and rhythm is taught and then students are expected to perform the piece at auditions. Professors look for coordination, technique, rhythm, degree of movement, and body structure. The dance faculty members also assess your ability to learn and your potential to complete the curriculum. Dance programs vary, so check with the college of your choice for specific information.

Art Portfolios

A portfolio is simply a collection of your best pieces of artwork. The pieces you select to put in your portfolio should demonstrate your interest and aptitude for a serious education in the arts. A well-developed portfolio can help you gain acceptance into a prestigious art college and increase your chances of being awarded a scholarship in national portfolio competitions. The pieces you select should show diversity in technique and variety in subject matter. You may show work in any medium (oils, photography, watercolors, pastels, etc.) and in either black-and-

white or color. Your portfolio can include classroom assignments as well as independent projects. You can also include your sketchbook.

Specialized art colleges request that you submit an average of ten pieces of art, but remember that quality is more important than quantity. The admission office staff will review your artwork and transcripts to assess your skill and potential for success. Usually, you will present your portfolio in person; however, some schools allow students to mail slides if distance is an issue. There is no simple formula for success other than hard work. In addition, there is no such thing as a "perfect portfolio," nor any specific style or direction to achieve one.

Tips to Pull Your Portfolio Together:

- Try to make your portfolio as clean and organized as possible.

- It is important to protect your work, but make sure the package you select is easy to handle and does not interfere with the viewing of the artwork.

- Drawings that have been rolled up are difficult for the jurors to handle and view. You may shrink-wrap the pieces, but it is not required.

- Avoid loose sheets of paper between pieces.

- If you choose to mount or mat your work (not required), use only neutral gray tones, black, or white.

- Never include framed pieces or three-dimensional work.

- Use spray fixative on pieces that could smudge.

- A slide portfolio should be presented in a standard 8 x 11 plastic slide sleeve, which can be purchased at any photo or camera supply store.

- Be sure paintings are completely dry before you place them in your portfolio.

Theater Auditions

Most liberal arts colleges do not require that students who audition be accepted into the theater department unless the college offers a Bachelor of Fine Arts (B.F.A.) degree in theater. You should apply to the college of your choice prior to scheduling an audition. You should also consider spending a full day on campus so that you may talk with theater faculty members and students, attend classes, meet with your admission counselor, and tour the facilities.

Although each college and university has different requirements, you should prepare two contrasting monologues taken from plays of your choice if you're auditioning for a B.F.A. acting program. The total length of both pieces should not exceed 5 minutes, and you should take a theater resume and photo to the audition with you.

Musical theater requirements generally consist of one up-tempo musical selection and one ballad as well as one monologue from a play or musical of your choice. The total of all your pieces should not exceed 5 minutes. Music for the accompanist, a resume of your theater experience, and a photo are also required.

Tips to Get You Successfully through an Audition:

- Choose material suitable for your age.

- If you choose your monologue from a book of monologues, you should read the entire play and be familiar with the context of your selection.

- Select a monologue that allows you to speak directly to another person; you should play only one character.

- Memorize your selection.

- Avoid using characterization or style, as they tend to trap you rather than tapping deeper into inner resources.

STUDENTS WITH DISABILITIES GO TO COLLEGE

Current estimates indicate that more than 49 million American citizens have been identified as having disabilities. With increased public awareness of the laws requiring access to every facet of community life, there has been an apparent rise in the number of students identified as having disabilities. Often, those students enter early intervention programs as infants or toddlers. Elementary and secondary programs for some disabilities continue through age 21.

Legal Rights of Students with Disabilities

Section 504 of the Rehabilitation Act of 1973 states that "no otherwise qualified individual . . . shall, solely by reason of . . . handicap, be excluded from participation in, be denied the benefits of, or be subject to discrimination under any program or activity receiving federal financial assistance."

Passage of that legislation mandated that colleges and universities receiving federal financial assistance could not discriminate in the recruitment, admission, or treatment of students.

In 1990, the Americans with Disabilities Act (ADA) extended and made more specific the rights and antidiscrimination legislation provided by Section 504. The ADA requires educational institutions at all levels, public and private, to provide equal access to programs, services, and facilities. Schools must be accessible to students, as well as to employees and the public, regardless of any disability. To ensure such accessibility, they must follow specific requirements for new construction, alterations or renovations, academic programs, and institutional policies, practices, and procedures.

Students with specific disabilities

have the right to request and expect accommodations, including auxiliary aids and services that enable them to participate in and benefit from all programs and activities offered by or related to a school.

To comply with ADA requirements, many high schools and universities offer programs and information to answer questions for students with disabilities and to assist them both in selecting appropriate colleges and in attaining full inclusion once they enter college. And most colleges and universities have disabilities services offices to help students negotiate the system. When it comes time to apply to colleges, write to the ones that you're interested in to find out what kinds of programs they have in place. When it comes time to narrow down your choices, make a request for a visit.

What is Considered a Disability?

A person is considered to have a disability if he or she meets at least one of three conditions. The individual must:

DIRECTORY FOR STUDENTS WITH DISABILITIES

THE FOLLOWING RESOURCES CAN HELP STUDENTS, FAMILIES, AND SCHOOLS WITH THE LEGAL REQUIREMENTS FOR ACCOMMODATING DISABILITIES. THEY CAN ALSO LINK YOU WITH OTHER GROUPS AND INDIVIDUALS THAT ARE KNOWLEDGEABLE IN STUDENTS' RIGHTS AND THE PROCESS OF TRANSITION INTO POSTSECONDARY EDUCATION.

ALSO, THERE ARE SPECIAL INTEREST, EDUCATION, SUPPORT, AND ADVOCACY ORGANIZATIONS FOR PERSONS WITH PARTICULAR DISABILITIES. CHECK WITH YOUR COUNSELOR OR CONTACT ONE OF THE FOLLOWING ORGANIZATIONS FOR INFORMATION:

ACT Assessment Administration
Special Testing
P.O. Box 4028
Iowa City, Iowa 52243
319-337-1332
www.act.org

Association on Higher Education and
Disability (AHEAD)
University of Massachusetts Boston
100 Morrissey Boulevard
Boston, Massachusetts 02125-3393
617-287-3880
www.ahead.org

Attention Deficit Disorder Association
(ADDA)
1788 Second Street, Suite 200
Highland Park, Illinois 60035
847-432-ADDA
www.add.org

Children and Adults with Attention Deficit
Disorders (CHADD)
8181 Professional Place, Suite 201
Landover, Maryland 20785
800-233-4050 (toll free)
www.chadd.org

ERIC Clearing House on Disabilities and
Gifted Children
1110 North Glebe Road
Arlington, Virginia 22201-5704
800-328-0272 (toll free)

Council for Learning Disabilities (CLD)
P.O. Box 40303
Overland Park, Kansas 66204
913-492-8755

HEATH Resource Center
National Clearinghouse on Postsecondary
Education for Individuals with Disabilities
American Council on Education
One Dupont Circle, NW, Suite 800
Washington, D.C. 20036
800-544-3284 (toll free)
www.heath-resource-center.org

International Dyslexia Association
The Chester Building
8600 LaSalle Road, Suite 382
Baltimore, Maryland 21286-2044
800-222-3123 (toll free)
www.interdys.org

Learning Disabilities Association of
America, Inc. (LDA)
4156 Library Road
Pittsburgh, Pennsylvania 15234-1349
412-341-1515
www.ldanatl.org

Learning Disabilities Association of
Canada (LDAC)
323 Chapel Street, Suite 200
Ottawa, Ontario K1N 7Z2
613-238-5721
www.ldac-taac.ca

National Center for Law and Learning
Disabilities (NCLLD)
P.O. Box 368
Cabin John, Maryland 20818
301-469-8308

National Center for Learning Disabilities
(NCLD)
381 Park Avenue South, Suite 1401
New York, New York 10016
888-575-7373 (toll free)
www.ncld.org

National Information Center for Children
and Youth with Disabilities
P.O. Box 1492
Washington, D.C. 20013
800-695-0285 (toll free)
www.nichcy.org

Recording for the Blind & Dyslexic
20 Roszel Road
Princeton, New Jersey 08540
609-452-0606
www.rfbd.org

SAT Services for Students with Disabilities
The College Board
P.O. Box 6226
Princeton, New Jersey 08541-6226
609-771-7137
www.collegeboard.com

1 have a documented physical or mental impairment that substantially limits one or more major life activities, such as personal self-care, walking, seeing, hearing, speaking, breathing, learning, working, or performing manual tasks;

2 have a record of such an impairment; or

3 be perceived as having such an impairment.

Physical disabilities include impairments of speech, vision, hearing, and mobility. Other disabilities, while less obvious, are similarly limiting; they include diabetes, asthma, multiple sclerosis, heart disease, cancer, mental illness, mental retardation, cerebral palsy, and learning disabilities.

Learning disabilities refer to an array of biological conditions that impede a person's ability to process and disseminate information. A learning disability is commonly recognized as a significant deficiency in one or more of the following areas: oral expression, listening comprehension, written expression, basic reading skills, reading comprehension, mathematical calculation, or problem solving. Individuals with learning disabilities also may have difficulty with sustained attention, time management, or social skills.

According to a 1999 report by the HEATH Resource Center of the American Council on Education, 154,520, or 9 percent, of the nation's 1.7 million full-time college freshmen identified themselves as having a learning disability.

Auxiliary Aids and Services

The ADA requires educational institutions to provide auxiliary aids and services to ensure that no individual is excluded or denied access to a program. Auxiliary aids and services encompass a wide range of devices and assistance, including acquisition or modification of equipment, devices, or action. Examples include, but are not limited to, the following items for specific disabilities:

Deaf/Hard of Hearing:

- qualified interpreter note takers
- computer-aided transcription services (real-time captioning)
- written materials
- telephone handset amplifiers
- assistive listening devices and systems
- telephones compatible with hearing aids
- closed-caption decoders
- open and closed captioning
- telecommunication devices for deaf persons (TDDs/TTYs)
- videotext displays

The ADA slightly revised the definition of a "qualified interpreter" as one who is able to interpret effectively, accurately, and impartially, both receptively and expressively, using any necessary specialized language. A qualified interpreter does not need to be a certified interpreter, and a certified interpreter may or may not be qualified in a given circumstance. The definition applies on a case-by-case basis.

Blind/Visually Impaired:

- qualified readers
- taped texts
- audio recordings
- Braille materials
- large print
- tactile and high-contrast signage or documents

Architectural barrier removal, especially for those with physical impairments, is also required and may include items such as:

- ramps
- curb cuts of sidewalks or entrances
- repositioning or rearranging of furniture or equipment
- installation of visual and auditory alarms
- renovation or construction of restrooms for accessibility (grab bars, widened stalls, raised toilet seats, lowered urinals, insulated pipes, lever handles, etc.)

Schools must provide what is adequate for inclusion at all levels, although the aids or services do not necessarily have to be the most expensive or complex.

Many of the auxiliary aids and services listed are actually assistive technology (AT). An AT device is any item, piece of equipment, or product system, whether acquired off-the-shelf, modified, or customized, that is used to increase, maintain, or improve functional capabilities of an individual with a disability. An AT service is any service that directly assists an individual with a disability in the selection, acquisition, or use of an assistive technology device.

The ADA opens doors for inclusion and educational success. Assistive technology devices and services are enablers that help you function once you get inside the door. See "Tips for Students with Disabilities" for more information.

Special Services for Students with Learning Disabilities

Some students with learning disabilities need only to connect with instructors who will afford them extra attention or extra time for assignments. Others need additional services, which may include tutoring, alternative test arrangements, note-taking, taped textbooks, basic skills remedia-

tion, diagnostic testing, priority registration, and advocates. Services change and are added regularly, so check with the school(s) in which you are interested to see if special services are offered.

Comprehensive Programs for Students with Learning Disabilities

A comprehensive program is one that is especially designed for students with learning disabilities. Often, special admissions procedures must be followed for students to be admitted to colleges with these programs.

Such a program may be more than some students need, however. Services change from year to year and even from semester to semester, so be sure to check with schools to see what they provide. You may find the book *Colleges with Programs for Students with Learning Disabilities or Attention Deficit Disorders* a useful resource. You can purchase it by visiting Peterson's online bookstore at www.petersons.com. For additional resources, refer to the Directory for

TIPS FOR STUDENTS WITH DISABILITIES

- Document your disability with letters from your physician(s), therapist, case manager, school psychologist, and other service providers.
- Get letters of support from teachers, family, friends, and service providers that detail how you have learned to work despite your disability.
- Learn the federal laws that apply to students with disabilities.
- Research support groups for peer information and advocacy.
- Visit several campuses.
- Determine the best point in the admissions process at which to identify yourself as having a disability.
- Look into the services available, the pace of campus life, and the college's expectations for students with disabilities.
- Ask about orientation programs, including specialized introductions for or about students with disabilities.
- Ask about flexible, individualized study plans.
- Ask if the school offers technology such as voice synthesizers, voice recognition, and/or visual learning equipment to its students.
- Ask about adapted intramural/social activities.
- Ask to talk with students who have similar disabilities to hear about their experiences on campus.
- Once you select a college, get a map of the campus and learn the entire layout.
- If you have a physical disability, make sure the buildings you need to be in are accessible to you. Some, even though they comply with the ADA, aren't as accessible as others.
- Be realistic. If you use a wheelchair, for example, a school with an exceptionally hilly campus may not be your best choice, no matter what other accommodations it has.

Students with Disabilities on page 71.

A Final Word

If you have a disability, you will take the same steps to choose and apply to a college as other students, but you should also evaluate each college based on your special need(s). Get organized, and meet with campus specialists to discuss your specific requirements. Then, explore whether the programs, policies, procedures, and facilities meet your specific situation.

It is usually best to describe your disability in a letter attached to the application so the proper fit can be made between you and the school. You may even want to have your psychoeducational evaluation and testing record sent to the school. Some colleges help with schedules and offer transition courses, reduced course loads, extra access to professors, and special study areas to help address your needs.

Remember, admission to college is a realistic goal for any motivated student. If you invest the time and effort, you can make it happen.

HOMESCHOOLERS GO TO COLLEGE

If you've been learning at home for the last few years, you might have some concerns about selecting the right college or university, the application process, and the overall change in learning environments. With an estimated 1.23 million students being homeschooled nationwide, these are valid concerns for institutions of higher education as well.

According to homeschooling consultant Rich Fairchild, "The bottom line is: Can you do the work, and can you pay the bill?" If so, the process of being admitted to college is no different for homeschoolers than it is for other students. At present, there are simply no set rules for admitting homeschoolers to the country's many colleges and universities. In fact, the phenomenon is so new that many of the institutions of higher learning are

only now in the process of establishing some guidelines in this area.

Cafi Cohen, homeschooling enthusiast and author of a book on the topic, agrees. Ninety-five percent of the colleges and universities have no protocol for evaluating applications from homeschoolers, she says. Cohen's book, *And What About College?: How Home Schooling Leads to Admissions to the Best Colleges and Universities*, offers homeschoolers some specific advice on the topic while sharing the experiences of getting her own children admitted to college.

Cohen's son and daughter were homeschooled since the sixth and seventh grades. Her son recently graduated from the Air Force Academy, while her daughter is attending California Polytechnic Institute. Homeschoolers apply to college like anyone else, she emphasizes. Cohen cautions, however, that the SAT I is more important for homeschoolers because it is the one benchmark that is used to compare homeschoolers with other students. Some admission officers say they require homeschoolers to also take several SAT IIs as well.

Cohen doesn't recommend that homeschoolers take the GED exam unless a college specifically asks for it. Instead, homeschoolers should create a transcript that resembles those from area high schools. According to Cohen, it's probably best to use a portfolio for the smaller, more specialized schools, conforming your document to what they are used to seeing. In her experiences with both children, she was never asked for a diploma.

Cohen believes that in five to ten years, most colleges and universities will have developed admission policies for homeschoolers. In the meantime, homeschooled students should take advantage of the same resources that regular students use—namely, high school guidance counselors, some of whom work on a freelance basis.

DISTANCE LEARNING STUDENTS GO TO COLLEGE

As a future college student, can you picture yourself in any of these scenarios?

1 You need some information, but the only place to find it is at a big state university. Trouble is, it's hundreds of miles away. No problem. You simply go to your local community college and hook up electronically with the university. Voila! The resources are brought to you.

2 That ten-page paper is due in a few days, but you still have some last-minute questions to ask the professor before you turn it in. Only one problem: you won't be able to see the professor until after the paper is due. Being a night owl, you also want to work on it when your roommate is asleep. Not to worry. Since you have the professor's e-mail address, just like all the other students in the class, you simply e-mail your question to her. She replies. You get your answer, finish the paper, and even turn it in electronically.

3 After graduating from high school, you can't go to college right away, but your employer has a neat hook up with a college that offers courses via the Internet. During your lunch hours, you and several of your work buddies log in to a class and get college credit.

Not too long ago, if you'd offered these scenarios to high school graduates as real possibilities, they would have thought you were a sci-fi freak. Distance education was not common at all—or if it was, it usually meant getting courses via snail mail or on videotape. Well, today you are in the right place at the right time. Distance education is a reality for countless high school graduates.

What distance education now means is that you can access educational programs and not have to physically be in a classroom on a campus. Through such technologies as cable or satellite television, videotapes and audiotapes, fax, computer modem, computer conferencing and video-conferencing, and other means of electronic delivery, the classroom comes to you—sometimes even if you're sitting in your room in your bunny slippers and it's 2 in the morning.

Distance learning expands the reach of the classroom by using various technologies to deliver university resources to off-campus sites, transmit college courses into the workplace, and enable you to view class lectures in the comfort of your home.

Where and How Can I Take Distance Learning Courses?

The technology for new, cheaper telecommunications technology is getting better all the time, and there is a growing demand for education by people who can't afford either the time or money to be a full-time, on-campus student. To fill that demand, educational networks also are growing and changing how and when you can access college courses.

Most states have established new distance learning systems to advance the delivery of instruction to schools, postsecondary institutions, and state government agencies. Colleges and universities are collaborating with commercial telecommunications entities, including online information services such as America Online and cable and telephone companies, to provide education to far-flung student constituencies. Professions such as law, medicine, and accounting, as well as knowledge-based industries, are utilizing telecommunications networks for the transmission of customized higher education programs to working professionals, technicians, and managers.

Ways in Which Distance Learning May Be Offered:

◷ Credit courses. In general, if these credit courses are completed successfully, they may be applied toward a degree.

◷ Noncredit courses and courses offered for professional certification. These programs can help you acquire specialized knowledge in a concentrated, time-efficient manner and stay on top of the latest developments in your field. They provide a flexible way for you to prepare for a new career or study for professional licensure and certification. Many of these university programs are created in cooperation with professional and trade associations so that courses are based on real life workforce needs, and the practical skills learned are immediately applicable in the field.

What Else Does Distance Learning Offer?

Distance learning comes in a variety of colors and flavors. Along with traditional college degrees, you can earn professional certification or continuing education credits (CEUs) in a particular field.

Professional Certification

Certificate programs often focus on employment specializations, such as hazardous waste management or electronic publishing, and can be helpful to those seeking to advance or change careers. Also, many states mandate continuing education for professionals such as teachers, nursing home administrators, or accountants. Distance learning offers a convenient way for many individuals to meet professional certification requirements. Health care, engineering, and education are just a few of the many professions that take advantage of distance learning to help their professionals maintain certification.

Many colleges offer a sequence of distance learning courses in a specific field of a profession. For instance, within the engineering profession, certificate programs in computer integrated manufacturing, systems engineering, test and evaluation, and waste management education and research consortium are offered via distance learning.

Business offerings include distance learning certification in information technology, total quality management, and health services management.

Within the field of education, you'll find distance learning certificate programs in areas such as early reading instruction and special education for learning handicapped. There are opportunities for you to earn degrees at a distance at the associate, baccalaureate, and graduate levels. Two-year community college students are now able to earn baccalaureate degrees—without relocating—by transferring to distance learning programs offered by four-year universities. Corporations are forming partnerships with universities to bring college courses to worksites and encourage employees to continue their education. Distance learning is especially popular among people who want to earn their degree part-time while continuing to work full-time. Although on-campus residencies are sometimes required for certain distance learning degree programs, they generally can be completed while employees are on short-term leave or vacation.

Continuing Education Units (CEUs)

If you choose to take a course on a noncredit basis, you may be able to earn continuing education units (CEUs). The CEU system is a nationally recognized system to provide a standardized measure for accumulating, transferring, and recognizing participation in continuing education programs. One CEU is defined as 10 contact hours of participation in an organized continuing education experience under responsible sponsorship, capable direction, and qualified instruction.

The Way Distance Learning Works

Enrolling in a distance learning course may simply involve filling out a registration form, making sure that you have access to the equipment needed, and paying the tuition and fees by check, money order, or credit card. In these cases your applications may be accepted without entrance examinations or proof of prior educational experience.

Other courses may involve educational prerequisites and access to equipment not found in all geographic locations. Some institutions offer detailed information about individual courses, such as a course outline, upon request. If you have access to the Internet and simply wish to review course descriptions, you may be able to peruse an institution's course catalogs electronically by accessing the institution's home page on the Web.

Time Requirements

Some courses allow you to enroll at your convenience and work at your own pace. Others closely adhere to a traditional classroom schedule. Specific policies and time limitations pertaining to withdrawals, refunds, transfers, and renewal periods can be found in the institutional catalog.

Admission to a Degree Program

If you plan to enter a degree program, you should consult the academic advising department of the institution of your choice to learn of entrance requirements and application procedures. You may find it necessary to develop a portfolio of your past experiences and of your accomplishments that may have resulted in college-level learning.

How Do I Communicate with My Instructor?

Student-faculty exchanges occur using electronic communication (through fax and e-mail). Many institutions offer their distance learning students access to toll-free numbers so students can talk to their professors or teaching assistants without incurring any long-distance charges.

Responses to your instructor's comments on your lessons, requests for clarification of comments, and all other exchanges between you and your instructor will take time. Interaction with your instructor—whether by computer, phone, or letter—is important, and you must be willing to take the initiative. ■

Spent a semester
studying in Paris –
"C'etait incroyable!"

Getting the education and experience
he'll need to compete in the real world.

Likes to rock and
roll around campus
with friends.

Picked the one school that gives him the
programs of a university, the personal
attention of a smaller college and a setting
that lets him explore and grow.

It fits him. See how it fits you.

Boston

Quinnipiac   Providence

New York

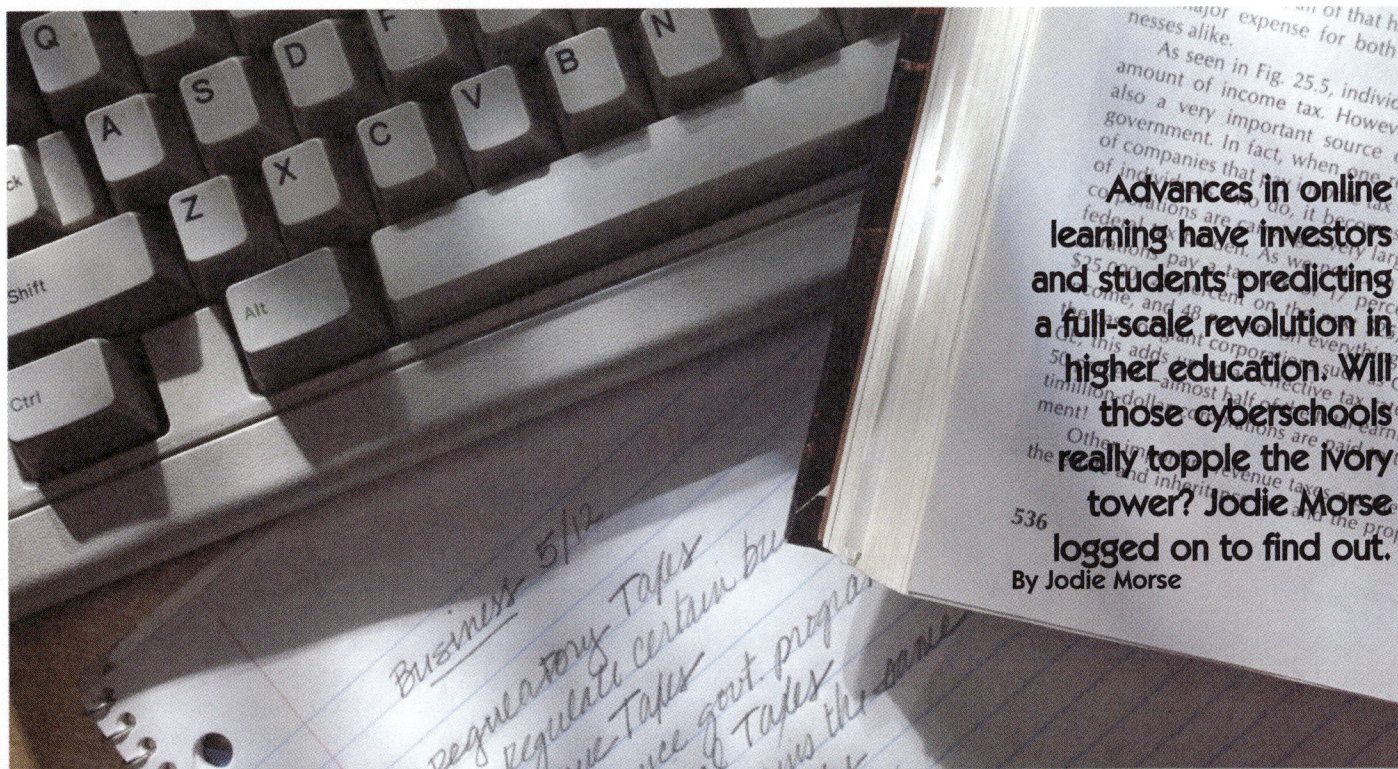

Advances in online learning have investors and students predicting a full-scale revolution in higher education. Will those cyberschools really topple the ivory tower? Jodie Morse logged on to find out.
By Jodie Morse

LOG ON TO LEARN

ALWAYS DREADED THE FIRST day of school. My parents like to remind me that I spent the first day of the first grade in denial, making repeated trips back to my kindergarten classroom. On the first day of my junior year in high school, after a summer of endless lobbying to be allowed to drive myself to school, I found myself in the parking lot talking to AAA when I locked my keys in the car with the engine running. During my first day at college, I got lost while looking for a premed placement test and wound up in a cemetery adjacent to the science complex. I took this as a glaring sign and dropped my medical aspirations, promptly enrolling in as many literature courses as possible.

So it was something of a relief to attend the first lecture of English XB17, a survey course of Shakespeare's major plays offered by the University of California, Berkeley's extension program. Other than the short commute from my bed to the laptop at the other end of my 500-sq.-ft. studio apartment, no travel was necessary. To find my actual classroom, I simply clicked onto an area of AOL that Berkeley used, where I'd been preregistered, to read and complete my first assignment. And when I worried that I was wasting a sunny July Saturday immersed in an introduction to social and cultural mores of the English Renaissance, I just stepped outside for a walk. Then I returned to my desk, leisurely phoned a friend and settled down to work.

I quickly learned why so many Americans are heading off to college without leaving their keyboards. They're logging on to sites set up by prestigious schools like Berkeley, Columbia and Stanford, as well as to a new breed of cyber-only institutions, such as Jones International University and Western Governors University. Online learning is especially appealing at a time when traditional college students—those 18-to-22-year-olds who spend four years living on campus and attending classes and keg parties—make up just 16% of total university enrollment. The vast majority of today's students are time-crunched adults who must pencil in college diplomas and graduate degrees between hectic jobs and kids' soccer games.

> **I quickly learned why so many Americans are heading off to college without leaving their keyboards.**

The upshot: during this academic year, some 2 million people will take online classes.

Investors are jumping at the opening. In 1999, online learning accounted for just $1.2 billion of the $249 billion higher-education industry; by 2003 that figure is projected to grow to $7 billion, according to Merrill Lynch. With the aid of eager venture capitalists, new virtual schools are sprouting up, and the old brick-and-mortar ones are appending for-profit Web arms and paying their professors in stock options. Even the U.S. Army has climbed into the online-learning trenches, budgeting $600 million over the next six years to enable recruits to get degrees from U.S. colleges, no matter where they're stationed.

Proponents of online learning predict that such advances will one day render academe about as relevant as ancient Greek. They contend that students in online classes get more faculty interaction than those packed into a cavernous lecture hall—and for much less money. And the gush about a not-so-distant scenario in which any student will be able to get higher education on demand and employers will give those online credentials the same stock as an Ivy League diploma.

Visions of tumbling ivory towers have naturally made many academics apoplectic. They fear that professors' livelihoods will be debased by upstart courses, often taught by "instructors" who lack Ph.D.s and work for cut rates. Self-preservation aside, they contend that no amount of technological know-how can approach four years of in-person pedagogy. Not to mention four years of priceless collegiate intangibles like late-night philosophizing sessions and first loves. "The real challenge as a teacher is to turn the lights on and get the pot boiling, and you can really only do that face to face," says David Noble, a history professor at Toronto's York University and a persistent critic of online learning. "At these digital diploma mills, all you get is a cyber-counterfeit education."

I decided to conduct an unscientific study of my own and take a class. (I paid my $505 and enrolled like any other student, but at the end of the course I told the professor I was a journalist.) I gravitated to Berkeley mainly because of its reputation, but also because its online courses are still fairly low-tech, requiring nothing more than the 56K modem I have on my laptop at home. And I enjoyed the catchy motto: "Bringing the university to you."

I briefly considered Classics of Children's Literature and History of Film, but I settled on Shakespeare. The description boasted that the course was the "winner of the 1997 Helen Williams Award for Excellence in Collegiate Independent Study." Whatever that was, I was sold. Plus, as a onetime English major, I'd read more than my share of Shakespeare and felt I had a fairly good basis to judge the quality of the instruction. I also thought my background might enable me to skimp on some of the reading if I got busy. Finally, I could think of no educational experience that better evoked my own undergraduate years than my two semesters of Shakespeare. Once in a while, I still get flashbacks of my Shakespeare professor, an old-fashioned curmudgeon, hand to his heart, belting out an impassioned *Hamlet* soliloquy to a rapt class.

My online class was of the so-called asynchronous variety, meaning that instead of convening at an appointed time each week to learn and discuss material, each student works at his or her own pace. Lectures typically are downloaded from the Internet or, as in my case, arrive in printed form through the mail. Discussions take the form of running commentaries snaking through topical message boards. Students are encouraged to arrange live chat discussions and, in lieu of weekly office hours, e-mail their professor whenever questions arise.

While it is a blessing for the eternally overbooked, like me, the asynchronous format did little to foster class unity. After reading each play, we were required to post a response on a message board and take up a question posed by one of our classmates. If a particularly spirited discussion was under way (example: cross-dressing Shakespearean actors), our professor, Mary Ann Koory, would send out an e-mail prodding us to log on. But other than those infrequent nudges, it was left up to us to decide how actively we participated.

Asynchronicity was liberating in at least one sense, however. As an undergrad, I detested those class drones who always monopolized the discussion. They're just as garrulous and annoying over e-mail, tending to post their observations in loud colors like fire-engine red, but here they're easier to avoid. Just don't click on them.

I'd be hard-pressed to tell anything about my classmates or even how many were in the class at one time, since we were all chugging through the lessons at such varied paces. I'd often find myself responding to a posting by a student who had no intention of returning to that topic—he'd already moved on to the next lesson. And my attempts at starting a live group discussion in our class chat room were equally fruitless: only one other person showed up for my chat on Richard III's villainy. And it was the professor.

The quality of her teaching more than made up for the flat class dynamic. The "lectures" were learned, lively and strewn

> At these digital diploma mills, all you get is a cyber-counterfeit education.
>
> David Noble, a history professor at Toronto's York University

throughout with entertaining pop-cultural allusions. (At one point, we were told to consider Shakespeare's folio of plays as a compilation of the best-ever Grateful Dead bootlegs.) Mary Ann (we were on a first-name basis from our very first e-mail) says she makes use of current events to connect with the varied backgrounds of her students. Most of the time the technique worked, though I could have done without the essay question asking us to compare and contrast Othello with O.J. Simpson.

The work load, as is often the case in online courses, was much heftier—for both students and professor—than in a typical college course. Here, each reading assignment had an essay of several "screens" followed by a three-hour final. After netting a string of B's and lukewarm comments, I realized my skimp-on-reading strategy wouldn't cut it. Mary Ann perceptively tagged my early work a "little light on the logical argument," noting that "you were more interested in your prose than in Shakespeare's work." After that zinger, I stepped up my scholarship. And though I never took the final, I was pulling A's by the course's end.

Mary Ann's best response time was just one hour after I handed in a paper, and her comments often engendered a string of follow-up e-mails. She says such one-on-one discussions are the norm—she often converses more with her online students than with those taking the in-person version. And those online discussions are often much more inclusive. "For shy people, the social barriers fall away online," she told me. "However attenuated, online conversations tend to be of higher quality and much more democratic in the best Jeffersonian sense of the word."

Even though my e-mails with Mary Ann were stimulating, I wondered if they would have been enough to keep me enthralled if I hadn't been writing this article. According to some estimates, the dropout rate from some online courses can be as high as 50%, compared with just 26% at traditional schools. "Older students'

lives are full of disruptions," says Vicky Phillips, CEO of Geteducated.com, a distance-learning research and consulting firm. "Work responsibilities change, kids get sick, people get divorced." My disruptions were less cataclysmic (cable TV and phone calls), but they often proved urgent enough to pull me off an essay for several hours or days.

Many online proponents are looking to the more cutting-edge technologies, such as live streaming video, to curb online student apathy. Other online programs, like Duke University's well-regarded M.B.A. program, require students to come together for a certain number of in-person classes. But schools without a campus don't have that luxury and must find other ways to gin up school spirit: Jones International University has opened an online school store and sends its students late-night snacks. Kentucky Virtual University is sponsoring a digital football league, and Kaplancollege.com has plans for online yearbooks and weekly mixers.

> **The work load, as is often the case in online courses, was much heftier—for both students and professor—than in a typical college course.**

Class bonding is much less of an obstacle for students who progress through a full-fledged online degree program together. Take Marilyn McKay, a marketing consultant in a two-year online M.B.A. program at the University of Maryland University College. McKay, who has a more than full-time job at her own firm and lives in the isolated California desert, chose online learning for its flexibility. "You really learn much more about people than in one of those crowded 200-person lectures where the professor uses the same notes he has for the past 10 years and no one speaks up," she says. Plus, she reminded me, meeting people in print can sometimes be more revealing than sharing small talk while filing into a classroom. "For starters," she says, "you learn quickly who knows how to spell and who uses bad grammar."

McKay is 53 and has grown children. For serious graduate students like her—or

even serious dabblers like me—online learning may work. But for the millions of wide-eyed 18-year-olds out there, it's still no contest. Which may explain why, after putting out calls to some of the major online programs, I could turn up only one student who was awarded an undergraduate diploma online. Tasha Overton, 23, got a B.S. in computer programming last year from University of Maryland University College. The primary interpersonal connections she says she made were in her sorority, which she joined during the semester she spent on campus at Tennessee's Austin Peay State University: "I was interested only in getting through my classes, and I didn't go to college to meet people. For me, online education meant the freedom from ever having to set foot in a classroom."

However, even the staunchest backers of online learning would curtail that freedom. According to Geteducated.com's Phillips, "Colleges will always exist as we know them as social rites of passage. People don't only go off to college to learn Plato, but to come of age." And they do so not just by hearing an inspired literary mind render *Hamlet*, but also by spending the first day of class dazed and confused in a field of tombstones. ∎

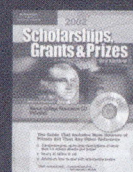

8 FINANCIAL AID DOLLARS AND SENSE

Getting financial aid can be intimidating—but don't let that stop you.

It's complicated, and there are a lot of parts to this puzzle. Leave a few out or put too many in, and the puzzle doesn't come out right. However, if you look at each piece separately rather than trying to understand the whole process all at once, it will be much easier to absorb. The trick is to start early, be organized, and plan ahead.

Finding the money you need to attend a two- or four-year institution or vocational or trade school is a challenge, but you can do it if you devise a strategy well before you actually start applying to college. Financial aid comes from a lot of different sources. But this is where *GAJ* comes in. You'll find lots of help here to locate those sources and find out where to get advice. Financial aid is available to help meet both direct educational costs (tuition, fees, books) and personal living expenses (food, housing, transportation).

Times have changed to favor the student in the financial aid process. Because the pool of potential traditional college students has diminished, colleges and universities are competing among themselves to attract good students. In fact, some colleges and universities no longer use financial aid primarily as a method to help students fund their college education but rather as a marketing and recruitment tool. This puts students and families at an advantage, one that should be recognized and used for bargaining power.

It used to be that colleges and universities offered need-based and merit-based financial aid to only needy and/or academically exceptional students. Now some schools offer what might be called incentive or discount aid to encourage students to choose them over another college. This aid, which is not necessarily based on need or merit, is aimed at students who meet the standards of the college but who wouldn't necessarily qualify for traditional kinds of aid.

If You're an Athlete, a Minority Student, or Planning to Go into the Military

If you plan to try for a athletic scholarship or you're a minority student, look at Section 7, *College Bound and More—For Those With Special Needs and Talents*, where you'll find financial information just for you. If you plan to finance your education through the military, please see Section 10, *Other Options after High School*.

A BIRD'S-EYE VIEW OF FINANCIAL AID

You and your family should be assertive in negotiating financial aid packages. It used to be that there was no room for such negotiation, but in today's environment, it is wise to be a comparison shopper. Families should wait until they've received all of their financial offers and then talk to their first-choice college to see if the college can match the better offers from other colleges. *(Continued on page 88)*

On Your Mark GET SET GO.

Congratulations on your decision to go on to higher education! It is just the first of many decisions that you'll be making over the next several months, but it is definitely the most important and will affect your entire future.

You may be feeling a bit overwhelmed at the moment. After all, there are many factors to getting ready for higher education. However, if you follow our simple timeline and take it one step at a time, you'll be attending your first class, free of financial worries, before you know it!

➲ Think about different jobs and careers that interest you. Then think about your own interests, skills and talents. The Internet is a great resource to help you get started. For example, AESmentor, found at www.aesmentor.org, offers a Career Center to help you find a career that best suits you. A comprehensive list of career examples is available, as well as My Mentor, which allows you to create a custom portfolio containing personal, academic, and career information. Another site to look at is Petersons.com, which includes a career education and guidance area where you can take a personality assessment and research

career schools and two- and four-year colleges that offer career training. Further, the U.S. government's Bureau of Labor Statistics produces a site that includes information on most careers in the United States (www.bls.gov/ocohome.htm).

➲ Start thinking about the type of school that you would like to attend. The AESMentor and Peterson's sites allow you to search for and compare colleges and universities across the nation in terms of total enrollment, campus setting, average class size, tuition, and the percentage of attending students who receive financial aid.

➲ Make sure that you have taken all of the necessary courses in school. Just as there are certain requirements you must fulfill to graduate from high school, there are requirements for going on to higher education. Talk with your high school counselor and check informational brochures on schools you are interested in attending.

➲ If you can, take Advanced Placement (AP) courses. These courses take a more in-depth look at the subject, and usually require more applied theory and preparation than a general-study course. However, if you accept the challenge you may be able to skip col-

For Higher Education!

lege introductory courses in that subject. AP tests are offered to first-year students, allowing them to "test out" of these classes. For example, if you take AP English while in high school, and pass the test, you could be taking a course directly relating to your major while other students are taking English 101 to fulfill the school's core requirements.

➲ Study hard! You don't have to be the smartest student in your school, or even earn the highest GPA, but you do need to work hard and meet your own potential. You should show admission counselors that you consistently earn high grades. However, you can also show an admission counselor dedication and initiative by working hard to earn high marks and showing improvement. Don't be discouraged, and keep working!

➲ Get involved in extracurricular activities. Don't over-do it and join several all at once; but select activities that interest you and allow you to exhibit your leadership skills. Consider sports teams, school clubs, community groups, and church activities. Most admissions counselors are looking for a well-rounded student—someone who can bring more than just "book smarts" to their school. Plus, it shows that you are responsible enough to handle the pressures of schooling while still taking part in other activities.

➲ Take advantage of your school counselor's experience. Your high school counselor has access to a great deal of information that you will need in planning for higher education. In addition to the information and advice that your counselor can offer, you will find postsecondary school brochures, scholarship applications, admission applications, financial aid applications, SAT dates, and much more. Your school counselor will also be sending your high school transcripts to the schools that you are applying to, so it is important to form a good relationship early on. He or she may also have connections with other agencies and institutions that may prove to be helpful.

Ok, so those are some of the long-term items that you will need to work on. Now, here is a more tangible list of things that you will need to do.

➲ You will be required to take standardized tests before enrolling in an institution of higher education. You should begin taking these tests in your junior year. These tests can be taken as many times as you want, and the highest score will be the score that is considered in the admission process. The PSAT is a practice test for the SAT and may qualify you for the National Merit Scholarship Program and National Scholarship Service and Fund for African American students. It also designates students for the National Hispanic Scholar Recognition Program. The SAT and the ACT Assessment are both nationally used tests; each takes about 3 hours to complete. The SAT measures developed verbal and math reasoning abilities as they relate to successful performance in college. The ACT Assessment measures knowledge and skills in English, math, reading, and science. Reservations at a scheduled test location are required, and testing fees are incurred. Check your guidance office for a list of the testing dates.

➲ For each school that you are interested in attending, you must complete and submit an admission form. Although schools vary in their admission policies, every college requires you to write an essay, usually meant to convey who you are and what communication skills you possess. Admission counselors consider several things when reviewing applications: GPA, class rank, strength of subjects, SAT/ACT scores, recommendations, activities/awards, personal essays, and interviews. There is a fee to file admission forms, although many schools will waive the application fee if you attend an Open House and bring your application with you. You may find the admission forms you need at your guidance office or you can download, complete, and submit them online at www.aesmentor.org.

➲ As you prepare for higher education, one of your

biggest concerns is probably financial aid. There are four types of financial aid available that can be combined to create financial aid packages.

1. Scholarships are money awarded that does not have to be paid back. They are given to students who show promise of high achievement in areas such as academics, athletics, music, art, or other fields.

You should exhaust all opportunities to receive a scholarship or grant since these do not need to be paid back. Scholarships are awarded by many private businesses and companies, professional associations or organizations, civic clubs, and labor unions. They have varying eligibility requirements; you may be surprised at the number of scholarships available that apply directly to you. Visit your local library and your school's guidance office, check the local newspaper, inquire at your church, and ask businesses in your area. You can also find an excellent source of scholarship information at www.aesmentor.org. This site includes a scholarship search engine, which provides you with a listing of scholarships that match your specific skills, interests, and background.

2. Grants are also money awarded that does not have to be paid back. However, aid is based on financial need.

In order to receive financial aid assistance from the federal or state government, you must complete the Free Application for Federal Student Aid (FAFSA). Most schools require that you complete this form, too. The form gathers information from you and your parents to determine the amount of aid you will be eligible to receive. There is no filing fee; however, there are filing deadlines that must be met. You can get this form from your guidance counselor, the school you plan to attend, or by calling the U.S. Department of Education toll-free at 800-4 FED-AID. You can also download the FAFSA form at www.ed.gov/offices/OSFAP/students/apply/express. html or apply directly on line at www.fafsa.ed.gov or www.aesmentor.org.

Be advised, though, that some states have separate applications for state grants. Contact your state's higher education agency for assistance.

3. Loans are money borrowed that must be paid back at specific interest rates.

Always exhaust your federal loan eligibility first because these loans tend to offer the lowest interest rates. However, all federal Stafford Loans are not the same. Different guarantors and lenders offer different benefits. For example,

aesBEST Stafford Loans can save a typical borrower nearly $1,100 compared to a standard Stafford Loan.

aesBEST is an affordable Stafford Loan that provides borrowers with immediate up-front and repayment benefits. A typical aesBEST borrower will pay only 1% in up-front fees. Most programs charge 4% of the total loan amount! Borrowers also reap long-term benefits; a 2% interest rate reduction after 48 consecutive on-time payments, a .25 % interest rate reduction for automatic direct debit of payment and a single point of customer service for the life of the loan.

Your parents may also assist you in paying for your education with a federal PLUS loan, through which your parents can borrow up to the difference between your educational costs and other financial aid each year from a bank or another lending institution.

Private loans are also available through various lenders. However, these often carry the highest interest rate for repayment. In most cases, obtaining a private loan should be your last course of action in acquiring financial aid for higher education.

4. Work-study awards provide students with on-campus or off-campus employment to help pay for school costs.

Work-study programs also allow students to gain career-related, hands-on work experience in high-tech and community service positions. Participants generally work from 10 to 15 hours per week during the academic year and up to 40 hours per week during the summer. There are filing deadlines for participants. For more information contact the financial aid office at the school you plan to attend.

Getting ready for higher education may seem overwhelming to you right now, but if you follow the timeline included below and the advice offered above, you'll be ready in no time!

Getting Ready...

Although college is two years away for juniors, there is plenty to do. Your junior year will be a busy time...

Fall

- If you haven't already chosen your major for your postsecondary schooling, begin narrowing your choices.
- Attend college fairs and meet with college representatives who visit your high school.

- Attend financial aid informational meetings with your parents.
- Request information brochures from those colleges that interest you the most.
- Take the PSAT in preparation for the SAT and for eligibility for National Merit Scholarships.
- Begin searching for potential scholarships on the Internet, at your local library, and through local businesses, associations, and municipalities.

Spring

- Take the SAT I or the ACT Assessment (depending on the requirements of the schools that you are interested in attending). If SAT II tests are required, this would also be a good time to take those.
- Narrow your list of choice colleges and make plans to visit those campuses. You may take advantage of open houses or schedule a one-on-one interview and tour with an admission counselor.
- Request information regarding those scholarships for which you are eligible. Scholarship search engines are available on sites such as AESmentor and FastWEB, and Peterson's
- Look for a summer job.

Summer

Complete admission application forms for the schools that you would like to attend. (If you attend an upcoming open house, many colleges will waive the application fee if you bring your application with you to the campus.)

Senior Year

Your senior year is the time for completing applications, applying for financial aid, and taking care of a lot of things you probably haven't thought about yet. Just remember, take it one step at a time.

August

- Request applications and information from those colleges in which you're most interested.
- Visit schools and/or plan fall visits to help narrow your choices.
- Look into fall overnight and weekend college visitation programs.

September

- Mark your calendar for college fairs and admissions representative visits.
- Meet with your counselor to develop a college admissions plan.
- Register for the SAT, ACT Assessment, and/or prep courses.
- Consider early decision/early action programs.

October

- Create a schedule of admissions and financial aid deadlines.
- Begin applications and admission essays.
- Request transcripts from your guidance office and letters of recommendation from teachers, activity leaders, coaches, and/or community members.
- Explore college and scholarship information on line, at the library, and throughout your community.

November

- Follow up to ensure that letters of recommendation are submitted.
- Complete essays and applications.
- Submit applications for early decision/early action programs.

December

- Complete, photocopy, and submit your applications. Keep the photocopies for your records.
- Obtain a Free Application for Student Financial Aid (FAFSA). You can do this on line by visiting www.aessuccess.org.
- Obtain any other financial aid forms that may be required by the schools to which you are applying.

January

- Talk to your parents about obtaining income tax information and/or completing their taxes early to help in completing the FAFSA.
- Complete, photocopy, and submit the FAFSA.

February

- Be sure that you have submitted all required financial aid forms.

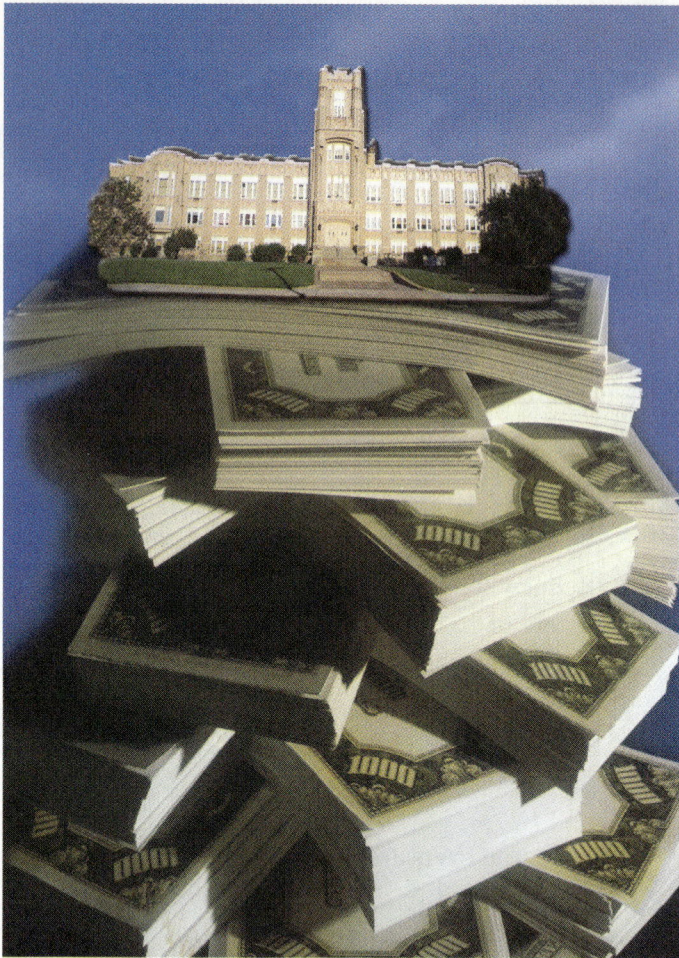

- If selected for verification, send copies of your income tax forms to financial aid offices.
- Watch the mail for your Student Aid Report (SAR).
- Time to look for a summer job.

April

- Receive admissions notifications.
- Compare financial aid awards relative to cost of attendance.
- Make your final enrollment decision and submit the enrollment deposit, if requested.
- Make a decision regarding your housing. If you will be living on campus, you need to apply for housing.
- Notify those schools that you will not be attending.
- Sign and return financial aid forms for the school that you will be attending.

May

- Take AP exams.
- Send final transcript and student loan applications to your chosen college.
- Contact your financial aid office to check your status.

June

- Complete any remaining financial aid forms.
- Plan for college orientation and transportation to school.

July

- Finalize college transportation and housing.

Planning for a Solid Future

If, in the course of planning for higher education and obtaining financial aid, you choose to take out a student loan, it is important to remember that you are entering into a long-term commitment that must be taken seriously. After your graduation from postsecondary schooling, you will be responsible for beginning to pay back your student loan, among other financial obligations such as a car, an apartment, etc. You have taken an important step in the right direction just by choosing to go on to higher education. The quickest way to undo that is to fail to manage your financial responsibilities properly. You must plan for the future financially and be prepared to repay debt. Mismanagement of debt can often lead to a downward spiral that is difficult to overcome. Why put yourself in that position to begin with?

Another way to plan for the future is to avoid credit card debt. Many campuses have booths where credit cards are readily available to students, and many students abuse this and soon find themselves drowning in debt. A credit card can help you to establish good credit if you keep the balance low and pay it off each month. Good credit can help you later on as you look to buy a car or rent an apartment. However, if you know that this responsibility could prove to be too much for you, the best thing to do is avoid credit cards altogether.

For more information on managing debt and the long-term implications of defaulting on your student loan, visit YouCanDealWithIt.com. This Web site was designed to help recent and soon-to-be college graduates deal with life after college. In addition to debt management information, the site offers job interview tips, advice on buying a car, career wardrobe pointers, and much more. Visit YouCanDealWithIt.com now to get a head start on your future!

Good luck!

FINANCIAL AID GLOSSARY

ASSETS. The amount a family has in savings and investments. This includes savings and checking accounts, a business, a farm or other real estate, and stocks, bonds, and trust funds. Cars are not considered assets, nor are such possessions as stamp collections or jewelry. The net value of the principal home is counted as an asset by some colleges in determining their own awards but is not included in the calculation for eligibility for federal funds.

CITIZENSHIP/ELIGIBILITY FOR AID. To be eligible to receive federally funded college aid, a student must be one of the following:

1. A United States citizen

2. A non-citizen national

3. A permanent resident with an I-151 or I-551 without conditions

4. A participant in a suspension of deportation case pending before Congress

5. A holder of an I-94 showing one of the following designations: "Refugee," "Asylum Granted," "Indefinite Parole" and/or "Humanitarian Parole," "Cuban Haitian Entrant, Status Pending," or "Conditional Entrant" (valid if issued before April 1, 1980).

Individuals in the U.S. on an F1 or F2 visa only or on a J1 or J2 exchange visa only cannot get federal aid.

COOPERATIVE EDUCATION. A program offered by many colleges in which students alternate periods of enrollment with periods of employment, usually paid, and which can lengthen the usual baccalaureate program to five years.

EXPECTED FAMILY CONTRIBUTION (EFC) OR PARENTAL CONTRIBUTION. A figure determined by a congressionally mandated formula that indicates how much of a family's resources should be considered "available" for college expenses. Factors such as taxable and nontaxable income and the value of family assets are taken into account to determine a family's financial strength. Allowances for maintaining a family and future financial needs are then taken into consideration before determining how much a family should be able to put toward the cost of college.

INDEPENDENT STUDENT. A student who reports only his or her own income (and that of a spouse, if relevant) when applying for federal financial aid. Students who will be 24 or older by December 31, 2001, will automatically be considered "independent" for 2001–2002. Students who are under 24 will be considered independent if they are:

- ❑ married and not claimed as a dependent on their parents' 2001 federal income tax return
- ❑ the supporter of a legal dependent other than a spouse
- ❑ a veteran of the U.S. Armed Forces
- ❑ an orphan or ward of the court
- ❑ classified as independent by a college's financial aid administrator because of other unusual circumstances
- ❑ a graduate or professional student

MERIT-BASED AID. Any form of financial aid awarded on the basis of personal achievement or individual characteristics without reference to financial need.

SUBSIDIZED LOAN. A loan for which the borrower is not responsible for all of the interest payments. For Subsidized Federal Stafford and/or Direct Loans, the government pays interest to the lender on behalf of the borrower while the student is in college and during approved grace periods.

To be eligible to receive federal/state financial aid, you must maintain satisfactory academic progress toward a degree or certificate. This criterion is established by each college or university. You'll also need a valid social security number, and all male students must register for selective service on their eighteenth birthday.

Once you apply for federal aid, your application will be processed in approximately four weeks (one week if applying electronically). You'll then receive a Student Aid Report (SAR) in the mail, which will report the information from your application and your expected family contribution (EFC—the number used in determining your eligibility for federal student aid). Each school you listed on the application will also receive your application information.

You must reapply for federal aid every year. Also, if you change schools, your aid doesn't necessarily go with you. Check with your new school to find out what steps you must take to continue receiving aid.

Once you've decided to which schools you want to apply, talk to the financial aid officers of those schools. There is no substitute for getting information from the source when it comes to understanding your financial aid options. That personal contact can lead you to substantial amounts of financial aid.

If you qualify, don't let the sticker price of the college or program scare you away, because you may get enough outside money to pay for the education you want. Don't rule out a private institution until you have received the financial aid package from the school. Private colleges, in order to attract students from all income levels, offer significant amounts of financial aid.

Public-supported institutions tend to offer less financial aid because the lower tuition acts as a form of assistance (see "Projected College Expenses"). In addition, students attending school in their home state often have more aid possibilities than if they attend an out-of-state college. Use the "College Funds Available" chart later in this section to determine how much you and your family can contribute to your education and the "College Cost Comparison" table at the end of this section to figure out which schools best suit you financially.

TYPES OF FINANCIAL AID

Be sure that you understand the differences between the types of financial aid so you are fully prepared to apply for each. One or more of these financial resources may make it possible to pursue the education you want.

Grants: Grants are given for athletics (Division I only), academics, demographics, special talent potential, and/or need. Repayment is not required.

Scholarships: Scholarships, also called "merit aid," are awarded for academic excellence. Repayment is not required.

Loans: Student loans, which have lower interest rates, may be college sponsored or federally sponsored or may be available through commercial financial institutions.

Loans must be repaid, generally after you have graduated or left school.

College work-study: College work-study is a federally sponsored program that enables colleges to hire students for employment. If eligible, students work a limited number of hours throughout the school year. Many private colleges offer forms of self-help employment aid as their own supplement to the diminishing supply of federally funded work-study.

FEDERAL FINANCIAL AID PROGRAMS

A number of sources of financial aid are available to students from the federal government, state governments, private lenders, foundations and private agencies, and the colleges and universities themselves. In addition, as discussed earlier, there are four different forms of aid: grants, scholarships, loans, and work-study.

The federal government is the single largest source of financial aid for students. In the 2000–01 academic year, the U.S. Department of Education's student financial aid programs made more than an estimated $42 billion available in loans, grants, and other aid to millions of students. Following are listings of federal financial aid programs available to you.

Federal Grants

The federal government offers a number of educational grants, which are outlined below:

Federal Pell Grant

The Federal Pell Grant is the largest grant program in the nation; about 4 million students receive awards annually. This grant is intended to be the base or starting point of assistance for lower-income families. Eligibility for a Federal Pell Grant depends on the EFC, or Expected Family Contribution. (See the "Financial Aid

Glossary" for a description of commonly used terms.) The amount you receive will depend on your EFC, the cost of education at the college or university you attend, and whether you attend full-time or part-time. The highest award depends on how much the program is funded. The maximum for the 1999–2000 school year was $3,125. How much you get will depend not only on your financial need but on your cost of attending school, whether you're a full-time or part-time student, and whether you attend school for a full academic year or less.

The law authorizes maximum annual Pell Grant awards ranging from $4,500 in the 1999–2000 academic year to as much as $5,800 in the 2003–04 academic year. Note that the actual maximum for each of these academic years will be determined by the amount Congress appropriates for the program. Historically, the amount appropriated has resulted in maximum awards that are greater than the awards in previous years, but less than the authorized award.

Federal Supplemental Educational Opportunity Grant

As its name implies, the Federal Supplemental Educational Opport-

(Continued on page 91)

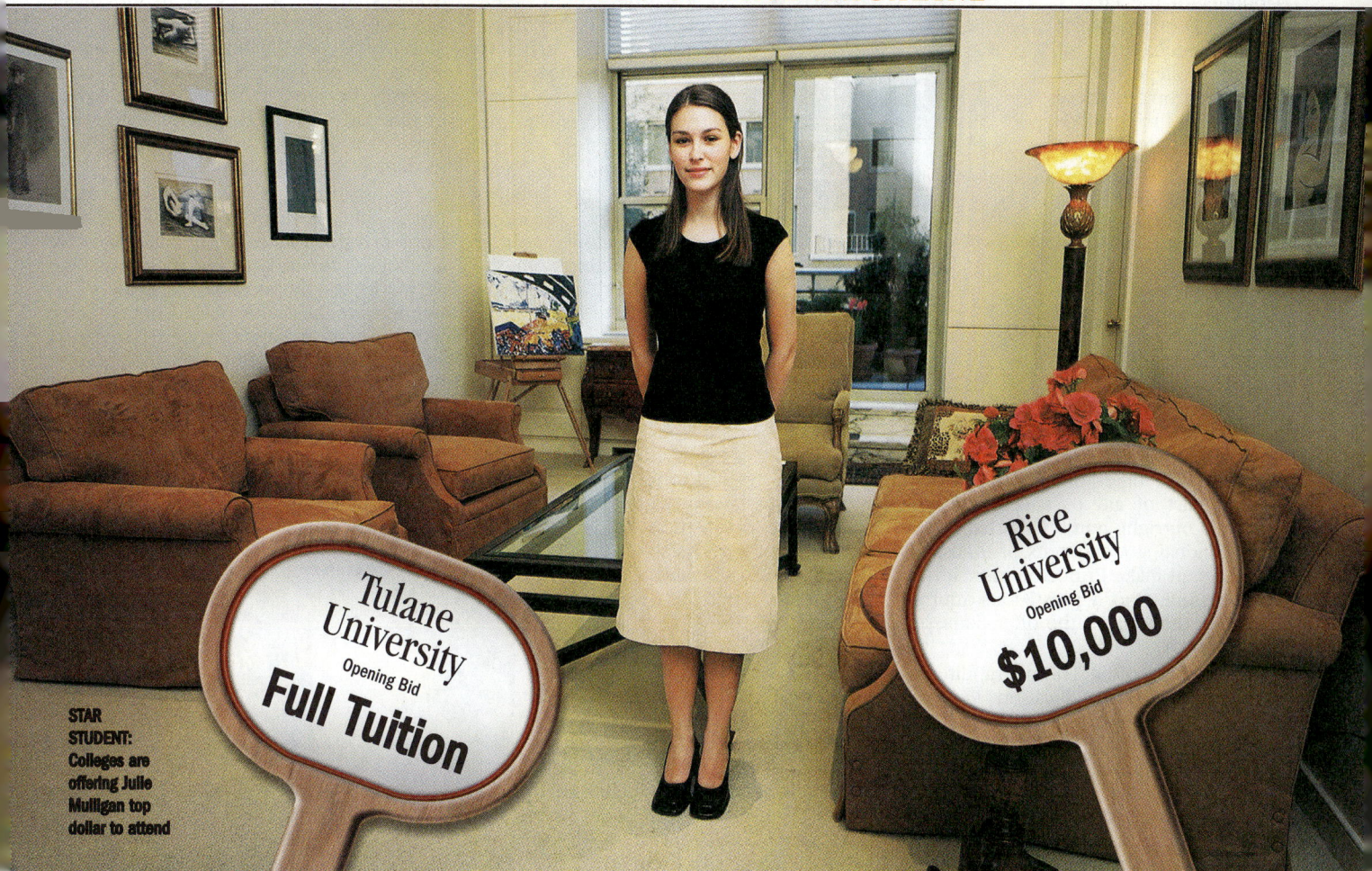

Tulane University
Opening Bid
Full Tuition

Rice University
Opening Bid
$10,000

STAR STUDENT: Colleges are offering Julie Mulligan top dollar to attend

HOW MUCH DO I HEAR FOR THIS STUDENT?

As colleges up their bids for the highest scorers, more scholarships go to kids who don't need them

By **BARRETT SEAMAN**

When Julie Mulligan was a senior at New York City's elite Spence School, she had a problem many of her college-bound contemporaries must have envied. Accepted at five prestigious universities, including Cornell in the Ivy League, she was weighing scholarship offers from two: $10,000 a year from Rice University in Houston, and $25,000 a year from Tulane in New Orleans. Julie's status as an A student with 1520 SATs attracted these offers, even though her father Jerry, a Manhattan lawyer, earned too much to qualify for a financial-aid package based on need.

The bidding war to sign Julie was good news for the Mulligans and other families of hard-working, high-scoring students. But many educators believe this competition poses a danger to the traditional, lower-income recipients of financial aid—and ultimately to some of the institutions themselves. Money awarded to high achievers, they say, will ultimately reduce funds that might have gone to needier students who,

while academically qualified for top colleges, are less likely to have the highest SAT scores or class rank. Yet many colleges feel compelled to spend what it takes to enroll anyone whose numbers will improve their standing in the national rankings, which often seal their reputations among applicants.

The result, some educators fear, will be a widening chasm between a few richly endowed institutions able to buy the very best applicants and a growing legion of poorer colleges, public and private, forced to use scarce money to attract good students—money that might be better spent on a new science lab or faculty salaries, as well as on scholarships for the needy. Says

Professor Gordon Winston, co-founder of the Project on the Economics of Higher Education at Williams College: "We're going to be using up these resources on the rich kids and not have any left over for the poor kids."

The weapons in this war are called "merit-based aid" and "preferential packages." The latest skirmish began in February, when Princeton University, whose $8.4 billion endowment is the largest per student of any U.S. college, announced that it would no longer require its scholarship recipients to take out loans as part of aid packages, replacing them with outright grants. This change will save individual students tens of thousands of dollars and make Princeton more attractive than some equally prestigious campuses—unless they match the offer. Some are doing just that.

According to Ron Ehrenberg, director of Cornell's Higher Education Research Institute and author of *Tuition Rising: Why College Costs So Much*, Princeton's move (a shift of $16 million a year in resources) is triggering similar deals at Harvard, Yale and M.I.T. Dartmouth announced that grants for next year's freshmen will increase an average of $1,750 per student. Jim Bock, acting admissions dean at Swarthmore, says Princeton's move "raises the bar," adding, "We're always refining our policies."

However, ripples are also being felt at institutions that, while selective, can ill afford to bid more for top students. Pennsylvania's Dickinson College has an endowment less than one-fiftieth the size of Princeton's and must carefully husband aid. "Princeton," says Dickinson vice president for enrollment and student life Robert Massa, "has reduced the maneuverability of making a financial-aid package competitive."

This is the second time in three years Princeton has stolen a march in the tuition wars. In 1998 the university announced it would no longer count the value of an applicant family's home as part of the formula it uses to determine financial need. That change allowed many applicants to qualify for a few thousand dollars more in aid.

For most of the past half-century, financial-aid officers at selective colleges—including M.I.T. and the eight Ivies—agreed among themselves on a single method of calculating a family's ability to pay. Applicants were told what their "expected family contribution" would be. But in 1990 the U.S. Justice Department charged these colleges with price fixing. The case was settled in 1993 when the colleges agreed to

Need vs. Know-How

How federal aid to college students is divided between merit and

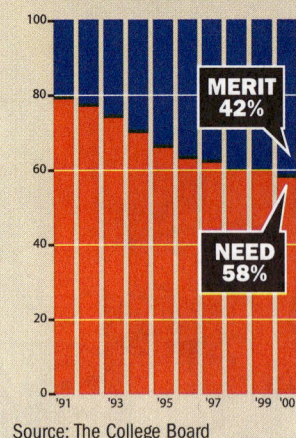

[chart showing stacked bars from '91 to '00, with MERIT 42% (top, blue) and NEED 58% (bottom, red), y-axis from 0 to 100]

Source: The College Board

stop swapping financial information about their applicants. Still, they insisted they would strive to confine aid to those who were in need.

At first, the collapse of the scholarship cartel seemed a good thing. With tuition at private colleges soaring nearly 75% during the 1990s alone, a little price competition among them seemed in order. In fact, market forces had been at work in college admissions for at least a couple of decades among the less competitive institutions, some of which needed to charge lower prices just to fill their classrooms. But since the lawsuit, a growing number of selective colleges—those whose applicants outnumber their available slots—have begun offering financial incentives regardless of need.

Ironically, the most selective colleges, often those that can best afford to give money away, benefit from a kind of Chivas Regal effect, in which buyers are willing to pay for cachet. While Princeton and a few other top colleges continue to limit aid to those in need, their actions are fueling a bidding war among schools eager to win kids away from Princeton—or any other college above them in the perceived pecking order. As a result, observes James Monks of M.I.T.'s Consortium on Financing Higher Education, "financial aid is no longer viewed as a charitable means of admitting a 'poor scholar,' but rather as a price discount to which an applicant is entitled and which is subject to negotiating and bargaining."

Most colleges play the merit-scholarship game with stealth. Many dodge the discount label by proffering merit scholarships that are endowed by private donors and have set qualifications: Emory offers the Scholars Program; Washington University in St. Louis, Mo., has its Honorary Scholars program. The private University of Rochester offers any New York State resident a $5,000 tuition break—one that just happens to make Rochester financially competitive with the better of the campuses of the State University of New York, to which it often loses applicants.

Now the game is getting even more complicated. "Each college kind of has its own stance on the degree to which it's willing to have those conversations" about financial aid, says Amy Grieger, college counselor at Northfield Mount Hermon, a presti-

gious Massachusetts prep school. What troubles Grieger as well as many college admissions officers is that the latest wave of merit-based scholarships is undermining efforts to promote economic and racial diversity, because it handicaps the lower-income kids, who might not be first in their class. "As a system, we're not serving those students very well," she admits.

Winston of Williams, noting that most of the colleges' financial-aid money comes from private donors, complains that "we are being pressured to use money we got as charity to compete like car dealers. The winners are the highly placed, high-income kids." The losers, says Cornell's Ehrenberg, will be "the low-income kids, those not at the top academically and students who do not have as much information on how to play the game." And the disparity will only get worse. The number of college applicants ages 18 to 24 is expected to increase a total of 1.6 million by 2015, and of those new applicants, 80% will come from minor-

> **Students may go to lesser schools simply because they are offered more money.**
> —RON EHRENBERG, Cornell University

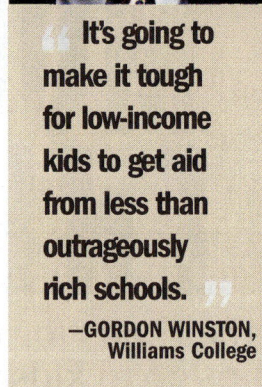

> **It's going to make it tough for low-income kids to get aid from less than outrageously rich schools.**
> —GORDON WINSTON, Williams College

ity groups that tend to be economically disadvantaged.

America's higher-education system, considered the most diversified on earth, is valued precisely because of its full menu of choices—from small Bible colleges to world-class universities. If the tuition wars spread further, that diversity will suffer. "In the short term," observes Dickinson's Massa, the merit-scholarship bidding "benefits colleges because we get our numbers. But if as a result we're not able to build new buildings or pay professors, it will cost us our future." ■

—*Reported by Heather Won Tesoriero*

unity Grant (FSEOG) provides additional need-based federal grant money to supplement the Federal Pell Grant. Each participating college is given funds to award to especially needy students. The maximum award is $4,000 per year, but the amount a student receives depends on the college's policy, the availability of FSEOG funds, the total cost of education, and the amount of other aid awarded.

Federal Scholarships

The following comprise the scholarships available through the federal government:

ROTC Scholarships

The Armed Forces (Army, Air Force, Navy, Marines) may offer up to a four-year scholarship that pays full college tuition plus a monthly allowance; however, these scholarships are very competitive and based upon GPA, class rank, ACT or SAT scores, and physical qualifications. Apply as soon as possible before December 1 of your senior year. Contact the headquarters of each of the armed forces for more information: Army, 800-USA-ROTC; Air Force, 800-423-USAF; Navy, 800-USA-NAVY; Marines, 800-MARINES (all numbers are toll-free).

Scholarships from Federal Agencies

Federal agencies, such as the CIA, NASA, Department of Agriculture, and Office of Naval Research, offer an annual stipend as well as a scholarship. In return, the student must work for the agency for a certain number of years or else repay all the financial support. See your counselor for more information.

Robert C. Byrd Honors Scholarship

To qualify for this scholarship, you must demonstrate outstanding academic achievement and excellence in high school as indicated by class rank, high school grades, test scores, and leadership activities. Award amounts of $1,500 are renewable for four years. Contact your high school counselor for application information. Deadlines may vary per state, so contact your state's Department of Education.

National Science Scholars Program (NSSP)

To qualify, you must be a graduating high school senior with a minimum 3.5 GPA and an ACT score of at least 25 or SAT I score of at least 1100 and demonstrate excellence and achievement in the physical, life, or computer sciences; mathematics; or engineering. Scholarships are as much as $5,000 per year or the student's cost of attendance, whichever is less, for up to five years of study. Awards are made to two students from each congressional district. Contact your high school counselor or NSSP coordinators at your state's Department of Education for application and deadline information.

Federal Loans

Following are methods through which you may borrow money from the federal government:

Federal Perkins Loan

This loan provides low-interest (5 percent) aid for students with exceptional financial need (students with the lowest expected family contribution). The Federal Perkins Loans are made through the college's financial aid office—that is, the college is the lender. For undergraduate study, you may borrow a maximum of $3,000 per year for up to five years of undergraduate study and may take up to ten years to repay the loan, beginning nine months after you graduate, leave school, or drop below half-time status. No interest accrues while you are in school and, under certain conditions (e.g., if you teach in a low-income area, work in law enforcement, are a full-time nurse or medical technician, or serve as a Peace Corps or VISTA volunteer), some or all of your loan can be canceled within 14 days after the date that your school sends notice of crediting the transaction, or by the first day of the payment period, whichever is later.

Payments also can be deferred under certain conditions, such as unemployment.

FFEL Stafford Student Loan

An FFEL Stafford Student Loan may be borrowed from a participating commercial lender, such as a bank, credit union, or savings and loan association. The interest rate varies annually (it has gone up to a maximum of 8.25 percent). If you qualify for a need-based subsidized FFEL Stafford Student Loan, the interest is paid by the federal government while you are enrolled in school. There is also an unsubsidized FFEL Stafford Student Loan that is not based on need and for which you are eligible, regardless of your family income.

The maximum amount you may borrow as a dependent in any one year is $2,625 when you're a freshman, $3,500 when you're a sophomore, and $5,500 when you're a junior or senior, with a maximum of $23,000 for the total undergraduate program. The maximum amount you may borrow as an independent is

$6,625 when you're a freshman (no more than $2,625 in subsidized Stafford Loans), $7,500 when you're a sophomore (no more than $3,500 in subsidized Stafford Loans), and $10,500 when you're a junior or senior (no more than $5,500 in subsidized Stafford Loans). You will be required to pay a 4 percent fee, which is deducted from the loan proceeds.

To apply for an FFEL Stafford Student Loan, you must first complete a FAFSA to determine eligibility for a subsidized loan and then complete a separate loan application that is submitted to a lender. The financial aid office can help you select a lender, or you can contact your state's Department of Higher Education to find a participating lender. The lender will send you or your parents a promissory note that you must sign indicating that you agree to repay the loan. The proceeds of the loan, less the origination fee, will be sent to your college to be either credited to your student account or paid to you directly.

If you qualify for a subsidized Stafford Loan, you don't have to pay interest while in school. For an unsubsidized FFEL Loan, you will be responsible for paying the interest from the time the loan is established. However, some FFEL lenders will

permit you to delay making payments and will add the interest to your loan. Once the repayment period starts, whether you're a borrower of either subsidized or unsubsidized FFEL Loans, you will have to pay a combination of interest and principal monthly for up to a ten-year period.

William D. Ford Direct Stafford Loans

The Federal Direct Student Loan is basically the same as the Federal Stafford Student Loan Program. The difference is that the U.S. Department of Education, rather than a bank, is the lender. If your college does not participate in this program, you can still apply for an FFEL Stafford Student Loan.

Many of the terms of the Direct Stafford Loan are similar to those of the FFEL Stafford Loan. In particular, the interest rate, loan maximums, deferments, and cancellation benefits are the same. However, under the terms of the Direct Stafford Student Loan, you have a choice of repayment plans. You may choose:

- A standard fixed monthly repayment for up to ten years

- An extended repayment plan with lower fixed monthly payments for twelve to thirty years at a rate

with a higher total amount of interest payment

- A graduated monthly repayment plan for twelve to thirty years in which payments grow from 50 percent to 150 percent of the standard plan

- Or an income contingent repayment plan with monthly payments based on your yearly income and family size

- You cannot receive both a Direct Stafford Loan and an FFEL Stafford Loan for the same period of time but may receive both in different enrollment periods.

PLUS Loans

The PLUS loans are for parents of dependent students and are designed to help families with cash-flow problems. There is no needs test to qualify, and the loans are made by FFEL lenders or directly by the Department of Education. The loan has a variable interest rate that cannot exceed 9 percent, and there is no specific yearly limit; your parents can borrow up to the cost of your education, less other financial aid received. Repayment begins 60 days after the money is advanced. A 4 percent fee is subtracted from the proceeds. Parent borrowers must generally have a good credit record to qualify for PLUS loans.

The PLUS loan will be processed under either the Direct or the FFEL system, depending on the type of loan program for which the college has contracted.

Federal Direct Lending

Provisions are identical to the Federal Stafford Student Loan programs. However, the primary lending institution is the college or university participating in the Federal Direct Lending Program, as opposed to a bank or other financial institution.

Lender of Last Resort

This program assists students who have tried to obtain a Federal Stafford student loan and have been denied by two lending institutions. Eligible stu-

(Continued on page 94)

Your College Cash

Section 529 plans offer tax-free growth and are the clear choice for most parents

By DANIEL KADLEC

Cynthia Johnson for TIME

The hardest part about saving for college ought to be the saving part, not choosing where to stash the savings. Stock-index funds? Zero-coupon bonds? Target maturity mutual funds? Custodial accounts? Prepaid tuition plans? Education IRAs? Each has advantages for folks staring at potential six-figure tuition bills down the road. It all amounts to a terrifying multiple-choice test that leads even straight-A parents to resort to guesswork or to cutting class altogether.

Take heart. This grind of a course just got a lot easier. The $1.35 trillion tax cut President Bush has signed may be loaded with numbing nuances on a broad range of tax fronts. But on the issue of saving for college, it's perfectly clear: so-called 529 plans, which allow tax-free withdrawals for college expenses, are a no-brainer for just about everyone.

Named after a section of the tax code, 529 plans are run by the states, and soon all 50 will have a version. These plans are open to everyone. Contributions are often deductible at the state level, and you can sock away as much as $250,000 per child. The plans are so popular that fund company American Century, one of the first to offer a tailored college-savings vehicle, scrapped its once popular program last year in favor of Learning Quest, a national 529 plan run through Kansas.

Yes, 529 plans reduce chances of getting financial aid, some charge high fees, and there is a penalty if you don't use the money for tuition, books or room and board. No, you don't have a lot of control over how the money is invested. Yet look at the upside: you retain total control over the money—unlike that in a custodial account, which becomes the property of your child at age 18 or 21. Better still, the savings have always grown tax-deferred before being taxed at the child's rate upon withdrawal. And here's great news: starting next year, there's no tax on withdrawals, tipping the scales in favor of 529 plans for most people.

Fund company T. Rowe Price found that the same $5,000 yearly investment by a taxpayer in the 28% bracket over 18 years resulted in total savings of $287,704 in a new 529 plan, $250,157 in a custodial account (under the Uniform Gift to Minors Act) and $224,527 in a taxable account, based on a 10% rate of return. The gap narrows over shorter durations. After just five years, the same investment produces $38,520 in a 529 plan, $37,368 in a custodial account and $34,587 in a taxable account.

If you have just a few years, 529 plans may not be best, given their relative inflexibility. Go with a taxable account invested in a broad stock index. That enhances your ability to get college aid and to use the Lifetime Learning and Hope Scholarship credits freely. It also puts you in full control of your money. But for early starters, you can't beat the new 529 plans, which make it even easier now to move assets among extended family members.

Note that Congress can giveth—and taketh. Critics view the new provision as a freebie to the rich and charge that the easy money will lead exclusive universities to raise rates, putting the very best education further out of reach. So the tax-free nature of 529s may not last. But don't let that stop you. Saving somewhere—anywhere—is the key to passing this class. ∎

THINKING AHEAD TO PAYING BACK YOUR STUDENT LOAN

MORE THAN EVER BEFORE, LOANS HAVE BECOME AN IMPORTANT PART OF FINANCIAL ASSISTANCE. THE MAJORITY OF STUDENTS FIND THAT THEY MUST BORROW MONEY TO FINANCE THEIR EDUCATION. IF YOU ACCEPT A LOAN, YOU ARE INCURRING A FINANCIAL OBLIGATION. YOU WILL HAVE TO REPAY THE LOAN IN FULL, ALONG WITH ALL OF THE INTEREST AND ANY ADDITIONAL FEES (COLLECTION, LEGAL, ETC.). SINCE YOU WILL BE MAKING LOAN PAYMENTS TO SATISFY THE LOAN OBLIGATION, CAREFULLY CONSIDER THE BURDEN YOUR LOAN AMOUNT WILL IMPOSE ON YOU AFTER YOU LEAVE COLLEGE. DEFAULTING ON A STUDENT LOAN CAN JEOPARDIZE YOUR FINANCIAL FUTURE. BORROW INTELLIGENTLY.

SOME REPAYMENT OPTIONS

A number of repayment options are available to borrowers of federally guaranteed student loans.

The Standard Repayment Plan: requires fixed monthly payments (at least $50) over a fixed period of time (up to ten years). The length of the repayment period depends on the loan amount. This plan usually results in the lowest total interest paid because the repayment period is shorter than under the other plans.

The Extended Repayment Plan: allows loan repayment to be extended over a period from generally twelve to thirty years, depending on the total amount borrowed. Borrowers still pay a fixed amount each month (at least $50), but usually monthly payments will be less than under the Standard Repayment Plan. This plan may make repayment more manageable; however, borrowers usually will pay more interest because the repayment period is longer.

The Graduated Repayment Plan: allows payments to start out low and increase every two years. This plan may be helpful to borrowers whose incomes are low initially but will increase steadily. A borrower's monthly payments must be at least half, but may not be more than one-and-a-half times what he or she would pay under Standard Repayment. As in the Extended Repayment Plan, the repayment period will usually vary from twelve to thirty years, depending on the total amount borrowed. Again, monthly payments may be more manageable at first because they are lower, but borrowers will pay more interest because the repayment period is longer.

The Income Contingent Repayment Plan: bases monthly payments on adjusted gross income (AGI) and the total amount borrowed. This is currently only available to students who participate in Direct Loans; however, some FFEL lenders and guaranty agencies provide income-sensitive repayment plans. As income rises or falls each year, monthly payments will be adjusted accordingly. The required monthly payment will not exceed 20 percent of the borrower's discretionary income as calculated under a published formula. Borrowers have up to twenty-five years to repay; after that time, any unpaid amount will be discharged, and borrowers must pay taxes on the amount discharged. In other words, if the federal government forgives the balance of a loan, the amount is considered to be part of the borrower's income for that year.

dents must be enrolled at an eligible postsecondary educational institution.

Nursing Student Loan Program

Awarded to nursing students with demonstrated financial need. This loan has a 5 percent interest rate, repayable after completion of studies. Repayment is to be completed within ten years. Contact your college's financial aid office for deadline and other information, including maximum borrowing amounts.

Other Federal Programs

The following programs offer alternative ways to earn money for college:

Federal Work-Study (FWS)

This program provides jobs for students who need financial aid for their educational expenses. The salary is paid by funds from the federal government and the college (or the employer). You work on an hourly basis in jobs on or off campus and must be paid at least the federal minimum wage. You may earn only up to the amount awarded, which depends on the calculated financial need and the total amount of money available to the college.

AmeriCorps

AmeriCorps is a national service program for a limited number of students. Participants work in a public or private nonprofit agency that provides service to the community in one of four priority areas: education, human services, the environment, and public safety. In exchange, they earn a stipend for living expenses and up to $4,725 for up to two years to apply toward college expenses. Students can work either before, during, or after they go to college and can use the funds to either pay current educational expenses or repay federal student loans. If you successfully complete one full-time term of service (at least 1,700 hours over one year or less), you will be eligible for an award of $4,725. If you successfully complete one part-time term of service (at least 900 hours over two years or less), you will be eligible for an award of $2,362.50. You should speak to your college's financial aid office for more details about this program and any other new initiatives available to students.

FAMILIES' GUIDE TO TAX CUTS FOR EDUCATION

Many new tax benefits for adults who want to return to school and for parents who are sending or planning to send their children to college will be available due to the balanced budget that was signed into law in 1997. These tax cuts effectively make the first two years of college universally available, and they give many more working Americans the financial means to go back to school if they want to choose a new career or upgrade their skills. About 12.9 million students benefit—5.8 million under the "HOPE Scholarship" tax credit and 7.1 million under the Lifetime Learning tax credit.

HOPE Scholarship Tax Credit

The HOPE Scholarship tax credit helps make the first two years of college or career school universally available. Students receive a 100 percent tax credit for the first $1,000 of tuition and required fees and a 50 percent credit on the second $1,000. This credit is available for tuition and required fees less grants, scholarships, and other tax-free educational assistance and became available for payments made after December 31, 1997, for college enrollment after that date.

This credit is phased out for joint filers who have between $80,000 and $100,000 of adjusted gross income, and for single filers who have between $40,000 and $50,000 of adjusted gross income. The credit can be claimed in two years for students who are in their first two years of college or career school and who are enrolled on at least a half-time basis in a degree or certificate program for any portion of the year. The taxpayer can claim a credit for his own tuition expense or for the expenses of his or her spouse or dependent children.

The Lifetime Learning Tax Credit

This tax credit is targeted at adults who want to go back to school, change careers, or take a course or two to upgrade their skills and to college juniors, seniors, graduate and professional degree students. A family will receive a 20 percent tax credit for the first $5,000 of tuition and required fees paid each year through 2002, and for the first $10,000 thereafter. Just like the HOPE Scholarship tax credit, the Lifetime Learning Tax Credit is available for tuition and required fees less grants, scholarships, and other tax-free educational assistance; families may claim the credit for amounts paid on or after July 1, 1998, for college or career school enrollment beginning on or after July 1, 1998. The maximum credit is determined on a per-taxpayer (family) basis, regardless of the number of postsec-ondary students in the family, and is phased out at the same income levels as the HOPE Scholarship tax credit. Families will be able to claim the Lifetime Learning tax credit for some members of their family and the HOPE Scholarship tax credit for others who qualify in the same year.

NATIONAL, STATEWIDE, AND LOCAL SCHOLARSHIPS

Requirements for the financial resources listed below are approximate and may vary. Check with your guidance counselor for the most up-to-date information regarding the availability of these resources and the requirements to qualify.

National Scholarships

Following is an abridged list of national scholarship program:

Coca-Cola Scholars Program

Awards to seniors planning to attend an accredited college or university. Based on academics, school and community activities, and motivation to serve and succeed in all endeavors. Call for deadline and application information at 800-306-2653 (toll-free) or check www.cocacola.com.

Duracell/National Science Teachers Association Scholarship Competition

Open to all students in grades 9 through 12. Student must design and build a device powered by Duracell batteries. Call 703-243-7100 for application and deadline information.

Elks National Scholarship

Awards more than $1 million to "most valuable students" nationwide. To qualify, you must be in the upper 5 percent of your class and have an A average. Awards are based upon scholarship, leadership, and financial need. Call 773-755-4732 for application and deadline information or visit their Web site at www.elks.org.

National Foundation for Advancement in the Arts/Arts

Recognition & Talent Search (NFAA/ARTS)

Awards are based on talent in dance, music, theater, visual arts, writing, voice, jazz, or photography. Call 800-970-2787 (toll-free). Early application is June 1 of junior year, and the final application deadline is October 1 of senior year.

National Merit Scholarship Program

Based on the PSAT exam taken in the junior year. Also investigate the National Honor Society Scholarship.

National Society of Professional Engineers

Awarded to high school seniors who plan to study engineering in college. Applications are accepted from August 1 through December 1, and the scholarships are awarded in January. Must be a U.S. citizen planning to attend an engineering program in the United States approved by the Accreditation Board for Engineering and Technology. Visit the NSPE's Web site at www.nspe.org for more information.

Prudential Spirit of Community Award

Nationwide program to honor exemplary, self-initiated community service by middle and high school students. Each school may nominate its top volunteer. Contact the National Association of Secondary School Principals at 703-860-0200 for application and deadline information, or visit their Web site at www.nassp.org.

Tylenol

Award based 40 percent on leadership in school and community, 50 percent on grade point average, and 10 percent on clear statement of goals. Call 800-676-8437 (toll-free) for an application. Deadline: January.

Statewide Scholarships

Please see the appendices for a listing of scholarships organized by each state in your region.

Local Scholarships

It is not possible within the scope of this book to list all of the sources of local scholarship dollars. The following are excellent resources for seeking local financial assistance:

- ☼ Your guidance counselor
- ☼ A high school teacher or coach
- ☼ Your high school and elementary school PTA (yes, many elementary school PTAs award scholarships to alumni)
- ☼ The local librarian
- ☼ College admissions office
- ☼ Your parents' alma mater
- ☼ Your employer
- ☼ Your parents' employer
- ☼ Professional and social organizations in your community

APPLYING FOR SCHOLARSHIPS

Here are some tips to help make a success of your scholarship hunt.

1 Start early. Your freshman year is not too early to plan for scholarships academically, choose extracurricular activities that will highlight your strengths, and get involved in your church and community—all things that are important to those who make scholarship decisions.

2 Search for scholarships. A couple of hours a week in the public library will help you learn about hundreds of scholarships and assess those for which you might qualify.

3 Apply, apply, apply. One student applied for nearly sixty scholarships and was fortunate enough to win seven. "Imagine if I'd applied for five and only gotten one," she says.

4 Plan ahead. It takes time to get transcripts and letters of recommendation. Letters from people who know you well are more effective than letters from prestigious names who know you only vaguely.

5 Be organized. In the homes of scholarship winners, you can often find a file box where all relevant information is stored. This method allows you to review deadlines and requirements every so often. Computerizing the information, if possible, allows you to change and update information quickly.

6 Follow directions. Make sure that you don't disqualify yourself by filling the forms out incorrectly, missing the deadline, or failing to supply important information. Type your applications, if possible, and have someone proofread them.

MYTHS AND MISCONCEPTIONS ABOUT SCHOLARSHIPS AND FINANCIAL AID

The scholarship and financial aid game is highly misunderstood by many high school students. And high school guidance counselors, overburdened with paperwork and complaints, often lack the time to fully investigate scholarship opportunities and to inform students about them. The myths and misconceptions persist while the truth about scholarships remains hidden, the glittering prizes and benefits unknown to many teenagers.

Myth #1: Scholarships are rare, elusive awards won only by valedictorians, geniuses, and whiz kids.

The truth is that with proper advice and strategies, private scholarships are very much within the grasp of high school students who possess talent and ability in almost any given field. Thousands of high school students like you compete and win.

Myth #2: My chances of being admitted to a college are reduced if I apply for financial aid.

The truth is that most colleges have a policy of "need-blind" admissions, which means that a student's financial need is not taken into account in the admission decision. However, there are a few colleges that do consider ability to pay before deciding whether or not to admit a student. There are a few more that look at ability to pay of those whom they placed on a waiting list to get in or those students who applied late. Some colleges will mention this in their literature, others may not. In making decisions about the college application and financing process, however, families should apply for financial aid if the student needs the aid to attend college.

Myth #3: All merit scholarships are based on a student's academic record.

The truth is that many of the best opportunities are in such areas as writing, public speaking, leadership, science, community service, music and the arts, foreign languages, and vocational-technical skills. So that means you don't always have to have a 3.99 GPA to win if you excel in a certain area.

Myth #4: You have to be a member of a minority group to get a scholarship.

The truth is that there are indeed some scholarships that are targeted toward women and minority students. There are also scholarships for which you must be a member of a specific national club or student organization (such as 4-H and the National Honor Society), which makes these scholarships just as exclusive. But most scholarship opportunities are not exclusive to any one segment of the population.

Myth #5: If you have need for and receive financial aid, it's useless to win a scholarship from some outside organization because the college will just take away the aid that the organization offered.

It's true that if you receive need-based aid, you can't receive more than the total cost of attendance (including room and board, books, and other expenses, not just tuition). If the financial aid that you've been awarded meets the total cost and you win an outside scholarship, colleges have to reduce something. But usually, they reduce the loan or work-study portion of your financial aid award before touching the grant portion that they've awarded you. This means that you won't have to borrow or earn as much. Also, most colleges don't meet your full financial need when you qualify for need-based financial aid. So, if you do win an outside scholarship, chances are that your other aid will not be taken away or reduced.

SCHOLARSHIP SCAMS

Unfortunately for prospective scholarship seekers, the private aid sector exists virtually without patterns or rules. Regrettably, the combination of the urgency to locate money, limited time, and a complex and bewildering system has created opportunities for fraud. Although most scholarship sponsors and most scholarship search services are legitimate, schemes that pose as either legitimate scholarship search services or scholarship sponsors have cheated thousands of families.

These fraudulent businesses advertise in campus newspapers, distribute flyers, mail letters and postcards, provide toll-free phone numbers, and even have sites on the Web. The most obvious frauds operate as scholarship search services or scholarship clearinghouses. Another quieter segment sets up as a scholarship sponsor, pockets the money from the fees and charges that are paid by thousands of hopeful scholarship seekers, and returns little, if anything, in proportion to the amount it collects. A few of these frauds inflict great harm by gaining access to individuals' credit or checking accounts with the intent to extort funds.

The Federal Trade Commission (FTC), in Washington, D.C., has a campaign called Project $cholar$cam to confront this type of fraudulent activity. There are legitimate services. However, a scholarship search service cannot truthfully guarantee that a

COLLEGE FUNDS AVAILABLE

USE THIS CHART TO ESTIMATE YOUR FAMILY'S RESOURCES THAT WILL BE AVAILABLE FOR COLLEGE EXPENSES. CHECK YOUR PROGRESS AT THE END OF YOUR SOPHOMORE AND JUNIOR YEARS TO SEE IF YOUR PLANS FOR SEEKING FINANCIAL AID NEED TO BE REVISED.

	Estimated amount available	Actual amount: 11th grade	Actual amount: 12th grade
YOUR RESOURCES			
Savings and other assets			
Summer earnings			
Part-time work during school year			
Miscellaneous			
PARENTS' RESOURCES			
From their current income			
From college savings			
Miscellaneous (insurance, annuities, stocks, trusts, home equity, property assets)			
TOTAL			

Source: American College Testing Program

student will receive a scholarship, and students almost always will fare as well or better by doing their own homework using a reliable scholarship information source, such as *Peterson's Scholarships, Grants & Prizes*, than by wasting money and time with a search service that promises a scholarship.

The FTC warns you to be alert for these six warning signs of a scam:

1 "This scholarship is guaranteed or your money back." No service can guarantee that it will get you a grant or scholarship. Refund guarantees often have impossible conditions attached. Review a service's refund policies in writing before you pay a fee.

2 "The scholarship service will do all the work." Unfortunately, nobody else can fill out the personal information forms, write the essays, and supply the references that many scholarships may require.

3 "The scholarship will cost some money." Be wary of any charges relat-

ed to scholarship information services or individual scholarship applications, especially in significant amounts. Before you send money to apply for a scholarship, investigate the sponsor.

4 "You can't get this information anywhere else." In addition to Peterson's, scholarship directories from other publishers are available in any large bookstore, public library, or high school guidance office.

5 "You are a finalist" or "You have been selected by a national foundation to receive a scholarship." Most legitimate scholarship programs almost never seek out particular applicants. Most scholarship sponsors will contact you only in response to an inquiry because they generally lack the budget to do anything more than this. Should you think that there is any real possibility that you may have been selected to receive a scholarship, before you send any money, investigate first to be sure that the sponsor or program is legitimate.

6 "The scholarship service needs your credit card or checking account number in advance." Never provide your credit card or bank account number on the

telephone to the representative of an organization that you do not know. Get information in writing first. An unscrupulous operation does not need your signature on a check. It will scheme to set up situations that will allow it to drain a victim's account with unauthorized withdrawals.

In addition to the FTC's six signs, here are some other points to keep in mind when considering a scholarship program:

- Fraudulent scholarship operations often use official-sounding names, containing words such as federal, national, administration, division, federation, and foundation. Their names are often a slight variant of the name of a legitimate government or private organization. Do not be fooled by a name that seems reputable or official, an official-looking seal, or a Washington, D.C., address.

- If you win a scholarship, you will receive written official notification by mail, not by telephone. If the sponsor calls to inform you, it will follow up with a letter in the mail. If a request for money is made by phone, the operation is probably fraudulent.

- Be wary if an organization's address is a box number or a residential address. If a bona fide scholarship program uses a post office box number, it usually will include a street address and telephone number on its stationery.

- Beware of telephone numbers with a 900-area code. These may charge you a fee of several dollars a minute for a call that could be a long recording that provides only a list of addresses or names.

- Watch for scholarships that ask you to "act now." A dishonest operation may put pressure on an applicant by saying that awards are on a "first-come, first-serve" basis. Some scholarship programs will give preference to the earlier qualified applications. However, if you are told, especially on the telephone, that you must respond quickly but that you will not hear about the results for several months, there may be a problem.

- Be wary of endorsements. Fraudulent operations will claim endorsements by groups with names similar to well-known private or government organizations. The Better Business Bureau (BBB) and government agencies do not endorse businesses.

- Don't pay money for a scholarship to an organization that you've never heard of before or whose legitimacy you can't verify. If you have already paid money to such an organization and find reason to doubt its authenticity, call your bank to stop payment on your check, if possible, or call your credit card company and tell it that you think you were the victim of consumer fraud.

To find out how to recognize, report, and stop a scholarship scam, you may write to the Federal Trade Commission's Consumer Response Center at 600 Pennsylvania Avenue NW, Washington, D.C. 20580. On the Web, go to www.ftc.gov, or call 877-FTC-HELP (toll-free). You can also check with the Better Business Bureau (BBB), which is an organization that maintains files of businesses about which it has received complaints. You should call both your local BBB office and the BBB office in the area of the organization in question; each local BBB has different records. Call 703-276-0100 to get

COLLEGE COST COMPARISON WORKSHEET

Chart your course to see which college or university best fits your financial resources. Your totals in expenses and funds available should be the same amount. If not, you have a funding gap, meaning that you have more expenses than funds available and will need to take out a loan (most likely), or vice versa (less likely).

	College 1	College 2	College 3	College 4
EXPENSES				
Tuition and fees	$	$	$	$
Books and supplies	$	$	$	$
Room and board	$	$	$	$
Transportation	$	$	$	$
Miscellaneous	$	$	$	$
TOTAL	$	$	$	$
FUNDS AVAILABLE				
Student and parent contributions	$	$	$	$
Grants	$	$	$	$
Scholarships	$	$	$	$
Work-study	$	$	$	$
TOTAL	$	$	$	$
FUNDING GAP	$	$	$	$

A CHECKLIST FOR SENIORS

Applying for financial aid can become confusing if you don't record what you've done and when. Use this chart to track important information. Remember to keep copies of all applications and related information.

	COLLEGE 1	COLLEGE 2	COLLEGE 3	COLLEGE 4
COLLEGE APPLICATIONS				
Application deadline				
Date sent				
Official transcript sent				
Letters of recommendation sent				
SAT/ACT scores sent				
Acceptance received				
INDIVIDUAL COLLEGE FINANCIAL AID AND SCHOLARSHIP APPLICATIONS				
Application deadline				
Date sent				
Acceptance received				
FREE APPLICATION FOR FEDERAL STUDENT AID (FAFSA), FINANCIAL AID FORM (FAF), AND/OR PROFILE				
Form required				
Date sent				
School's priority deadline				
FAFSA ACKNOWLEDGMENT				
Date received				
Correct (Y/N)				
Date changes made, if needed				
Date changes were submitted				
STUDENT AID REPORT				
Date received				
Correct (Y/N)				
Date changes made, if needed				
Date changes were submitted				
Date sent to colleges				
FINANCIAL AWARD LETTERS				
Date received				
Accepted (Y/N)				

Source: The Dayton-Montgomery County Scholarship Program

the telephone number of your local BBB, or look at www.bbb.org for a directory of local BBBs and downloadable BBB complaint forms.

APPLYING FOR FINANCIAL AID

Applying for financial aid is a process that can be made easier when you take it step by step.

1 You must complete the Free application for Federal Student Aid (FAFSA) to be considered for federal financial aid. Pick up the FAFSA from your high school guidance counselor or college financial aid office or download it from the Department of Education's Web site at www.fafsa.ed. gov. The FAFSA is due any time after January 1 of the year you will be attending school. Submit the form as soon as possible, but never before the first of the year. If you need to estimate income tax information, it is easily amended later in the year.

2 Apply for any state grants.

3 Complete the PROFILE in addition to the FAFSA, because many four-year private colleges and some public universities require it. The PROFILE is a need analysis report, not an aid application. Some institutions have developed their own need analysis report. Check with your college or university to see what is required. The PROFILE registration is a one-page form available from your guidance counselor or through the College Board at www. collegeboard.com.

4 Complete individual colleges' required financial aid application forms on time. These deadlines are usually before March 15, but check with your institution to be sure.

5 Make sure your family completes the required forms during your senior year of high school.

6 Always apply for grants and scholarships before applying for student loans. Grants and scholarships are essentially free money. Loans must be repaid with interest.

Use the "Checklist for Seniors" on this page to keep track of the financial aid application process.

FINANCIAL AID DIRECTORY

You can use these numbers for direct access to federal and state agencies and processing services. However, your guidance counselor may have the answers or information you need.

FEDERAL STUDENT AID INFORMATION CENTER

Provides duplicate student aid reports and aid applications to students. Also answers questions on student aid, mails Department of Education publications, makes corrections to applications, and verifies college federal aid participation. Write to the Federal Student Aid Information Center, P.O. Box 84, Washington, D.C. 20044-0084 or call 800-4-Fed-Aid.

UNITED STUDENT AID FUNDS (USAF)

Provides aid application forms and information on loan amounts. Also provides information on guarantee dates and assists students in filling out application forms. Write to P.O. Box 6180, Indianapolis, Indiana 46206-6180, or call 877-USA-Group.

VETERANS BENEFITS ADMINISTRATION

Provides dependent education assistance for children of disabled veterans. College-bound students should call the VBRO to determine whether or not they qualify for assistance, what the benefits are, and if a parent's disability qualifies them for benefits. Call 800-827-1000 or visit their Web site at www.gibill.va.gov.

ACT FINANCIAL AID NEED ESTIMATOR (FANE)

Mails financial tabloids to students, provides information on filling out financial aid forms, and estimates financial aid amounts. Also mails financial need estimator forms. Forms are also accessible on line. Go to www.ACT.org or write to P.O. Box 4029, Iowa City, Iowa 52243-4029, or call 319-337-1615.

COLLEGE SCHOLARSHIP SERVICE (PROFILE)

Provides free applications and registration forms for federal student aid. Helps students fill out applications. Write to P.O. Box 6350, Princeton, NJ 08541-6350 or call 800-239-5888.

Student Financial Assistance Information, Department of Education

This page takes you to some of the major publications on student aid, including the latest edition of the Student Guide. Visit www.ed.gov/finaid.html.

College Board Online

In addition to several financial aid interactive calculators and access to FUND FINDER (the College Board's database of more than 3,000 sources of scholarships, internships, contests, and loans), this site provides a wealth of information, such as a glossary of financial aid terms, a bibliography of financial aid books, and financial planning and borrowing tips and tools for students and parents. Visit www.collegeboard.com.

Petersons.com

Get advice in finding sources to pay for college and search for scholarships at www.petersons.com/resources/finance.html.

SRN Express

A free Web version of the Scholarship Resource Network (SRN) database, SRN Express focuses on portable, private-sector, non-need-based aid. The award listings here contain more detailed information than most scholarship databases and scholarship listing books. The Web address is www.srnexpress.com. ∎

FINANCIAL AID ON THE WEB

A number of good financial aid resources exist on the Web. It is quick and simple to access general financial aid information, links to relevant Web sites, loan information, employment and career information, advice, scholarship search services, interactive worksheets, forms, and free expected family contribution (EFC) calculators.

Also visit the Web sites of individual colleges to find more school-specific financial aid information.

FAFSA Online

The Free Application for Federal Student Aid can be downloaded from the U.S. Department of Education's World Wide Web page and filed electronically. The address is www.ed.gov/offices/OSFAP/Students/apply/express.html.

The Education Resource Institute (TERI)

TERI is a private, not-for-profit organization that was founded to help middle-income Americans afford a college education. This site contains a database describing more than 150 programs that aim to increase college attendance from underrepresented groups. (The target population includes students from low-income families and those who are the first in their family to pursue postsecondary education.) Visit TERI's Web site at www.teri.org.

FinAid

Sponsored by the National Association of Student Financial Aid Administrators, it includes a comprehensive alphabetical index of all financial aid resources on the Web. You can find the site at www.finaid.org.

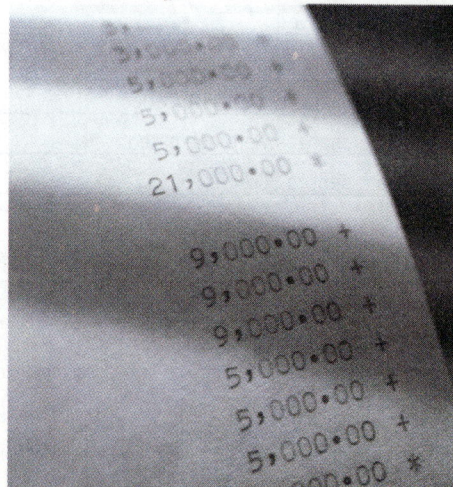

WHAT TO EXPECT IN COLLEGE

If you were going on a long trip, wouldn't you want to know what to expect once you reached your destination? Same with college.

Of course *GAJ* can't fill in all the details of what you'll find once you begin college. However, we can give you information about some of the bigger questions you might have, such as choosing a major, the decision to become part of Greek life, and transferring.

How to Choose a Major

A major is the area that you will study in-depth in college. You will take up to two thirds of your classes in that subject. However, your major is only part of your undergraduate studies, as colleges and universities generally require a core curriculum in addition to your major course work.

You can choose from hundreds of majors—from accounting to zoology—but which is right for you? Should you choose something traditional or select a major from an emerging area? Perhaps you already know what career you want, so you can work backwards to decide which major will best help you achieve your goals.

If you know what you want to do early, you will have more time to plan your high school curriculum, extracurricular activities, jobs, and community service to coincide with your major. Your selection of a college may also depend upon the college providing a strong academic program in a certain major.

What if I Don't Know What I Want to Do With My Life?

It's okay if you have not decided upon a major yet. In fact, more than half of all college freshmen are undecided and prefer to get a feel for what's available at college before making a decision. Most four-year colleges don't require students to formally declare a major until the end of their sophomore year or beginning of their junior year.

Can I Change My Major if I Change My Mind?

Choosing a major does not set your future in stone, nor does it necessarily disrupt your life if you need to change your major. However, there are advantages to choosing a major sooner rather than later. If you wait too long to choose, you may have to take additional classes to satisfy the requirements, which may cost you additional time and money.

Where Do I Begin?

Choosing a major usually begins with an assessment of your career interests. Once you have taken the self-assessment test provided in Section 1, you should have a clearer understanding of your interests, talents, values, and goals. Then review possible majors, and try several on for size. Picture yourself taking classes, writing papers, making presentations, conducting research, or working in a related field. Talk to people you know who work in your fields of interest and see if you like what you hear. Also, try reading the classified ads in your local newspaper. What jobs sound interesting to you? Which ones pay the salary that you'd like to make? What level of education is required in the ads you find interesting? Select a few jobs

that you think you'd like and then consult the following list of majors to see which major(s) coincide. If your area of interest does not appear here, talk to your counselor or teacher about where to find information on that particular subject.

A Major List of Majors

Agriculture

- Agricultural Business and Management
- Agricultural Mechanization

- Agricultural Supplies and Related Services
- Horticulture Services Operations and Management
- Agriculture/Agricultural Sciences
- Animal Sciences
- Food Sciences and Technology
- Plant Sciences

Many agriculture majors apply their knowledge directly on farms and ranches. Others work in industry (food, farm equipment, and agricultural supply companies), federal agencies (primarily in the Departments of Agriculture and the Interior), and state and local farm and agricultural agencies. Jobs might be in research and lab work, marketing and sales, advertising and public relations, or journalism and radio/TV (for farm communications media).

Agriculture majors also pursue further training in biological sciences, animal health, veterinary medicine, agribusiness, management, vocational agriculture education, nutrition and dietetics, and rural sociology.

Architecture

- Architecture
- Architectural Environmental Design
- City/Urban, Community, and Regional Planning
- Landscape Architecture

Architecture and related design fields focus on the built environment as distinct from the natural environment of the agriculturist or the conservationist. The four-year architecture degree is a preprofessional one; professional practice requires a five-year bachelor's degree or a six-year program leading to a master's degree.

Career possibilities include drafting, design, and project administration in architectural, engineering, landscape design, interior design, industrial design, planning, real estate, and construction firms; government agencies involved in construction, housing, highways, and parks and recreation; and government and nonprofit organizations interested in historic or architectural preservation.

These studies also provide a good background for further training in architectural, civil, and structural engineering; public administration; city management; and business management.

Area/Ethnic Studies

- Area Studies
- Ethnic and Cultural Studies

Area and ethnic studies majors provide a background that is useful in a wide variety of work settings. The important skills acquired through these majors—research, writing, analysis, critical thinking, and cultural awareness—combined with the expertise gained in a particular area make this group of majors valuable in a number of professional careers. Area and ethnic studies majors who know the language of the area they study are often viewed more favorably by prospective employers. For that reason, a second major that includes that language is recommended.

Ethnic studies majors find positions in administration, education, public relations, and communications in such organizations as cultural, government, international, and (ethnic) community agencies; international trade (import-export); social service agencies; and the communications industry (journalism, radio, and TV). These studies also provide a good background for further training in law, business management, public administration, education, social work, museum and library work, and international relations.

Arts

- Crafts, Folk Art, and Artisanry
- Dance
- Design and Applied Arts
- Dramatic/Theater Arts and Stagecraft
- Film/Video and Photographic Arts
- Fine Arts and Art Studies
- Music
- Visual and Performing Arts

Art majors most often use their training to become practicing artists, though the settings in which they work vary. People with knowledge and appreciation of the arts can find work in both the business and the not-for-profit sectors—many people with art training work in non-art-related fields or fields in which art is useful but not essential. An advanced degree is necessary for research and scholarship.

Aside from the most obvious art-related career—that of the self-employed artist or craftsperson—many fields require the skills of a visual artist. These include advertising; public relations; publishing; journalism; museum work; television, movies, and theater; community and social service agencies concerned with education, recreation, and entertainment; and teaching, both in schools (which usually require education courses) and independently.

A background in art is also useful if a student wishes to pursue art therapy, arts or museum administration, or library work.

Biological Sciences

- Biochemistry and Biophysics
- Biology, General
- Botany
- Cell and Molecular Biology
- Microbiology/Bacteriology
- Miscellaneous Biological Specializations
- Zoology

The biological sciences include the study of living organisms from the level of molecules to that of populations. A bachelor's degree is adequate preparation for some entry-level jobs, but a career in the biological sciences often requires an advanced degree in either a life science specialty or a related discipline within the fields of agriculture, engineering, health, physical science, or social science.

Biological science majors find jobs in industry; government agencies; technical writing, editing, or illustrating; science reporting; secondary school teaching (which usually requires education courses); and research and laboratory analysis and testing. Biological sciences are also a sound foundation for further study in medicine, psychology, health and hospital administration, and biologically oriented engineering.

Business

- Accounting
- Administrative and Secretarial Services
- Apparel and Accessories Marketing Operations
- Business
- Business Administration and Management
- Business Communications
- Business Information and Data Processing Services
- Business Quantitative Methods and Management Science
- Business/Managerial Economics
- Enterprise Management and Operation
- Entrepreneurship
- Financial Management and Services
- Food Products Retailing and Wholesaling Operations
- Hospitality and Recreation
- Hospitality Services Management
- Human Resources Management
- International Business
- Marketing Management and Research
- Marketing Operations
- Real Estate
- Tourism and Travel Services

Business majors comprise all the basic business disciplines. At the undergraduate level, students can major in a general business administration program or specialize in a particular area, such as marketing or accounting. These studies lead not only to positions in business and industry but also to management positions in other sectors. Management-related studies include the general management areas (accounting, finance, marketing, and management) as well as special studies related to a particular type of organization or industry. Management-related majors may be offered in a business school or in a department dealing with the area in which the management skills are to be applied.

Communication

- Advertising
- Communications, General
- Communication Technologies
- Journalism and Mass Communications
- Public Relations and Organizational Communications
- Radio and Television Broadcasting

Majors in communication usually focus on either print media (journalism, publishing) or electronic media (radio, TV). Career areas tend to follow this split and to further divide into the creative side (writing, editing, and programming) and the business side (sales, marketing, advertising, finance, and management). An M.B.A. is becoming increasingly necessary for advancement on the business side, whereas experience still seems to be the best upward route on the creative side (although a master's degree may help you get your first job).

Jobs in communication range from reporting (news and special features), copywriting, technical writing, copyediting, and programming to advertising, public relations, media sales, and market research. Such positions can be found at newspapers, radio and TV stations, publishing houses (book and magazine), advertising agencies, corporate communications departments, government agencies, universities, and firms that specialize in educational and training materials. Freelancing your skills is an alternative way to get started, although it's usually easier to start your freelance career after you've gained some experience working for someone else.

Communication students also go on for further training in law, business management, public administration, arts management, social work, educational media, journalism, radio/TV, and library and archival work.

Computer, Information, and Library Sciences

- Computer and Information Sciences, General
- Computer Programming
- Computer Science
- Data Processing Technology
- Information Sciences and Systems
- Library Science/Librarianship

Computer and information science and systems majors stress the theoretical aspects of the computer and emphasize mathematical and scientific disciplines. Data processing, programming, and computer technology programs tend to be more practical; they are more oriented toward business than to scientific applications and to working directly with the computer or with peripheral equipment.

Career possibilities for computer and information sciences include data processing, programming, and systems development or maintenance in almost any setting: business and industry, banking and finance, government, colleges and universities, libraries, software firms, service bureaus, computer manufacturers, publishing, and communications.

Library science gives preprofessional background in library work and provides valuable knowledge of research sources, indexing, abstracting, computer technology, and media technology, which is useful for further study in any professional field. In most cases, a master's degree in library science is necessary to obtain a job as a librarian.

Library science majors find positions in public, school, college, corporate, and government libraries and research centers; book publishing (especially reference books); database and information retrieval services; and communications (especially audiovisual media).

Computer, information, and library sciences all provide good backgrounds for further training in management-related areas (business, government, health, nonprofit organizations), engineering, archival work, and systems analysis.

Education

◌ Bilingual/Bicultural Education

◌ Education Administration and Supervision

◌ Education, General

◌ Educational/Instructional Media Design

◌ General Teacher Education

◌ Special Education

◌ Student Counseling and Personnel Services

◌ Teacher Assistant/Aide

◌ Teacher Education, Specific Academic and Vocational Programs

◌ Teaching English as a Second Language/Foreign Language

If you want to teach a particular subject at the elementary or secondary level, you will generally have to become certified to teach in your field. This is not necessarily the case for private and parochial schools, where the pay is often lower than in public schools. Nevertheless, even in these settings, certification is usually preferred. Generally, if you want to make a career of teaching, you should go to a college that offers certification sequences—education, secondary education, or elementary education—and the academic major you

wish to teach. So, if you wanted to teach secondary-level English, you would look into colleges that offer either education or secondary education and also offer English. Certification is done by state, so you will need to find out whether the program at a specific college will be acceptable preparation for the state in which you plan to teach.

On the other hand, if the education field you are interested in requires extensive or very specialized course work in education and relatively little advanced study in other areas (such as physical, reading, or special education), you should choose only the specific education major that applies.

If you want to major in education, you should be prepared to consider working in related fields (of which there are many) in case jobs are scarce in your particular teaching specialty. Although the current situation is competitive in most teaching fields, the demand is highest for teachers of math, science, special education, and vocational subjects. Master's degrees are recommended for teachers and are almost always required for positions as guidance counselors, principals, and curriculum specialists. Teacher aides, who are assistants to the classroom teacher, generally don't require a degree or certification in education.

Positions as teachers in public elementary and secondary schools, private day and boarding schools, religious and parochial schools, vocational schools, and proprietary schools are the jobs most often filled by education majors. However, teaching positions also exist in noneducational institutions, such as museums, historical societies, prisons, hospitals, and nursing homes as well as jobs as educators and trainers in government and industry. Administrative (nonteaching) positions in employee relations and personnel, public relations, marketing and sales, educational publishing, TV and film media, test development firms, and government and community social service agencies also tap the skills and interests of education majors.

Course work in education also provides a good background for further training in school psychology, social work, library and museum work, personnel and labor relations, public administration, business management, college student personnel work (admissions, financial aid, and student activities), and training and management development.

Engineering and Engineering Technologies

◌ Aerospace, Aeronautics, and Astronautical Engineering

◌ Agricultural Engineering

◌ Architectural Engineering

◌ Bioengineering and Biomedical Engineering

◌ Ceramic Sciences and Engineering

◌ Chemical Engineering

- Civil Engineering
- Civil Engineering/Civil Technologies
- Computer Engineering
- Construction/Building Technology
- Electrical and Electronic Engineering-Related Technology
- Electrical, Electronics, and Communications Engineering
- Electromechanical Instrumentation and Maintenance Technology
- Environmental Control Technologies
- Engineering Design
- Engineering Mechanics
- Engineering Physics
- Engineering Science
- Engineering, General
- Engineering/Industrial Management
- Environmental/Environmental Health Engineering
- Geological Engineering
- Industrial Production Technologies
- Industrial/Manufacturing Engineering
- Materials Engineering
- Materials Science
- Mechanical Engineering
- Mechanical Engineering-Related Technologies
- Metallurgical Engineering
- Mining and Petroleum Technologies
- Nuclear Engineering
- Petroleum Engineering
- Polymer/Plastics Engineering
- Quality Control and Safety Technologies
- Systems Engineering

Engineering is one of the few professional fields in which a bachelor's degree is sufficient career prepara-

tion. Many engineers, however, go on for a master's degree in a new technology or to move into management. Engineering technology and science technology majors prepare students for practical design and production work rather than for jobs that require more theoretical, scientific, and mathematical knowledge.

Industry, research labs, and government agencies where technology plays a key role, such as in manufacturing, electronics, construction communications, transportation, and utilities, hire engineering as well as engineering technology and science technology graduates regularly. Work may be in technical activities (research, development, design, production, testing, scientific programming, or systems analysis) or in nontechnical areas where a technical degree is needed, such as marketing, sales, or administration.

These studies provide a good background for further training in the disciplines listed above as well as in business management, public administration, urban planning, city management, medicine, public health, environmental design, and law (especially patent law).

Foreign Language and Literature

- Classical and Ancient Near Eastern Languages and Literatures
- East and Southeast Asian Languages and Literatures
- East European Languages and Literatures
- Foreign Languages and Literatures
- Germanic Languages and Literatures
- Greek Languages and Literatures (Modern)
- Middle Eastern Languages and Literatures
- Romance Languages and Literatures

Knowledge of foreign languages and cultures is becoming increasingly recognized as important in today's

international world. Language majors possess a skill that is used in organizations with international dealings as well as in career fields and geographical areas where languages other than English are prominent. However, a greater variety of career possibilities exists if facility with a foreign language is combined with other skills, knowledge, and interests than if it is relied on alone as an entry to the job market. You might want to consider a dual major or a concentration of courses in another field as well as a language major to enhance your job prospects. A Ph.D. is generally necessary for college teaching and research positions in these disciplines.

Career possibilities include positions with business firms with international subsidiaries; import-export firms; international banking; travel agencies; airlines; tourist services; government and international agencies dealing with international affairs, foreign trade, diplomacy, customs, or immigration; secondary school foreign language teaching and bilingual education (which usually require education courses); freelance translating and interpreting (high level of skill necessary); foreign language publishing; and computer programming (especially for linguistics majors).

Foreign languages also provide a good background for further training in law, international affairs and diplomacy, international trade, international social service, professional specialized translating and interpreting, library and archival work, and museum work.

Health Sciences

- Communication Disorders Sciences and Services
- Dental Services
- Health and Medical Administrative Services
- Health and Medical Assistants
- Health and Medical Diagnostic and Treatment Services
- Health and Medical Laboratory Technologies

Continued on page 107

MAKING THAT MAJOR DECISION—REAL-LIFE ADVICE FROM COLLEGE SENIORS

SOMEWHERE BETWEEN HER JUNIOR AND SENIOR YEAR IN HIGH SCHOOL, KAREN GLIEBE GOT THE PSYCHOLOGY BUG. WHEN CHOOSING A MAJOR IN COLLEGE, SHE KNEW JUST WHAT SHE WANTED. JUSTIN BINTRIM, ON THE OTHER HAND, DID A COMPLETE 180. HE THOUGHT HE'D STUDY PHYSICS, THEN VEERED TOWARD PHILOSOPHY. IT WASN'T UNTIL HE TOOK SURVEY COURSES IN LITERATURE THAT HE FOUND WHERE HIS HEART REALLY LAY, AND NOW HE'S GRADUATING WITH A DEGREE IN ENGLISH.

YOU MIGHT FIND YOURSELF AT EITHER END OF THIS SPECTRUM WHEN CHOOSING A MAJOR. EITHER YOU'LL KNOW JUST WHAT YOU WANT OR YOU'LL TRY ON A NUMBER OF DIFFERENT HATS BEFORE FINALLY SETTLING ON ONE. TO GIVE YOU A TASTE OF WHAT IT COULD BE LIKE FOR YOU, MEET FOUR COLLEGE SENIORS WHO HAVE BEEN THROUGH THE TRIALS AND ERRORS OF CHOOSING THEIR MAJORS. HOPEFULLY YOU'LL PICK UP SOME POINTERS FROM THEM OR AT LEAST FIND OUT THAT YOU DON'T HAVE TO WORRY SO MUCH ABOUT WHAT YOUR MAJOR WILL BE.

FROM GROVE CITY COLLEGE, A LIBERAL ARTS SCHOOL IN PENNSYLVANIA, MEET KAREN GLIEBE, WHO WILL GRADUATE WITH A DEGREE IN PSYCHOLOGY, AND ENGLISH MAJOR JUSTIN BINTRIM. FROM MICHIGAN STATE UNIVERSITY, MEET COMPUTER ENGINEERING MAJOR SETH MOSIER AND KIM TROUTEN, WHO IS FINISHING UP A ZOOLOGY DEGREE. HERE'S WHAT THEY HAD TO SAY:

HOW THEY CHOSE THEIR MAJORS

Karen
During high school, I volunteered at a retirement center, and my supervisor gave me a lot of exposure to applied psychology. After my freshman year in college, I talked to people who were using a psychology degree. You put in a lot of work for a degree and can wonder if it's worth all the work. It helps to talk to someone who has gone through it so you can see if that's what you want to be doing when you graduate.

Justin
I wasn't sure about what my major would be. One professor told me to take survey courses to see if I was interested in the subject. I took English literature, math, psychology, and philosophy. I liked English the best and did well in it. The next semester I took two English courses and decided to switch my major. My professors told me not to worry about choosing a major. They said to get my feet wet and we'll talk about your major in two years. I decided that if they're not worried about a major I wouldn't be either, but I still had it on my mind. I was around older students who were thinking about their careers so I talked to them about the jobs they had lined up.

Seth
I liked computers in high school. In college, I started out in computer science but got sick of coding. My interest in computers made me pick computer science right off the bat. I didn't know about computer engineering until I got to college.

Kim
I wanted to be a veterinarian but after two years decided that I didn't want to go to school for that long. I was still interested in animals and had two options. One was in animal science, which is working more with farm animals, or going into zoology. I decided to concentrate on zoo and aquarium science. Besides being a vet, the closest interaction with animals would be being a zookeeper.

THE ELECTIVES THEY TOOK AND WHY

Karen
My adviser told me to take different classes, so I took philosophy, art, religion, and extra psychology classes that weren't required.

Justin
I was planning to do a double major, but my professors said to take what interested me. English majors have lots of freedom to take different courses, unlike science majors.

Seth
Because I'm in computer engineering, I don't get to take a lot of electives. I am taking a swimming class right now and took a critical incident analysis class where we look at major accidents. I wanted something that wasn't computer engineering-related but extremely technical.

Kim
I took some kinesiology classes, which was pretty much an aerobics class. I needed to work out and figured I could get credit for it. I also took sign language because I'm interested in it.

WHAT THEY'RE GOING TO DO WITH THEIR DEGREES

Karen
I want to go to graduate school and hopefully get some experience working with kids.

Justin
I'm applying to graduate school in English literature and cultural studies. I want to do research and become a college professor.

Seth
I'm going to work for the defense department. It's not the highest offer I've gotten, but it will be the most fun, which is more important to me than the money.

Kim
My goals have changed again. I don't plan on using my degree. I just got married a year ago, and my husband and I want to go into full-time ministry. I'll use my degree to get a job and then we'll go overseas.

THE CHANGES THEY WOULD MAKE IN THE CLASSES THEY TOOK IF THEY COULD

Karen
There are classes I wouldn't necessarily take again. But even though I didn't learn as much as I wanted to, it was worth it. I learned how

to work and how to organize my efforts.

Justin

I should have worried less about choosing a major when I first started college. I didn't have the perspective as to how much time I had to choose.

Seth

I have friends who would change the order in which they took their humanities classes. I was lucky enough to think ahead and spread those classes out over the entire time. Most [engineering] students take them their freshman year to get them all out of the way. Later on they're locked in the engineering building all day. Because I didn't, it was nice for me to get my mind off engineering.

Kim

Something I can't change are the labs. They require a lot of work, and you only get one credit for three hours. Some labs take a lot of work outside of class hours. I had a comparative anatomy lab, which kept me busy over entire weekends. I suggest you don't take a lot of classes that require labs all at once.

THEIR ADVICE FOR YOU

Karen

You don't have to know what you want to do with the rest of your life when you get to college. Most people don't even stay with the major they first choose. Colleges recognize that you will see things you may have not considered at first. Some high school students say they won't go to college unless they know what they want to do.

Justin

If it's possible, take a little of this and a little of that. If you're an engineering student, you'll have it all planned out [for you], but if you're a liberal arts major and are not sure,

you probably can take something from each department.

Seth

If possible, take AP exams in high school. You'll be able to make a decision about a major. Freshmen who think they want to do engineering suffer through math and physics classes. Then by their sophomore or junior year they realize they don't want to be engineers. If they'd taken AP classes, they'd know by their freshman year.

Kim

When I changed my major I was worried that I might have spent a year in classes that wouldn't count toward my new major. But you shouldn't be scared to change majors because if you stick with something you don't like, you'll have to go back and take other classes anyway.

THOUGH THESE FOUR SENIORS ARRIVED AT A DECISION ABOUT WHICH MAJOR THEY WANTED IN DIFFERENT WAYS, THEY HAD SIMILAR THINGS TO SAY.

➢ It's okay to change your mind about what you want out of college.

➢ To find out which major you might want, start with what you like to do.

➢ Talk to professionals who have jobs in the fields that interest you.

➢ Ask your professors about what kinds of jobs you could get with the degree you're considering.

➢ Talk to seniors who will be graduating with a degree in the major you're considering.

➢ Take electives in areas that interest you, even though they may have nothing to do with your major.

➢ College is a time to explore many different options, so take advantage of the opportunity.

☯ Health and Medical Preparatory Programs

☯ Mental Health Services

☯ Miscellaneous Health Professions

☯ Nursing

☯ Pharmacy

☯ Physical/Occupational Therapy

☯ Public Health

Health professions majors, while having a scientific core, are more focused on applying the results of scientific investigation than on the scientific disciplines themselves. A bachelor's degree is adequate preparation for some beginning-level jobs, but a master's degree is increasingly necessary for career advancement. Allied health majors prepare graduates to assist health professionals in providing diagnostics, therapeutics, and rehabilitation.

Medical science majors, such as

optometry, pharmacy, and the premedical profession sequences, are, for the most part, preprofessional studies that compose the scientific disciplines necessary for admission to graduate or professional school in the health or medical fields. A bachelor's degree is adequate for some beginning-level jobs, but a career in these major fields requires an advanced degree.

Health service and technology majors prepare students for positions in the health fields that primarily involve services to patients or working with complex machinery and materials. Medical technologies cover a wide range of fields, such as cytotechnology, biomedical technologies, and operating room technology.

Administrative, professional, or research assistant positions in health agencies, hospitals, occupational health units in industry, community and school health departments, government agencies (public health, environmental protection), and international health organizations are available to majors in health fields as are jobs in marketing and sales of health-related products and services, health education (with education courses), advertising and public relations, journalism and publishing, and technical writing.

Home Economics and Social Services

☯ Community Organization, Resources, and Services

☯ Consumer and Homemaking

☯ Education

☯ Family and Community Studies

☯ Family/Consumer Resource Management

☯ Foods and Nutrition Studies

☯ Home Economics, General

☯ Housing Studies

☯ Individual and Family Development Studies

☯ Public Administration

☯ Public Policy Analysis

☯ Social Work

Home economics encompasses many different fields—basic studies in foods and textiles as well as new areas, such as consumer economics and leisure studies, that overlap with aspects of agriculture, social science, and education. Career areas are emerging in which a background in home economics provides the advantage of an interdisciplinary viewpoint.

Jobs for home economics majors can be found in government and community agencies (especially those concerned with education, health, housing, or human services), nursing homes, child-care centers, journalism, radio/TV, educational media, and publishing. Types of work also include marketing, sales, and customer service in consumer-related industries, such as food processing and packaging, appliance manufacturing, utilities, textiles, and secondary school home economics teaching (which usually requires education courses).

Majors in social services find administrative aide or assistant positions in government and community health, welfare, and social service agencies, such as hospitals, clinics, YMCAs and YWCAs, recreation commissions, welfare agencies, and employment services. See the "Law and Legal Studies" section for information on more law-related social services.

Home economics and social services studies also provide a good background for further training in business management, hotel and institutional management, public health, food technology, environmental design and urban planning, social work, marriage and family counseling, public administration, and personnel.

Humanities (Miscellaneous)

- Comparative Literature
- Creative Writing
- English Language and Literature, General
- English Language and Literature/ Letters
- English Technical and Business Writing
- Liberal Arts and Sciences, General Studies, and Humanities
- Philosophy
- Speech and Rhetorical Studies

The majors that constitute the humanities (sometimes called "letters") are the most general and widely applicable and the least vocationally oriented of the liberal arts. They are essentially studies of the ideas and concerns of human kind. These include classics, history of philosophy, history of science, linguistics, and medieval studies.

The skills and knowledge that the study of these subjects imparts are truly enduring and relevant to any field of endeavor, especially where the ability to understand ideas, think logically, and write and speak clearly is crucial. A major in philosophy—or in any other of the humanities—doesn't lead automatically to a job labeled philosopher or writer; rather it provides an excellent foundation for many generalized careers and for further training in a variety of fields. Some think that the humanities are the ideal preprofessional preparation for law school. Research and teaching in any of these fields at the university level usually require a Ph.D.

Career possibilities for humanities majors can be found in business firms, government and community agencies, advertising and public relations, marketing and sales, publishing, journalism and radio/TV, secondary school teaching in English and literature (which usually requires education courses), freelance writing and editing, and computer programming (especially for those with a background in logic or linguistics).

Law and Legal Studies

Students of legal studies can use their knowledge of law and government in fields involving the making, breaking, and enforcement of laws; the crimes, trials, and punishment of law breakers; and the running of all branches of government at local, state, and federal levels. Advanced degrees are needed for research and

scholarship and for practicing law.

Students in legal areas find positions in all types in law firms, legal departments of other organizations, the court or prison system, government agencies (such as law enforcement agencies or offices of state and federal attorneys general), and police departments. In addition, the skills acquired in this field, such as research and writing, can be useful in most careers, especially those listed in the "Social Sciences" section.

Mathematics and Physical Sciences

- Applied Mathematics
- Astronomy
- Atmospheric Sciences and Meterology
- Chemistry
- Geological and Related Sciences
- Mathematical Statistics
- Mathematics
- Physical Sciences, General
- Physics

Mathematics is the science of numbers and the abstract formulation of their operations. Physical sciences involve the study of the laws and structures of physical matter. A bachelor's degree is adequate preparation for some entry-level jobs, but for career advancement to high-level positions, a graduate degree is necessary in either a physical science specialty or a related discipline within the fields of biological sciences, engineering, health and medicine, or social sciences. The quantitative skills acquired through the study of science and mathematics are especially useful for computer-related careers.

Career possibilities include positions in industry (manufacturing and processing companies, electronics firms, defense contractors, consulting firms); government agencies (defense, environmental protection, law enforcement); scientific/technical writing, editing, or illustrating; journalism (science reporting); secondary school teaching (usually requiring education courses); research and laboratory analysis and testing; statistical analysis; computer programming; systems analysis; surveying and mapping; weather forecasting; and technical sales.

These studies also provide a good background for further training in engineering (any field), actuarial work (insurance), operations research, business management, and public administration.

Natural Resources

- ⏀ Conservation and Renewable Natural Resources
- ⏀ Fishing and Fisheries Sciences and Management
- ⏀ Forest Production and Processing
- ⏀ Forestry and Related Sciences
- ⏀ Health and Physical Education/ Fitness
- ⏀ Natural Resources Conversation
- ⏀ Natural Resources Management and Protective Services
- ⏀ Parks, Recreation, and Leisure Facilities Management
- ⏀ Parks, Recreation, and Leisure Studies
- ⏀ Wildlife and Wildlands Management

A major in the natural resources field prepares students for work in areas as generalized as environmental conservation and as specialized as groundwater contamination.

Jobs are available in industry (food, energy, natural resources, and pulp and paper companies), consulting firms, state and federal government agencies (primarily the Departments of Agriculture and the Interior), and public and private conservation agencies. See also the Agriculture and Biological Sciences sections for more information on natural resources-related fields.

Course work in natural resources provides a good background for further training in biological sciences, environmental education, environ-

mental or natural resources engineering, and resources management.

Psychology

- ⏀ Clinical Psychology
- ⏀ Cognitive Psychology and Psycholinguistics
- ⏀ Developmental and Child Psychology
- ⏀ Experimental Psychology
- ⏀ Industrial and Organizational Psychology
- ⏀ Physiological Psychology/ Psychobiology
- ⏀ Psychology

Psychology majors involve the study of behavior and can range from the biological to the sociological. Students can study individual behavior, usually that of humans, or the behavior of crowds. Students of psychology do not always go into the more obvious clinical fields, the fields in which psychologists work with patients. Certain areas of psychology, such as industrial/organizational, experimental, and social, are not clinically oriented.

Psychology and counseling careers can be in government (such as mental health agencies), schools, hospitals, clinics, private practice, industry, test development firms, social work, and personnel. The careers listed in the general "Social Sciences" section are also pursued by psychology and counseling majors.

With advanced study, psychology graduates teach at the college level, do research, and become psychiatrists (medical school required) and psychologists.

Religion

- ⏀ Bible/Biblical Studies
- ⏀ Biblical and Other Theological Languages and Literatures
- ⏀ Missions/Missionary Studies and Missiology
- ⏀ Pastoral Counseling and Specialized Ministries

- ⏀ Religion/Religious Studies
- ⏀ Religious Education
- ⏀ Religious/Sacred Music
- ⏀ Theological Studies and Ministerial Studies

Religion majors are usually seen as preprofessional studies for those who are interested in entering the ministry. Graduate study in a seminary is required for practice in most religious denominations. However, other professional fields, as well as the career opportunities listed below, are open to those who want to pursue these majors at the bachelor's level only. In contrast to the academic study of religion, which takes a neutral stance, theology is usually studied from the perspective of those committed to a particular religious belief.

Career possibilities for religion include casework, youth counseling, administration in community and social service organizations, teaching in religious educational institutions, and writing for religious and lay publications. Religious studies also prepare students for the kinds of jobs other humanities majors often pursue.

Social Sciences

- ⏀ Anthropology
- ⏀ Archaeology
- ⏀ Criminology
- ⏀ Economics
- ⏀ Geography
- ⏀ History
- ⏀ International Relations and Affairs
- ⏀ Political Science and Government
- ⏀ Social Sciences, General
- ⏀ Sociology
- ⏀ Urban Affairs/Studies

Social sciences majors study people in relation to their society. Thus, social science majors can apply their education to a wide range of occupations that deal with social issues and activities. A Ph.D. is required for research and teaching positions in most of the social sciences.

Career opportunities are varied. People with degrees in the social sciences find careers in government, business, community agencies (serving children, youth, senior citizens), advertising and public relations, marketing and sales, secondary school social studies teaching (with education courses), casework, law enforcement, parks and recreation, museum work (especially for anthropology, archaeology, geography, and history majors), preservation (especially for anthropology, archaeology, geography, and history majors), banking and finance (especially for economics majors), market and survey research, statistical analysis, publishing, fundraising and development, and political campaigning. For more specific information, see the sections on "Area/Ethnic Studies," "Home Economics and Social Services," "Law and Legal Studies, and Psychology."

The social sciences are also useful for further training in law, business management, public administration, city management, counseling (vocational, school, rehabilitation, family, personal), international relations, journalism and radio/TV, library and archival work, personnel and labor relations, medicine, urban planning, student personnel work, public health, and criminology.

Technologies

- ☼ Biological Technology
- ☼ Nuclear and Industrial Radiologic Technologies
- ☼ Technology Education/Industrial Arts

Technology majors, along with trade fields, are most often offered as two-year programs. Majors in technology fields prepare students directly for jobs; however, positions are in practical design and production work rather than in areas that require more theoretical, scientific, and mathematical knowledge.

Technology fields are also very diverse. Engineering technologies prepare students with the basic training in specific fields (e.g., electronics, mechanics, or chemistry) that are necessary to become technicians on the support staffs of engineers. Other technology majors center more on maintenance and repair. Work may be in technical activities, such as production or testing, or in nontechnical areas where a technical degree is needed, such as marketing, sales, or administration.

In any case, a technology major can provide the training that is necessary for graduates to work in that field after only two years of courses. However, some technology-oriented majors, such as nuclear technology and aircraft and missile maintenance, may require additional study or certification for many positions. In addition, more training is generally required for complex technical areas, such as research, development, design, scientific programming, and systems analysis. However, technology program credits do not necessarily transfer to upper-level programs, so finding out about specific programs before you enroll is important.

Industries, research labs, and government agencies in which technology plays a key role—such as in manufacturing, electronics, construction, communications, transportation, and utilities—hire technology graduates regularly. Also see the "Health Sciences" section for information on health-related technologies.

Technological studies also provide a good background for further training in the disciplines listed above as well as in specific engineering fields, business management, public administration, urban planning, city management, public health, and environmental design.

GREEK LIFE

At the National Interfraternity Council in Indianapolis, four predominant qualities are stressed when speaking about fraternities and sororities: scholarship, friendship, leadership, and service. High school students who already have experience in these four areas have a jump on Greek life. What's more important, however, is that students who decide to pledge a fraternity or sorority gain additional opportunities in these four areas. For ease of reading the rest of this section, the word fraternity will be used to apply to sororities as well.

Scholarship

A fraternity experience helps you make the academic transition from high school to college. Although the classes taken in high school are challenging, they'll be even harder in college. While there are no overall academic requirements for entering a fraternity, each fraternity may require certain academic standards for their members. Many hold mandatory study times, and the Interfraternity Council requires all fraternity members to carry a minimum grade point average of 2.0. A network system among members exists in which older members can assist younger students. Old class notes and exams are usually kept on file for study purposes, and personal tutors are often available. Members of a fraternity have a natural vested interest in seeing that other members succeed academically.

Friendship

Social life is an important component of Greek life. Social functions offer an excellent opportunity for freshmen to become better acquainted with others in the chapter. Whether it is a Halloween party or a formal dance, there are numerous chances for members to develop poise and confidence. By participating in these many functions, students enrich friendships and build memories that will last a lifetime. Remember, social functions aren't only parties; they can include such activities as intramural sports and Homecoming.

Leadership

Because fraternities are self-governing organizations, leadership opportunities abound. Students are given hands-on experience in leading committees, managing budgets, and interacting with faculty members and administrators. Most houses have as many as ten officers, along with an array of committee members. For instance, a fraternity treasurer gains invaluable experience by working with a budget that may exceed $200,000. There are also numerous officer positions available on the Interfraternity Council.

In today's world, employers are looking for well-rounded individuals with leadership skills. By becoming actively involved in leadership roles while still in high school as well as after joining a fraternity, students gain valuable experience that is essential for a successful career. Interestingly, although Greeks represent less than 10 percent of the undergraduate student population, they hold the majority of leadership positions on campus.

Service

According to the North-American Interfraternity Council, fraternities are increasingly becoming involved in various philanthropies and hands-on service projects. Helping less fortunate people has become a major focus of Greek life. This can vary from work with Easter Seals, blood drives, and food pantry collections to community upkeep, such as picking up trash, painting houses, or cleaning up area parks. Greeks also get involved in projects with organizations such as Habitat for Humanity, the American Heart Association, and Children's Miracle Network. By being involved in philanthropic projects, students not only raise money for worthwhile causes, but they also gain a deeper insight into themselves and their responsibility to the community.

Pledging

Most fraternities require students to pledge or interview for acceptance into its organization. Although requirements vary from fraternity to fraternity, these two tips can apply across the board.

1 Fraternities like to accept individuals with a strong commitment to academics. The better your grades, the better your chances for getting in. A student who has been actively involved in the community as well as at his or her high school has an added advantage.

2 A major misconception of Greek life is that it revolves around wild parties and alcohol. Students should not mention either of these elements when seeking membership in a fraternity.

For more information about fraternities and sororities on the campus of your choice, contact the Office of Greek Affairs at that campus location.

WHAT IF YOU DON'T LIKE THE COLLEGE YOU PICK

In the best of worlds, you compile a list of colleges, find the most compatible one, and are accepted. You have a great time, learn a lot, graduate, and head off to a budding career. However, you may find the college you chose isn't the best of worlds. Imagine these scenarios:

1 Halfway through your first semester of college you come to the distressing conclusion that you can't stand being there for whatever reason. The courses don't match your interests. The campus is out in the boonies and you don't ever want to see another cow. The selection of extracurricular activities doesn't cut it.

2 You have methodically planned to go to a community college for two years and move to a four-year college to complete your degree. Transferring takes you nearer to your goal.

3 You thought you wanted to major in art, but by the end of the first semester you find yourself more interested in English lit. Things get confusing, so you drop out of college to sort out your thoughts and now you want to drop back in, hoping to rescue some of those credits.

4 You didn't do that well in high school—socializing got in the way of studying. But you've wised up, have gotten serious about your future, and two years of community college have brightened your prospects of transferring to a four-year institution.

Circumstances shift, people change, and, realistically speaking, it's not all that uncommon to transfer. Many people do. The reasons why students transfer run the gamut, as do the institutional policies that govern them. The most common transfers are students who move from a two-year to a four-year university or the person who opts for a career change midstream.

Whatever reasons you might have for wanting to transfer, you will be doing more than just switching academic gears. Aside from losing credits, time, and money, transferring brings up the problem of adjusting to a new situation. This affects just about all transfer students, from those who made a mistake in choosing a college to those who planned to go to a two-year college and then transferred to a four-year campus. People can choose colleges for arbitrary reasons. That's why admissions departments try to ensure a good match between the student and campus before classes begin. Unfortunately, sometimes students don't realize they've made a mistake until it's too late.

The best way to avoid having to transfer is to extensively research a college or university before choosing it. Visit the campus and stay overnight, talk to admissions and faculty members, and try to learn as much as you can. ■

[TIME'S COLLEGES OF THE YEAR]

Welcome, Freshmen!

As a huge wave of first-year students surges into dorms, TIME honors four colleges that know how to help newcomers survive and thrive

By ELLIE MCGRATH

"FINIS ORIGINE PENDET," THE ROMAN POET MANLIUS WROTE. "The end depends on the beginning." Success in life hinges on how well we are reared—and what we learn in school. More than ever these days, getting off to a good start in college can make the difference between getting a degree and giving up. That makes the passage from teenager at home to first-year college student one of the most stressful and important transitions in life.

Many popular guides to American colleges rate them on such factors as the number of volumes in the library, the percentage of faculty with Ph.D.s and the SAT scores of incoming freshmen. There is, however, an essential component that most guidebooks ignore, or have not figured out how to measure: Are the students engaged by their courses? How well do they learn?

In recent years, in our own separately published guidebook, TIME has named a group of Colleges of the Year, selected not as anointed "winners" of a ranking exercise but rather as exemplars—schools that have taken laudable steps to improve their undergraduate education. Each year our criterion has had a different focus—from promoting minority access to providing academic opportunities for residents of the surrounding community. Last year we used the teaching of writing across the curriculum as our measure of success, and we named four Colleges of the Year that reflected the variety of postsecondary institutions in America: a large university with research facilities, a state university with courses up to the master's level, a liberal arts college and a community college.

This year TIME recognizes four institutions with highly effective programs to help first-year students make a successful transition into college life. Helping new students survive has, in our judgment, become an essential responsibility of every college. That task takes on new urgency this year, as the children of baby boomers swell the freshman classes of many universities to record numbers in a dorm-bursting wave that won't peak until the end of the decade.

The profile of American college students has changed dramatically over the past 20 years as the proportion of high school graduates going to college has increased from 49% to 63%. There are more minority students, more first-generation students—and more students who lack basic skills. Far more students must take jobs to cover college costs. Add to all that the sudden freedom of college life, and the stage is set for emotional turmoil, binge drinking and academic failure.

At highly selective institutions, the vast majority of students graduate. But at public universities, which educate most U.S. students getting bachelor's degrees, nearly 60% fail to complete degrees within five years—and half of those leave during the first year. The dropout rate is even higher at many community colleges, where students are juggling jobs with their course work.

"We operate under the assumption that students know how to do it—or if they don't, they'll flunk out and it's their problem," says John Gardner, executive director of the Policy Center on the First Year of College and the leader—along with Russell Edgerton of the Pew Forum on Undergraduate Learning—of a panel of higher-education experts that advised us during our selection process.°

Thanks to Gardner and other higher-education experts, a movement is spreading to ensure that students exit with degrees. Backed by 30 years of experimentation and data, Gardner and other academics have established that colleges can boost freshman retention by:

➤ training faculty to mentor and support new students;

➤ creating first-year seminars, orientation courses and intimate "learning communities;"

➤ teaching students organizational and study skills; and

➤ arranging dorms so that freshmen live among students with similar academic interests.

First-year seminars have entered the higher-education mainstream, with 71% of the more than 4,000 accredited U.S.

RITUAL GREETING:
Freshmen parade
into William Jewell
College in Missouri

campuses offering such courses. About 85% of freshmen take them, and the survival rate of students who take the courses is 3% to 10% better than that of students who do not. These courses often provide the basis for cohesive learning communities, which spark intellectual confidence among their members. At Drury University in Missouri, for instance, orientation groups of 20 students meet with a faculty mentor three times a week during freshman year to analyze the ideas that shape life in America.

Residential colleges face the challenge of assimilating a diverse student body and seeing that the students live as well as learn in harmony. Harvard requires incoming freshmen to read a booklet of essays on diversity by such writers as Henry Louis Gates and Ralph Waldo Emerson. During orientation, they are put in small groups to discuss the essays with faculty. "Students rate this one of the most powerful events of the entire orientation," says Richard Light, professor of education at Harvard and author of *Making the Most of College: Students Speak Their Minds*.

In selecting our 2001 Colleges of the Year from among candidates recommended by our advisory board, the editors sought institutions with comprehensive freshman programs that have improved retention rates and created a sense of community for students. Amid a rapidly growing movement, the hardest part was choosing among so many impressive candidates. We believe they offer good news for other colleges looking for ways to turn raw freshmen into studious sophomores—and ultimately into productive alumni. ■

—With reporting by Constance E. Richards/Brevard, N.C.

*OTHER PANELISTS: Richard Guarasci, provost and senior vice president, Wagner College; **George Kuh**, chancellor's professor and director of the National Survey of Student Engagement, Indiana University, Bloomington; **Cecilia López**, associate director of the Higher Learning Commission of the North Central Association of Colleges and Schools; **Roberta Matthews**, provost and vice president for academic affairs, Brooklyn College; and **Kay McClenney**, senior associate of the Pew Forum on Undergraduate Learning.

Indiana University

A web of friendly interest groups makes this big research institution feel less intimidating

By HARRIET BAROVICK BLOOMINGTON

JUSTIN GREIS, AN AMBITIOUS BUSINESS major in his junior year at Indiana University, Bloomington, wants to be a partner at a major law or accounting firm. Yet when Ernst & Young, the accounting giant, offered him a rare post-sophomore year summer internship, he turned it down. Instead, he helped

HOMEWORK HELP: A freshman and tutor talk calculus

teach a rigorous summer seminar to incoming freshmen for $100 a week. Greis attributes his 3.9 GPA, among other accomplishments, to the sense of belonging he developed two years ago in the university's Intensive Freshman Seminar program. "I learned how to study there and made some of my best friends. It was important to feel I was giving back some of what I got."

In the Intensive Freshman Seminar program, open to all, about 300 of I.U.'s 6,700 first-year students get a jump on college by spending three weeks in August in tiny classes taught by senior professors with whom they form valuable relationships. They live and bond with

peers and older students who help teach courses. They learn time-management and study skills. And they often become campus leaders. Alumni of the program half-jokingly describe it as a cult.

The program is relatively tiny at this 36,000-student university, a sprawling campus with doctoral programs and research facilities. But it's only one part of a comprehensive effort to make the university's freshmen feel connected and equipped to succeed. In the late 1980s the state's relatively low rate of college graduation spurred administrators to better engage I.U.'s freshmen. Those efforts got a boost in 1997 when the Indianapolis-based Lilly Endowment gave the university $2.5 million to increase graduation rates. I.U. dedicated the funds primarily to retaining freshmen.

The university has launched several small, targeted efforts rather than a one-size-fits-all solution. Students who aren't attracted to the 12-year-old Intensive Freshman Seminar can join "freshman interest groups"; they live and study with students who share their academic interests. Minority freshmen can get mentors from among senior faculty. Drop-in academic support centers, open until 11 p.m., offer writing and math tutors at three residence halls.

The results of these disparate efforts are encouraging. The percentage of freshmen returning for their sophomore year has risen to 85%, from 80% in 1994. Freshman retention among African-

Photographs for TIME by Ryan Schick

DISCOVERY: A syringe of food for salamander embryos helps illustrate an Intensive Freshman Seminar class on cloning tech-

American and Latino students has jumped to 82%, from 64% in 1994. "There are a whole bunch of life buoys out there," says Travis Paulin, director of the university's summer freshman programs. "We want them to feel they can latch on to one or two that work for them."

More than 200 senior faculty members have taken part in freshman programs. Biologist Craig Nelson, a Carnegie Foundation U.S. Professor of the Year for 2000, whose focus is collaborative learning, takes students on team-building expeditions to scale rock-climbing walls at the start of his August course on evolution. One rotating group of 10 faculty members, the Freshman Learning Project, works on ways to make their large, introductory lecture classes more effective. To learn how to better empathize with baffled freshmen, an art-history scholar might sit through a painfully unfamiliar class on finite math.

What matters most, many freshmen say, is knowing that someone cares about

OTHER NOTABLES

Harvard University, Cambridge, Mass. A freshman seminar founded in 1959 has been expanded to 60 courses this year **University of Michigan, Ann Arbor** Professors get 600 freshmen to help with research like identifying the breast-cancer gene **Stanford University, Palo Alto, Calif.** A seminar helps freshmen bond with professors

them. For sophomore Patrick Dumas, from West Lafayette, Ind., the university inspired a "terror about getting lost" in the high-powered machinery. But early, close contact with his seminar professor, who met with him regularly for meals, made other professors less intimidating. Dumas now serves as a supreme court justice in the student government and enjoys mentoring freshmen.

For minority students, who constitute 8% of the student body, getting early support is especially important. "A girl on my floor last year said she didn't like black people or fat people," says Cherie Wardell, an African-American senior from Indianapolis, who is able to laugh at the memory. Wardell has for the past two summers been a resident assistant in a program called Groups—open to all classes but focused on first-year students—that offers a summer course and financial and academic support throughout the year for 300 low-income and first-generation freshmen. Wardell dis-

covered that with a "family" of people who had been through similar experiences, she could feel more comfortable at the university.

Joaquin Jara, a sophomore sports-marketing major from Whiting, Ind., is part of the first generation in his family to attend college and says his parents at first discouraged him from enrolling. He says the Groups program inspired him to persevere. His three younger siblings now e-mail him daily, proudly recounting what they're learning in school. They all plan to attend college.

The university's freshman efforts are well targeted but sometimes confusing. "We could use a little more work on getting freshmen to know all their options," concedes Michael Wilkerson, coordinator of academic affairs. "It's not always easy, but it's a challenge we're constantly working on."

Yet for all the patchwork quality, I.U.'s efforts on behalf of its freshmen are creating something valuable: small communities that effectively humanize the gargantuan institution. Says summer-programs director Paulin: "It's a lot of fun every year to watch the freshmen arrive, all nervous and excited, and have a hand in getting them on their way." ∎

—With reporting by Matt Baron/Bloomington

GROUP GROPE: A freshman-seminar student completes a "trust fall," designed to forge bonds and hone problem-solving skills

Photographs for TIME by Andre Lambertson

Appalachian State

This regional university throws the book at freshmen to get them on the same page

By MEGAN RUTHERFORD BOONE

AS HE HELPED HIS SON RICH MOVE into his dorm at Appalachian State University in August, Bruce Withrow, 52, remembered how he and his classmates were greeted when they first arrived at another North Carolina university 33 years earlier, when baby boomers were swelling enrollments. "We've got too many of you here," they were told by an administrator. "And we're going to get rid of a bunch of you." That's a far cry from the message that Rich and other incoming students are given at Appalachian. "All of you have the ability

to do well here," Joe Watts, an associate vice chancellor, assured a group of freshmen. "You'll have problems—but we'll help you out."

Appalachian backs that promise with action. As it has grown from a rural grammar school with 53 pupils in 1899 into a state university—it is what educators call a masters' institution—with 12,800 students, the school has worked hard to retain its cozy sense of community so that every student feels known, nurtured and challenged.

Consider Sarah Jusiewicz, now a sophomore. After becoming hooked as a teenager on such crime dramas as

Dragnet and *Diagnosis Murder*, Jusiewicz knew she wanted to work in an FBI lab specializing in fingerprint analysis, ballistics and fiber comparison. So the New Jersey teenager applied to Appalachian, which offers a chemistry major with a forensic science concentration. The university's picturesque setting in the Blue Ridge Mountains didn't hurt its appeal.

Jusiewicz was accepted but still worried about her preparation. Her high school didn't offer a chemistry lab. But her determination to pursue a career in science was bolstered by the book assigned to her Appalachian freshman class to read before they showed up last year. Rodney Barker's *And the Waters Turned to Blood* traces the investigation by botanist JoAnn Burkholder of a mysterious microorganism linked to massive fish kills in North Carolina waters in the 1990s. Jusiewicz felt further inspired when Burkholder delivered the convocation address. "To see a woman who's got her doctorate and become an expert in her field made me feel that I could do it too," Jusiewicz recalls.

Her adviser steered Jusiewicz into a forensic science "learning community" of 11 students, all enrolled together in a freshman seminar and in chemistry and criminal-justice classes that included students from outside the group. Their seminar was far cozier than either the chemistry class of 50 students or the criminal-justice course (more than 30). It fostered new friendships, honed their study skills and brought in working professionals to familiarize them with the forensics field. It also served as a ready-made study group for the other two courses.

Her chemistry professor, Dale Wheeler, invited the forensics group to dinner, which made Jusiewicz feel more comfortable about asking him questions after class. She could also attend sessions led three times a week by a senior chemistry major whose assignment was to reinforce the lectures. When she had trouble with a math course, she signed up for free one-on-one tutoring. The results: a B in chemistry and an A in math.

Students enrolled in small freshman seminars and learning communities return to Appalachian for their sophomore year at a higher rate than do their peers who don't partake in the program (90% vs. 84% for 1999's freshmen). So the school is expanding the program, which is offered on a first-come, first-served basis. More than 50% of the incoming class will take part in freshman seminars this year, up from about 40% last year. And students in each freshman seminar are enrolled together in at least one other course to form a learning community.

When freshmen arrive for one of the two-day orientation sessions held over the summer, their parents are invited to come along. About half do. While the kids take placement tests and register for courses, their parents attend lectures on the development of young adults, confer with parents of current students and get tips on how to gauge their kids' academic progress. ("Ask your students their professors' names two or three weeks into

the semester" is one piece of advice from freshman seminars director Rennie Brantz. "If they don't know, they're not engaged.") During orientation, kids are required to bunk on campus. That's optional for parents, but about half seize the opportunity to sample dorm life. Sarah's mom, Merry Jusiewicz, 49, arrived with concerns about sending her daughter so far from home but left reassured: "I got a real feeling of a genuinely caring faculty."

Some faculty members resent the focus on freshmen, accusing the administration of "hand holding." Joni Petschauer, director of freshman learning communities, pleads guilty: "Yes! That's exactly what we're doing. We're extending our hands to them for the first semester. I embrace that."

In August, instead of asking their new

APPALACHIAN FALL: Professor Rennie Brantz entertains freshmen, above, and Sarah Jusiewicz conquers lab fear

classmates "Where are you from?" many freshmen arriving on the Appalachian campus asked one another "Have you read the book?" The following day, the 2,321 freshmen broke into small groups for discussions led by faculty and administrators of *A Lesson Before Dying*, Ernest Gaines' acclaimed 1993 novel about a black man condemned to die for a crime he did not commit and the black teacher who visits him in jail. Author Gaines was scheduled to deliver the convocation address at the university. And the theater department is staging a play adapted from the book.

But those are just the planned events. It is the spontaneous eruptions of interest that are the most gratifying to the freshman advocates at Appalachian. Jeffrey Grubbs, 18, a freshman from Charlotte, said that he rarely reads for pleasure but tore through *A Lesson Before Dying*, savoring the rich evocation of 1940s Louisiana. "It's just drenched in setting," he marveled. One evening after the formal book discussion, he found himself persuading some visiting friends to give the book a try. As the school year began, Appalachian had its freshmen on the same page—and spreading the word. ∎

OTHER NOTABLES

Kean University, Union, N.J. This commuter college requires a course on time management, study skills and human relations **Kennesaw State University, Kennesaw, Ga.** Small learning communities help freshmen bond **X**-A mostly black school gets parents involved and provides frequent advising

Keith Philpott for TIME (2)

GETTING TO KNOW YOU: A student mentor learns about each freshman's family, social fears and favorite candy

William Jewell College

At a Missouri liberal-arts school, many
shepherds watch over the freshman flock

By REBECCA WINTERS LIBERTY

IT WOULD BE TOUGH FOR A FRESH-man to slip through the cracks at William Jewell College. That's because this 1,400-student Baptist liberal-arts school in Liberty, Mo., has caulked up every crevice where a newcomer might stumble. Jewell's mentor program reaches out to incoming students even before they pack their bags. Its introductory freshmen seminar has all the first-year students highlighting their copies of St.Augustine's *Confessions* on the same night. And the college assigns all newcomers as many as five contacts—

two faculty members and three students—to check on their adjustment.

"There are so many people looking out for you here it would be almost impossible to sit in your room and sulk," says Melanie Anstine, a sophomore elementary-education major from Holden, Mo., who is mentoring seven freshmen.

Eliminating the sulk factor is exactly the point of the school's interventionist efforts to nurture newcomers, says Kathy Sheppard Nasteff, 36, the dean for first-year students. She is one of the two faculty contacts for each freshman; the other is the student's academic adviser. "These young

adults are entering a whole new world," says Nasteff. "We want to help them find an immediate comfort zone." It seems to be working. Since the mentor program started four years ago, retention rates at Jewell have risen to 86%, from 72%.

The process starts in May when high school seniors and transfer students get a letter from a student mentor, the first of several communications they will receive over the summer. The mentors, selected through a rigorous application process, are sophomores or juniors who still have vivid memories of the emotional turbulence of their freshman year. Anstine, an A student in high school, recalls the shock of getting her first college D. "I bawled," she says.

Each mentor contacts eight to 10

incoming students and their parents. They probe for key information: whose parents just got divorced, whose family is having trouble paying tuition and who is petrified of sorority rush (42% of Jewell students join fraternities and sororities). The mentors answer questions like "Should I bring a microwave?" or "What's the reading load?" They also find out little details from Mom and Dad, like their

Day. Upperclassmen lead the groups and a faculty or staff member through a series of team-building exercises designed to help the "first years" overcome their shyness. In one exercise they must get every team member and a full glass of water to an "island" several feet away by swinging on a rope. In another they have to turn over a small tarp they are standing on, without touching the imaginary "poison-

students Nasteff, the freshmen are introduced to that traditional student counselor, the resident adviser, and one more peer contact that reflects the college's Baptist background—a student called a shepherd, whose role is spiritual guidance. That guidance can mean helping freshmen study for midterms or praying with them. Jewell's campus is ecumenical—no religion courses or pledge of faith is required, and the student-senate leader is Jewish—but the school's Christian focus is evident. You're more apt to see young people praying over their dinners in the dining hall than you might at a state school, and classroom discussions can get heated when biology majors are also fierce creationists. Jewell is also 90% white, with most of its students hailing from the Midwest.

A HELLO ON HELIUM: Mentors, sounding like a chipmunk choir, teach freshmen the alma mater

daughter's favorite candy. The mentors leave the favorite candy in front of their charge's door that first day on campus, with other goodies like a William Jewell car sticker and a handmade welcome sign. "It's a way of saying, 'You have a friend here already and you haven't even finished unpacking,'" says mentor Erin Stein, a sophomore.

After the mini-fridges and extra-long sheets are unloaded, the books bought and the parents pried away, the freshmen meet their mentor groups for an event called Adventure

OTHER NOTABLES

Drury University, Springfield, Mo. Orientation begins with a summer reading assignment to prepare for the August seminar **Elon University, Elon, N.C.** Students can rough it together during summer leadership programs in the nearby mountains **Wagner College, New York City** Freshmen work at social agencies, charities or museums

ous goo" outside the tarp. "You get comfortable with a group of people really quickly when you have to squeeze onto a 2-by-4 with them," says Stein.

Each exercise is followed by a discussion of how it relates to such typical freshman experiences as meeting seemingly impossible challenges and identifying human and material resources.

As students settle in over the weekend, they meet the rest of their five-person intervention team. In addition to their mentor, their academic adviser and dean for first-year

Many of the first-year students' first exploration of different worldviews comes in the required freshman seminar called The Responsible Self. "It sounds like a course in shampooing your hair," groans junior Andy Johnson, who nevertheless feels the course "taught me a lot about myself."

Students read books like the Bhagavad Gita and John Stuart Mill's *On Liberty* with the goal of looking at themselves and their society in new ways. The one-semester course has achieved mythic status among Jewell students. Freshmen sweat it; sophomores freak the freshmen out about it; juniors grudgingly approve of it; and seniors reflect on it as life changing.

Stein checked in on a few of the freshmen she was mentoring after their first day of Responsible Self, a deed she will repeat throughout the year—formally with gatherings for ice cream or pizza, and informally with quick hellos in the dining hall. "They screamed my name across the quad," Stein says. "It's hard to believe these are the same quiet people who stared back at me at the beginning of the weekend. I guess they feel at home." Mission accomplished. ■

Photographs for Time by Dan Lamont—Corbis Sygma

JUGGLING her kids, work and classes, Hunter, a former crack addict, says her first year at Seattle Central was worth the extra effort

Seattle Central

This community college pushes diverse students to work together in small teams

By ANDREW GOLDSTEIN SEATTLE

COLLEGE RECRUITMENT BROCHURES typically look like Benetton ads. Come to our school, they seem to proclaim, and you'll learn as much from your multicolored classmates as you will from your professors. In most cases this is a fiction. Colleges tend to do a poor job of attracting minority students, and it's rare to see genuine interaction among different groups. If you were to visit Seattle Central Community College, however, you might just find a 40-year-old Hispanic mom designing computer software with a lanky, blond, 24-year-old snowboarder. Or maybe you will run into Gil Reynosa, 31, a deaf student from Mexico, building a boat with Rhonda Pence, 50, a former teacher. At Seattle Central, diversity is real, and so are its benefits.

The secret is a first-year curriculum that is carefully designed to inspire repeated, meaningful interactions among its students, both inside and outside the classroom. This is no easy task: as with many community colleges, everyone at Seattle Central lives off campus, and 80% hold full-time or part-time jobs. In many places with such an untethered, multitasking student body, it can be easy for freshmen to feel lost and alone. So Seattle Central encourages faculty to emphasize group work and keeps all its classes small. Average size: 22. (At the University of Washington, which receives more than twice as much state funding per pupil as Seattle Central, the average size of a first-year class is 40.)

Seattle Central has also created one of the nation's most expansive programs of "learning communities"—courses that are centered on a common theme and bring together students and faculty from different disciplines. And the college gives course credit for community-service projects tied to classes. Culinary-arts students help train homeless men and women for jobs in the restaurant industry; students preparing to become opticians go to rural Thailand to distribute eyeglasses.

All this group work wouldn't be so important if most of Seattle Central's 10,000 students were alike. But with 52% from minority groups, the school is one of the most diverse colleges in the U.S. And the diversity goes beyond race: 26% of the students are age 35 or older, 25% are immigrants, and about 65% are the first in their family to go to college. It helps that Seattle Central is situated at the meeting point of Seattle's historically black Central district, the mostly Asian International district and the mostly white business district. But just as important are the nearly 200 scholarships the school gives each year—thanks to alums who are far more loyal than most community-college grads. Seattle Central also boasts a faculty that's 28% minority, nearly three times the national average.

The most bustling spot on campus is the computer center, which offers the open space and frantic energy of a brokerage trading floor. Most Seattle Central students don't have their own computers, so they come here to work, socialize and surf the Web. They also come for the free tutoring, available in every subject—a program that college President Charles Mitchell credits with keeping many freshmen from dropping out. This is where Dora Hunter, 37, a business-technology student, became friends with fellow freshman Nhu-y Pham, 60, who came to Seattle from Vietnam in 1993.

Hunter, a former crack addict, is a single mother with five boys, ages 19, 17, 6, 4 and 1. To make ends meet, she works for a collection agency from 8 a.m. until 1 p.m., when her classes begin. She often thinks about quitting college to earn more money. But her friendship with Pham has kept her focused on her goal: to get a bachelor's degree in business. "For the first time since I can remember," says Hunter, "there are people besides my family that I can talk to."

Mixing all sorts of different people together in their first year of college doesn't always turn out so smoothly, however. And that may be part of the point. One of Seattle Central's learning communities is called Integrated Media Communications, in which 70 students from the departments of photography, graphic design and printing meet for six hours every Friday. For the final project in May, instructors divided the class into teams and matched students with others from different fields. Each group had to create an original brochure for a real nonprofit organization.

Mary Cunningham, 40, a mother of three, found herself teamed with Jenna Geary, 23, a professional printer, and Jake Dehnert, 19, a talented, carefree high school graduate hoping to become a graphic designer. The trio's brochure, for a diabetes-research group, turned out brilliantly: the nonprofit is planning to distribute it widely. But getting there involved a series of sometimes bitter clashes, with Dehnert's becoming fed up with Cunningham's bossiness and both women's lashing out at what the two considered Dehnert's lack of responsibility. Says Cunningham: "When you're a mother, you're a mother. You tell people what to do. I had to learn to be more flexible." Dehnert, whose artistic talent helped make the brochure a success but who also slept through the group's final presentation, says working so closely with Cunningham changed him. "Mary raised the bar. I'm more professional because of her."

Nearly 650 Seattle Central students a year sign up for learning communities, and for these students the retention rate is a remarkable 97%. The college's overall retention rate is 70%, a strong number for a community college serving such a low-income population. But there's no numerical formula for measuring how much students learn from the diversity of their peers. Consider Jennifer Strickland, 17, a humanities student from Bainbridge Island, a wealthy, secluded suburb of Seattle. By the spring of her first year, she had become so involved in the college community that she joined a group of students in a march to protest the fatal police shooting of an unarmed black man. "Seattle Central has kind of made me realize I had been living in a bubble for the past 10 years," says Strickland. "Now I see political injustices and want to change them." ∎

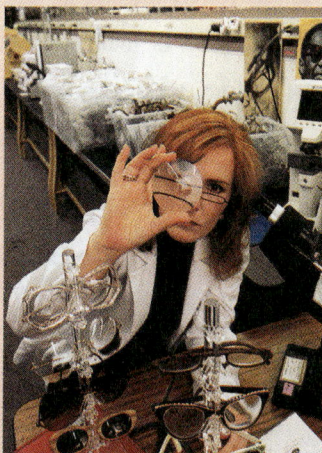

EYE OPENER: Students get life lessons, fixing glasses for the poor and working in groups

OTHER NOTABLES

Community College of Denver Four-fifths of students are the first in their family to go to college. A summer program teaches them study skills

Mesa Community College, Mesa, Ariz. Returning students greet and advise newcomers

Valencia Community College, Orlando, Fla. Tough starter classes get underperformers up to speed

10 OTHER OPTIONS AFTER HIGH SCHOOL

Somehow you just don't fit the ivy-covered campus image, but you're not sure about what other choices are open to you.

Perhaps the idea of spending four more years in a classroom studying stuff doesn't interest you. Besides, maybe your grades aren't the greatest. Or maybe the money isn't there for college tuition. Are you out of luck?

Not at all. You have plenty of options—from taking courses in a community college to help you decide what to do, to charging full speed ahead into training for a specific career in a vocational school or career college, to joining the military or entering an apprentice program.

COMMUNITY COLLEGES, CAREER COLLEGES, AND TECHNICAL EDUCATION

Many of you might be stuck in the "going to a traditional four-year college is the only way to go" rut. If you can get out of that mindset, you'll find that there are a number of paths that you can take to a well-paying and satisfying career. Here are some facts about college students that might surprise you. According to Shannon McBride, Program Director of the Golden Crescent Tech Prep School-to-Career Partnership in Victoria, Texas, "Only 40 percent of high school graduates attempt to go to a four-year college, and of those, only 25 percent get their degree. And of that 25 percent, only 37 percent use the degree they got in that area."

What's happening to the 60 percent of students who don't choose a four-year college? Well, a lot of them are getting trained for careers elsewhere. It's a good thing they are.

McBride talks about the skills that are needed in today's workplace. It used to be that you could get a good job that paid well with only a high school degree. That has changed dramatically. Today, 65 percent of the labor force must have training beyond a high school diploma, but that doesn't mean they must have a four-year degree. Says McBride, "We were a nontechnical society. You could get a great job connecting a widget to a wadget. Now a robot can do that, but we need someone to fix that robot."

If not college, then what?

Aside from joining the military or going into an apprenticeship, you have other educational directions you can take: community colleges, public and private vocational/career schools, and trade programs. Each has its own advantages. Let's look at each one.

Community Colleges

Community colleges are excellent places to get ready for a career. Unfortunately, many people have the idea that two-year colleges are second best. Think again. Community colleges offer a comprehensive range of classes that could lead to a four-year degree or right into a great career. An associate degree from a two-year college can prepare you for a number of jobs that pay well if not better than a four-year degree. (See the list on page 136 for jobs that don't call for a four-year degree.)

If you aren't sure what you want to do or what talents you have, community colleges allow you the free-

dom to explore different career interests at a low cost. Community colleges also allow those students who didn't pay attention in math or

(Continued on page 126)

WAY BEYOND SHOP CLASS

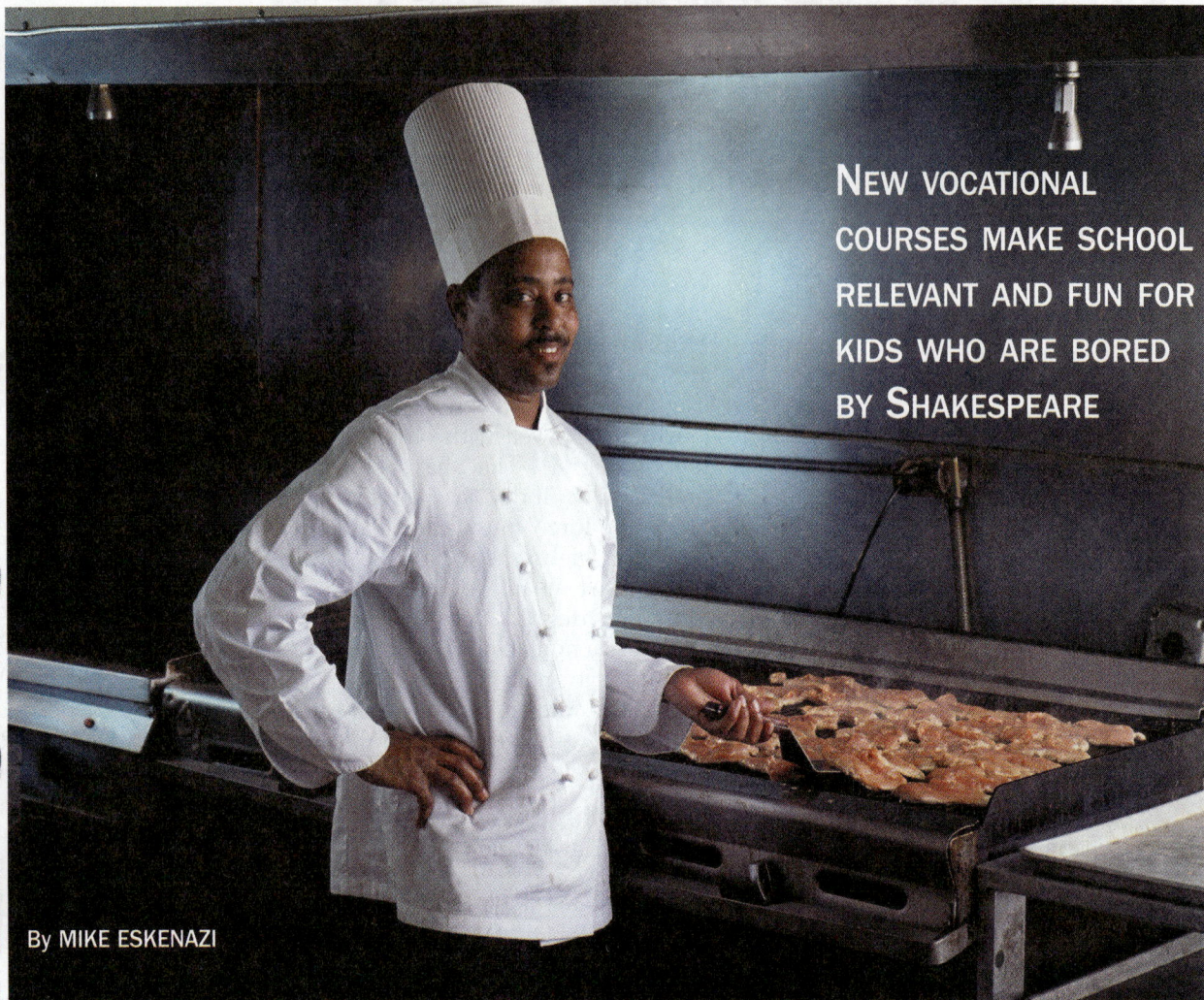

NEW VOCATIONAL COURSES MAKE SCHOOL RELEVANT AND FUN FOR KIDS WHO ARE BORED BY SHAKESPEARE

By MIKE ESKENAZI

Matt Grohnke wasn't dumb; he just couldn't get interested in English literature or American history. During his first two years at Robinson High School in Fairfax, Va., Matt would count the minutes until he could get home and focus on his real passion—computers. So after some prodding from his guidance counselor, Matt applied to the career academy located within a high school in nearby Chantilly, Va. At the Chantilly Academy, students earn coveted technical certifications in courses designed by Cisco Systems, Microsoft and Nortel. Surrounded by like-minded classmates and encouraged to pursue something he loved, Matt quickly blossomed from a bit of an outcast who couldn't get his GPA above C level to a motivated and popular A student.

Stories like Matt's have caught the eye of school administrators, leading to a nationwide movement toward career academies. For many kids, especially those who feel disconnected from traditional coursework and don't excel at things like sports or drama club, these "schools within schools" provide an exciting connection between classwork and a fulfilling career. They also manage, through the breadth of their recruiting and their subject offerings, to avoid much of the stigma once associated with shop and vocational classes.

During a recent open house, guidance counselors from across Fairfax County toured the 18 career clusters at Chantilly Academy, popping into the Animal Sciences classroom to watch students groom dogs and visiting the Hotel Management and Dental Careers courses. The counselors then settled into an annex off the high school cafeteria, where students in Culinary Arts served a four-course meal.

those aspiring toward other medical careers, such as physical therapy or nursing, are offered more practical training.

Most of the nation's 1,500 career academies are all-day schools that focus on one area of study. In a typical medical academy, students would fulfill all of their core academic work at the academy, but it would be tailored to their areas of specialization. In a comprehensive long-term study of these academies, the Manpower Demonstration Research Corp. found that the programs were especially beneficial to underperforming students. One key benefit was reducing the dropout rate.

Whittman describes half of the Chantilly Academy's students as "at risk." He doesn't mean that they have grown up amid poverty and violence but rather that they, like Matt Grohnke, were not previously interested in their high school work and weren't headed for college or a career. But at the academy, says Grohnke, "you're doing something you love. Then you get a good feeling by getting a good grade, and then you want that feeling everywhere, in all your other classes." ■

Top Left: Floral Designer
Bottom Right: Information Technology Specialist

Until 1993, Fairfax had a dual-track system, in which some students were prepped for college and others were dumped into vocational schools, which were viewed as dead-end depositories for underperforming teens. Now, though, Fairfax has five distinct career academies that bus juniors and seniors in from across this sprawling and diverse county for two-hour courses each school day and then bus them back to their home schools for regular coursework. John Whittman, Chantilly Academy's principal, estimates that 15% of the students are in advanced-placement or honors courses, 25% are special-needs or learning-disabled students, and the rest are "just regular kids who are bored in traditional classrooms."

In the Medical Health Technologies cluster, all first-year students learn basic physiology, including how to take a patient's blood pressure. Teachers counsel kids on goals and career paths, and career coordinators help place them in internships with hospitals, medical practices and physical-therapy centers. In their second year, students are given lessons more customized to their career track. Those thinking about college pre-med are urged to take advanced biology, while

SNAPSHOT OF A CAREER COLLEGE STUDENT

Katrina Dew
Network Systems Administration
Silicon Valley College
Fremont, California

WHAT I LIKE ABOUT BEING A CAREER STUDENT:
"Career colleges are for fast-track oriented students who want to get out in the work field and still feel that they have an appropriate education."

ABOUT KATRINA
Right after high school, Katrina headed for junior college, but she felt like she was spinning her wheels. She wanted something that was goal-oriented. Community college offered too many options. She needed to be focused in one direction.

At first Katrina thought she would become a physical therapist. Then she realized how much schooling she would need to begin working. Turning to the computer field, she saw some definite benefits. For one, she had messed around with them in high school. She could get a degree and get out in two years. She saw that computer careers are big and getting bigger. Plus, there weren't a lot of women in that field, which signaled more potential for her. But before she switched schools, she visited the career college, talked to students, sat in on lectures. She really liked the way the teachers related to their students. Along with her technical classes, she's taken algebra, psychology, English composition, and management communication.

Nicholas Cecere
Automotive Techniques Management
Education America/Vale Technical Institute
Blairsville, Pennsylvania

WHAT I LIKE ABOUT BEING A CAREER STUDENT:
"I compare career college to a magnifying glass that takes the sun and focuses it. You learn just what you need to learn."

ABOUT NICHOLAS
So far, Nicholas has completely repainted his 1988 Mercury Topaz, redone all the brakes, put in a brand-new exhaust system, and lots of smaller stuff here and there. But he says that's nothing compared to the completely totaled cars some of his classmates haul into the school. Talk about hands-on; they're able to completely restore them while going through the program.

Nicholas didn't always have gasoline running through his veins. In fact, he just recently discovered how much he likes automotives. After graduating from high school, he went to a community college, and after one semester left to work at a personal care home. Standing over a sink of dirty dishes made him realize he wanted more than just a job. He started thinking about what he wanted to do and visited a few schools, including the body shop where his brother worked. Where others might see twisted car frames, Nicholas saw opportunity and enrolled in the program.

English classes the chance to catch up and move on, whether to good jobs or more education. Judy Rosenthal, a college counselor at East Brunswick High School in East Brunswick, New Jersey, calls community colleges a great stepping stone because those students who don't have strong grades in high school can easily get into community college and pull up their grades.

For those students who can't afford the high cost of university tuition, community colleges let them take care of their basic classes before transferring to a four-year institution. Other students get associate degrees from community colleges because of the lower cost of overall tuition as well as living expenses. They live at home while getting their degree. William Tomasco, the Principal of Furness High School in Philadelphia, Pennsylvania, points out that not everyone is able to jump right into college. Community colleges give you the chance to take a look at what you want to do or, if you have already decided, give you a springboard into your future.

Vocational/Career Schools

Another educational option is to get specific job training at either a public or private career or technical school. Different states have different names for these educational institutions—tech-prep schools, technical institutes,

WHAT TO LOOK FOR IN A CAREER COLLEGE

A TOUR OF THE COLLEGE IS A MUST! WHILE VISITING THE CAMPUS DO THE FOLLOWING:

➢ Get a full explanation of the curriculum, including finding out how you will be trained.

➢ Take a physical tour of the classrooms and laboratories and look for cleanliness, modern equipment/computers, and size of classes. Observe the activity in classes: are students engaged in class, are lectures dynamic?

➢ Ask about employment opportunities after graduation. What are the placement rates (most current) and list of employers? Inquire about specific placement assistance: resume preparation, job leads, etc. Look for "success stories" on bulletin boards, placement boards, and newsletters.

➢ Find out about tuition and other costs associated with the program. Ask about the financial aid assistance provided to students

➢ Find out if an externship is part of the training program. How are externships assigned? Does the student have any input as to externship assignment?

➢ Ask if national certification and registration in your chosen field is available upon graduation.

➢ Inquire about the college's accreditation and certification.

➢ Also find out the associations and organizations the college belongs to. Ask what awards or honors the college has achieved.

➢ Ask if the college utilizes an advisory board to develop employer relationships.

➢ Ask about the rules and regulations. What GPA must be maintained? What is the attendance policy? What are grounds for termination? What is the refund policy if the student drops or is terminated? Is there a dress code? What are holidays of the college?

Source: Arizona College of Allied Health, Phoenix, Arizona

vocational/business schools, career colleges. Some are supported by the state, and some are private.

Generally, these schools prepare you for a specific career. Some will require you to take academic courses such as English or history. Others will relate every class you take to a specific job, such as computer-aided drafting or interior design. Some focus specifically on business or technical fields. Bob Sullivan, a career counselor at East Brunswick High School in East Brunswick, New Jersey, points out that the negative side to this kind of education is that if you haven't carefully researched what you want to do, you could waste a lot of time and money. "There's no room for exploration or finding yourself as opposed to a community college where you can go to find yourself and feel your way around," he explains.

Trade Programs

Majors in trade specialties are as straightforward as they are diverse. For the most part, graduates of a particular trade program go on to practice that trade. Carpentry majors work as carpenters, culinary arts majors as cooks and chefs.

Although for most vocational positions an associate degree is sufficient to start in the field, some jobs might require further study or some kind of licensing or certification. Sometimes this special licensing can be obtained through a college program. In addition, a period of apprenticeship must be served for most trade specialties before a worker can practice independently.

FINANCIAL AID OPTIONS FOR CAREER AND COMMUNITY COLLEGES

The financial aid process is basically the same for students attending a community college, a career college, or a technical institute as it is for students attending a four-year college. However, there are some details that can make the difference between getting the maximum amount of financial aid and only scraping by.

As with four-year students, the federal government is still your best source of financial aid. Most community colleges and career and technical schools participate in federal financial aid programs. To get detailed information about federal financial aid programs and how to apply for them, read through Section 8: "Financial Aid Dollars and Sense. "Here are some quick tips on where to look for education money.

Investigate federal financial aid programs. You should definitely check out a Federal Pell Grant, which is a need-based grant available to those who can't pay the entire tuition themselves. The Federal Supplemental Educational Opportunity Grant (FSEOG) is for those students with exceptional financial need. You also can take advantage of the Federal Work-Study programs that provide jobs for students with financial aid eligibility to work in return for part of their tuition. Many two-year institutions offer work-study, but the number of jobs tends to be limited. Also, federal loans make up a substantial part of financial aid for two-year students. Student loans, which have lower interest rates, may be sponsored by the institution or federally sponsored, or they may be available through commercial financial institutions. They are basically the same as those for the traditional four-year college student such as the Federal Perkins Loan, the Subsidized and Unsubsidized Federal Stafford Student Loans. In fact, some private career colleges and technical institutes only offer federal loans. You also can find more specific information about federal loans in Section 8.

Don't overlook scholarships. What many two-year students don't realize is that they could be eligible for scholarships. Regrettably, many make the assumption that scholarships are only for very smart students attending prestigious universities. You'd be surprised to learn how many community and career colleges have scholarships. It's critical to talk to the financial aid office of each school you plan to attend to find out what scholarships might be available. The Imagine America scholarship program is offered to students who attend select career colleges around the country. See "A Scholarship for Career College Students" on page 123 for more information.

Check in with your state. Two-year students should find out how their states can help them pay for tuition. Every state in the union has some level of state financial aid that goes to community college students. The amounts are dependent on which state you live in, and most are in the form of grants.

THE ARMED SERVICES

You can take the following three paths into the armed services—all of which provide opportunities for financial assistance for college.

1 Enlisted personnel. All five branches of the armed services offer college-credit courses on base. Enlisted personnel can also take college courses at civilian colleges while on active duty.

2 ROTC. More than 40,000 college students participate in Reserve officers' Training Corps (ROTC). Some students participate to receive ROTC scholarships. However, even those students who participate without scholarships learn the following skills that prepare them for life after college:

- How to earn the respect of others
- How to make tough decisions under pressure
- How to confidently express themselves
- How to speak effectively to groups of people

- ⏰ How to motivate others to get a job done

- ⏰ How to work in a team

Two-, three-, and four-year ROTC scholarships are available to outstanding students. You can try ROTC at no obligation for two years or, if you have a four-year scholarship, for one year. Normally, all ROTC classes, uniforms, and books are free. ROTC graduates

are required to serve in the military for a set period of time, either full-time on active duty or part-time in the Reserve or National Guard. Qualifying graduates can delay their service to go to graduate or professional school first.

3 **Officer Candidate School.** Openings at the U.S. service academies are few, so it pays to get information early. Every student is on a full scholarship, but free does not mean easy—these intense programs train graduates to meet the demands of leadership and success.

- ⏰ **West Point.** The U.S. Army Academy offers a broad-based academic program with nineteen majors in twenty-five fields of study. Extensive training and leadership experience go hand in hand with academics.

- ⏰ **Annapolis.** The U.S. Naval Academy is a unique blend of tradition and state-of-the-art technology. Its core curriculum includes eighteen major fields of study, and classroom work is supported by practical experience in leadership and professional operations.

- ⏰ **Air Force Academy.** The U.S. Air Force Academy prepares and motivates cadets for careers as Air Force officers. The academy offers a B.S. degree in twenty-six majors. Graduates receive a reserve commission as a second lieutenant in the Air Force.

- ⏰ **Coast Guard Academy.** This broad-based education, which leads to a B.S. degree in eight technical or professional majors, includes a thorough grounding in the professional skills necessary for the Coast Guard's work.

ARMED SERVICES VOCATIONAL APTITUDE BATTERY (ASVAB)

In the 1960s, the Department of Defense decided to develop a common selection and classification test, the ASVAB, for use in the nation's

high schools. ASVAB testing in high schools began in 1968. ASVAB was first used by all military services for selection and classification of recruits in 1976.

General Information

The ASVAB 18/19, a multiple aptitude battery designed for use with students in their junior or senior year in high school or in a postsecondary school, was developed to yield results useful to both students and the military. The school testing program helps the military attract well-qualified volunteers. Schools use ASVAB 18/19 test results to assist their students in identifying their aptitudes and developing future educational and career plans. The military services use the results to help determine the qualifications of young people for enlistment and to help place them in military occupational programs.

Composites

ASVAB results are reported by composite scores, which are combinations of test scores. ASVAB 18/19 yields three academic and two general ability-loaded composite scores.

The three academic composites—academic ability, verbal ability, and math ability—measure a student's potential for further formal education and predict performance in general areas requiring verbal and mathematic skills.

The two career exploration composite scores are ASVAB codes and Military Careers Scores. Ranges of Academic Ability Composite scores are converted into a primary ASVAB code and a secondary ASVAB code that enable students to identify occupations in which successful workers have aptitude levels similar to their own. The Military Career Score is a combination of the scores from the Academic Ability Composite and the Mechanical Comprehension and the Electronics Information tests. It is used to estimate a candidate's likelihood of qualifying for various enlisted occupations described in *Military Careers*, a Department of Defense publication that details occupations available in the military. The Military Career Score is reported in a range between 140 and 240 with a mean of 200.

Frequently Asked Questions About ASVAB

What is the Armed Services Vocational Aptitude Battery (ASVAB)? The ASVAB, sponsored by the Department of Defense, is a multi-aptitude test battery consisting of ten short individual tests covering Word Knowledge, Paragraph Comprehension, Arithmetic Reasoning, Mathematic Knowledge, General Science, Auto & Shop Information, Mechanical Comprehension, Electronics Information, Numerical Operations, and Coding Speed. Your ASVAB results provide scores for each individual test, as well as three academic composite scores—Verbal, Math, and Academic Ability—and two career exploration composite scores.

What is an aptitude? An aptitude is a readiness to become proficient in a type of activity, given the opportunity. This may refer to your capacity to learn one type of work or your potential for general training. The ASVAB measures aptitudes that are related to success in different jobs.

Why should I take the ASVAB? As a high school student nearing graduation, you are faced with important career choices. Should you go on to college, technical, or vocational school? Would it be better to enter the job market? Should you consider a military career? Your ASVAB scores are measures of aptitude. Three of the composite scores measure your aptitude for higher academic learning. The other two general ability-loaded composite scores are provided for career exploration purposes.

What is ASVAB 18/19? ASVAB 18/19 is the multiple aptitude test battery used solely in the school testing program. Approximately 1 million students take the ASVAB annually. ASVAB is one of the most widely used aptitude tests in America.

When and where is the ASVAB given? ASVAB is administered annually or semiannually at more than 14,000 high schools and postsecondary schools in the United States.

Is there a charge or fee to take the ASVAB? ASVAB is administered at no cost to the school or to the student.

How long does it take to complete the ASVAB? ASVAB testing takes approximately three hours. If you miss class, it will be with your school's approval.

If I wish to take the ASVAB but my school doesn't offer it (or I missed it), what should I do? See your school counselor. In some cases, arrangements may be made for you to take it at another high school. Your counselor should telephone 800-323-0513 (or in Illinois, 708-688-4922) for additional information.

How do I find out what my scores mean and how to use them? Your scores will be provided to you on a report called the ASVAB Student Results Sheet. Along with your scores, you should receive a copy of *Exploring Careers: The ASVAB Workbook*, which contains information that will help you understand your ASVAB results and show you how to use them for career exploration. Test results are returned to participating schools within 30 days.

What is a passing score on the ASVAB? No one "passes" or "fails" the ASVAB. The ASVAB enables you to compare your scores to those of other students at your grade level.

If I take the ASVAB, am I obligated to join the military? No. Taking the ASVAB does not obligate you to the military in any way. You are free to use your test results in whatever manner you wish.

Is there any relationship between taking the ASVAB and Selective Service registration? There is no relationship between taking the ASVAB and Selective Service registration. ASVAB information is not available to the Selective Service System.

If I am planning to go to college, should I take the ASVAB? Yes. ASVAB results provide you with information that can help you determine your capacity for advanced academic education. You can also use your ASVAB results, along with other personal information, to identify areas for career exploration.

If I take the ASVAB in school, can my scores be used if I decide to enlist in the military? Yes. You may use the ASVAB results for up to two years for military enlistment if you are a junior, a senior, or a postsecondary school student. The military services encourage all young people to finish high school before joining the armed forces.

Should I take the ASVAB if I plan to become a commissioned officer? Yes. Taking the ASVAB is a valuable experience for any student who aspires to become a military officer. The aptitude information you receive could assist you in career planning.

Should I take the ASVAB if I am considering entering the Reserve or National Guard? Yes. These military organizations also use the ASVAB for enlistment purposes.

What should I do if a service recruiter contacts me? You may be contacted by a service recruiter before you graduate. If you want to learn about the many opportunities available through the military service, arrange for a follow-up meeting. However, you are under no obligation to the military as a result of taking the ASVAB.

Is the ASVAB administered other than in the school testing program? Yes. ASVAB is also used in the regular military enlistment program. It is administered at approximately sixty-five Military Entrance Processing Stations located throughout the United States. Each year, hundreds of thousands of young men and women who are interested in enlisting in the uniformed services (Army, Navy, Air Force, Marines, and Coast Guard) but who did not take the ASVAB while in high school or post-secondary school are examined and processed at these military stations.

Is the ASVAB used in the regular military enlistment program the same as ASVAB 18/19? No. ASVAB, Forms 20-22 are currently used in the regular military enlistment program. However, these forms are equivalent in scope of test and level of difficulty to ASVAB 18/19 used in the school testing program.

ASVAB Forms 20-22 are used in the Computerized Adaptive Testing program known as CAT-ASVAB. These tests are not paper-and-pencil tests but are computer administered.

How are those tested in the regular military enlisted program advised of their ASVAB scores? With the CAT-ASVAB, the computer is programmed to automatically compute and print a score report for each individual tested. This report contains raw and standard scores for each subtest, as well as composite scores. Results are used to determine whether the test-taker obtained a score high enough to be eligible for enlistment. Those who qualify are told the same day when to return for further processing. The score report is used to assist in counseling and classification.

Is any special preparation necessary before taking the ASVAB? Yes. A certain amount of preparation is required for taking any examination. Whether it is an athletic competition or a written test, preparation is a must in order to achieve the best results. Your test scores reflect not only your ability but also the time and effort in preparing for the test. The uniformed services use ASVAB to help determine a person's qualification for enlistment and to help indicate the vocational areas for which the person is best suited. Achieving your maximum score will increase your vocational opportunities.

Financing Higher Education through the U.S. Armed Forces

The U.S. military provides a number of options to help students and their parents get financial aid.

The Montgomery G.I. Bill

Available to enlistees in all branches of the service, the G.I. Bill pays up to $19,296 toward education costs at any accredited two- or four-year college or vocational school, for up to ten years after discharge.

There are two options under the bill:

1 Active Duty. If you serve on active duty, you will allocate $1,200 of your pay ($100 a month for twelve months) to your education fund. Then, under the G.I. Bill, the federal government pays out up to $19,296.

2 Reserve Duty. If you join a Reserve unit, you can receive up to $9,180 to offset your education costs.

You can visit the Veterans Affairs Web page at www.va.gov.

The Department of Defense The U.S. Department of Defense offers a large number of education benefits to those enrolled in the U.S. military or employed by the Department of Defense, including scholarships, grants, tuition assistance, and internships. Visit their Web site at http://198.3.128.64/edugate for complete information.

Reserve Officers' Training Corps (ROTC) The ROTC offers college scholarships that pay most of the recipient's tuition and other expenses and includes a monthly allowance of $150. The Army, for example, provides an ROTC scholarship of up to $16,000 a year, depending upon the tuition of the school, plus a living allowance of $150 per month for the academic year. After graduation, most trainees enter the service as officers and complete a four-year tour of duty. For the most current information about eligibility, applications, and deadlines, call 800-USA-ROTC (toll-free).

Tuition Assistance All branches of the military pay up to 75 percent of tuition for full-time, active-duty enlistees who take courses at community colleges or by correspondence during their tours of duty. Details vary by service.

The Community College of the Air Force Members of the Air Force, Air National Guard, or Air Force Reserves can convert their technical training and military experience into academic credit, earning an associate degree, an occupational instructor's certificate, or a trade school certificate. Participants receive an official transcript from this fully accredited program. You can visit the Community College of the Air Force on line at www.au.af.mil/au/ccaf/.

Educational Loan-Repayment Program The Armed Services can help repay government-insured and other approved loans. One third of the loan will be repaid for each year served on active duty.

Other Forms of Tuition Assistance
Each branch of the military offers its own education incentives. To find out more, check with a local recruiting office.

APPRENTICESHIPS

Some students like working with their hands and have the skill, patience, and temperament to become expert mechanics, carpenters, or electronic repair technicians. If you think you'd enjoy a profession like this and feel that college training isn't for you, then you might want to think about a job that requires apprenticeship training.

To stay competitive, America needs highly skilled workers. But if you're looking for a soft job, forget it. An apprenticeship is no snap. It demands hard work and has tough competition, so you've got to have the will to see it through. An apprenticeship is a program formally agreed upon between a worker and an employer where the employee learns a skilled trade through classroom work and on-the-job training. Apprenticeship programs vary in length, pay, and intensity among the various trades. A person completing an apprenticeship program generally becomes a journeyperson (skilled craftsperson) in that trade.

The advantages of apprenticeships are numerous. First and foremost, an apprenticeship leads to a lasting lifetime skill. As a highly trained worker, you can take your skill anywhere you decide to go. The more creative, exciting, and challenging jobs are put in the hands of the fully skilled worker, the all-around person who knows his or her trade inside out.

Skilled workers advance much faster than those who are semiskilled or whose skills are not broad enough to equip them to assume additional responsibilities in a career. Those who complete an apprenticeship have also

BUREAU OF APPRENTICESHIP AND TRAINING OFFICES

NATIONAL OFFICE:
U.S. Department of Labor
Frances Perkins Building
200 Constitution Avenue, NW
Washington, D.C. 20210
202-693-3813

Northeast Regional Office
Suite 1815 East
170 South Independence Mall West
Philadelphia, Pennsylvania 19106
412-395-5037

Southern Regional Office
Room 6T71
61 Forsyth Street, SW
Atlanta, Georgia 30303
404-562-2335

Midwestern Regional Office
Room 656
230 South Dearborn Street
Chicago, Illinois
312-353-7205

Southwestern Regional Office
Room 317
Federal Building
525 Griffin Street
Dallas, Texas 75202
214-767-4993

Western Regional Office
Room 465721
US Custom House
19th Street
Denver, Colorado 80202
303-844-4792

acquired the skills and judgment that are necessary to go into business for themselves if they choose.

What to Do if You're Interested in an Apprenticeship

If you want to begin an apprenticeship, you have to be at least 16 years old, and you must fill out an application for employment. These applications may be available year-round or at certain times during the year, depending on the trade you're interested in. Because an apprentice must be trained in an area where work actually exists and where a certain pay scale is guaranteed upon completion of the program, the wait for application acceptance may be pretty long in areas of low employment. This standard works to your advantage, however. Just think: you wouldn't want to spend one to six years of your life learning a job where no work exists or where the wage is the same as, or just a little above, that of common laborer.

Federal regulations prohibit anyone under the age of 16 from being considered for an apprenticeship. Some programs require a high school degree or certain course work. Other requirements may include passing certain aptitude tests, proof of physi-

cal ability to perform the duties of the trade, and possession of a valid driver's license.

Once you have met the basic program entrance requirements, you'll be interviewed and awarded points on your interest in the trade, your attitude toward work in general, and personal traits, such as appearance, sincerity, character, and habits. Openings are awarded to those who have achieved the most points.

If you're considering an apprenticeship, the best sources of assistance and information are vocational or career counselors, local state employment security agencies, field offices of state apprenticeship agencies, and regional offices of the Bureau of Apprenticeship and Training (BAT). Apprenticeships are usually registered with the BAT or a state apprenticeship council. Some apprenticeships are not registered at all, although that doesn't necessarily mean that the program isn't valid. To find out if a certain apprenticeship is legitimate, contact your state's apprenticeship agency or a regional office of the BAT. Addresses and phone numbers for these regional offices are listed above. You can also visit the Bureau's Web site at www.doleta.gov/atels_bat. ■

PART 3

Some of you will go to college first and then look for jobs. Some of you might work for a few years and then go to college. And many of you will go immediately into the workplace and bypass college altogether. Whenever you become an employee, you'll want to know what you can do to succeed on the job and move to both higher levels of responsibility and more pay.

YOU AND THE WORKPLACE

11
JUMP INTO WORK

Almost everyone ends up in the workplace at some point. No matter when you plan to receive that first full-time paycheck, there are some things you'll need to do to prepare yourself for the world of work.

At each grade level, there are specific steps you should take regardless of whether or not you plan to attend college immediately following high school. In fact, college and career timelines should coincide, according to guidance counselors and career specialists. The focus nowadays is on "school-to-work," and although many of you may plan to attend a college or university right after high school, you should have some specific career goals in mind. You need to be able to focus on the relationship between school and work—and specifically on how much education you need and why you are going to college. Career specialists all over the nation recommend that students take college-preparatory courses, even if they aren't planning on attending college.

THE CAREER TIME LINE

This time line will help you meet college requirements and still prepare for work. In an effort to make sure that you are adequately preparing for both school and work, incorporate these five steps into your career/college time line:

1 Take an interest survey or aptitude test. You can do this as early as the sixth grade, but even if you're in high school now, it's not too late. By doing so, you will begin to get a feel for what areas you might be good at and enjoy.

2 Beginning in middle school, you should start considering what your options are after high school. However, if you're only starting to think about this in high

school, that's okay, too. Keep a notebook of information gathered from field trips, job-shadowing experiences, mentoring programs, and career fairs to help you make sense of the possibilities open to you. This process should continue through high school. Many schools offer job shadowing and internship programs for students to explore different vocational avenues. Take advantage of these opportunities if you can. Too often, students don't explore the workplace until after they've taken the courses necessary to enter a particular profession, only to discover it wasn't the career they dreamed of after all.

3 No later than the tenth grade, visit a vocational center to look at the train-

TAKING A BREAK BETWEEN HIGH SCHOOL AND COLLEGE

Because of the soaring costs of college tuition today, college is no longer a place to "find yourself." It is a costly investment in your future. The career you choose to pursue may or may not require additional education; your research will determine whether or not it's required or preferred. If you decide not to attend college immediately after high school, however, don't consider it to be a closed door. Taking some time off between high school and college is considered perfectly acceptable by employers. Many students simply need a break after twelve years of schooling. Most experts agree that it's better to be ready and prepared for college; many adults get more out of their classes after they've had a few years to mature.

Source: Street Smart Career Guide: A Step-by-Step Program for Your Career Development.

ing programs offered. Some public school systems send students to vocational and career program centers for career exploration.

4 During your junior and senior years, be sure to create a portfolio of practice resumes, writing samples, and a list of work skills. This portfolio should also include your high school transcript and letters of recommendation. It will serve
(Continued on page 138)

CAREERS WITHOUT A FOUR-YEAR DEGREE

SOME STUDENTS SPEND A FEW YEARS IN THE WORKPLACE BEFORE GOING TO COLLEGE. OTHERS BEGIN THEIR CAREER WITH A HIGH SCHOOL DIPLOMA, A VOCATIONAL CERTIFICATE, OR UP TO TWO YEARS OF EDUCATION OR TRAINING AFTER HIGH SCHOOL.

WITH THAT IN MIND, SOMETIMES IT'S EASIER TO KNOW WHAT YOU DON'T WANT THAN WHAT YOU DO WANT. TAKE A LOOK AT THE LIST BELOW, AND CHECK OFF THE CAREERS THAT INTEREST YOU. PERHAPS YOU'VE THOUGHT OF SOMETHING YOU'D LIKE TO DO THAT ISN'T ON THIS LIST. WELL, DON'T DUMP YOUR HOPES. THERE ARE MANY DIFFERENT LEVELS OF TRAINING AND EDUCATION THAT CAN LEAD YOU TO THE CAREER OF YOUR DREAMS. SINCE THIS LIST IS NOT ALL-INCLUSIVE, YOU SHOULD CHECK WITH YOUR HIGH SCHOOL COUNSELOR OR GO ON LINE TO RESEARCH THE TRAINING YOU'LL NEED TO ACHIEVE THE JOB OR CAREER YOU WANT—WITHOUT A FOUR-YEAR DEGREE.

THEN TALK TO YOUR GUIDANCE COUNSELOR, TEACHER, LIBRARIAN, OR CAREER COUNSELOR FOR MORE INFORMATION ABOUT THE CAREERS ON THE LIST BELOW OR THOSE YOU'VE RESEARCHED ON YOUR OWN.

AGRICULTURE AND NATURAL RESOURCES
High school/vocational diploma
- ☐ Fisher
- ☐ Groundskeeper
- ☐ Logger
- ☐ Pest Controller

Up to two years beyond high school
- ☐ Fish and Game Warden
- ☐ Tree Surgeon

APPLIED ARTS (VISUAL)
High school/vocational diploma
- ☐ Floral Arranger
- ☐ Merchandise Displayer
- ☐ Painter (artist)

Up to two years beyond high school
- ☐ Cartoonist
- ☐ Commercial Artist
- ☐ Fashion Designer
- ☐ Interior Decorator
- ☐ Photographer

APPLIED ARTS (WRITTEN AND SPOKEN)
High school/vocational diploma
- ☐ Proofreader

Up to two years beyond high school
- ☐ Advertising copywriter
- ☐ Legal assistant

BUSINESS MACHINE/COMPUTER OPERATION
High school/vocational diploma
- ☐ Data Entry
- ☐ Statistical Clerk
- ☐ Telephone Operator
- ☐ Typist

Up to two years beyond high school
- ☐ Computer Operator
- ☐ Motion Picture Projectionist
- ☐ Word Processing Machine Operator

CONSTRUCTION AND MAINTENANCE
High school/vocational diploma
- ☐ Bricklayer
- ☐ Construction Laborer
- ☐ Elevator Mechanic
- ☐ Floor Covering Installer
- ☐ Heavy Equipment Operator
- ☐ Janitor
- ☐ Maintenance Mechanic

Up to two years beyond high school
- ☐ Building Inspector
- ☐ Carpenter
- ☐ Electrician
- ☐ Insulation Worker
- ☐ Lather
- ☐ Painter (construction)
- ☐ Pipefitter
- ☐ Plumber
- ☐ Roofer
- ☐ Sheet Metal Worker
- ☐ Structural Steel Worker
- ☐ Tile Setter

CRAFTS AND RELATED SERVICES
High school/vocational diploma
- ☐ Baker/Cook/Chef
- ☐ Butcher
- ☐ Furniture Upholsterer
- ☐ Housekeeper (hotel)
- ☐ Tailor/Dressmaker

Up to two years beyond high school
- ☐ Dry Cleaner
- ☐ Jeweler
- ☐ Locksmith
- ☐ Musical Instrument Repairer

CREATIVE/PERFORMING ARTS
High school/vocational diploma
- ☐ Singer
- ☐ Stunt Performer

Up to two years beyond high school
- ☐ Actor/Actress
- ☐ Dancer/Choreographer
- ☐ Musician
- ☐ Writer/Author

EDUCATION AND RELATED SERVICES
High school/vocational diploma
- ☐ Nursery School Attendant
- ☐ Teacher's Aide

ENGINEERING AND RELATED TECHNOLOGIES
High school/vocational diploma
- ☐ Biomedical Equipment Technician
- ☐ Laser Technician

Up to two years beyond high school
- ☐ Aerospace Engineer Technician
- ☐ Broadcast Technician
- ☐ Chemical Laboratory Technician
- ☐ Civil Engineering Technician
- ☐ Computer Programmer
- ☐ Computer Service Technician
- ☐ Electronic Technician
- ☐ Energy Conservation Technician
- ☐ Industrial Engineering Technician
- ☐ Laboratory Tester
- ☐ Mechanical Engineering Technician
- ☐ Metallurgical Technician
- ☐ Pollution Control Technician
- ☐ Quality Control Technician
- ☐ Robot Technician
- ☐ Surveyor (land)
- ☐ Technical Illustrator
- ☐ Tool Designer
- ☐ Weather Observer

FINANCIAL TRANSACTIONS
High school/vocational diploma
- ☐ Accounting Clerk
- ☐ Bank Teller
- ☐ Cashier
- ☐ Payroll Clerk
- ☐ Travel Agent

Up to two years beyond high school
- ☐ Bookkeeper
- ☐ Loan Officer

HEALTH CARE (GENERAL)
High school/vocational diploma
- ☐ Dental Assistant
- ☐ Medical Assistant
- ☐ Nursing/Psychiatric Aide

Up to two years beyond high school
- ☐ Dietetic Technician
- ☐ Nurse (practical)
- ☐ Nurse (registered)
- ☐ Optometric Assistant
- ☐ Physical Therapist's Assistant
- ☐ Physician's Assistant
- ☐ Recreation Therapist

HEALTH-CARE SPECIALTIES AND TECHNOLOGIES
High school/vocational diploma
- ☐ Dialysis Technician

Up to two years beyond high school
- ☐ Dental Hygienist
- ☐ Dental Laboratory Technician
- ☐ EEG Technologist
- ☐ EKG Technician
- ☐ Emergency Medical Technician
- ☐ Medical Laboratory Technician
- ☐ Medical Technologist

- ☐ Nuclear Medicine Technologist
- ☐ Operating Room Technician
- ☐ Optician
- ☐ Radiation Therapy Technologist
- ☐ Radiologic Technologist
- ☐ Respiratory Therapist
- ☐ Sonographer

HOME/BUSINESS EQUIPMENT REPAIR
High school/vocational diploma
- ☐ Air-Conditioning/Refrigeration/Heating Mechanic
- ☐ Appliance Servicer
- ☐ Coin Machine Mechanic
Up to two years beyond high school
- ☐ Communications Equipment Mechanic
- ☐ Line Installer/Splicer
- ☐ Office Machine Servicer
- ☐ Radio/TV Repairer
- ☐ Telephone Installer

INDUSTRIAL EQUIPMENT OPERATIONS AND REPAIR
High school/vocational diploma
- ☐ Assembler
- ☐ Blaster
- ☐ Boilermaker
- ☐ Coal Equipment Operator
- ☐ Compressor House Operator
- ☐ Crater
- ☐ Dock Worker
- ☐ Forging Press Operator
- ☐ Furnace Operator
- ☐ Heat Treater
- ☐ Machine Tool Operator
- ☐ Material Handler
- ☐ Miner
- ☐ Sailor
- ☐ Sewing Machine Operator
Up to two years beyond high school
- ☐ Bookbinder
- ☐ Compositor/Typesetter
- ☐ Electronic Equipment Repairer
- ☐ Electroplater
- ☐ Firefighter
- ☐ Instrument Mechanic
- ☐ Lithographer
- ☐ Machine Repairer
- ☐ Machinist
- ☐ Millwright
- ☐ Molder
- ☐ Nuclear Reactor Operator
- ☐ Patternmaker
- ☐ Photoengraver
- ☐ Power House Mechanic
- ☐ Power Plant Operator
- ☐ Printing Press Operator
- ☐ Stationery Engineer
- ☐ Tool and Die Maker
- ☐ Water Plant Operator
- ☐ Welder
- ☐ Wire Drawer

MANAGEMENT AND PLANNING
High school/vocational diploma
- ☐ Administrative Assistant
- ☐ Food Service Supervisor

- ☐ Postmaster
- ☐ Service Station Manager
Up to two years beyond high school
- ☐ Benefits Manager
- ☐ Building Manager
- ☐ Caterer
- ☐ Contractor
- ☐ Credit Manager
- ☐ Customer Service Coordinator
- ☐ Employment Interviewer
- ☐ Executive Housekeeper
- ☐ Funeral Director
- ☐ Hotel/Motel Manager
- ☐ Importer/Exporter
- ☐ Insurance Manager
- ☐ Manager (small business)
- ☐ Office Manager
- ☐ Personnel Manager
- ☐ Restaurant/Bar Manager
- ☐ Store Manager
- ☐ Supermarket Manager

MARKETING AND SALES
High school/vocational diploma
- ☐ Auctioneer
- ☐ Bill Collector
- ☐ Driver (route)
- ☐ Fashion Model
- ☐ Product Demonstrator
- ☐ Salesperson (general)
- ☐ Sample Distributor
Up to two years beyond high school
- ☐ Claims Adjuster
- ☐ Insurance Worker
- ☐ Manufacturer's Representative
- ☐ Real Estate Agent
- ☐ Sales Manager
- ☐ Travel Agent
- ☐ Travel Guide

PERSONAL AND CUSTOMER SERVICE
High school/vocational diploma
- ☐ Barber
- ☐ Bartender
- ☐ Beautician
- ☐ Child-care Worker
- ☐ Counter Attendant
- ☐ Dining Room Attendant
- ☐ Electrologist
- ☐ Flight Attendant
- ☐ Host/Hostess
- ☐ Houseparent
- ☐ Manicurist
- ☐ Parking Lot Attendant
- ☐ Porter
- ☐ Private Household Worker
- ☐ Waiter/Waitress

RECORDS AND COMMUNICATIONS
High school/vocational diploma
- ☐ Billing Clerk
- ☐ Clerk (general)
- ☐ File Clerk

- ☐ Foreign Trade Clerk
- ☐ Hotel Clerk
- ☐ Meter Reader
- ☐ Postal Clerk
- ☐ Receptionist
- ☐ Stenographer
Up to two years beyond high school
- ☐ Court Reporter
- ☐ Legal Secretary
- ☐ Library Assistant
- ☐ Library Technician
- ☐ Medical Records Technician
- ☐ Medical Secretary
- ☐ Personnel Assistant
- ☐ Secretary
- ☐ Travel Clerk

SOCIAL AND GOVERNMENT
High school/vocational diploma
- ☐ Corrections Officer
- ☐ Police Officer
- ☐ Security Guard
- ☐ Store Detective
Up to two years beyond high school
- ☐ Detective (police)
- ☐ Hazardous Waste Technician
- ☐ Recreation Leader
- ☐ Personal/Customer Services

STORAGE AND DISPATCHING
High school/vocational diploma
- ☐ Dispatcher
- ☐ Mail Carrier
- ☐ Railroad Conductor
- ☐ Shipping/Receiving Clerk
- ☐ Stock Clerk
- ☐ Tool Crib Attendant
- ☐ Warehouse Worker
Up to two years beyond high school
- ☐ Warehouse Supervisor

VEHICLE OPERATION AND REPAIR
High school/vocational diploma
- ☐ Automotive Painter
- ☐ Bus Driver
- ☐ Chauffeur
- ☐ Diesel Mechanic
- ☐ Farm Equipment Mechanic
- ☐ Forklift Operator
- ☐ Heavy Equipment Mechanic
- ☐ Locomotive Engineer
- ☐ Railroad Braker
- ☐ Refuse Collector
- ☐ Service Station Attendant
- ☐ Taxicab Driver
- ☐ Truck Driver
Up to two years beyond high school
- ☐ Aircraft Mechanic
- ☐ Airplane Pilot
- ☐ Auto Body Repairer
- ☐ Automotive Mechanic
- ☐ Garage Supervisor
- ☐ Motorcycle Mechanic

as a valuable reference tool when it comes time to apply for jobs.

5 By tenth or eleventh grade, you should begin honing in on a specific career path. More employers today are looking for employees who have both the education and work experience that relates to the career field for which they're interviewing. If you are looking for part-time employment, you should consider jobs that pertain to your field of study. Until you start interacting with people in the field, you won't have a realistic feel of what's involved in that profession. It adds to the importance of the learning. For a list of careers and related college majors, refer back to Section 5. If you're planning on heading into the workplace right after high school, take a look at the previous two pages for a list of careers that don't require a four-year degree.

WRITING YOUR RESUME

Resumes are a critical part of getting a job. Chances are you'll have to submit one before you get interviewed. A resume is an introduction of your skills to a potential employer. For that reason, your resume must stand out in a crowd because some employers receive dozens of resumes in the mail each week. A resume that is too long, cluttered, or disorganized may find its way to the "circular file," also known as the trash can. You can avoid this hazard by creating a resume that is short, presentable, and easy to read.

Remember that a resume is a summary of who you are and an outline of your experiences, skills, and goals. While writing it, you may discover some talents that you weren't aware you had and that will help boost your confidence for the job search.

Begin by collecting facts about yourself, including where you went to high school, your past and present jobs, activities, interests, and leadership roles. Next to the individual activities, write down what responsibilities you had. For example, something as simple as babysitting requires the ability to settle disagreements and supervise others.

Next, decide on how you would like to format your resume. Most hiring managers expect to see one of two types of resumes: chronological or functional. The chronological resume is the most traditional, supplying the reader with a sequential listing (from present to past) of your accomplishments. Because the emphasis here is on past employment experience, high school and college students with little or no employment history might want to avoid this type. A functional resume, on the other hand, highlights a person's abilities rather than his or her work history. Entry-level candidates who want to focus on skills rather than credentials should consider using a functional resume.

SAMPLE FUNCTIONAL RESUME

Michele A. Thomas
3467 Main Street
Atlanta, Georgia 30308
404-555-3423
E-mail: mthomas_987654321@yahoo.com

OBJECTIVE
Seeking a sales position in the wireless phone industry

EDUCATION
High School Diploma, June 2002
John F. Kennedy High School, Atlanta, Georgia

SKILLS
Computer literate, IBM: MS Works, MS Word, WordPerfect, Netscape; Macintosh: MS Word, Excel

ACTIVITIES/LEADERSHIP
Student Government secretary, 2001-2002
Key Club vice president, 2000–2001
Future Business Leaders of America

AWARDS
Varsity Swim Club (Captain; MVP Junior, Senior; Sportsmanship Award)
Outstanding Community Service Award, 2001

EXPERIENCE
Sales Clerk, The Limited, Atlanta, Georgia; part-time, September 2000 to present
Cashier, Winn-Dixie Supermarkets, Atlanta, Georgia, Summers 1999 and 2000

INTERESTS
Swimming, reading, computers

REFERENCES
Available upon request

PARTS OF A RESUME

At the very least, your resume should include the following components:

Heading: Centered at the top of the page should be your name, address, phone number, and e-mail address.

Objective: In one sentence, tell the employer what type of work you are looking for.

Education: Beginning with your most recent school or program, include the date (or expected date) of completion, the degree or certificate earned, and the address of the institution.

Don't overlook any workshops or seminars, self-study, or on-the-job training in which you have been involved. If any courses particularly lend themselves to the type of work you'd be doing on that job, include them. Mention grade point averages and class rank when they are especially impressive.

Skills and abilities: Until you've actually listed these on paper, you can easily overlook many of them. They may be as varied as the ability to work with computers or being captain of the girl's basketball team.

Work experience: If you don't have any, skip this section. If you do, begin with your most recent employer and include the date you left the job, your job title, the company name, and the company address. If you are still employed there, simply enter your start date and "to present" for the date. Include notable accomplishments for each job. High school and college students with little work experience shouldn't be shy about including summer, part-time, and volunteer jobs, such as lifeguarding, babysitting, delivering pizzas, or volunteering at the local parks and recreation department.

Personal: Here's your opportunity to include your special talents and interests as well as notable accomplishments or experiences.

References: Most experts agree that it's best to simply state that references are available upon request. However, if you do decide to list names, addresses, and phone numbers, limit yourself to no more than three. Make sure you inform any people whom you have listed that they may be contacted. Take a look at the sample resume on the previous page, and use it as a model when you create your resume.

Resume-Writing Tips

These tips will help as you begin constructing your resume.

- Keep the resume short and simple. Although senior executives may use as many as two or three pages, recent graduates should limit themselves to one page.
- Capitalize headings.
- Keep sentences short; avoid writing in paragraphs.
- Use language that is simple, not flowery or complex.
- Be specific, and offer examples when appropriate.
- Emphasize achievements.
- Be honest.
- Don't include information about salary or wages.
- Use high-quality, white, beige, or gray, 8½" x 11" paper.
- Make good use of white space by leaving adequate side and top margins on the paper.
- Make what you write presentable, using good business style and typing it on a computer or word processor.
- Because your resume should be a reflection of your personality, write it yourself.
- Avoid gimmicks such as colored paper, photos, or clip art.
- Make good use of bullets or asterisks, underlining, and bold print.
- Proofread your work, and have someone you trust proofread it also.
- Be neat and accurate.
- Never send a resume without a cover letter.

THE COVER LETTER

Every resume should be accompanied by a cover letter. This is often the most crucial part of your job search because the letter will be the first thing that a potential employer reads. When you include a cover letter, you're showing the employer that you care enough to take the time to address him or her personally and that you are genuinely interested in the job.

Always call the company and verify the name and title of the person to whom you are addressing the letter. Although you will want to keep your letter brief, introduce yourself and begin with a statement that will catch the reader's attention. Indicate the position you are applying for and mention if someone referred you or if you are simply responding to a newspaper ad. Draw attention to yourself by including something that will arouse the employer's curiosity about your experience and accomplishments. A cover letter should request something, most commonly an interview. Sign and date your letter. Then follow up with a phone call a few days after you're sure the letter has been received. Persistence pays. The sample cover letter on the next page can help you as you begin writing your cover letter.

JOB HUNTING 101

High school is a time for taking classes and learning, developing relationships with others, becoming involved in extracurricular activities that teach valuable life skills, and generally preparing for college or a job. Regardless of where you're headed after high school, you need to learn how to create a favorable impression. That can mean setting some clear, attainable goals for yourself, putting them down on paper in the form of a resume and cover letter, and convincing interviewers that you are, indeed, the person for whom they are looking. In short, learn how to sell yourself. A brief course in Job Hunting 101 will help you do just that.

Marketing Yourself

You can use several approaches to market yourself successfully. Networking, the continual process of contacting friends and relatives, is a great way to get information about job openings. Seventy-five percent of the job openings in this country are not advertised but are filled by friends, relatives, and acquaintances of peo-

SAMPLE COVER LETTER

Take a look at how this student applied the facts outlined in her resume to the job she's applying for in the cover letter below. You can use this letter to help you get started on your own cover letters. Text that appears in all caps below indicates the kind of information you need to include in that section. Before you send your letter, proofread it for mistakes and ask a parent or friend you trust to look it over as well.

(DATE)
June 29, 2002

(YOUR ADDRESS)
3467 Main Street
Atlanta, Georgia 30308
E-mail: mthomas_987654321@yahoo.com
Phone: 404-555-6721

(PERSON—BY NAME—TO WHOM YOU'RE SENDING THE LETTER)
Mr. Charles E. Pence
Manager, Human Resources
NexAir Wireless
20201 East Sixth Street
Atlanta, Georgia 30372

Dear Mr. Pence:

(HOW YOU HEARD OF THE POSITION)
Your job announcement in the Atlantan Gazette for an entry-level sales position asked for someone who has both computer and sales skills. (SOMETHING EXTRA THAT WILL INTEREST THE READER) My training and past job experience fit both of those categories. I also bring an enthusiasm and desire to begin my career in a communications firm such as NexAir.

(WHAT PRACTICAL SKILLS YOU CAN BRING TO THE POSITION)
A few weeks ago, I graduated from John F. Kennedy High School here in Atlanta. While in school, I concentrated on gaining computer skills on both IBM and Macintosh machines and participated in organizations such as the Key Club, in which I was vice president, and the Future Business Leaders of America.

(RELATE PAST EXPERIENCE TO DESIRED JOB)
As you will see from my resume, I worked as a cashier at Winn-Dixie Supermarket for two summers and am currently employed as a sales clerk at The Limited. From these two positions, I have gained valuable customer service skills and an attention to detail, qualities which I'm sure are of utmost importance to you as you make your hiring decision.

I would very much like to interview for the position and am available at your convenience. I look forward to hearing from you soon.

Sincerely,

Michele A. Thomas

---

ple who already work there. From the employer's perspective, there is less risk associated with hiring someone recommended by an employee than by hiring someone unknown. Networking is powerful. Everyone has a primary network of people they know and talk to frequently. Those acquaintances know and talk to networks of their own, thereby creating a secondary network for you and multiplying the number of individuals who know what you're looking for in a job.

Broadcasting is another marketing method in which you gather a list of companies that interest you and then mail them letters asking for job interviews. Although the rate of return on your mailings is small, two thirds of all job hunters use this approach, and half of those who use it find a job. You will increase your response rate by addressing your letter to a particular person—the one who has the power to hire you—and by following up with a phone call a few days after the letter has been received. To obtain the manager's name, simply call the company and ask the receptionist for the person's name, job title, and correct spelling. Good resources for finding potential employers include referrals, community agencies, job fairs, newspaper ads, trade directories, trade journals, state indexes, the local chamber of commerce, the Yellow Pages, and the Web. See page 141 for a listing of career Web resources. These tips can help as you begin hunting for the perfect job.

- Job-hunting is time intensive. Do your homework, and take it seriously by using every opportunity available to you.
- Prepare yourself for the fact that there will be far more rejections than acceptances.
- Consider taking a temporary job while you continue the job hunt. It will help pay the bills and boost your morale at the same time.
- Research the activities of potential employers, and show that you have studied them when you're being interviewed.
- Keep careful records of all contacts and follow-up activities.
- Don't ignore any job leads—act on every tip you get.
- Stay positive.

With all these thoughts in mind, you should be ready to begin the process of making people believe in you, and that's a major part of being successful in your job hunt.

The Job Interview

Boost your confidence. You can prevent some of the preinterview jitters by adequately preparing. Remember that you have nothing to lose and that you, too, are doing the choosing. Just as you are waiting and hoping to be offered a job, you have the option of choosing whether or not to accept an offer. It's all right to feel somewhat anxious, but keep everything in perspective. This is an adventure, and you are in control. Most important, remember to be yourself. With all of this in mind, consider some of the following points of the interview process.

- Speak up during the interview, and furnish the interviewer with the information he or she needs in order to make an informed decision. It is especially impressive if you can remember the names of people to whom you've been introduced. People like to be called by name, and it shows that you took the initiative to remember them.

- Always arrive a few minutes early for the interview, and look your best. The way you act and dress tells the interviewer plenty about your attitude and personality. Sloppy dress, chewing gum, and cigarettes have no place at an interview and will probably cut your interview short. Instead, dress professionally and appropriately for the job. Avoid heavy makeup, short skirts, jeans, and untidy or flashy clothing of any kind. Although a business suit may be appropriate for certain jobs, a person who is applying for an outdoor position should probably interview in clean, neatly pressed dress slacks and a golf shirt or a skirt and blouse.

The best way to prepare for the interview is to practice. Have a friend or relative play the role of the interviewer, and go over some of the most commonly asked questions. Learn as much as you can about the company you're interviewing with—it pays to do your homework. When you show a potential employer that you've taken the time and initiative to learn about his or her company, you're showing that you will be a motivated and hard-working employee. Employers fear laziness and minimal effort, looking instead for workers who don't always have to be told what to do and when to do it.

Here is a list of interview questions you can expect to have to answer:

- Tell me a little bit about yourself.
- What qualifications do you have?
- Why do you want to work for us?
- Tell me about your current (or last) job.
- Why are you leaving that job?
- What did you like most about that job?
- What would you change about that job?
- Do you enjoy school? Why or why not?
- Do you plan to continue your education?
- What do you plan to be doing for work five years from today?
- What is your greatest strength?
- What is your greatest weakness?
- What motivates you to do a good job?
- Are you at your best when working alone or in a group?
- What are your goals?
- Do you have any questions for me?

Take the time to prepare some answers to these commonly asked questions. For instance, if you haven't set at least

one goal for yourself, do it now. Be ready to describe it to the interviewer. Likewise, you should be able to talk about your last job, including what you liked the most and the least. Adapt your answers so they apply to the job for which you are presently interviewing.

If you are seeking a job as a manager, you might respond by saying you

(Continued on page 145)

WHAT WILL OUR OFF

BY DANIEL EISENBERG

As technology becomes part of the furniture, cramped cubicles will give way to flexible work spaces that adapt to your job—or mood

WHAT IN THE HELL WAS BOB PROPST thinking? It's a reasonable question to ask as you survey the cramped confines of your standard-issue corporate cubicle and bathe in the dull glow of overhead fluorescent lights, all the while trying to ignore the sound of your colleagues' clipping their fingernails or blathering away on a speakerphone.

Propst is the guy who, three decades ago, dreamed up these modular boxes for furniture giant Herman Miller. As he envisioned it, the system of wafer-thin, movable walls would be a revolutionary tool that would break down rigid hierarchies, spur creativity and free work spaces from the shackles of uniformity. Unfortunately, he didn't count on the square-foot police. Those FORTUNE 500 facility managers arrested his innovation and reformed it into an impersonal, white-collar assembly line, one that can make a genuine gear-head long for the good, old days of windowless offices and rotary phones.

With that record of innovation, workers are a bit skeptical about the office of the future. What will the geniuses in real estate come up with in the next quarter-century? If current trends are any indication, hide. Consider "hoteling," the latest workplace experiment, which treats employees as though they were visiting nomads who are assigned a phone and portable desk by a concierge. Or perhaps the "head cubicle," as imagined by Dilbert creator Scott Adams, a square helmet that will let CEOs "stack us up like firewood in a warehouse on the outskirts of town, where rents are low."

Millions of telecommuters, of course, don't intend to wait for such an outcome. They have already set up quarters wherever they set down their laptops. "Today's office is an aging concept, 150 years old, that people have been hanging on to," argues Stevan Alburty, who runs WorkVirtual, an office-consulting shop. It's only a matter of time, telecommuting true believers claim, before city skyscrapers and suburban office parks are abandoned altogether, left as archaeological curiosities for future generations.

Left inset, right and below courtesy of Haworth

Bounce Haworth's prototypes include the pogo stool, right, to keep you on your toes, and the Drift workstation and tricycle desk, above and below, meant to organize work better and let you roam free

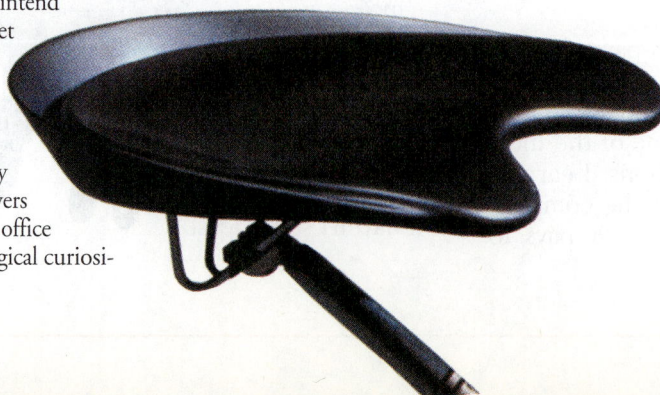

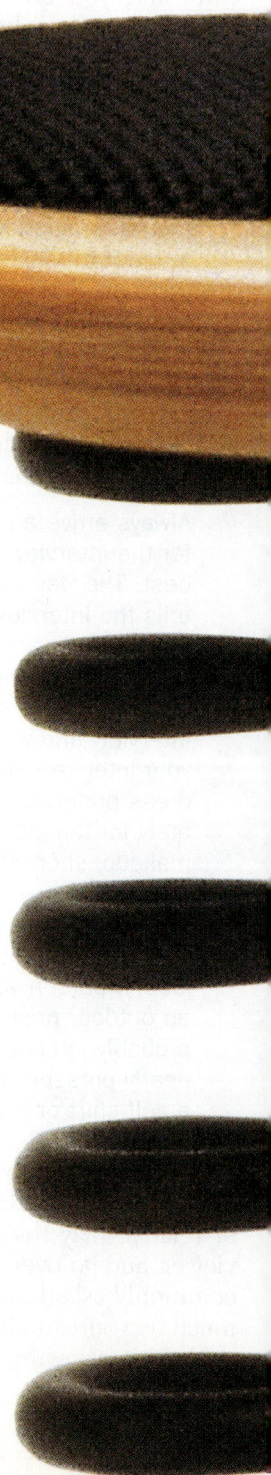

ICES **LOOK LIKE?**

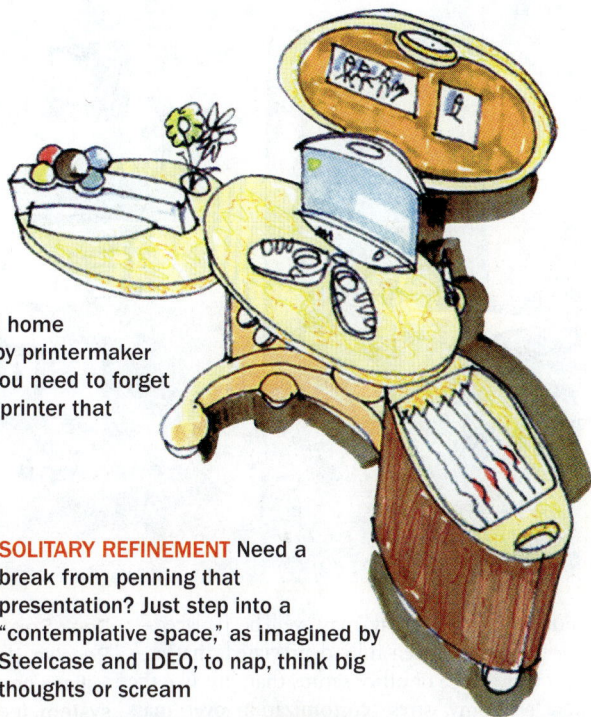

IN THE DEN The proposed home workstation, right, made by printermaker Lexmark, folds up when you need to forget about your job and has a printer that produces its own paper

SOLITARY REFINEMENT Need a break from penning that presentation? Just step into a "contemplative space," as imagined by Steelcase and IDEO, to nap, think big thoughts or scream

GROUP EFFORT When they need to collaborate, workers can flock to areas like Steelcase's "team space," above, to chat in the flesh or have a lifelike videoconference

Clockwise from bottom: Inset, Illustration by Rodger Eich, Haworth; middle and left-inset illustrations, design by Iain Thorp, IDEO; top right, illustration by Pete Mendel and Tom Pangburn, Lexmark International.

Well, don't start your dig just yet. PCs may be great for solitary pursuits, composing Powerpoint presentations or writing. But as long as co-workers need to brainstorm, bat around ideas and just plain gossip, they will always return to the water cooler, choosing a little face-to-face time over e-mail and the Web. Says Christine Albertini, vice president of advanced concepts at office-furniture maker Steelcase: "The basic nature of work is social."

Clueless corporations, which have typically approached the office as a storage site for people and paper, are only just starting to think outside the cubicle, imagining work spaces that foster interaction, not isolation. By 2025, though, the standard-issue, gloomy maze of hallways

Smith, manager of appliance platforms at H-P Labs. When you arrive at work, you could simply stroll through a secure, smart door and listen as your desktop virtual assistant reads aloud your schedule for the day. The temperature and lighting will adjust automatically to your preferences. Though we probably won't attain the mythical paperless office, there will likely be less of the messy stuff lying about, thanks to high-tech, rewritable parchment. And forget about typing: sophisticated voice recognition will let you tell your PC what to do (though all that yakking could just as easily make you hoarse).

The harsh right angles and rigid grid layout so despised by hapless cubicle-ites are also likely to vanish. In their place, workers might find themselves in a tentlike structure with a retractable roof, pitched right in the middle of a vast, open commons area. Screens stretching from poles could shift from transparent to opaque, depending on your mood and need for privacy. Don't worry about the noise from your next-door neighbor; acoustics technology can block that out. And don't fret about fighting for a windowed office either; with walls of flat-screen monitors raining down images and data from all directions, you will be able to enjoy any number of stunning virtual views from your cockpit. To chat with a co-worker a continent away, just call him or her on a lifelike, 3-D video-conferencing system. If you need to get busy on a project with a few of your colleagues, simply fold up your movable workstation and roll over to them. You won't have to knock. "We'll blur the line between furniture and technology," says Rick Duffy, director of the knowledge-resource group at Herman Miller. "Instead of building walls of metal and wood, what if they inflated with air or water?"

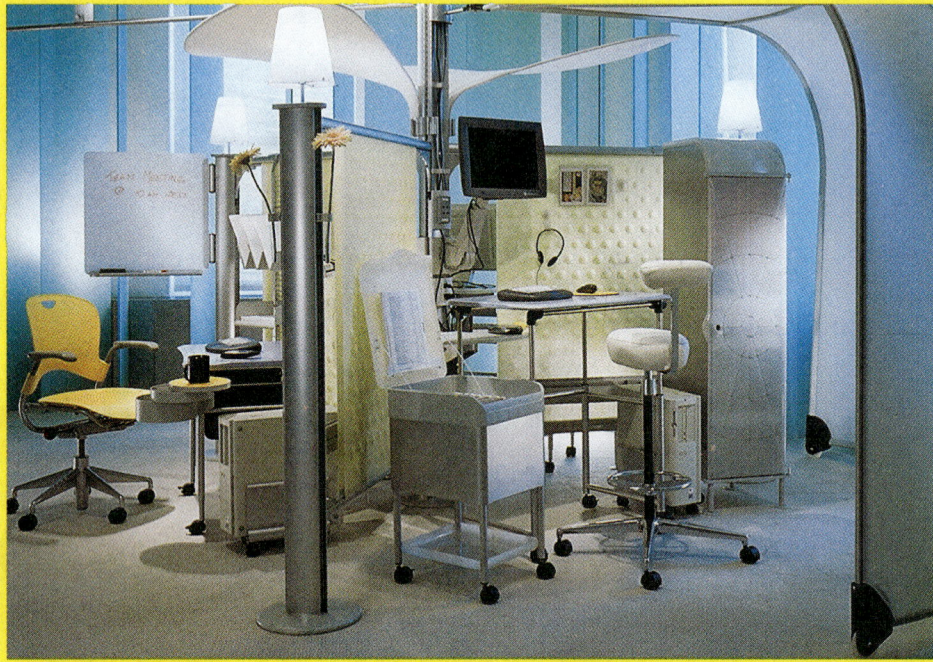

and bullpens of today may well be replaced—once they have been fully depreciated, that is—by a wide range of office setups that, just like the new economy, stress customization over mass appeal. In this newfangled, dynamic working environment, employees should be able to personalize their work spaces and constantly reconfigure their surroundings to suit the changing needs of business.

"Think of the buildings as stage sets, where you can play out any technological or organizational scheme," muses Volker Hartkopf, professor of architecture at Carnegie Mellon University.

So what might this workers' paradise look and feel like? Well, for starters, technology will be "invisible but unavoidable," as Bob Arko of industrial designer IDEO puts it. The tangled cables that snake through every office, for instance, should disappear, replaced by wireless systems that zap voice, data and video through the air. Smart materials could make any surface or gadget feel like wood one day and metal the next. Intelligent chairs might conform perfectly to your posture, giving you a much needed back rub in the process. Embedded systems and biometric, body-sensing technology will enable every piece of hardware, from cell phones and PDAs to PCs, to know exactly who you are and where, as well as to communicate with every other piece.

"You'll walk into the building like you own the place," says Mark

Don't Box Me In
Resolve, Herman Miller's new office system, features translucent screens that stick out from poles to form an open environment

We won't hold our breath for that one. Just as important as personal space, though, will be group space. Rather than a couple of conference rooms decked out with imposing mahogany tables, picture multiple areas for groups to convene and collaborate—from indoor gardens, playgrounds and cafés to what designers term contemplative caves. Even the lowly office kitchenette might be wired by 2025. Say you're having a spirited debate with a colleague about a pitch to a prospective client just as you're grabbing a cup of joe. By 2025, according to John Seely, director of Xerox's Palo Alto Research Center, you should be able to expand the conversation right there on digital whiteboards that line the walls and then have your ideas instantly e-mailed to your computer.

The boss, mind you, will probably be clued in to your little chat as well. Privacy, as we all know well, is rapidly eroding in the workplace, and the situation only stands to get worse. From reading employees' e-mail to tracking their Web surfing, more corporations are keeping a close eye on their human capital. In another quarter-century, we will probably be forced to carry badges that let our superiors know where we are at all times, from the bathroom to the vending machines. Then again, crafty folks who want to spend the day at the movies might just fashion counterfeit badges and have colleagues pass them around to throw security off the trail. "It could be the greatest boon to goofing off ever," says Adams. After all, as Bob Propst learned when he tried to build the flexible office more than 30 years ago, workplace innovations don't always work out as planned. ∎

liked the varied responsibilities of your past job. Recall that you enjoyed the unexpected challenges and flexible schedule. And when describing what you liked least, make sure you respond with some function or area of responsibility that has nothing to do with the responsibilities of the job you hope to get.

More than likely, the first question you'll be asked is to tell the interviewer something about yourself. This is your chance to "toot your horn," but don't ramble. You might ask the interviewer specifically what he or she would like to hear about: your educational background or recent experiences and responsibilities in your present or last job. After he or she chooses, stick to the basics; the next move belongs to the interviewer.

When asked about personal strengths and weaknesses, given that the question is two parts, begin with a weakness so you can end on a strong note with your strengths. Again, try to connect your description of a strength or weakness with the requirements for the job. Naturally, it wouldn't be wise to reveal a serious weakness about yourself, but you can mention how you have changed your shortcomings. You might say, "I like to get my work done fast, but I consciously try to slow down a little to make sure I'm careful and accurate." When it comes to strengths, don't exaggerate, but don't sell yourself short.

Asking Questions

You can ask questions, too. In fact, the interviewer expects you to ask questions to determine if the job is right for you, just as he or she will be trying to find out if you'll be successful working for his or her company. When you ask questions, it shows that you're interested and want to learn more. When the type of question you ask indicates that you've done your homework regarding the job and the company, your interviewer will be impressed. Avoid asking questions about salary or fringe benefits, anything adversarial, or questions that

SAMPLE THANK-YOU LETTER

AFTER YOU'VE INTERVIEWED FOR A JOB, IT'S IMPORTANT TO REITERATE YOUR INTEREST IN THE POSITION BY SENDING A THANK-YOU LETTER TO THOSE WHO INTERVIEWED YOU. TAKE A LOOK AT MICHELE'S LETTER TO THE MANAGER SHE INTERVIEWED WITH AT NEXAIR. YOU CAN USE THIS LETTER AS A MODEL WHEN THE TIME COMES FOR YOU TO WRITE SOME THANK-YOU LETTERS.

July 17, 2001

Michele A. Thomas
3467 Main Street
Atlanta, Georgia 30308
E-mail: mthomas_987654321@yahoo.com
Phone: 404-555-6721

Mr. Charles E. Pence
Manager, Human Resources
NexAir Wireless
20201 East Sixth Street
Atlanta, Georgia 30372

Dear Mr. Pence:

It was a pleasure meeting with you Monday to discuss the sales opportunity at NexAir's downtown location. After learning more about the position, it is clear to me that with my background and enthusiasm, I would be an asset to your organization.

As we discussed, my experiences as a cashier at Winn-Dixie Supermarket and as a sales clerk at The Limited have provided me with the basic skills necessary to perform the responsibilities required of a sales representative at NexAir. I believe that with my ability to learn quickly and communicate effectively, I can help NexAir increase sales of its wireless products.

Thank you for the opportunity to interview with your organization. If there is any additional information I can provide about myself, please do not hesitate to call me. I look forward to hearing your decision soon.

Sincerely,

Michele A. Thomas

show you have a negative opinion of the company. It's all right to list your questions on a piece of paper; it's the quality of the question that's important, not whether you can remember it.

Following Up

After the interview, follow up with a thank-you note to the interviewer. Not only is it a thoughtful gesture, it triggers the interviewer's memory about you and shows that you have a genuine interest in the job. Your thank-you note should be written in a business letter format and should highlight the key points in your interview. The sample thank-you note above can help.

During the interview process, remember that you will not appeal to everyone who interviews you. If your first experience doesn't work out, don't get discouraged. Keep trying.

What Employers Expect from Employees

As part of the National City Bank personnel team in Columbus, Ohio, Rose Graham works with Co-operative Business Education (CBE) coordinators in the area who are trying to place high school students in the workplace. When asked what skills she looks for in potential employees, she quickly replies that basic communication skills are at the top of her list. She stresses, "The ability to construct a sentence and put together words cannot be overemphasized." She cites knowledge of the personal computer, with good keyboarding skills, as essential.

In an article published in the *Nashville Business Journal*, Donna Cobble of Staffing Solutions outlined these basic skills for everyday life in the workplace:

Communication: Being a good communicator not only means having the ability to express oneself properly in the English language, it also means being a good listener. If you feel inferior in any of these areas, it's a good idea to sign up for a public speaking class, read books on the subject, and borrow techniques from professional speakers.

Organization: Organization is the key to success in any occupation or facet of life. The ability to plan, prioritize, and complete a task in a timely fashion is a valuable skill. Check out the next section for tips on improving your time-management skills.

Problem solving: Companies are looking for creative problem solvers, people who aren't afraid to act on a situation and follow through with their decision. Experience and practice play a major role in your ability to determine the best solution. You can learn these techniques by talking with others about how they solve problems as well as observing others in the problem-solving process.

Sensitivity: In addition to being kind and courteous to their fellow workers, employees need to be sensitive to a coworker's perspective. That might mean putting yourself in the other person's shoes to gain a better understanding of that person's feelings. Employers look for individuals who are able to work on a team instead of those concerned only with their own personal gain.

Judgment: Although closely related to problem solving, good judgment shows up on many different levels in the workplace. It is the ability of a person to assess a situation, weigh the options, consider the risks, and make the necessary decision. Good judgment is built on experience and self-confidence.

Concentration: Concentration is the ability to focus on one thing at a time. Learning to tune out distractions and relate solely to the task at hand is a valuable asset for anyone.

Cooperation: Remember that you're being paid to do a job, so cooperate.

Honesty: Dishonesty shows up in many different ways, ranging from stealing time or property to divulging company secrets. Stay honest.

Initiative: Don't always wait to be told exactly what to do. Show some initiative and look around to see what needs to be done next.

Willingness to learn: Be willing to learn how things are done at the company instead of doing things the way you want to do them.

Dependability: Arrive at work on time every day, and meet your deadlines.

Enthusiasm: Although not every task you're assigned will be stimulating, continue to show enthusiasm for your work at all times.

Acceptance of criticism: Corrective criticism is necessary for any employee to learn how things should be done. Employees who view criticism as a way to improve themselves will benefit from it.

Loyalty: There is no place for negativity in the workplace. You simply won't be happy working for an employer to whom you're not loyal.

Never fail to show pride in your work, the place where you work, and your appearance. By making these traits a part of your personality and daily performance, you will demonstrate that you are a cut above other employees with equal or better qualifications.

Jumping on the Salary Fast-Track

So the job offer comes, and it's time to talk about money. Unless you are

an undiscovered genius, you most likely will start near the bottom of the salary scale if you're heading straight to the workplace after graduating from high school. There's not much room to negotiate a salary since you probably won't be able to say, "Well, I've done this, this, and this. I know what my experience is worth." You will find that most people hiring first-time employees will have a "take-it-or-leave-it" attitude about salary offers. However, according to Amryl Ward, a human resources consultant who has been hiring employees for twenty-five years in various human resource positions, there are some things that entry-level employees can do to make themselves more easily hired and, once hired, to get themselves on the fast-track toward more pay.

1 As you interview for the job, be prepared to tell a potential employer why you're worth hiring. "Bring your skills to the table," says Ward. For instance, you might not think that the job you had during the summer at that big office supply store did anything more than earn you spending money. On the contrary, you learned valuable skills, such as how to be part of a team and how to deal with customers. What about that after-school office job you had? You learned how to answer the phones and how to work with certain software. Think carefully about the jobs you had in high school and what you learned from them. Those are called transferable skills.

2 Once you're hired, be willing to do more than just what the job requires. Sure, you may be frying fries at the start. But if you come in early and stay late, if you pitch in to help another employee with his or her job, or if you voluntarily clean up the counters and sweep the floor, that says to management, "This employee is a winner. Let's keep him or her in mind the next time a promotion comes up." Soon, you might be managing a crew, then the store.

ON THE JOB

Once you snag that perfect job, there's no time to rest easy. You need to keep your manager happy and

instill trust in your coworkers. And at the same time you're doing this, you'll want to watch out for yourself, keep yourself happy, and stay ahead of the learning curve. Here are some ways for you to do just that.

Minding Your Office Etiquette

Okay, so maybe you didn't know which was the salad fork at your cousin Sally's wedding reception. Most likely, though, you can name a few basic rules of etiquette, like not chewing with your mouth open at the dinner table. Now, what about when it comes to the manners you're supposed to have in the workplace? That usually draws a blank if you've never worked in an office setting. How would you know what's the right way to answer the phone or talk to your boss or customers?

Shannon McBride, the Program Director at the Golden Crescent Tech Prep School to Career Partnership in Victoria, Texas, has seen many students come through his program and land good jobs. He's also seen many of them succeed because they knew how to present themselves in a professional situation. Unfortunately, he can also relate stories of high school graduates who had no clue how to act in the workplace. They didn't realize that when they're working in an office with a group of people, they have to go out of their way to get along and follow the unwritten rules of that workplace. They didn't realize that the office is not the place to make personal statements about their individuality in how they dress or in how they conduct themselves that conflict with the environment.

McBride says that means you'll

have to size up how others are dressing and match what the office is geared to. For instance, if you work in a business office, most likely you'd wear slacks and a button-down shirt or a nice skirt and top. If you worked in a golf pro shop, you'd wear a golf shirt and shorts. "As much as you want to be an individual," says McBride, "you have to fit in when you're in a business setting. If you want an adult job, you have to act like an adult."

A lot of young people don't grasp how important office etiquette is and blow it off as just some silly rules imposed by adults. But McBride cautions that not following the norms of office etiquette can make or break a job. You can have all the technical talent and know all the latest software applications, but if you're not up on how people dress, talk, and conduct business, your job probably won't last very long. When it comes to getting a job, McBride warns, "First impressions are so important. Bad office etiquette can hurt that first impression." The best advice that we can give is that if you're not sure what the policy is about answering phones, using e-mail or the Internet on the job, or dress codes, you should ask your boss. He or she won't steer you wrong and will be pleased that you were concerned enough to ask.

Finding a Friendly Face at Work

There you are on the first day of a new job. Everyone looks like they know what they're doing while you stand there feeling really dumb. Even for the most seasoned employee, those first few weeks on the job are tough. Of course, everyone else looks like they know what they're doing because they've been doing it for quite some time. Wouldn't it be nice, though, if you had someone to help you adjust? Someone who would give you those little inside tips everyone else learns with experience. Someone to caution you about things that could go wrong or to give you a heads-up when you're doing something that could lead to a reprimand. If you look around the office, you'll find such a person, says Robert Fait, Career Counselor and Instructional Specialist, who is associated with Career and Technology Education in the Katy Independent School district in Katy, Texas.

You might not realize that such a person is a mentor, but in the strict definition of the word, that's what he or she is. Or, as Fait puts it, "Mentors are role models who are willing to assist others with personal education and career goal setting and planning. This caring person shares a listening ear, a comforting shoulder, and an understanding heart." In other words, a mentor is someone who will make you feel comfortable in a new working environment, show you the procedures, and, in the end, help you become more productive.

Unless the company you're working for has a formal mentoring program, mentors don't come with huge signs around their necks that read, "Look here. I'm a mentor. Ask me anything." You have to look for them. Fait advises new employees to look closely at their coworkers and take notice of who demonstrates positive behavior, has strong work habits, and seems trustworthy. Those are the people to approach. "Such workers are usually willing to share their knowledge and insights with others," says Fait.

Who knows? Given some time, you could become a mentor yourself after you've been on the job for a while. Maybe you'll be able to help some new employee who looks kind of bewildered and in need of a friendly hand because you'll remember what it was like to be the new person.

MOVING OUT ON YOUR OWN?

As you consider moving away from home either to a college dorm or your own place, some pretty wonderful expectations of what it will be like no doubt will come floating into your head. No more parental rules. On your own. Making your own decisions. Hamburgers forever. Coming and going when you want to. Oops, what's this? Looks like you're out of clothes to wear. No more cereal bowls—they're all in the sink, and they're dirty. Out of milk and the refrigerator's empty. Yikes! What happened to all those warm, fuzzy thoughts about freedom?

Sure, it's nice to be able to come and go as you please, but before you get too far into that pleasant—and unrealistic—mind mode, here are some thoughts you might want to consider as you make plans to become independent. Ozzie Hashley, a guidance counselor at Clinton Community Schools in Clinton, Michigan, works with juniors and seniors in high school. Here is what he says to inform students about the realities of independent life.

1 If you rent your own place, have you thought about the extra charges in addition to the rent? Says Hashley, "Many students think only of paying the rent. They don't realize that they'll be responsible for utilities in many cases. Or the money it will take to wash and dry your clothes."

2 Subsisting on hamburgers and fries sounds yummy, but as you watch a fast food diet eat its way into your paycheck, you'll most likely think about cooking up something yourself. What will you cook? Who will buy the food? More importantly, who will do the dishes? Dividing up the responsibilities of preparing food is a big aspect of being on your own, especially when sharing a living space.

3 Medical insurance may not be on your mind as you prepare to graduate—you're probably on your parent's insurance plans right now. However, once you are established as an independent person at age 18 and you're living on your own, insurance becomes a big consideration. If you need health care and don't have medical insurance, the bills will be big. So when you get a job, make sure that you have medical coverage. If you're going off to college after high school, you'll most likely be covered under your parent's insurance until age 23.

4 There's no one to tell you when to come home when you're on your own. There's also no one to tell you that you're really disorganized when it comes to managing your time. Time management might not sound like a big deal now, but when you have to juggle all the facets of being independent—your job, taking care of your living space and car, your social life—then being able to manage time becomes an important part of life. The last section of this publication can help you with this skill.

5 Managing your money moves into a whole other realm when you are on your own. You have to make sure you have enough to pay the rent, your car loan, and insurance, not to mention that movie you wanted to see, the CD you wanted to buy, or those funky jeans you saw at the mall last week. If you want to eat at the end of the month, budgeting will become an important part of your new independent vocabulary. Ask your parents or an adult you trust to help you set up your budget. ∎

12 SURVIVAL SKILLS

Whether you're headed to college or work, you're going to come face to face with some intimidating stuff after graduation.

Your level of stress will most likely increase due to the demands of your classes or job and to your exposure to alcohol or drugs; various forms of conflict will rise, and you're going to have to keep up with your own health and nutrition. Seem daunting? It's really not if you keep a level head about you and stick to your core values. This section will help you work through the muddier side of life after high school.

SKILLS TO MAKE YOU STRESS-HARDY

Jump out of bed and into the shower. What to wear? Throw that on. Yuck—what's that stain? "Mom, where are my clean socks?" Tick, tock. No time to grab a bite if you want to make the homeroom bell. Skid around the corner and race for the classroom just as the final bell rings. Whoops, forgot your bio book. Sports, clubs, job, homework, friends on the phone, and finally (sigh) sleep.

Sound like your life? If you're like most high school students, that description probably hits pretty close to home. So now we'll take your already hectic schedule and throw in the fact that you'll soon be graduating and have to figure out what to do with your life. Can you say "stress"?

Some people say that stress actually motivates them to perform better, but we won't talk about those perfect people. For most of you, stress means that you may snap at the dog, slam a few doors, get mad at your mom, and feel down. Maybe you'll even have physical symptoms—stomach disturbances, rapid heartbeat, sweaty palms, dizziness. The list goes on. Not a good place to be when you're dealing with a huge list of things to do, plus graduation is staring you in the face.

How to handle stress has been written about countless times, but out of all the advice that's out there, a few simple pointers can really help you prevent the sweaty palms and nauseated feeling in the pit of your stomach.

French fries out, good food in. Eat at least one hot, balanced meal a day. Healthy, as in veggies, fruits, meats, cheese, grains. Read further along in this section for more information about nutrition and health.

Sleep. Seven, eight, ten hours a day. Easier said than done, but well worth it. Sleep will not only get you through high school but also your college and career lives, and it will help you stop feeling like such a frazzled bunch of nerve endings.

Hug your dog, cat, rabbit, friend, or mom. Loneliness breeds stress because then all you've got is yourself and those stressed-out thoughts zooming around in your head.

Get with friends. That takes time, but being with people you like and doing fun things eases stress—as long as you don't overdo it.

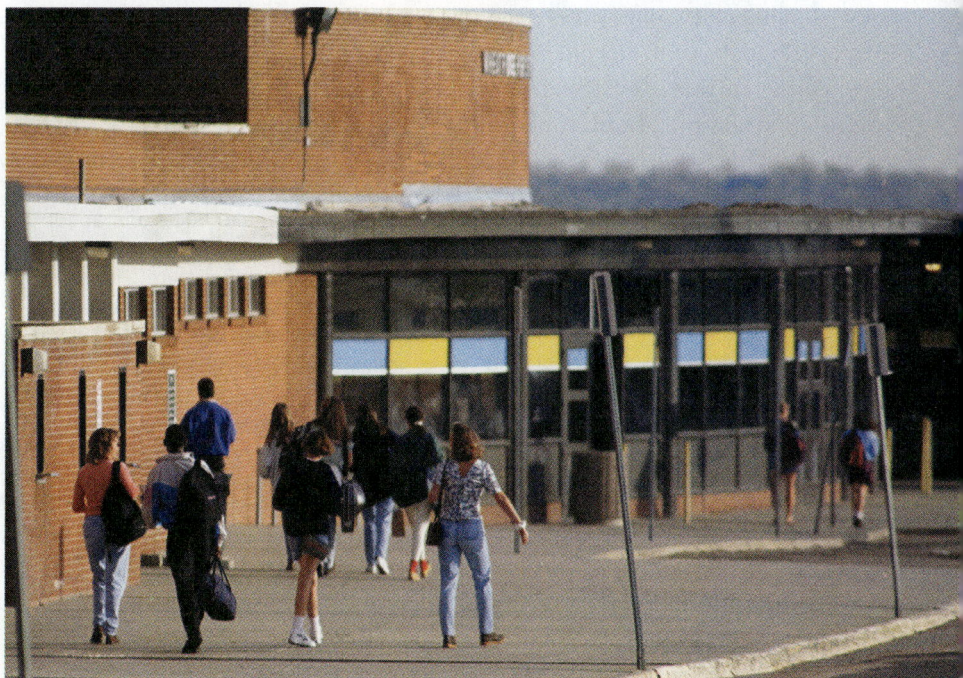

Exercise. This does not include running down the hall to make the bell. We're talking 20 minutes of heart-pounding perspiration at least three times a week. It's amazing what a little sweat can do to relax you. Believe it or not, good posture helps too.

Don't smoke, drink, or use excessive amounts of caffeine. Whoever told you that partying is the way to relieve stress got it all wrong. Nicotine and alcohol actually take away the things your body needs to fight stress.

Simplify your expenses. Money can be a big stress factor. Think of ways to eliminate where you're spending money so that the money you have doesn't have to be stretched so far. Be creative. Share resources. Sell items you no longer use. Maybe put off buying something you've been wanting.

Let your feelings out of your head. It takes time and energy to keep them bottled up inside. Have regular conversations with your parents and siblings so that minor annoyances can be solved when they're still small.

Organize your time. As in prioritizing and dealing with one small part of your life instead of trying to solve everything in one shot. Read on for more information about time management. This is just a teaser.

Lighten up. When you've graduated and are into whatever it is you'll end up doing, you'll look back and realize that this was a teensy little part of your life. So look on the bright side. The decisions you'll be making about your future are heavy, but they won't be cut in stone. You can change them if they don't work out.

Stress Busters

Most people get stressed when things are out of control—too many things to do, too many decisions to make, or too much information to digest. If you add not having enough time, enough money, or enough energy to get it all done, you have the perfect recipe for stress. Try these three stress busters on for size.

In the space below, identify what's causing you stress:

_____
_____
_____
_____

Then choose from these three options:

1 **Alter the situation.** Some things you can't control, some things you can. Change the ones you can. If you have too much on your plate and can't possibly do it all, push a few things aside. There's got to be something on the list you can get rid of. (And no, homework is not an acceptable answer.) Maybe you need to be able to say no to extra demands. Concentrate on what is important. Make a list of your priorities from the most important to the least, and work your way down.

2 **Avoid the situation—for now.** Step back and ask, "Is this really a problem? Do I really need to solve it now?" This doesn't mean you should procrastinate on things that need to get done. Think of this stress buster as buying some time, taking a break, catching your breath, getting advice, and airing out the situation so that you can deal with it when you're more prepared to handle it.

3 **Accept the situation.** How you perceive your circumstances has a lot to do with how you make decisions about them. Put whatever is stressing you in the perspective of the big picture. How will this really affect me next year or even ten years from now? Look at your circumstances through the lens of your personal values. Think about what feels right to you, not someone else.

Quick Fixes for Stressful Moments

So, you've done all the things we talked about earlier in this section, and you're still feeling like you're being pulled in a million directions. If your stress thermometer has hit the top, use these quick fixes to help calm you down.

- Make the world slow down for a bit. Take a walk. Take a shower. Listen to some soothing music.

- Breathe deeply. Get in tune with the rhythm of your own breathing. Lie or sit down for fifteen minutes and just concentrate on relaxing.

- Relax those little knots of tension. Start at your head and work down to your toes.

- Close your eyes and clear your mind. Oops, there comes that nagging thought. Out, out, out. Get rid of the clutter. Imagine yourself in your favorite place: the beach, under a tree, whatever works.

- Close the door to your bedroom, and let out a blood-curdling scream. Walt Whitman knew what he was talking about when he said, "I sound my barbaric yawp over the roofs of the world." Just let your family know what you're doing so they don't come running to your room in fear. You'll be amazed at how much better you feel.

- When all else fails, watch a funny movie. Read the comics. Get in a giggly frame of mind. Those big challenges will quickly be brought down to size.

WINNING THE TIME MANAGEMENT GAME

What is the value of time? Six dollars an hour? The price of a scholarship because the application is a day late? Time can be a very expensive resource or something you can use to your advantage. Even if you recognize the value of time, managing it is a challenge.

When you live with enough time, life is relaxed and balanced. In order to find that balance, you have to prioritize and plan. Decide what you want and what is important to you. Organize logically and schedule realistically. Overcome obstacles. Change bad habits. Simplify and streamline. Save time when you can. Sound impossible? It's not easy, but you can do it. The secret is held in a Chinese proverb: The wisdom of life is the elimination of nonessentials.

It's All about Control

The good thing about time is that much of it is yours to do with as you wish. You may feel out of control and as if you must run to keep up with the conflicting demands and expectations of your life. But we all have the same number of hours in each day. The key is in how we spend them. The following tips are designed to help you spend your time wisely and to keep you in control of your life.

Prepare a list of your goals and the tasks necessary to accomplish them. This could be by day, week, month, semester, or even year. You may also want to break the list into sections, such as friends and family, school, work, sports, health and fitness, home, personal development, and college preparation.

Prioritize based on time-sensitive deadlines. Use a grading system to code how important each task is. A is "Do It Now," B is "Do It Soon," C is "Do It Later." Understand the difference between "important" and "urgent."

Be realistic about how much you can really do. Analyze how you spend your time now. What can you cut? How much time do you truly have for each task?

Think ahead. How many times have you underestimated how long it will take to do something? Plan for roadblocks, and give yourself some breathing space.

Accept responsibility. Once you decide to do something, commit yourself to it. That doesn't mean that a task that was on the "A" list can't be moved to the "C" list. But be consistent and specific about what you want to accomplish.

Divide and conquer. You may need to form a committee, delegate tasks to your parents, or ask for help from a friend. That is why it is called time management.

Take advantage of your personal prime time. Don't schedule yourself to get up and do homework at 6 a.m. if you are a night owl. It won't work. Instead, plan complex tasks when you are most efficient.

Avoid procrastination. There are a million ways to procrastinate. And not one of them is a good reason if you really want to get something done. Have you ever noticed that you always find time to do the things you enjoy?

Do the most unpleasant task first. Get it over with. Then it will be all downhill from there.

Don't over-prepare. That is just another way to procrastinate.

Learn to say no to the demands on your time that you cannot afford.

Be enthusiastic, and share your goals with others.

If you set too many goals at once, you will overwhelm yourself from the start. Remember, what is important is the quality of the time you spend on a task, not the quantity. It doesn't make any difference if you study for 10 hours if you don't recall a thing you've reviewed. The overall goal is to be productive, efficient, and effective, not just busy. You'll also need to pace yourself. All work and no play makes for an unbalanced person.

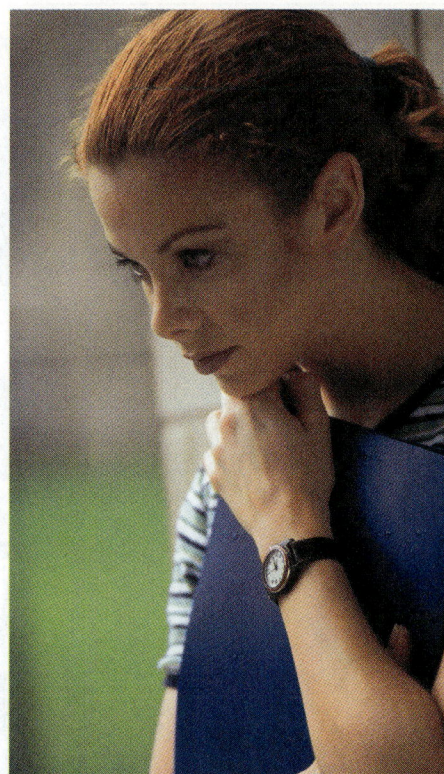

Use all the benefits of modern technology to help you manage time. You can save lots of time by using a fax, e-mail, or voice mail. If you don't already use a day planner or calendar, you would be wise to invest in one. Write in all the important deadlines, and refer to it often. Block out commitments you know you have so you won't over-schedule yourself. When you do over-schedule yourself or underestimate the time it takes to accomplish a task, learn from your mistakes. But don't get too down on yourself. Give yourself a pep talk every now and then to keep yourself positive and motivated.

DRUGS AND ALCOHOL: ARE YOU AT RISK?

At risk? Wait a minute. How could you be at risk when the legal drinking age in all fifty states is 21? Chances are, if you're reading this, you're not 21 yet. It's also illegal to smoke or buy any tobacco product before age 18, and possession of any drug for recre-

(Continued on page 154)

THE WASTED DAYS OF YOUTH

Five now-sober young adults talk about their teen experiences with alcohol

By AMANDA BOWER

TIME talked to five young adults about teen drinking. Their names have been changed to protect their identities. The accompanying photographs are of models.

Jenn, 23, San Francisco

Social worker, plans to go to law school next year

Sobriety date: April 24, 1994

"Around 10 or 11, I would come home from school, and in the couple of hours before my mom came home drink gin and cranberry juice. I managed to stay holed up in my room so that she didn't notice. At 13, I discovered social drinking, and found a whole new world. I didn't feel too fat. I didn't feel my hair wasn't right. My goal was always to be the most drunk person at the party.

By 14, I was running away from home. I would stay in downtown Portland with all the street kids. We'd go to clubs. Sometimes somebody had an apartment we could stay in. Sometimes we'd sleep in parks. Sometimes we wouldn't sleep at all. The summer before I turned 15, I left home for good and was on the streets for most of the summer. I would panhandle, sit somewhere downtown and ask people for money. My priority was alcohol first, cigarettes and food second. Pretty much from the time I got up to the time I went to sleep I was drunk, I was loaded in some way.

My mom was really scared. She didn't know what was going on. She didn't think I was drinking. On my 15th birthday I was picked up by the cops on runaway charges and was sent to live with my dad. I was pretty much loaded the entire time I lived there, and I realized later that my dad thought that me loaded was me sober. He didn't know me any different. Eventually I ended up in treatment, and was sober for almost a year. Then I took one sip of beer and my life fell apart instantly. Within 24 hours of that first drink I was in tears because I had to wait three more hours to have another drink. Any question I had about being an alcoholic went out the window. And I knew a better way of life. I knew what AA offered."

Alex, 20, New York City

Freelance graphic designer

Sobriety date: March 23, 1998

"When I was 12, my boss—he was 25—asked if I wanted to go drink with him. If he'd asked me to kill the mayor I would have said okay, because he was like a god to me. I went to see my friends afterward, and I was tall enough, I was good looking enough, I was smart enough, they were laughing with me, or at least I thought so, and all the attention was on me. All my insecurities vanished.

By the time I was 15, I always kept liquor in the sock drawer, and I was drinking alone. I didn't want to have to share. I didn't want to have to deal with other people. By the end of that year, I was drinking hard alcohol five or six days a week. I started to steal to pay for it, money, things to pawn. I never stole from my family. By the time I was 17, I dropped out of school. I had my own apartment. I'd wake up around noon, and drink bourbon and coffee, in that order. Then I'd go to work bussing

tables, finish at midnight, and go to a bar. Closing time was 2:30 a.m., so I'd go home to drink. If I didn't have anything at home, I'd stay at a coffee shop until it was time to catch a bus to the airport. The bars there opened at 7 a.m.

I didn't really have any friends, and my mother's ability to deny was pretty strong.

Then I got in a lot of trouble with the law for stealing, and was offered the option of treatment. It sounded a lot better than five to 10 years in the penitentiary. One night I went to an Oscars party and I knew that if I got caught drinking, I could go to jail.

Knowing that full well, I walked into the party—my friend offered me a martini, I said, 'Yeah,' and I got loaded. That night, having learned a little bit about alcoholism at treatment, I started to see the patterns inside myself. That was the last night I drank."

Kate, 21, moved to New York City earlier this year

Sales executive, planning on career in social work

Sobriety date: January 20, 1999

"The first night I drank, my friends had to carry me back to our sleepover. I ended up wetting the bed. I drank again the next weekend and blacked out for the first time. In senior year I started drinking three times a week. A friend's brother got us alcohol. Friends' parents had alcohol we snuck. And I was sold alcohol a few times, even when I was 13. Sexual things happened that I wouldn't have done in my right mind. I was with friends' boyfriends. I told people I didn't like them. I started lying more.

By end of senior year I was drinking every day. High school was nothing compared to what I did in college. I just stopped caring. I would wake up at 3 in the afternoon. I would have missed all my classes. I'd be in

this dark dorm room I didn't want to leave, because I was scared to hear what I'd done the night before. I didn't answer the phone. But I wrote in my journal that I was the happiest that I'd ever been, because I was partying. I was put on academic probation.

Eventually I called my sister and I said I think I have a problem. I went into treatment. I was 19 years old, and I remember crying to the counselor saying, 'You're telling me I'm never going to drink again? How? I'm going to get married one day, graduate from college, there's New Year's Eve, St. Patrick's Day, friends' birthdays.' My counselor looked at me and said, 'You can drink any time you want. Just not today.' It's that whole day at a time thing. I had to go back to college to get my stuff. I relapsed in 24 hours. I went home, started going to AA meetings. And continued to get drunk.

Then I got a service position [at AA] and all I could think about was how I had this service position, I can't mess up."

Tony, 24, Pacific Northwest

Graduate computer science student

Sobriety date: January 2, 1994

"I started drinking at the age of six. My family, we were on a road trip to visit relatives back east, and I just started to steal drinks from my relatives. I really can't tell you much more about my youth than that first day drinking. It was the middle of summer. It was June. It was a bright day. I can almost describe every detail. But I can't tell you anything from grade school. I drank pretty much any time that I could. I would steal wine from my parents, and by the time I was 10 or 11, I was drinking weekly, every other week, daily if I could. My parents quit buying wine, but I had older sisters who visited from college, and they would always bring me whatever they had left over. In high school, we either stole alcohol from the liquor store or we found people to buy it for us. Every alcoholic is resourceful.

I would end up at parties, tell my friends I loved them, and then minutes later start a fight. I was failing out of school, drinking every day, ditching classes. I stole a lot from my parents. I couldn't hold down jobs. I was big into either cutting myself or drinking a lot with aspirin or taking a lot of poisons. I managed to hide those suicide attempts from my parents. When I'd wake up in the morning, I couldn't look at myself in the mirror.

When my parents took me to the treatment center, everything broke down. I was bawling. I started out in an [AA] meeting where the average age was in the 40s. I didn't

want to relate to these people talking about losing their families, their jobs, their houses. I was 17. But when they started talking about trying to commit suicide, drinking on a daily basis, blacking out, I had to relate to those things. I still go to as many meetings as I did when I first got sober—around five a week."

Betty, 21, of New York City Student

Sobriety date: October 29, 2000

"My first drink was when I was 14. I went to my grandparents' house and filled the water bottle on my bike with bits of everything they had. My friend was supposed to come over, but he bailed on me. My mom was at her boyfriend's. I sat on the couch, alone, sipping, and thought I would feel something right away. I drank the whole thing and woke up in the hospital. Even after it almost killed me, I definitely wanted to have it again.

Soon I was coming home at 4 a.m., head in the toilet, without my car, but on paper I looked good so my mom could deny it. I was in the top 5% of my class, I was the editor in chief of the school paper, the student council secretary. I burned out my friends. I woke up one morning at college, with vomit on the floor, and a call from some guy who had my bag and would only give it back if I gave him $500. That's when I got the AA number. I wrote down the address, the time of a meeting, and didn't go. I started dating a drug dealer. That was the beginning of the end, and I realized I had to face up to my addiction. I was only a few months sober when I spent my 21st birthday in Ireland. They were having St. Patrick's Day celebrations, delayed because of foot and mouth disease. The first

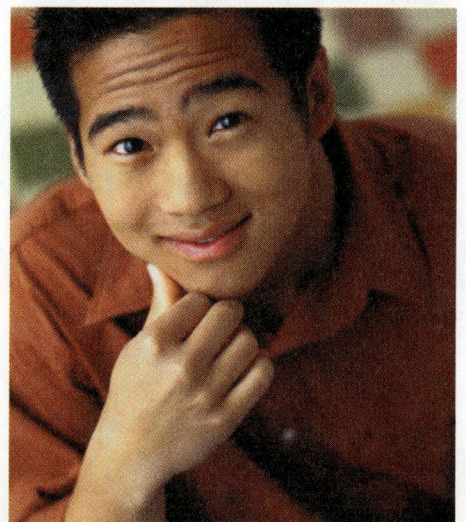

ational use is illegal, period. So if you drink alcohol before age 21; smoke or buy cigarettes, cigars, or chewing tobacco before age 18; or take any illegal drugs, you could:

- be arrested for driving under the influence (DUI)
- be convicted
- be required to pay steep fines
- have your driving privileges suspended
- get kicked out of school (that's any kind of school, college included)
- get fired
- go to jail
- have a criminal record

A criminal record. . . so what?

Consider this true story. A 29-year-old man who recently received his graduate degree in business was offered a job with a major Fortune-100 corporation. We're talking big bucks, stock options, reserved parking space—the whole nine yards. When the company did a background check and found that he was arrested for a DUI during his freshman year of college, they rescinded their offer. The past can and will come back to haunt you. Let's not even think about what would happen down the line if you decide to run for public office.

Think about why you might want to try drinking or doing drugs. For fun? To forget your troubles? To be cool? Are your reasons good enough? Remember the consequences before you make a decision.

DID YOU KNOW...

... that nicotine is as addictive as cocaine and heroin, according to the American Cancer Society?
... that drinking a lot of alcohol fast can kill you on the spot, according to Keystone College?
... that MDMA (Ecstasy, X, Adam, Clarity, Lover's Speed), according to NIDA, may permanently damage your memory?

DO I HAVE A PROBLEM?

TAKE THE QUIZ BELOW TO SEE IF YOU'RE IN REAL TROUBLE WITH DRUGS OR ALCOHOL.

1. Do you look forward to drinking or using drugs?
2. Do most of your friends drink or do drugs?
3. Do you keep a secret supply of alcohol or drugs?
4. Can you drink a lot without appearing drunk?
5. Do you "power-hit" to get high faster, by binge-drinking, funneling, or slamming?
6. Do you ever drink or do drugs alone, including in a group where no one else is doing so?
7. Do you ever drink or use drugs when you hadn't planned to?
8. Do you ever have blackouts where you can't remember things that happened when you were drunk or high?

If you answered yes to any of these questions, you probably need help. If you have a friend who fits the picture, find a respectful way to bring up your concerns. Don't be surprised if he or she tells you to back off—but don't give up, either. If someone in your family has an alcohol or drug problem, be aware that you may be prone to the same tendency.

Source: Keystone College, La Plume, Pennsylvania

How Can I Say No without Looking like a Geek?

"It takes a lot more guts to stay sober, awake, and aware than to just get high, get numb, and learn nothing about life," says one former user. "Laugh at people who suggest you drink or take drugs, and then avoid them like the plague."

Friends worth having will respect your decision to say no. And girls—if a guy pressures you to drink or get high, ditch him pronto. You can vice-versa that for guys, too. According to the National Institute on Drug Abuse (NIDA), alcohol and club drugs like GHB or Rohypnol® (roofies) make you an easy target for date rape.

The Nitty Gritty

Along with the temporary pleasure they may give you, all drugs (including club drugs, alcohol, and nicotine) have a downside. Alcohol, for example, is a depressant. Even one drink slows down the part of your brain that controls your reasoning. So your judgment gets dull just when you're wondering, "Should I drive my friends home? Should I talk to this guy? Should I have another drink?"

Your body needs about an hour to burn up the alcohol in one drink. Nothing, including coffee, will sober you up any faster. Here's what "one drink" means: one shot of hard liquor (straight or mixed in a cocktail), one glass of wine, one 12-ounce beer, or one wine cooler.

Alcohol helps smart people make bad decisions. In fact, many drugs make you believe that you're thinking even more clearly than usual. Well, guess what? You aren't. Depending on what drug you take, how much, and what you do while you're on it, you're also risking confusion, nausea, headache, sleep problems, depression, paranoia, rape (especially "date rape"), unwanted pregnancy, sexually transmitted diseases (STDs) ranging from herpes to HIV/AIDS, having a baby with a birth defect, memory impairment, persistent psychosis, lung damage, cancer, injuring or killing someone else, and death.

Take a moment now, when your brain is razor sharp, to decide if those consequences are worth the escape you get for 20 minutes one night. You may be saying, "Oh, come on. Only addicts have problems like that." Getting drunk or high doesn't necessarily mean that you're an alcoholic or an addict—but it always means a loss of control.

"So much of addiction is about denial," says one member of Alcoholics Anonymous. "I just didn't think I looked or acted or thought or smelled or lied or cheated or failed like an alcoholic or addict. It was when the drugs and alcohol use started to cause problems in multiple areas of my life that I began to think the problem might reside with me.

Friends leaving—in disgust—was what opened my eyes."

Where Can I Get Help?

If you think you have a problem, or if you think a friend has a problem, try Alcoholics Anonymous or Narcotics Anonymous. If you're not sure, ask yourself the questions in "Do I Have a Problem" on the previous page.

Talk to any adult you trust: maybe your doctor, a clergy member, a counselor, or your parents. Health clinics and hospitals offer information and treatment. The American Cancer Society can help you quit smoking. These are only a few places to turn—check out the Yellow Pages and the Web for more.

Alcoholics Anonymous
212-870-3400
www.aa.org

American Cancer Society
800-ACS-2345
www.cancer.org

Narcotics Anonymous
818-773-9999
www.na.org

So, that's the straight stuff. You're at a tough but wonderful age, when your life is finally your own and your decisions really matter. Think about what you value most—and then make your choices.

CONFLICT: HOW TO AVOID IT AND DEFUSE IT

You're walking along and you see a group of kids up ahead . . . and suddenly you're afraid. Or you're about to talk to someone you have a disagreement with, and already you're tense. Or your boyfriend's jealousy is spooking you. What should you do?

All of these situations involve potential conflicts that could get out of hand. Even if you never get into a violent situation, you'll face conflicts with others, as we all do. Learning to spot the warning signs of violence and to handle conflicts well will bring you lifelong benefits.

What's Your Style?

What do you do when you're faced with a potential conflict? Do you try to get away, no matter what? Do you find yourself bowing to pressure from others? Do you feel like you have to stand and fight, even if you don't want to? Do you wish you had some new ways to handle conflict?

Different situations call for different strategies. First, let's talk about situations where violence is a real possibility. Most of us get a bad feeling before things get violent, but too often, we ignore the feeling. Trust your gut feeling! And whether you're on the street or in school, Fred Barfoot of the Crime Prevention Association of Philadelphia suggests that you keep in mind these tips for avoiding violence:

- Walk like you're in charge and you know where you're going.

- Stick to lighted areas.

- Travel with a trusted friend when possible. On campus, get an escort from security at night. Loners are targets.

- If a person or group up ahead makes you nervous, cross the street immediately—and calmly—as if you'd intended to anyway.

- Call out to an imaginary friend, "Hey, Joe! Wait up!" and then run toward your "friend," away from whoever is scaring you.

- Go right up to the nearest house and ring the bell. Pretend you're expected: "Hey Joe, it's me!" You can explain later.

- If someone threatens you physically, scream.

- If someone assaults you, scream, kick where it hurts, scratch—anything.

- Don't ever get in a car with someone you don't know well or trust, even if you've seen that person around a lot.

- Strike up a conversation with an innocent bystander if you feel threatened by someone else, just to make yourself less vulnerable for a few minutes.

- Wear a whistle around your neck or carry a personal alarm or pepper spray.

- If someone mugs you, hand over your purse, wallet, jewelry—whatever he or she asks for. None of it is worth your life.

- Don't go along with something your gut says is wrong, no matter who says it's okay.

Remember that it's not a sign of weakness to back down if someone's egging you on to fight. Bill Tomasco, principal of Furness High School in Philadelphia, says that pressure from other kids to fight creates much of the violence in schools. If you're being pushed to fight, show true strength: Know that your opponent has a good side too, speak only to that good side, and don't give in to the pressure of the crowd.

Are You Safe at Home?

Locking doors and windows makes sense—but sometimes the danger lies within. A lot of violence occurs in abusive relationships, says Amy Gottlieb, a marriage family therapist intern at the California Family Counseling Center in Encino. To find out if you're at risk, ask yourself whether your partner, roommate, or family member:

- uses jealousy to justify controlling you

- puts you down, humiliates you, or pulls guilt trips on you

- threatens to reveal your secrets or tells lies about you

- makes all the decisions

- frightens you, especially if it's on purpose

- threatens you in any way

- uses force, drugs, or drink to get you to have sex

makes light of abusive behavior or says you provoked it.

If any of these things are going on in your relationship, talk about it to an adult you trust, and ask for help.

Talking It Out

If your instincts tell you to get away from a situation, do it. But you can resolve many actual or potential conflicts face to face and gracefully so that everyone walks away feeling good. Read on for some tips on handling conflict from Kare Anderson, a communications expert in Sausalito, California.

Most of us make the mistake of reacting quickly, thinking only of our own needs, and not listening, says Anderson. Try doing the opposite. First and foremost, think about what you really want from the situation, and keep your goal in mind the whole time. But bring up the other person's concerns first. Then, discuss how the situation affects you both. Offer a solution that will benefit you both—and only then talk about how your solution addresses your own needs.

When the other person is talking, really listen—don't just come up with retorts in your head. Always show that you've heard the person before you give your response, especially if you're talking with someone of a different sex, size, or race. Those differences can distract us so much that we actually hear less. If you're female, you may need to s-l-o-w yourself down. Say less than you think you need to. Guys, don't shut down altogether—keep the communication going.

Even if the other person acts like a jerk, be gracious and respectful. Ask questions instead of criticizing. Let someone save face instead of looking like a fool. If you insult or embarrass someone, you may never have that person's full attention again. In short, treat the other person as you'd like to be treated.

What should you do if you're really angry? One teen said, "Thinking about things calms me down." Another said, "Once in a while, we have to cool off for a day and then come back to the discussion." Anger almost always covers up fear. What are you afraid of? Is the reward you want out of this negotiation bigger than your fear? Focus on that reward. Don't forget to breathe—long, slow breaths.

Think about these strategies often, so you'll be more likely to use them when a situation gets hot, instead of just reacting blindly. Use them to plan for negotiations ahead of time, too. Learning to resolve problems with people takes most of us a lifetime—get a jump on it now!

THE LOWDOWN ON SEXUAL HARASSMENT

Has someone ever looked at you, talked to you, or touched you in a way that gave you the creeps, made you self-conscious about your body, or created a sexual mood when it wasn't appropriate? And did you begin to dread seeing this person because he or she just wouldn't quit?

If so, you've encountered sexual harassment. Sexual harassment is inappropriate behavior that

- is happening to you because of your sex
- is unwanted (you don't like it)
- is objectively offensive (to a hypothetical "reasonable" man or woman)
- is either severe, persistent, or pervasive
- interferes with your work or school experience.

Paul Edison, a domestic and sexual violence prevention educator in Portland, Oregon, says that mostly—just as with crimes like rape—men harass women. But teenage girls are a bit more likely than older women to sexually harass someone, more girl-on-girl harassment goes on with teens, and guys get harassed, too. In some of the most brutal cases coming to light now, gay men (or men perceived to be gay) are the targets.

People who sexually harass others fall into three camps, says Edison. Some just seem to be misguided and insensitive. Others get turned on by harassing someone. And a third group does it to intimidate—for example, to drive someone away from a job or just to make them feel bad about themselves.

So What Do I Do if Someone's Harassing Me?

Experts in self-defense say the best technique is to name the behavior that's bugging you and request that it stop. You might say, "Your hand is on my knee. Please remove it." If the person doesn't quit, you might try writing a letter spelling out what's bothering you and requesting that the person stop—this way, you've confronted the situation directly and you also have a record of your complaint.

But here's the good news, says Edison: You are not expected to handle harassment on your own, especially if the person harassing you is in a position of authority over you, such as a teacher, sergeant, or boss. The authorities at your school or your job should handle it—but they can't do that unless you tell them what's going on.

If you file a complaint, be prepared to describe what happened, when, and where. And make sure you report your concerns to someone who has clear authority to handle sexual harassment complaints, such as the principal or the personnel director.

Often, the person harassing you will stop as soon as he or she gets the clear message that the behavior isn't okay with you, especially if your complaint goes to someone higher up as well. Edison notes that most harassment cases don't end up involving lawyers and lawsuits. You may choose, in serious cases, to register your complaint with the Office of Civil Rights (if you're being harassed at school) or the Equal Employment Opportunity Commission (if you're being harassed at work). You can also file your complaint on different levels at the same about whom and how you touch. You may be comfortable touching people casually—perhaps you'll touch someone's hand or shoulder in conversation—but remember that other people's boundaries may differ from yours.

Pay attention to the person's reactions to you. Are you getting clear green signals when you do or say things around this person, or does the person seem to shrink away from you? Does the person shut down or seem upset when you do or say certain things? Of course, if someone's told you clearly that she or he doesn't like it when you do or say certain things, apologize and stop at once. And remember, no means no.

So, if you're faced with something that feels like sexual harassment, remember to trust your feelings, convey them clearly, and get help promptly if you need it.

STAYING HEALTHY IN SPITE OF YOURSELF

When someone—like your mom—asks if you're eating right, do you ever want to say, "Hey, have you looked at my life lately? Do you see a lot of time there for eating right?" Well, how about exercise—are you getting enough? "Yeah, right. I bench-press my backpack when I'm not doing wind sprints to my next class," may be how you reply.

If you're feeling like you can't escape your stress and fatigue, you might be surprised by how much better you'll feel if you keep active and don't just eat junk. Your workload will seem easier. You'll sleep better. You'll look fantastic. And you can stay healthy—even if your time and money are in short supply.

But Really, Who Has Time to Exercise?

As one teen says, "Schoolwork gets in the way, and then I want to relax when I have a moment that isn't filled with schoolwork." You can make time for anything, if you choose to. But if you aren't athletic by nature or your

time: for example, with your school and the police.

You have the legal right to a school and workplace free from discrimination based on your race, color, religion, sex, national origin, and—depending on where you live, as state and local laws vary—your sexual orientation. You have the right to protection from retaliation if you file a complaint of harassment. So don't be afraid to report a situation if it truly offends you and interferes with your life.

What if I'm Just Being Hypersensitive?

If someone's words or actions make you uncomfortable, that's all the reason you need to ask that person to stop the behavior, no matter how innocent the behavior may be. Trust your feelings—especially if you find you're trying to convince yourself that nothing is wrong.

What Will Happen to the Person Who Has Been Harassing Me?

If your complaint is successfully handled, says Edison, the main thing

that will happen is that the person will stop harassing you. People aren't "charged" with sexual harassment unless their behavior includes criminal conduct. But your harasser may face disciplinary action, loss of privileges, suspension, expulsion, lawsuits, or criminal action, depending on the severity of his or her behavior.

How Can I Avoid Harassing Someone?

Sometimes the line between harmless flirting, joking, or complimenting and harassment is pretty thin. How can you stay on the right side of that line?

First, pay attention to your own motives. Be honest with yourself. Do you enjoy watching someone get uncomfortable when you say or do certain things? Do you feel angry with the person for some reason? Do you enjoy exercising your authority over this person in some way? Do you find yourself obsessing about the person? If any of these are true, whatever you're saying or doing probably isn't harmless.

Even if your motives seem harmless to you, be extraordinarily careful school or work keeps you going non-stop, exercise is the first thing to go out the window.

However, you don't have to become a gym rat or run miles to get enough exercise. Longer workouts are great if you do them consistently, but you're better off getting little bits of regular exercise than just doing a huge workout every so often or never doing anything. And by "little bits," we mean 15- to 20-minute chunks. Add that to a fast walk to the bus, a frenzied private dance session in your room, or running up the stairs instead of taking the elevator, and you're exercising!

Regardless of how you choose to pump that muscle in the middle of your chest, the important thing is that you're doing something. You'll not only feel better about yourself, but you'll have increased energy to do other things, like study, go to work, or go out with friends.

What Does "Eating Right" Mean Anyway?

Eating right means eating a balance of good foods in moderate amounts. Your diet needn't be complicated or expensive. Dr. Michele Wilson, a specialist in adolescent medicine at the Children's Hospital of Philadelphia, notes that a teen's diet should be heavy in grains—especially whole grains—and light in sugars and fats. It should include a lot of fruits and vegetables and provide you with plenty of protein, calcium, vitamin A, B vitamins, iron, and zinc. Sound complicated?

Well, what's complicated about a bean burrito with cheese? How about pasta with vegetables, meat, or both in the sauce? A banana or some cantaloupe? Stir-fried vegetables with tofu? Carrot sticks with peanut butter? Yogurt? Cereal with milk and fruit? All of these are cheap, quick to make, and great for you.

One teen swears by microwaveable veggie burgers and adds, "Staying away from deep-fried anything is a good plan." Try to avoid things like chips and sweets, says Dr. Wilson, adding that if you're a vegetarian—and especially if you don't eat dairy products or fish—you should make sure you're getting enough protein and iron. And no matter what your diet, drink water—eight glasses a day.

As Long as I'm in Control of What I Eat, I'm Okay, Right?

That depends. Of course, having no control over what you eat is a problem. But "in control" can be good or bad. How severely do you control what and how you eat? Are you obsessed with getting thinner? Do people who love you tell you that you're too thin, and do you take that as a compliment? Do you ever binge secretly or make yourself throw up after a meal? If any of these are true, you may be suffering from anorexia or bulimia.

According to the National Association of Anorexia Nervosa and Associated Disorders (ANAD), eating disorders affect about 7 million women and 1 million men in this country and can lead to serious health problems—even death. "The thing that convinced me to get help was fear—I had to be hospitalized, as I was literally dying from my anorexia," says one woman. Most Americans who are anorexic or bulimic developed their eating disorders in their teens.

We asked some women being treated for eating disorders what they used to see when they looked in the mirror. "Total ugliness," said one. "The smallest dimple in my flesh looked immense," said another. And a third said, "I got rid of the mirrors because they would set me off to where I wouldn't eat for days." Their advice to teens struggling with an eating disorder? "Treat yourself as you wish your parents had treated you," "Ask people you feel close to not to discuss your weight with you," and "Find ways outside of yourself to feel in control." Above all—get help! That means going to someone you trust, whether it be a parent, relative, sibling, friend, doctor, or teacher. Or call ANAD's national hotline at 847-831-3438 for a listing of support groups and referrals in your area.

So If I Eat Right and Exercise, I'm Healthy?

Well, probably. But Dr. Wilson suggests that you keep a few other things in mind too. If you smoke, drink, or do drugs, you're asking for trouble. Aside from their many scarier side effects, all these habits can steal nutrients that you need. If all this sounds like the recipe for a dull and totally uncool life, remember that feeling and looking great are never boring and that vomiting (or dying) after downing the most tequilas in the fastest time looks really uncool. If you're making short-term decisions that will hurt you in the long run, take some time to figure out why. Good health is priceless—just ask any grandparent. ■

PART 4

Now that you have decided what types of opportunities you wish to pursue after graduation, you need a jumping-off point for getting more information. The appendices that follow will provide you with additional data to help you with your decision-making process. In these pages, you'll find the following:

APPENDICES

- IN-DEPTH DESCRIPTIONS OF SELECTED EDUCATION PROVIDERS FROM ACROSS THE COUNTRY
- A MAP OF THE MAJOR CITIES AND TOWNS LOCATED IN YOUR REGION.
- HIGH SCHOOL GRADUATION REQUIREMENTS FOR YOUR STATE
- IMPORTANT INFORMATION FOR YOUR REGION OF THE COUNTRY, INCLUDING:
  - A TABLE OF ALL 2- AND 4-YEAR COLLEGES AND UNIVERSITIES AS WELL AS SPECIAL MESSAGES FROM INSTITUTIONS THAT WISH TO PROVIDE MORE INFORMATION ABOUT THEMSELVES
  - CONTACT INFORMATION FOR CAREER AND VOCATIONAL SCHOOLS
  - SCHOLARSHIPS AND FINANCIAL AID PROGRAMS
  - DESCRIPTIONS OF INTERNSHIPS
  - OPPORTUNITIES FOR SUMMER ENRICHMENT

Note: Because of Peterson's comprehensive editorial review and because all material comes directly from institution or organization officials, we believe that the information presented in these appendices is accurate. Nonetheless, errors and omissions are possible in a data collection and processing endeavor of this scope. You should check with the specific institution or organization at the time of application to verify pertinent data that may have changed since the publication of this book.

BARRY UNIVERSITY

Miami Shores, Florida

About the University

Founded in 1940 by the Dominican Sisters of Adrian, Michigan, Barry University has grown significantly; yet it remains true to its mission of providing high-quality academics, a caring environment, a religious dimension, and community service. In 2000, Barry enrolled 8,358 students (2,544 full-time undergraduates) from forty-nine states and territories and more than eighty countries. The University is accredited by the Southern Association of Colleges and Schools to award bachelor's, master's, specialist, and doctoral degrees.

Seven residence halls accommodate 700 undergraduate students. Student services available on campus include counseling, career development and placement, campus ministry, and health services. The University has a snack bar, a cafeteria, a post office, a student center, a performing arts center, a television studio, a radio station, an athletic training room, a human performance lab, a biomechanics lab, a health and sports center, and an outdoor recreation center.

Intercollegiate sports (NCAA Division II) for men include baseball, basketball, golf, soccer, and tennis; women's teams include basketball, crew, golf, soccer, softball, tennis, and volleyball.

Academic Program

The University operates on a semester plan. The first semester extends from the end of August to mid-December, and the second semester extends from mid-January to early May. Two 6-week sessions are offered during the summer. A student must earn a minimum of 120 credits for a degree. Of these 120 credits, 9 must be in philosophy and theology, 9 in communication, 9 in humanities and arts, 9 in physical or natural sciences and mathematics, and 9 in social and behavioral sciences. The traditional full-time academic load is 12 to 18 credits each semester and 6 credits each summer term. Exceptionally well-qualified seniors may earn up to 6 hours of graduate credit with the recommendation of the department chairperson and the dean. Internships are required for many majors. The University also offers an active honors program designed to add breadth and depth to the educational experience. The approach is interdisciplinary.

The Clinical Center for Advanced Learning offers a program designed to assist students with learning disabilities who have the intellectual potential and motivation to complete a four-year degree.

Costs

For 2000-01, tuition for full-time undergraduate students for the academic year was $16,600. Room and board costs were $6400 (double room).

Financial Aid

Barry University offers an excellent scholarship and grant program, awarding scholarships each year to students who have demonstrated academic success and promise. These scholarships and grants may be renewed for up to four years as long as the students meet the renewal criteria. Barry need-based grants and athletic scholarships are also available.

The University also participates in the Federal Pell and Federal Supplemental Educational Opportunity Grant programs, the Federal Perkins Loan Program, the Federal Work-Study Program, the Florida Resident Access Grant Program, the Florida Student Assistance Grant, Florida Bright Futures Scholarships, and the Federal Family Educational Loan Program. Barry awards financial assistance on the basis of financial need and academic excellence. Applicants must submit the Free Application for Federal Student Aid (FAFSA) in order to be considered for aid. More than 85 percent of undergraduate full-time students receive assistance from the University. Additional information may be obtained by calling the Office of Financial Aid at 305-899-3673 or 800-495-2279 (toll-free).

Application and Information

The University reviews applications as they are completed. Students are advised of their acceptance once the Admissions Committee has reviewed all required documents. Students may apply any time after completion of the junior year in high school. It is advisable to apply early. The student's completed application form and supporting credentials should be sent to the address below. Students may also apply online at the University's Web site (listed below).

Ms. Marcia Nance
Dean of Enrollment Services
Barry University
11300 Northeast Second Avenue
Miami Shores, Florida 33161-6695
Telephone: 305-899-3100
800-695-2279 (toll-free)
Fax: 305-899-2971
E-mail: admissions@mail.barry.edu
World Wide Web: http://www.barry.edu

IGNITE YOUR POTENTIAL!

Business
Administration

Computer Applications

Computer
Information Systems

Graphic Design

Legal Assistant

Networking and
Computer Technology

Office Technologies

Telecommunications

DAY AND EVENING CLASSES

**PLACEMENT ASSISTANCE
FOR GRADUATES**

**FINANCIAL AID FOR THOSE
WHO QUALIFY**

REGIONALLY ACCREDITED

**BACHELOR'S & ASSOCIATE
DEGREE PROGRAMS**

BRIARCLIFFE COLLEGE

2 LOCATIONS IN BETHPAGE AND PATCHOGUE, NY

1.800.906.3200 · www.briarcliffe.edu

BRIARCLIFFE COLLEGE

Bethpage, New York

About the College

Briarcliffe College was established in 1966 to serve the educational needs of Long Island residents. The College has grown from an original enrollment of 18 women to the current coeducational enrollment of more than 2,500 students per year. Day, evening, weekend, and summer classes are offered.

A wide range of student activities is coordinated through the College's division of student affairs. Briarcliffe students have many opportunities to participate in college life through academic, social, service, and athletic programs. Typical events include theater trips, guest speakers, community service and charitable activities, concerts, and dances. The athletic department sponsors intercollegiate and intramural sports. Scholarships are awarded for men's baseball, women's softball, women's soccer, and men's and women's bowling.

A high-technology, small-business incubator is located on the main campus. The incubator provides up to twenty young companies with a supportive environment in which to grow. The companies are able to share resources, access the research and intellectual strengths of Briarcliffe College, and provide internship experiences for students.

Academic Program

The multilevel structure of the academic program enables students to enroll immediately in four-year programs or to earn a credential by completing short-term diploma or associate degree programs. Briarcliffe College provides a rich, career-oriented curriculum that prepares students to initiate or advance in their careers.

A minimum of 120 credits is required to earn a bachelor's degree, and 60 credits are required for an associate degree. Diploma programs may be completed in two semesters of full-time study by successfully finishing prescribed course work.

In addition to courses directly related to the major field of study, there is a general education requirement for each degree program. A minimum of 42 general education credits is required for the B.B.A. degree, and a minimum of 21 credits in general education are required for the A.A.S. degree.

The College operates on a traditional two-semester calendar for day classes and an innovative evening schedule that enables students to begin classes at four points during the year to earn semester-hour credits.

Costs

The tuition for full-time students during the 2000-01 academic year was $4950 per semester. Full-time tuition charges apply to students enrolled in 12 to 18 credits. Tuition for part-time students was $412.50 per credit.

Financial Aid

Briarcliffe College offers a wide variety of financial aid programs, including scholarships, grants, loans, and work-study. All applicants for financial aid are expected to complete the Briarcliffe College Financial Aid Application and the Free Application for Federal Student Aid (FAFSA). New York State residents receive an Express Tuition Assistance Program Application (ETA), which must also be completed.

Briarcliffe College directly funds several scholarship programs. The Presidential Scholarship is awarded to first-time college students who have earned at least an 80 high school average and have cumulative math and verbal SAT I scores of at least 1075. Daniel Turan Memorial Scholarships are competitive awards for students who have completed a sequence of business courses in high school. An Alumni Scholarship exam is administered twice each year for high school seniors. Alumni Scholarships may award as much as $9000 for a bachelor's degree program. Program-Specific Scholarships are competitive awards valued up to $6000 in each major program offered at Briarcliffe College. Athletic scholarships are awarded to outstanding athletes in baseball, bowling, soccer, and softball.

Application and Information

Students who are applying for fall semester admission are encouraged to submit their applications before January 1. The College has a rolling admissions policy. Applications for the spring and summer terms should be submitted at least sixty days before classes are scheduled to begin. Late applications are considered on a space-available basis.

Additional information and application materials are available by contacting Briarcliffe College at the following address:

Admissions Office
Briarcliffe College
1055 Stewart Avenue
Bethpage, New York 11714-3545
Telephone: 516-918-3600
888-333-1150 (toll-free)
Fax: 516-470-6020
E-mail: info@bcl.edu
World Wide Web: http://www.briarcliffe.edu

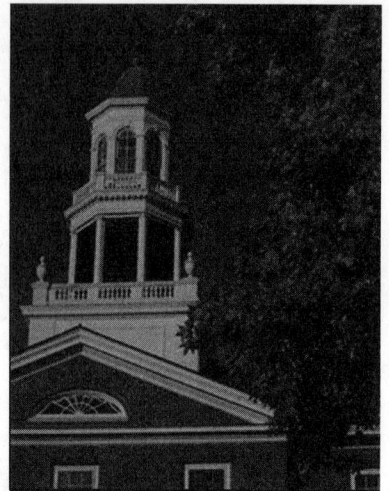

COLBY-SAWYER COLLEGE

New London, New Hampshire

About the College

Colby-Sawyer College, a coeducational, residential, undergraduate college provides programs of study that innovatively integrate the liberal arts and sciences with professional preparation. Students come from all over the United States and eight other countries, with 68 percent of the students coming from outside of New Hampshire. Within the last five years, an apartment-style and a suite-style residence hall have been built to accommodate the College's steady growth in enrollment.

Student athletic involvement occurs at the varsity, club, intramural, and recreational levels. There are nine varsity sports for women (NCAA Division III basketball, lacrosse, soccer, swimming, tennis, track and field, and volleyball; ECSC Alpine ski racing; and IHSA riding) and eight for men (NCAA Division III baseball, basketball, soccer, swimming, tennis, and track and field; ECSC Alpine ski racing; and IHSA riding). The Colby-Sawyer Chargers compete as a member of the Commonwealth Coast Conference.

The College is accredited by the New England Association of Schools and Colleges, and professional programs also carry the appropriate accreditations. Colby-Sawyer has consistently received recognition as one of the top colleges in its category.

Academic Program

At Colby-Sawyer College, it is believed that knowledge and experience nurture each other. Therefore, the combination of classroom learning and professional experience is an integral part of each student's education. Through a carefully crafted program offered by the Harrington Center for Career Development, all students are encouraged throughout their four years of study to continue to clarify their interests and goals and to gain practical experiences through student employment, internships, and voluntary service to the community.

Colby-Sawyer has an impressive roster of internship opportunities available. Organizations that have recently accepted Colby-Sawyer interns include Merrill Lynch, Continental Cable, Beth Israel Hospital, Blue Cross/Blue Shield, Harvard University Athletic Department, the Buffalo Bisons, the New England Patriots, the Currier Gallery of Art, the Basketball Hall of Fame, the Olympic Regional Development Authority, Channel 7 (Boston), the Appalachian Mountain Club, and CNN.

Costs

Tuition, room, and board for 2000-01 were $26,200. In addition to this comprehensive fee, which includes the cost of all student services, there was a $200 technology fee. Approximately $1500 should be allowed for books, supplies, personal expenses, and travel, depending on where students live.

Financial Aid

Through its Financial Aid Program, Colby-Sawyer encourages the attendance of students from a variety of ethnic and cultural backgrounds, economic levels, and geographic regions. Seventy-seven percent of the students currently receive some form of financial assistance, and Colby-Sawyer provides more than $4.5 million a year in grant assistance to its students. Both need-based and merit awards are available, including merit awards for outstanding academic achievement or student leadership. Applicants who wish to be considered for merit awards must be accepted for admission by February 1. Each applicant for need-based aid must submit the Free Application for Federal Student Aid (FAFSA) and the Colby-Sawyer Application for Financial Aid. Priority will be given to students whose completed forms are received before the March 1 deadline.

Application and Information

Colby-Sawyer receives and considers applications throughout the year. Beginning in December, applications are reviewed as soon as they become complete, and candidates are notified as soon as the admissions decision is finalized. A completed application includes a transcript of the candidate's high school work (including first-quarter grades for the senior year), SAT I or ACT scores, two letters of recommendation (one from a teacher and one from a guidance professional), a personal statement, and a $40 nonrefundable application fee. Application forms and additional information may be obtained by contacting:

Office of Admissions
Colby-Sawyer College
100 Main Street
New London, New Hampshire 03257
Telephone: 603-526-3700
800-272-1015 (toll-free)
Fax: 603-526-3452
E-mail: csadmiss@colby-sawyer.edu
World Wide Web: http://www.colby-sawyer.edu

COOKING AND HOSPITALITY INSTITUTE OF CHICAGO

Chicago, Illinois

About the Institute

The Cooking and Hospitality Institute of Chicago (CHIC), founded in 1983, was established to provide culinary education using the traditional European hands-on approach. In 1991, the Institute received degree-granting authority from the Illinois Board of Higher Education and began offering an Associate of Applied Science degree in culinary arts. In June 2000, CHIC introduced the Le Cordon Bleu Culinary Program to its Associate of Applied Science degree program. The Institute is accredited by the Accrediting Commission of Career Schools and Colleges of Technology (ACCSCT) and the American Culinary Federation (ACF) and is a candidate for accreditation from the Commission on Institutions of Higher Education of the North Central Association of Colleges and Schools.

Academic Program

CHIC operates on a trisemester basis with rolling midsemester starts. Students may begin their studies every other month (January, March, April, July, August, or October). Classes are offered seven days a week and five evenings a week.

CHIC offers a certificate program in baking and pastry. This program teaches the principles and techniques of professional pastry and baking production and is intended for students who have an interest in large-quantity baking or who want to work for establishments that have in-house baking and pastry operations.

An Associate of Applied Science degree is offered in Le Cordon Bleu culinary arts. The program includes professional cooking skills, baking and pastry skills, restaurant management skills, nutrition sciences, and general education. This well-rounded program is designed to give students the technical skills and theoretical expertise that are necessary for a career in the food service industry. Graduates can expect immediate employment in entry-level to midlevel positions as well as rapid advancement into management and sous chef positions and further. Students with or without prior experience find that this program offers everything that they need to begin a fast-track career in the fastest-growing industry in the United States.

CHIC offers a series of specialty classes that are designed for the person who wishes to learn professional techniques that can be used at home. CHIC also offers select professional courses for those interested in learning more in-depth professional techniques and for those who would like to sample the Institute's courses before committing to a full program.

Costs

For the 2000-01 academic year, tuition was $380 per credit hour. In addition, students can expect a one-time purchase of a supply kit ($800 for the associate degree program and $700 for the baking and pastry certificate program). Books can cost up to approximately $1500 per year.

Financial Aid

The Institute participates in federal financial aid programs such as student loans, Federal Pell Grants, Federal Supplemental Educational Opportunity Grants, and Federal Work-Study. Students may also receive funding from a variety of institutional and industry-related scholarships, which include the Nancy Abrams Academic Excellence Scholarship, Charlie Trotter's Culinary Education Foundation, the Educational Foundation's ProMgmt. Scholarship, and the Career College Association's Imagine America Scholarships for high school seniors as well as scholarships from the James Beard Foundation, the International Association of Cooking Professionals, the Illinois Restaurant Association, and the National Restaurant Association. Scholarships range from $500 to $10,000. Current students are invited to join the Student Advantage program, which matches students with employers who offer them part-time positions to help support their education during their course of study.

Nongovernmental loans are available through Sallie Mae and the National Loan Servicing Center. These loans may be used to supplement federal financial aid and in cases where students do not qualify for federal aid. The loan terms are similar to federal student loans, but the application procedure is greatly simplified.

Application and Information

Applications are accepted on an ongoing basis. Prospective students should contact:

Director of Admissions
Cooking and Hospitality Institute of Chicago
361 West Chestnut
Chicago, Illinois 60610
Telephone: 312-944-2725
877-828-7772 (toll-free)
Fax: 312-944-8557
E-mail: chic@chicnet.org
World Wide Web: http://www.chicnet.org

FLORIDA METROPOLITAN UNIVERSITY (FMU)

About the University

With more than 8,000 students enrolled, Florida Metropolitan University (FMU) is currently one of the largest private universities in Florida. FMU, Tampa Campus traces its roots back to 1890, making it the oldest business college in the state. FMU is a private university operating nine campuses in Florida. FMU offers various associate and bachelor's degree programs, master's degrees in business administration and criminal justice, as well as Associate of Business and Bachelor of Business Administration degrees on line. FMU is accredited by the Accrediting Council for Independent Colleges and Schools (ACICS).

Academic Program

Courses of study are available in the following areas: accounting, business, computers, commercial art, criminal justice, film and video, health care, hospitality, legal, management/marketing, network administration, and travel. A 2.0 cumulative grade point average and successful completion of all required courses for the particular program and degree level are required.

Students are provided the skills and knowledge to enter the work force with confidence. The University has its computer lab connected to the Internet, allowing students access to a vast source of information and research materials. Faculty members are experienced in their particular academic fields beyond teaching, thus bringing a "real-world" atmosphere to the instruction. The staff and faculty members are committed to helping each student reach his or her full potential by starting their experience off with a confidence building seminar and a mentoring program that help students realize they always have someone to assist them.

Costs

Per credit hours are assessed based on amount of classes taken per quarter and differ for selected programs. A registration fee of $25 is assessed per quarter. Books average $200 per quarter.

Financial Aid

A number of financial aid options are available to students, including Federal Pell Grant, Federal Supplemental Educational Opportunity Grant (FSEOG), Federal Work study Program (FWS), Florida Student Assistance Grant (FSAG), Federal Family Educational Loan Program (FFELP), Subsidized and Unsubsidized Federal Stafford Loans, and institutional scholarships. Financial aid is available for those who qualify.

Application and Information

Graduation from high school, or its equivalent (GED), is a prerequisite for admission. Applicants not completing a secondary program or not having a diploma will be considered for admission on the basis of the GED test or other equivalency. All applicants are required to successfully complete an assessment examination.

For further information, call 888-208-1577 toll-free.

Programs Eligible for Scholarship	Tuition and Fees	Course Length/ Credit Hours	Credential Earned
Accounting	$196-$219/credit hour	96/192 credit hours	AS/BS
Business Administration	$196-$219 credit hour	96/192 credit hours	AB/BBA
Computer Information Science	$196-$219/credit hour	96/192 credit hours	AS/BS
Commercial Art	$212-$235 credit hour	96 credit hours	AS
Criminal Justice	$196-$219/credit hour	96/192 credit hours	AS/BS
Film and Video	$214-$238/credit hour	96 credit hours	AS
Legal Assistant/Paralegal	$196-$219/credit hour	96/192 credit hours	AS/BS
Health Care Administration	$196-$219/credit hour	192 credit hours	BS
Hospitality Management	]$196-$219/credit hour	96 / 192 credit hours	AS/BS
International Business	$196-$219/credit hour	96/192 credit hours	AS/BS
Management/Marketing	$196-$219/credit hour	96 / 192 credit hours	AS/BS
Medical Assisting	$205-$228/credit hour	97 credit hours	AS
Microsoft Office User Specialist	$233/credit hour	96 credit hours	AS
Network Administration	$286/credit hour	98 credit hours	AS
Office Technologies	$196-219/credit hour	96 credit hours	AS
Pharmacy Technician	$205-228/credit hour	97 credit hours	AS
Surgical Technologist	$233/credit hour	101 credit hours	AS
Master of Business Administration	$315/credit hour	56 credit hours	MBA
Master of Science Criminal Justice	$331/credit hour	54-58 credit hours	MS

HAWAII PACIFIC UNIVERSITY

Honolulu, Hawaii

About the University

Hawaii Pacific University (HPU) is an independent, coeducational, career-oriented, comprehensive university with a foundation in the liberal arts. Undergraduate and graduate degrees are offered in close to fifty different areas. Hawaii Pacific prides itself on maintaining small class size (averaging 25 students) and individual attention to students.

Students at HPU come from every state in the union and more than 100 countries around the world. The diversity of the student body stimulates learning about other cultures firsthand, both in and out of the classroom. There is no majority population at HPU. Students are encouraged to examine the values, customs, traditions, and principles of others to gain a clearer understanding of their own perspectives. HPU students develop friendships with students from throughout the United States and the world, important connections for success in the global economy of the twenty-first century.

HPU has NCAA intercollegiate sports. Men's athletic programs include baseball, basketball, cheerleading, cross-country, and tennis. Women's athletics include cheerleading, cross-country, softball, tennis, and volleyball.

The Housing Office at HPU offers many services and options for students. Residence halls with cafeteria service are available on the Windward campus, while University-sponsored apartments are available in the Waikiki area for those seeking more independent living arrangements.

Academic Program

The baccalaureate student must complete at least 124 semester hours of credit. Forty-five of these credits provide the student with a strong foundation in the liberal arts, with the remaining credits composed of appropriate upper-division classes in the student's major and related areas. The academic year operates on a modified 4-1-4 semester system, featuring a five-week winter intersession. The University also offers extensive summer sessions. A student can earn up to 15 semester hours of credit during the summer. By attending these supplemental sessions, a student may complete the baccalaureate degree program in three years. A five-year B.S.B.A./M.B.A. program is also available.

Costs

For the 2001-02 academic year, tuition is $9360 (for most majors), and books and supplies cost approximately $1400. For students who live in residence halls, room and board are $7210. University-leased apartments rent for $2465 per semester. (There is an additional $400 refundable security deposit required for residence halls and University-leased apartments.) Tuition for marine science majors is $11,460, and tuition for nursing majors who are in their junior or senior year is $13,760.

Financial Aid

The University provides financial aid for qualified students through institutional, state, and federal aid programs. Approximately 50 percent of the University's students receive financial aid. Among the forms of aid available are Federal Perkins Loans, Federal Stafford Student Loans, Guaranteed Parental Loans, Federal Pell Grants, and Federal Supplemental Educational Opportunity Grants. To apply for aid, students must submit the Free Application for Federal Student Aid (FAFSA). The FAFSA may be submitted at any time, but the priority deadline is March 1.

Application and Information

Candidates are notified of admission decisions on a rolling basis, usually within two weeks of receipt of application materials. Early entrance and deferred entrance are available. HPU accepts the Common Application form.

For further information and for application materials, students should contact:

Office of Admissions
Hawaii Pacific University
1164 Bishop Street, Suite 200
Honolulu, Hawaii 96813
Telephone: 808-544-0238
866-225-5478
Fax: 808-544-1136
E-mail: admissions@hpu.edu
World Wide Web: http://www.hpu.edu/

HESSER COLLEGE

HESSER COLLEGE

Manchester, New Hampshire

About the College

Hesser College's innovative approach to higher education provides students increased flexibility compared to traditional colleges. After two years of college, students earn an associate degree and are prepared to enter the workplace, or, if they prefer, students can continue on in one of Hesser's bachelor's degree programs.

Hesser College was established in 1900 as Hesser Business College, a private, nonsectarian college. Since 1972, Hesser College has expanded and enriched its curricula in keeping with its tradition of providing an affordable career education of high quality. The physical building encompasses more than fifteen different businesses that all create the Hesser Center of Commerce and Education. This is an unusual and beneficial partnership of business and education.

Hesser College is fully accredited by the New England Association of Schools and Colleges. The association is the official accrediting agency for schools and colleges in the six New England states and is widely considered to hold the strictest academic standards. Students who choose Hesser College are assured of a high-quality education.

Academic Program

The primary goal of the curricula is to prepare students for success in specific career areas. The general education requirements are designed to provide the skills necessary for career growth and lifelong learning. Internships, practicums, and opportunities for part-time work experience are available in all majors. An education from Hesser College provides a solid career foundation. The College's goal is quite simple: to prepare people for careers and career advancement.

Many of the Hesser College programs are for the career-minded student who wants to concentrate on the skills required to be successful in the workplace. Seventy-five percent of the courses that students take are directly related to their career choices. Upon completion of the associate degree program, a student may pursue a four-year degree by enrolling in one of Hesser's bachelor's degree programs.

Hesser offers a wide range of associate degree programs that prepare students for high-demand careers. They include accounting; business administration; business computer applications; business science/individualized studies; child-care studies; communications and public relations; corrections, probation, and parole; early childhood education; hotel and restaurant management; human services; interior design; international business; law enforcement; liberal studies; marketing; medical assistant studies; medical office management; microcomputer support specialist studies; network engineer studies; paralegal studies; physical therapist assistant studies; psychology; radio and video production and broadcasting; small-business management/entrepreneurship; solutions developer studies; sports management; and travel and tourism. In addition, the College offers bachelor's degree programs in accounting, criminal justice, management, and marketing.

Costs

Part-time students are billed at the rate of $355 per credit for most majors. Information technology credit rates vary. Full-time expenses per semester in 2000-01 were as follows: tuition (12-16 credits), $4665; room, $1650; and meal plan (optional), $1125.

Financial Aid

Hesser College offers financial assistance to students based on demonstrated financial need. Seventy percent of students receive some form of aid. More than fifty scholarships are awarded each year to freshman and senior students. The College offers low-interest loans from both internal and external sources. Federal Supplemental Educational Opportunity Grants, the Federal Work-Study Program, Federal Perkins Loans, Federal Stafford Student Loans, and state scholarship programs are available to those who qualify. In order to apply for financial aid and scholarships at Hesser College, students must complete a FAFSA and a Hesser College Institutional Financial Aid Application.

Application and Information

Applicants must submit an application form with a $10 nonrefundable fee. Applications are reviewed on a first-come, first-served basis and normally take seven to fourteen days to be fully reviewed upon receipt of all required information.

Requests for additional information and application forms should be addressed to:
Director of Admissions
Hesser College
3 Sundial Avenue
Manchester, New Hampshire 03103
Telephone: 603-668-6660
800-526-9231 (toll-free)
Fax: 603-666-4722
E-mail: admissions@hesser.edu
World Wide Web: http://www.hesser.edu

ITT TECHNICAL INSTITUTE

About the Institute

ITT Technical Institute is owned and operated by ITT Educational Services, Inc. (ESI), a leading private college system focused on technology-oriented programs of study. ESI operates seventy ITT Technical Institutes in twenty-eight states, providing career-focused degree programs to approximately 29,000 students. Headquartered in Indianapolis, Indiana, ESI has been actively involved in the higher education community in the United States since 1969.

Curriculum offerings are designed to help students prepare for career opportunities in technology. Students attend classes year-round with convenient breaks provided throughout the year. Classes are generally offered in four-hour sessions three or four days a week and are typically available in the morning, afternoon and evening, depending on student enrollment. This class schedule offers flexibility to students to pursue part-time employment opportunities.

Academic Program

Programs are available in areas such as information technology, computer and electronics engineering technology, and computer drafting and design.

The IT Computer Network Systems program prepares students to perform tasks associated with upgrading computer systems and developing wide area and local area capabilities. Additional curriculum topics include global system integration, network system design, and implementation of network systems.

The IT Multimedia program prepares students to perform tasks associated with software application development and modification. Students acquire skills in software scripting, multimedia languages, database development, and other related technical subjects.

The IT Web Development program prepares students to perform tasks associated with software application development and its modification. Students acquire skills in Web development languages, software scripting, database development, and other related technical subjects.

The IT Software Applications and Programming program prepares students to perform tasks associated with software application development and modification. Students acquire skills in programming languages, software scripting, database development, and other related technical subjects.

The Computer and Electronics Technology program prepares students for careers in entry-level positions in modern electronics and computer technology. The program acquaints students with certain circuits, systems, and specialized techniques used in electronics and computer technology fields.

The Computer Drafting and Design program combines computer-aided drafting with conventional methods of graphic communication to solve drafting and basic design-related problems.

Costs

Refer to the school catalog, as tuition varies.

Financial Aid

ITT Technical Institute maintains a Finance Department on campus. The campus is designated as an eligible institution by the U.S. Department of Education for participation in the following programs: Federal Pell Grant Program, Federal Perkins Loan Program, Federal Stafford Loan Program, Federal PLUS Loan Program, and Federal Work Study Program. The school also offers non-federal loans available through Bank One for eligible students.

Application and Information

For information regarding application procedures, please call ITT at the number listed below or visit ITT's Web site.

World Wide Web: http://www.itt-tech.edu
Telephone: 800-ITT-TECH

THE OCEAN CORPORATION, HOUSTON

About the Institution

The Ocean Corporation has been in the education field since 1969. The school provides instruction in commercial diving and related fields. Courses include the Ultimate Diver Training Course, Nondestructive Testing/Inspection Training Course, and Medical Technician Training Course. The campus is on 4.2 acres located in Houston on the Gulf of Mexico in the hub of the diving industry. The school draws students nationally and internationally and offers job placement.

Academic Program

The following courses are available: The Ultimate Diver Training Course, Nondestructive Testing/Inspection Training Course, and Medical Technician Training Course. The Ultimate Diver Training Course trains students to be able to enter the Commercial Diving Industry. The Nondestructive Testing/Inspection Training Course trains students to be able to enter any industry that uses nondestructive testing. The Medical Technician Training is further education for commercial divers.

Costs

Tuition for the Ocean Corporation's Ultimate Diver Training program is $11,500. The cost includes books, some tools, and supplies. The cost for the Nondestructive Testing/Inspection Training Course is $2,500, and the Medical Technician Training Course costs $2,500.

Financial Aid

From its on-campus office, The Ocean Corporation offers Title IV Funding through the Federal Government—The Subsidized and Unsubsidized Stafford Loans, the Plus Loan, and the Pell Grant. The school also participates in the Veteran's Administration Educational Benefits, JTPA, Vocational Rehabilitation Educational Programs, Imagine America, and CCSCT.

Application and Information

For information regarding applications, please contact:
John Wood, President
10840 Rockley Road
Houston, TX 77099
Phone: (800) 321-0298
Fax (281) 530-9143
E-mail: Admissions@ocorp.com
World Wide Web: http://www.ocorp.com

Programs Eligible for Scholarship	Tuition and Fees	Course Length/ Credit Hours	Credential Earned
Ultimate Diver Training	$11,500	944 clock hours	Certificate
Nondestructive Testing/Inspector Training	$2,500	160 clock hours	Certificate
Medical Technician Training	$2,500	215 clock hours	Certificate

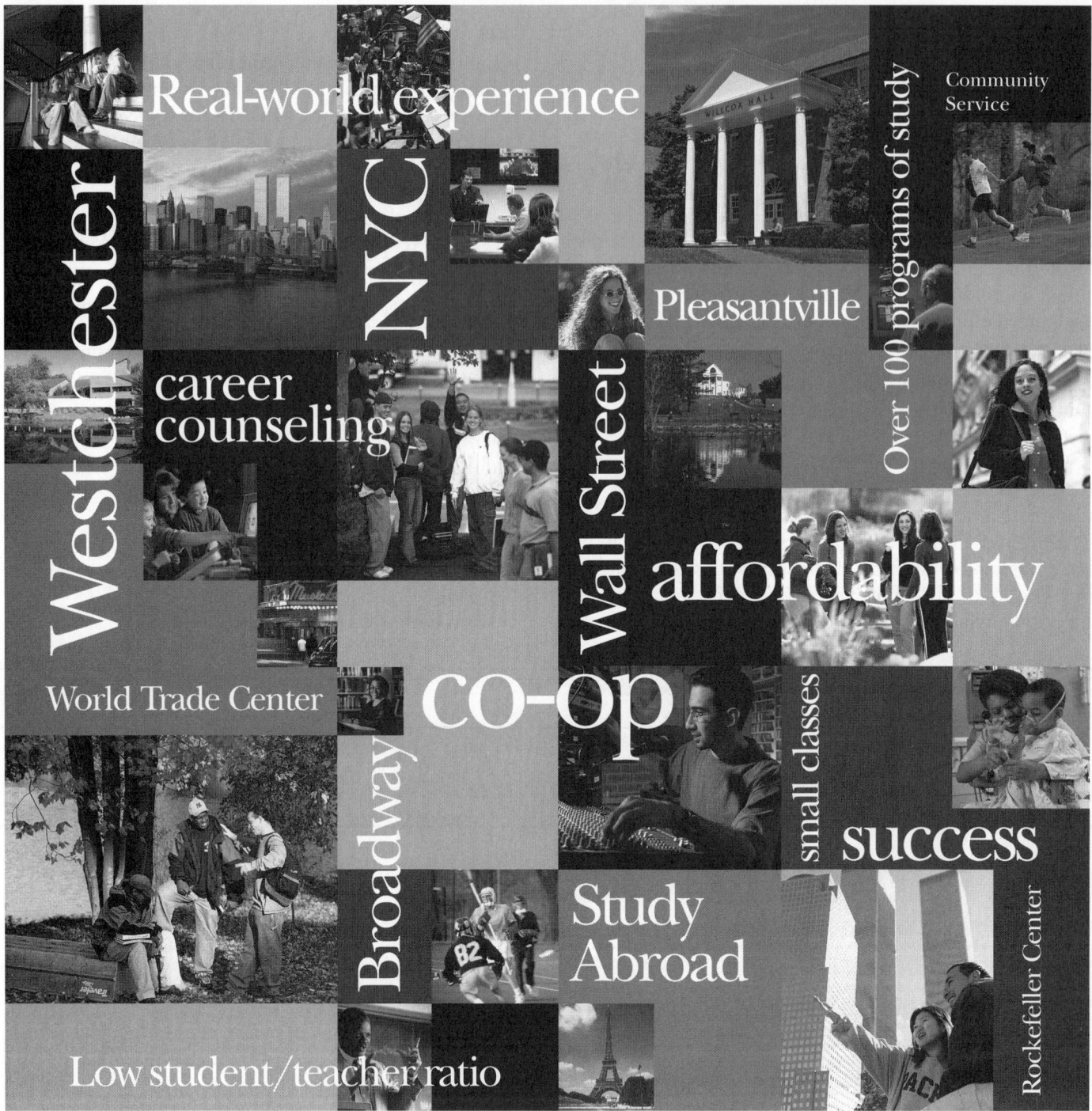

Opportunity is waiting for you at Pace University.
The opportunity to study in the buzzing, energetic atmosphere of New York City or in suburban Pleasantville. The opportunity to choose from over 100 degree programs. The opportunity to engage in real-world experiences through study abroad programs, internships, and co-op positions in some of the most fascinating places with the most exciting people. The opportunity to receive a quality education that you can afford. The opportunity to succeed here at Pace, and beyond.

PACE

Opportunity is

Call 1-800-874-PACE for more information, or visit our web site at www.pace.edu.

PACE UNIVERSITY

New York City and Pleasantville, New York

About the University

Pace University was founded in 1906 by two brothers, Homer and Charles Pace. The vision they had in 1906 is reflected in Pace's motto: "Opportunitas." Pace provides a remarkable array of learning, living, and working opportunities to all students. More than 100 majors and 3,000 courses of study are offered in the following five undergraduate schools: the Dyson College of Arts and Sciences, the Lubin School of Business, the School of Computer Science and Information Systems, the School of Education, and the Lienhard School of Nursing.

There are many activities and clubs to choose from, including the Black Students Organization, the Chinese Club, the Caribbean Students Association, student government associations, fraternities, sororities, two campus newspapers, two literary magazines, two yearbooks, two campus radio stations, and intercollegiate baseball, basketball, cross-country running, equestrian sports, football, golf, lacrosse, soccer (women's), softball, tennis, and volleyball (women's).

In 2000-01, approximately 9,100 undergraduate students were enrolled at Pace. The student body is diversified, with students coming from across the United States and from more than seventy-two countries.

Academic Program

The pattern of study at Pace University emphasizes the breadth of the core curriculum and involves taking prerequisites in the first two years and major courses plus electives in the junior and senior years. Selective academic programs in the University are preparatory to professional training in dentistry, law, medicine, and veterinary science.

The University honors program is designed to foster the intellectual life of outstanding students by enabling them to take greater responsibility and initiative in their academic work. Honors advisers assist students through individual advising. The Open Curriculum privilege permits an honors program member to choose courses in arts and sciences with a greater degree of freedom. The Independent Study Program encourages qualified students to undertake research and study to a depth beyond the normal course requirements. Pace participates in the Advanced Placement program of the College Board.

The Cooperative Education Program offers qualified students the opportunity to gain experience in their field while earning a four-year degree. Students can choose full-time, part-time, or summer schedules, working in an area directly related to their major course of study. It is recommended that admission to the program take place during the first year at the University.

Costs

Tuition for 2000-01 was $15,870 per year, a room was $4900 per year, and board was $2000 per year. Additional fees were $500, and books and supplies averaged $720.

Financial Aid

Financial aid is available through scholarships, institutional grants-in-aid, athletic scholarships, Federal Pell Grants, Federal Supplemental Educational Opportunity Grants, Federal Perkins Loans, Federal Stafford Student Loans, New York State Tuition Assistance Program awards (as well as awards from other states' incentive grant programs), Federal Work-Study awards, federal nursing scholarships and loans, and Law Enforcement Education Program awards. Further information on these programs may be obtained by contacting the Office of Financial Aid at the appropriate campus.

Application and Information

Requests for application forms and information for both the Pleasantville and New York City campuses should be addressed to the Student Information Center at the following address.

Student Information Center
Pace University
1 Pace Plaza
New York City, New York 10038
Telephone: 800-874-7223 Ext. UPGI
Fax: 212-346-1821
E-mail: infoctr@pace.edu
World Wide Web: http://www.pace.edu

SHENANDOAH UNIVERSITY

Winchester, Virginia

About the University

Shenandoah University was founded in 1875. By 1888 an unusual blend of educational opportunities had been formulated that included arts, sciences, music, medical arts, and business management. These programs, on a much more sophisticated basis, are found at Shenandoah today. The main campus is now more than 100 acres with nineteen buildings, including six residence halls. There are five additional buildings at off-campus locations. Shenandoah's historical relationship with the United Methodist Church does not place sectarian obligations on any student.

Shenandoah's students have the distinct advantage of being on a small campus near large metropolitan cultural centers. Such student organizations as academic fraternities, service and honor organizations, and various departmental clubs provide opportunities for leadership and recreation. Students come to Shenandoah because they want an educational experience of superior quality and believe that the facilities of a small campus, with a personal atmosphere, are the most conducive to achieving this experience. Fifty-five percent of the 2,428 students are from Virginia; the remaining 45 percent represent forty-one states and twenty-nine countries.

Shenandoah University is accredited by the Commission on Colleges of the Southern Association of Colleges and Schools (1866 Southern Lane, Decatur, GA 30033-4097; telephone: 404-679-4501) to award associate, bachelor's, master's, and doctoral degrees. Shenandoah holds membership in a number of professional organizations, including the National Association of Schools of Music, the National League for Nursing, the National Association of Music Therapy, the American Physical Therapy Association, the American Occupational Therapy Association, and the American Council on Pharmaceutical Education.

Academic Program

Shenandoah's academic calendar is divided into fall and spring semesters. Summer terms, ranging in length from two to eleven weeks, are also available. Each academic division (arts and sciences, business, conservatory, and health professions) offers diversified programs, with specific courses required by the various accreditation agencies. Credit is available through the tests of the College-Level Examination Program (CLEP), Proficiency Examination Program (PEP), and Advanced Placement (AP) Program and through various departmental challenge examinations.

Costs

The 2000-01 comprehensive annual fee (two semesters) for resident full-time undergraduate students was $22,300, which included tuition and room and board. The comprehensive annual tuition (two semesters) for commuting (day) full-time undergraduate students was $16,300. Undergraduate part-time tuition was $500 per credit hour. There is no difference in the cost of tuition and fees for out-of-state students. The Board of Trustees reserves the right to alter charges at any time.

Financial Aid

Shenandoah makes every effort to assist students in finding resources to finance their education. Approximately 91 percent of the University's students receive some type of financial aid. Shenandoah annually awards more than $18 million in aid to students in the form of grants, loans, scholarships, and employment on the campus. Previous financial aid packages have averaged approximately $13,000 per undergraduate student per year. To qualify for scholarships and financial aid, students must submit the Free Application for Federal Student Aid (FAFSA). Aid is awarded on a first-come, first-served basis, as funds are available. A student must be accepted for admission to a degree program before a financial aid offer is made. Specific information regarding financial aid should be requested from the Director of Financial Aid.

Application and Information

To apply, a student must submit an application with a $30 nonrefundable application fee, SAT I or ACT scores, and an official high school transcript. Applicants are notified of the admission decision after receipt of all credentials. An application, financial aid information, and other materials may be obtained by contacting:

Director of Admissions
Shenandoah University
1460 University Drive
Winchester, Virginia 22601
Telephone: 540-665-4581
800-432-2266 (toll-free)
Fax: 540-665-4627
E-mail: admit@su.edu

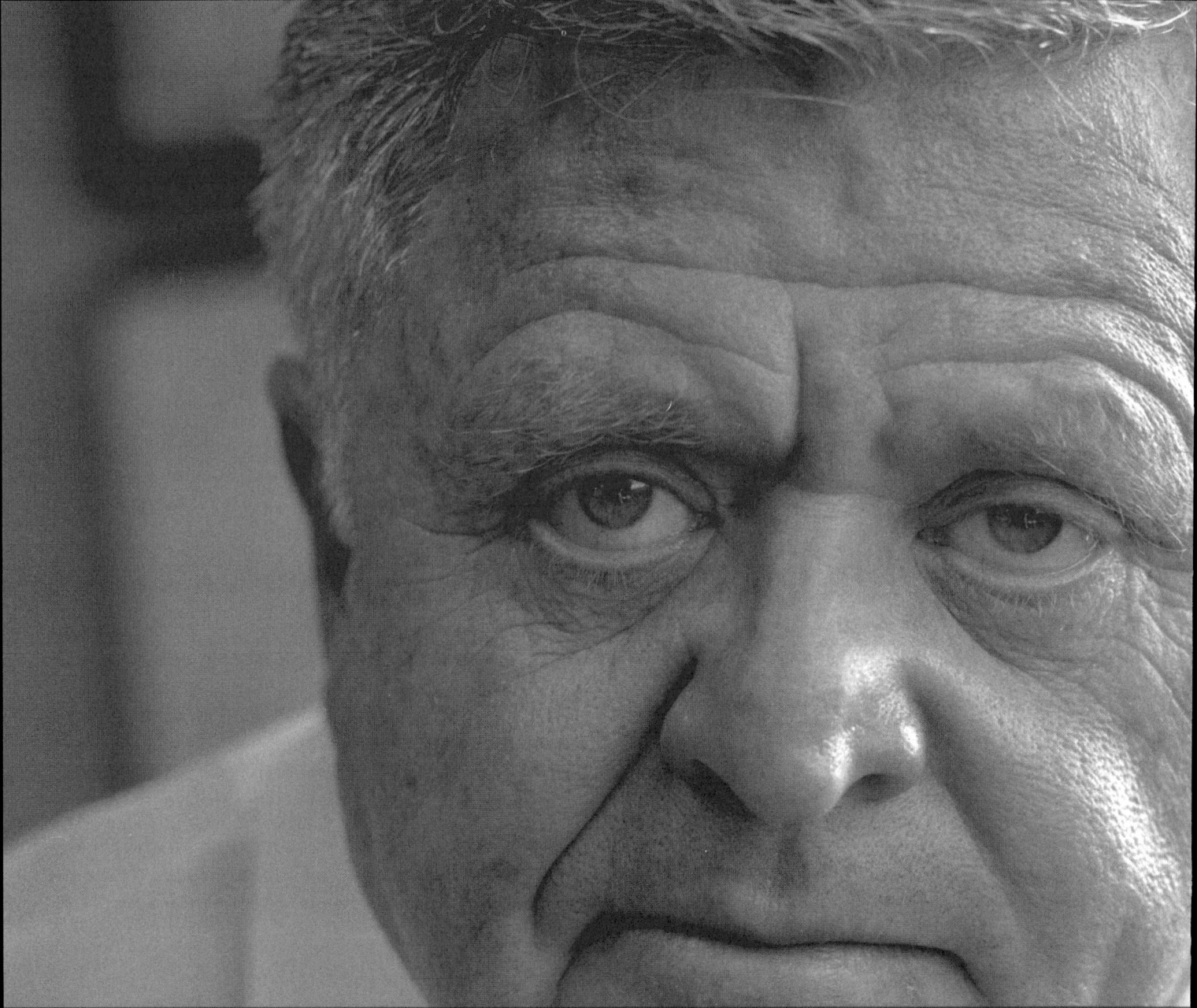

DR. WAYNE ISOM. TEXAS TECH. GROWING LEADER.

DUBBED "MEDICINE'S CARDIAC COWBOY," Dr. Wayne Isom already was a brilliant heart surgeon before he became famous earlier this year for conducting bypass surgery on late-night television star David Letterman. Isom was a pre-med major at Texas Tech University before going on to medical school. He always remembers his West Texas roots in his work at New York's Cornell Medical Center. He has operated on celebrity patients, like Larry King and Walter Cronkite, and many non-celebrities alike, finding ways to keep their hearts beating. He is what makes Texas Tech extraordinary. People are our strength. We are growing leaders. **www.texastech.edu.**

TEXAS TECH UNIVERSITY

Lubbock, Texas

About the University

Texas Tech University, founded in 1923, is a residential state university with a population of 25,000 students who come from all fifty states and ninety-nine other countries. Students at Texas Tech have the opportunity to study from more than 300 graduate and undergraduate degree programs.

The University is built around eight colleges: Agricultural Sciences and Natural Resources, Architecture, Arts and Sciences, Business Administration, Education, Engineering, Honors, and Human Sciences. A law school, which often boasts the highest number of students passing the bar exam in Texas, is conveniently located on the main campus. Also present is the Texas Tech University Health Sciences Center with its Schools of Medicine, Nursing, Pharmacy, and Allied Health.

Texas Tech has become a leader in academic programs ranging from pioneering research with the U.S. Department of Agriculture to improving alternative fuel capabilities for the nation's leading auto makers. Wind engineering research at the University has led to the creation of shelters that withstand the nation's most deadly tornadoes. In addition, students also find opportunities to master the arts with instruction from classically trained musicians as well as unique study abroad programs. A new addition to the academic programs includes the creation of the Institute for Environmental and Human Health. The institute offers graduate and undergraduate education in environmental science, toxicology, and environmental health.

The University competes in the Big XII Conference for intercollegiate athletics. Women participate in basketball, track and field, golf, tennis, volleyball, soccer, and softball while men participate in football, basketball, tennis, track and field, golf, and baseball. In addition, the University offers twenty-two club sports.

Academic Program

Texas Tech's undergraduate curriculum provides a broad range of courses in more than 150 majors. Recently, students at Texas Tech have seen an increase in competitive scholarships as well as the creation of the University's Honors College. Students accepted into the college find unparalleled undergraduate research opportunities for students in all major disciplines. As a result,

Texas Tech students are consistently awarded the prestigious Barry M. Goldwater Scholarship for science, engineering, and mathematics.

Costs

Texas Tech is listed in *The 100 Best College Buys for 1999 and 2000*, which is a directory of the top colleges and universities in the country whose costs are below the national average but whose academics are above the national average. In 1999-2000, the average cost for 30 undergraduate credit hours including books and nine-month room and board was $8574 for Texas residents. Residents of Arkansas, New Mexico, and Oklahoma living in bordering counties to Texas paid in-state tuition; residents of non-bordering counties paid an additional $900 per year. Students from other states paid an additional $6450 per year for out-of-state tuition. It is important to note that students who receive a $1000 scholarship from Texas Tech are exempt from out-of-state tuition. Costs are subject to change.

Financial Aid

A variety of financial aid is offered in the form of scholarships, grants, and loans. Competitive scholarships are awarded on academic merit, SAT or ACT scores, and class rank. More than 300 Presidential Endowed Scholarships are awarded to students each year. Need-based assistance is also available in the form of scholarships, government and private loans, grants, and work-study. Students' need for assistance is determined from the Free Application for Federal Student Aid (FAFSA). For a guide to scholarships and deadlines, students should contact the Office of Financial Aid (telephone: 806-742-3681).

Application and Information

All students should submit the *State of Texas Common Application*, a high school transcript, SAT I or ACT test scores, and the $40 application fee.

Requests for applications and other information should be directed to:

Office of Admissions and School Relations
Texas Tech University
Box 45005
Lubbock, Texas 79409-5005
Telephone: 806-742-1480
Fax: 806-742-0980
E-mail: admissions@ttu.edu
World Wide Web: http://www.texastech.edu

THE UNIVERSITY OF FINDLAY

Findlay, Ohio

About the University

The University of Findlay is a private coeducational institution with 4,525 full- and part-time students. Founded in 1882 by the Churches of God, General Conference, it emphasizes preparation for careers and professions in an educational program that blends liberal arts and career education. Students of many denominations attend Findlay, and religious participation is a matter of personal choice.

Bachelor of Arts degree programs are available in forty different majors. The Associate of Arts degree is awarded in nearly twenty areas. The largest programs at Findlay are in natural sciences, business, and social sciences. Majors in the sciences include athletic training, equestrian studies (English, Western, and equine management), nuclear medicine, occupational therapy, physical therapy, physician assistant studies, and pre-veterinary medicine. Business degrees are founded in a three-year comprehensive core program with eight different majors, including an individualized major option.

Most of Findlay's students come from Ohio and the surrounding states of Michigan, Indiana, and Pennsylvania. More than thirty other states are also represented.

Resident students live in six modern residence halls. All students eat their meals in an attractive dining hall. Social life at Findlay centers on student organizations, fraternities, and sororities. Organizations include department and special interest clubs, the newspaper, yearbook, musical groups, a radio station, Circle K, and Aristos Eklektos (honors).

Athletic programs are affiliated with NCAA Division II and the Great Lakes Intercollegiate Athletic Conference. Men's hockey, women's hockey, and men's volleyball are making a transition to Division I. Athletic scholarships are available.

Academic Program

Findlay operates on the semester system. Students must complete at least 124 semester hours with a minimum overall grade point average of 2.0 to earn a bachelor's degree. The Freshman Seminar introduces students to living and learning at Findlay and gives them the opportunity to work with the same teachers and student group in two related courses. The Honors Program provides additional challenge to those students who qualify on the basis of academic credentials. Study- and travel-abroad programs are offered by various departments. Credit and/or placement can be earned through Advanced Placement (AP) exams.

The Equestrian Program serves approximately 200 students from throughout the United States and abroad. Majors in equine management and in English and Western riding are offered. The pre-veterinary medicine program, using the farm facilities, offers the advantages of hands-on experience with livestock and an internship program in a distinctive curriculum. The Nuclear Medicine Institute provides the training necessary to qualify students for careers in nuclear medicine technology, a growing health-related career field. The Health Professions Program provides eleven majors, including athletic training, nuclear medicine, physical education, and recreational therapy.

Costs

Tuition for the 2001-02 academic year totals $17,088 for most programs, $19,988 for the equestrian programs, and $18,140 for the pre-veterinary medicine program. Room and board cost $6434. The estimated cost for transportation, books, and supplies is $1500.

Financial Aid

Eighty percent of Findlay students receive financial aid. Assistance is based on need as well as scholastic achievement. Factors used in determining aid are the Free Application for Federal Student Aid (FAFSA), grade point average, and ACT or SAT I results. Federal and state programs are used with institution grants and scholarships, including sibling grants. The FAFSA must be filed. Notification of aid awards is made on a rolling basis. Work-study jobs are available. Scholarships for high-achieving students and student athletes are offered.

Application and Information

Application forms and other information may be obtained by contacting:
Office of Undergraduate Admissions
The University of Findlay
1000 North Main Street
Findlay, Ohio 45840
Telephone: 419-424-4732
800-548-0932 (toll-free)
E-mail: admissions@findlay.edu
World Wide Web: http://www.findlay.edu

UNIVERSITY OF HOUSTON

Houston, Texas

About the University

The University of Houston (UH), a leading institution in the state-assisted system of higher education in Texas, stands on the forefront of education, research, and service. The largest and most comprehensive component of the University of Houston System, the UH main campus serves more than 32,000 students in fourteen colleges and a host of schools and programs offering more than 300 undergraduate, graduate, and special professional degrees.

UH conducts basic research in each academic department and operates more than forty research centers and institutes on campus. Through these facilities the University maintains creative partnerships with government and private industry, and the research conducted breaks new ground in such vital areas as superconductivity, space commercialization, chemical engineering, economics, and education. The Conrad N. Hilton College of Hotel and Restaurant Management attracts students from all over the country. The University's advanced professional programs include architecture, law, pharmacy, and optometry.

Sponsored research was at $45.5 million for fiscal year 1998. Considering its commitment to excellence, the University anticipates continued support and growth in the amount of grants and awards.

Outstanding faculty and facilities draw students from across the country and around the world. As a result, UH is characterized by a rich mix of cultural backgrounds in a student body that is 48 percent white, 17 percent Asian/Pacific Islander, 16 percent Hispanic, 12 percent African American, 7 percent international students who represent countries across the globe, and .5 percent Native American.

University of Houston public service and community activities, such as cultural offerings, clinical services, policy studies, and small-business initiatives, serve a diverse metropolitan population. Likewise, the resources of the Gulf Coast region complement and enrich the University's academic programs, providing students with professional expertise, practical experience, and career opportunities and allowing them to secure career-level jobs soon after graduation.

Academic Program

UH offers an undergraduate curriculum that provides students with a broad base in the liberal arts complemented by in-depth studies in disciplines of their choice,

affording students a foundation for lifelong learning. UH enrolls a substantial number of National Merit Scholars each year, and the quality of UH students is further reflected in the growing enrollment in the Honors College. Created to serve the intellectual needs of gifted undergraduates in more than 100 fields of study, the Honors College provides the careful guidance, flexibility, and personal instruction that nurture individual excellence. The Honors College offers all the advantages of a small college without sacrificing the wealth of resources and the rich diversity of a large university.

Costs

The estimated average total cost per semester for the 2000-01 school year was $1232 for Texas residents and $3800 for nonresidents. Costs are subject to change. Students should go to the University's Web site (listed below) for updated tuition information.

Financial Aid

Several types of student financial assistance are offered, including scholarships, which are generally based on measures of academic performance such as GPA, class rank, and SAT I or ACT scores, and need-based (as determined from the Free Application for Federal Student Aid) assistance, which includes loans, grants, and part-time employment. For applications and materials, students should write directly to: Office of Scholarships and Financial Aid, University of Houston, 4800 Calhoun Road, Houston, Texas 77204-2160.

Application and Information

Notifications of acceptance are based on a review of an applicant's complete file and continue on a rolling admission basis. An application fee of $40 is required. Students are urged to apply early. Deadlines are fall, May 11 for freshmen and June 1 for transfer students; spring, December 11; and summer, May 11.

Applicants are strongly encouraged to apply for admission using the Internet at the address listed below and are reminded to select the University of Houston as the receiving institution.

Requests for an application for admission, freshman and transfer scholarship applications, and information should be directed to:

Office of Admissions
University of Houston
4800 Calhoun Road
Houston, Texas 77204-2161
Telephone: 713-743-1010
E-mail: admissions@uh.edu
World Wide Web: http://www.uh.edu

UNIVERSITY OF SOUTH CAROLINA

Columbia, South Carolina

About the University

The University of South Carolina's Columbia campus, founded in 1801 as South Carolina College, quickly achieved a reputation of academic excellence in the classical tradition and became one of the most distinguished colleges in the United States. Today's University of South Carolina continues this tradition of excellence.

The location of the campus is ideal for students participating in internships related to their majors or seeking part-time employment in the area. Columbia offers a wide variety of restaurants, entertainment, and shopping, all within walking distance of the campus. Columbia is also home to a philharmonic orchestra, a symphony, ballet and dance companies, theaters, and galleries.

More than 260 student organizations on campus offer a niche for any student interest from backpacking to politics, including fraternities, sororities, service, and honors organizations. There are also 120 intramural sports teams. The University's varsity athletic teams, the Gamecocks and Lady Gamecocks, compete in Division I of the NCAA and play national schedules. The University of South Carolina is a member of the Southeastern Conference (SEC).

The Office of Disability Services assists physically challenged students with student orientation, registration, housing, library use, transportation, and classroom adaptation and provides sign language interpreters, readers and note takers, and personal, academic, and vocational counseling.

South Carolina has an all-campus enrollment of nearly 40,000. Of these, about 23,000 students are on the Columbia campus. About 78 percent are South Carolinians, while 22 percent represent the remaining forty-nine states and more than 100 other countries.

South Carolina is a comprehensive university that offers students more than seventy undergraduate majors ranging from traditional disciplines to technical and professional areas of study. The University is fully accredited by the Southern Association of Colleges and Schools to award baccalaureate, master's, and doctoral degrees.

Highly motivated, exceptional students find a distinctive educational niche in the University's South Carolina Honors College—rated one of the best in the United States. Also of special note is the University 101 program ("The Student in the University"), which is designed to acquaint new students with the University and its academic resources. South Carolina's program is recognized as a model for other colleges and universities both in the United States and abroad.

Academic Program

Completion of the baccalaureate degree requires acceptance from one of the schools or colleges granting undergraduate degrees, each of which has its own standards, prerequisites, and degree requirements. Minimum grade point average requirements for graduation vary depending upon the degree sought.

Costs

For 2001-02, expenses for in-state students total approximately $10,230 (including tuition and fees, room and board, and books and supplies). The total estimated expenses for out-of-state students are $16,700.

Financial Aid

Nearly half of the University's students receive some type of financial assistance, including financial aid, loans, work-study opportunities, and/or scholarships. Applicants must complete the Free Application for Federal Student Aid (FAFSA) before they may be considered for financial aid. The FAFSA should be submitted to the processor four to six weeks prior to the University's April 1 deadline. Generally, students considered for scholarships rank in the top 10 percent of their high school class and score 1300 or better on the SAT I. Scholarships based upon merit and strong academic potential are available, with awards from $1500 to $9000 per year. Several of the University's departments also award scholarships to outstanding entering freshmen.

Application and Information

High school seniors applying for admission should do so during the fall of their senior year. Transfer students are advised to apply at least three months prior to the semester in which they plan to enter. The application fee is $40.

For additional information about the University, students may contact:

Office of Undergraduate Admissions
University of South Carolina
Columbia, South Carolina 29208
Telephone: 803-777-7700
800-868-5USC (toll-free)
E-mail: admissions-ugrad@sc.edu
World Wide Web: http://www.sc.edu/admissions

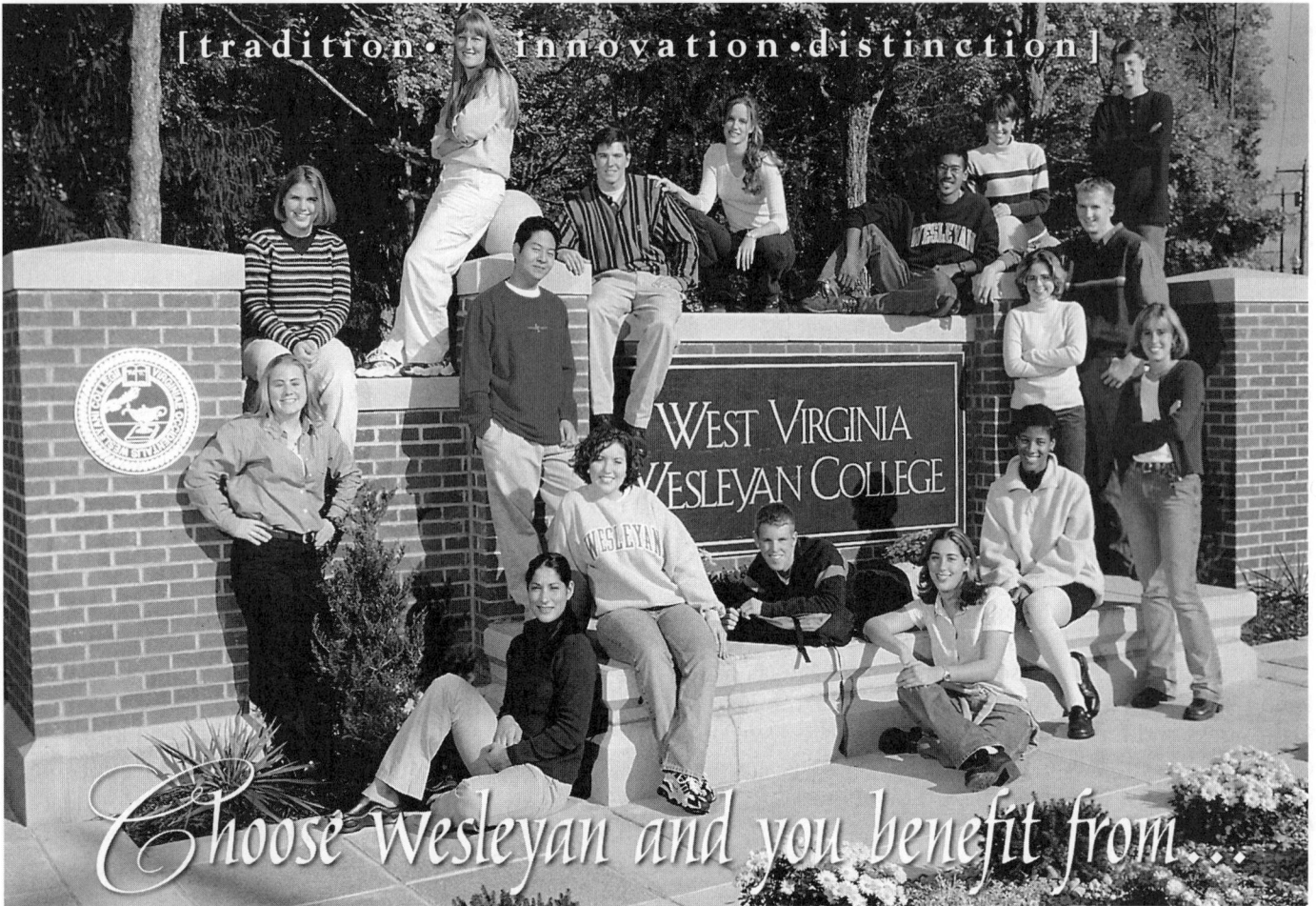

WEST VIRGINIA WESLEYAN COLLEGE

Buckhannon, West Virginia

About the College

Founded by the United Methodist Church in 1890, West Virginia Wesleyan College welcomes students of all geographic, religious, and ethnic backgrounds. The four-year liberal arts program encourages students to develop an understanding of their own individuality, a commitment to the surrounding community, and an involvement in curricular and cocurricular resources.

Wesleyan is accredited by the North Central Association of Colleges and Schools and approved by the University Senate of the United Methodist Church. The nursing program is accredited by the National League for Nursing Accrediting Commission, the teacher education program is accredited by the National Council for Accreditation of Teacher Education (NCATE), the music program is accredited by the National Association of Schools of Music, and the athletic training program is accredited by the Commission on Accreditation of Allied Health Education Programs (CAAHEP).

Wesleyan's more than 1,500 students originate from thirty-six states and twenty-nine countries. Forty-five percent of the student body come from West Virginia. Approximately 10 percent of the students are minority or international students. Eighty-five percent reside on campus in a variety of housing options, including residence halls, apartments, and substance-free housing.

The dynamic student life program offers more than seventy clubs and organizations in which students may participate, including student governance clubs, the campus radio station, the newspaper and yearbook clubs, six fraternities and five sororities, seventeen NCAA Division II sports teams, intramurals, Christian Life Council, and the Campus Activities Board, which schedules nightly weekend entertainment.

As a participant in the IBM ThinkPad University Program, Wesleyan provides students with a laptop computer for all four years of undergraduate study. Students use the computer in classrooms as well as the residence halls. The campus fiber-optic system allows for rapid Internet and e-mail access from all academic buildings and residence hall rooms.

Academic Program

Students are required to complete 120 credit hours of course work to become eligible for graduation. Approximately one third of those hours are taken in a student's major, one third in the general studies curriculum requirement, and one third in electives.

The 4-1-4 academic calendar is another feature at Wesleyan. During the optional January Term, students can focus on one class for the whole term, either as part of their major concentration or to fulfill a general studies or elective requirement. These classes may be taken on campus, but there are also opportunities for study abroad.

The honors program is offered for superior students who meet the specific requirements and are willing to commit themselves to a rigorous and enriching program that affirms the highest ideals of a liberal arts institution. Challenging classes and cultural outings are an integral part of the honors program and are offered throughout the academic year.

Costs

The 2001-02 costs at Wesleyan are $17,300 for tuition, $4400 for room and board, and $1400 for student fees, which include a student activity fee and technology fee.

Financial Aid

Wesleyan awards financial aid on the basis of scholastic achievements, special talents and abilities, and financial need. A number of scholarships are available, including awards for academics, athletics, community service, leadership, and performing and visual arts. Students may apply for low-cost federal loans. Students should file the Free Application for Federal Student Aid by February 15.

Application and Information

A completed online application form must be submitted through wvwc.edu along with a nonrefundable $30 application fee anytime after the junior year or during the senior year of high school. Admission offers are made on a rolling admission basis. The regular application deadline is March 1.

Requests for online application instructions, viewbook, and other information should be addressed to:

Office of Admission
West Virginia Wesleyan College
59 College Avenue
Buckhannon, West Virginia 26201
Telephone: 304-473-8510
800-722-9933 (toll-free)
E-mail: admission@wvwc.edu
World Wide Web: http://www.wvwc.edu

Distinguished Scholars Dedicated Teachers

William Paterson's Fulbright Scholars exemplify a tradition of academic excellence and commitment to student success.

William Paterson offers

- nationally renowned undergraduate and graduate programs
- access to state-of-the-art information and communications technology
- low student to faculty ratio (12:1)
- small class size (21.2)
- flexible scheduling—evenings and weekends
- student research and honors programs
- national and international student exchanges, internships, and leadership opportunities
- scholarships and financial assistance packages

From left to right, top to bottom: Vincent Parrillo, Sociology; Sara Nalle, History; William Small, Political Science; Martin Laurence, Economics (recipient of two awards); George Robb, History; Ching-Yeh Hu, Biology; Melvin Edelstein, History; Vernon McClean, African, African American, and Caribbean Studies; Theodore Cook, History; Isabel Tirado, History; Carol Gruber, History; Reynold Weidenaar, Communication; Bruce Williams, Languages and Cultures; Leslie Agard-Jones, African, African American, and Caribbean Studies; Martin Weinstein, Political Science; John Livingston, History; Michael Principe, Political Science; Krista O'Donnell, History; Lois Wolf, Political Science; Joanne Cho, History; Catarina Edinger, English; Charlotte Nekola, English; Mytheli Sreenivas, Women's Studies; Geoffrey Pope, Anthropology; John Mason, Political Science

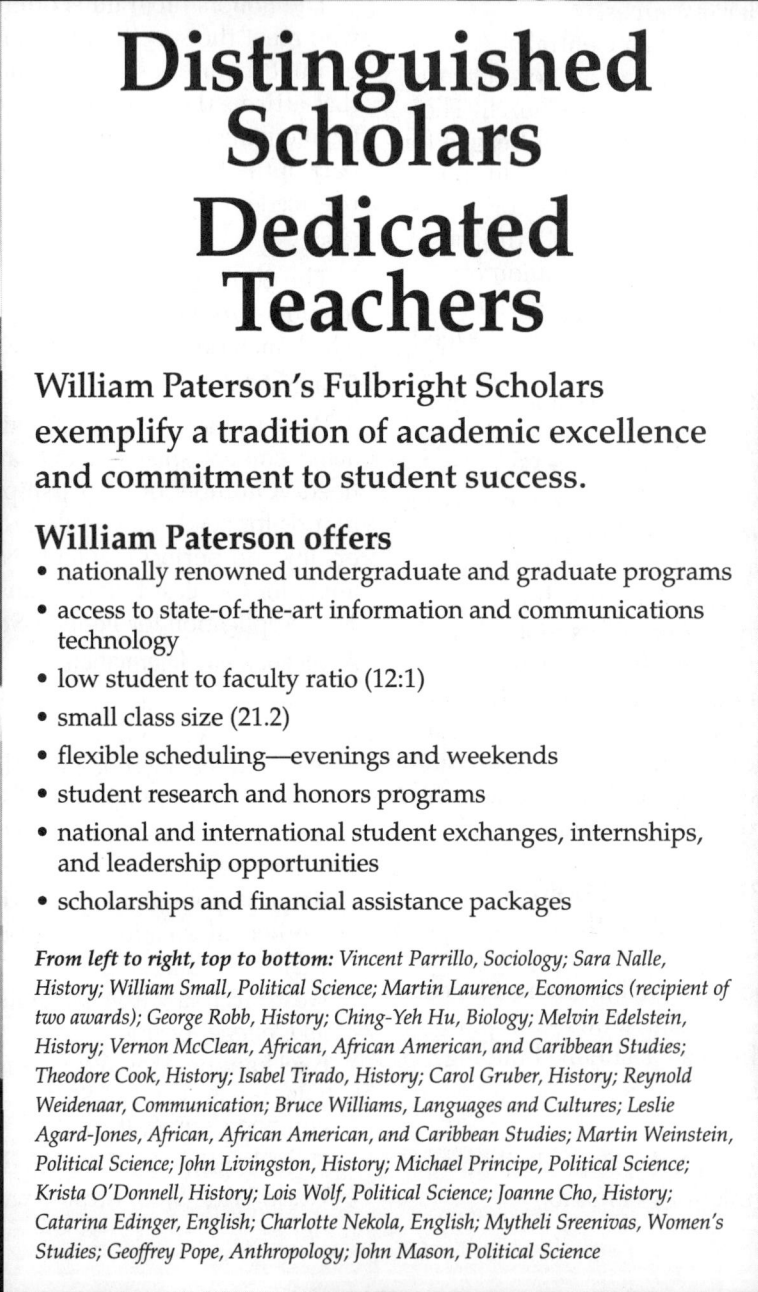

WILLIAM PATERSON UNIVERSITY

WAYNE, NEW JERSEY 07470
1.877.WPU.EXCEL • WWW.WPUNJ.EDU

WILLIAM PATERSON UNIVERSITY OF NEW JERSEY

Wayne, New Jersey

About the University

Since its founding in 1855, William Paterson University has grown into a comprehensive state institution whose programs reflect the area's need for challenging, affordable educational options. Ideally midsized (the total enrollment is 9,945, of whom 8,454 are degree-seeking undergraduates), William Paterson offers a wider variety of academic programs than smaller universities, yet provides students with a more personalized atmosphere than larger institutions. Although the majority of the University's students come from the New Jersey and New York vicinity, some international and out-of-state students enroll each year.

Social, cultural, and recreational activities complement the academic programs. Cultural events take place throughout the year, featuring both William Paterson's own talent and renowned professional artists. The most popular spot for social activities is the Student Center, which contains an art gallery, a performing arts lounge, a game room, and several auxiliary dining areas. The Student Activities Programming Board helps the more than fifty clubs and organizations to develop diverse activities for the entire student body. William Paterson has twenty-six social fraternities and sororities and eleven honor societies. The University has eighteen intercollegiate sports teams, nine for men and nine for women, including successful NCAA teams in men's baseball and women's softball.

Academic Program

Students must complete a minimum of 128 credits to earn a baccalaureate degree. Degree programs include a 60-credit general education requirement, 30-60 credits in a major, and 20-40 in elective courses. (In specialized degree programs, such as the B.F.A. and the B.M., general education and major course requirements may differ.) Diagnostic testing and career seminars, provided by the Career Development Office, also ensure that students receive the guidance necessary to make wise course selections and career decisions.

William Paterson offers honors programs for hose ambitious and well-qualified students who want to add a challenging dimension to their major. Currently, there are seven honors programs—in biopsychology, cognitive sciences, humanities, life science and environmental ethics, music, nursing, and performance studies.

Students who successfully complete Advanced Placement tests and/or College-Level Examination Program tests may receive credit for acceptable scores. In addition, credit may be awarded for military training and experience.

William Paterson University operates on a two-semester and two-summer-session system.

Costs

Annual tuition (including fees) for the 2001-02 academic year is $5150 for full-time (12 credits or more) students who are New Jersey residents and $8010 for full-time nonresident students. Room and board cost approximately $6400 per year. All charges are subject to change per the Board of Trustees.

Financial Aid

Financial aid is available through a number of federal and state grant, loan, scholarship, and work-study programs. To apply for need-based aid, students must file the Free Application for Federal Student Aid (FAFSA) with the United States Department of Education by the priority date of April 1.

Both the University and the Alumni Association award a number of competitive scholarships, based solely on academic merit, to entering freshmen. They are the Scholarships for Academic Excellence, scholarships for African-American and Hispanic students, and Trustee and Presidential Scholarships. Academic Achievement Scholarships are awarded only on a competitive basis to continuing students.

Application and Information

Application forms and transcripts from candidates for freshman status must be received by May 1 for fall admission and November 1 for spring admission. However, the University closes the application process earlier when the number of new and continuing students strains its ability to provide effective programs and services. A $35 application fee is required. Applications are reviewed on a rolling basis. Campus tours are available during the fall and spring semesters on weekdays by appointment when classes are in session.

For additional information and to apply online, go to the undergraduate admissions site at the address listed below or contact:

Office of Admissions
William Paterson University of New Jersey
Wayne, New Jersey 07470
Telephone: 973-720-2125
877-WPU-EXCEL (toll-free)
World Wide Web: http://www.wpunj.edu

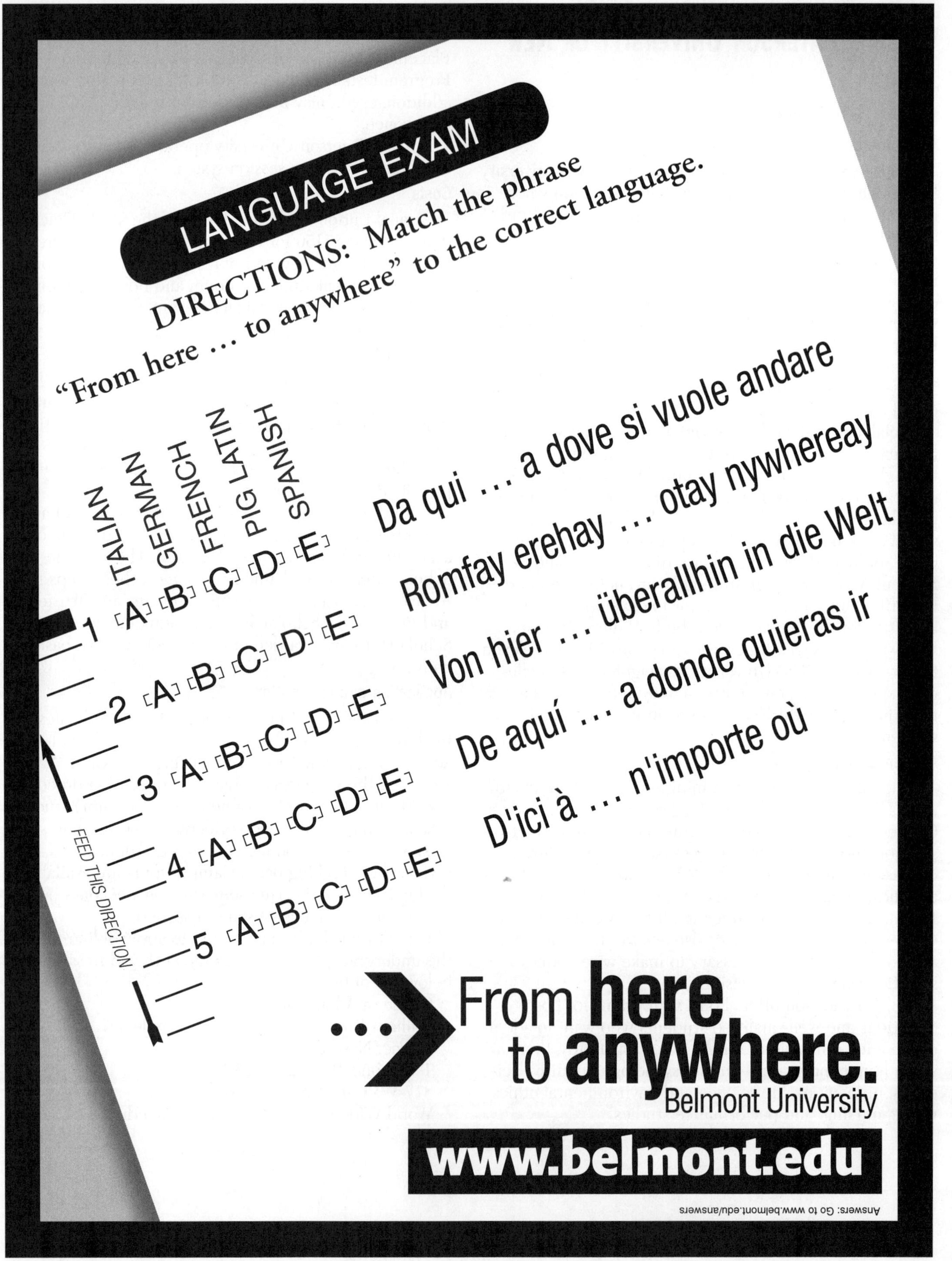

LANGUAGE EXAM
DIRECTIONS: Match the phrase
"From here … to anywhere" to the correct language.
ITALIAN
GERMAN
FRENCH
PIG LATIN
SPANISH
1 A B C D E Da qui … a dove si vuole andare
2 A B C D E Romfay erehay … otay nywhereay
3 A B C D E Von hier … überallhin in die Welt
4 A B C D E De aquí … a donde quieras ir
5 A B C D E D'ici à … n'importe où
FEED THIS DIRECTION
From here to anywhere.
Belmont University
www.belmont.edu
Answers: Go to www.belmont.edu/answers

Not only is our Allendale campus a nice place to visit, it's a great place to live. Which is why many of the young people who complete a university tour end up living here.

Best of all, students learn from professors committed to teaching. Which is why all classes are taught by professors, not graduate students or assistants. It's the kind of personalized instruction that better prepares students for graduate school or a more fulfilling professional career.

In addition to a superb teaching staff and beautiful campus, GVSU offers students and parents many

Discover why students from all over the country are turning a one-day visit to Grand Valley into a four-year stay.

More than 3,900 students live on campus in some of the newest housing in the state. Choices include suite-based living centers, residence halls, apartments, and special housing for Honors, Foreign Language, and Art students. And all students enjoy a picturesque campus and participate in a great variety of academic, social, cultural, and athletic activities.

Many people visit for a day and end up staying four years.

Call our Admissions Office for more information about degree programs, scholarships, and financial aid. You can also visit us on the Web at www.gvsu.edu.

other advantages, including:

- More than 75 bachelor's and master's degree programs.
- Class sizes that average just 28 students.
- Generous financial aid and scholarship packages.
- State-of-the-art science, music, art, and athletic facilities.
- Tuition rates among the lowest of any university in Michigan.
- Named one of the 100 most wired universities by *Yahoo! Internet Life* magazine.

GRAND VALLEY STATE UNIVERSITY

Allendale Campus

616.895.2025
800.748.0246
www.gvsu.edu

NEW ENGLAND MAP

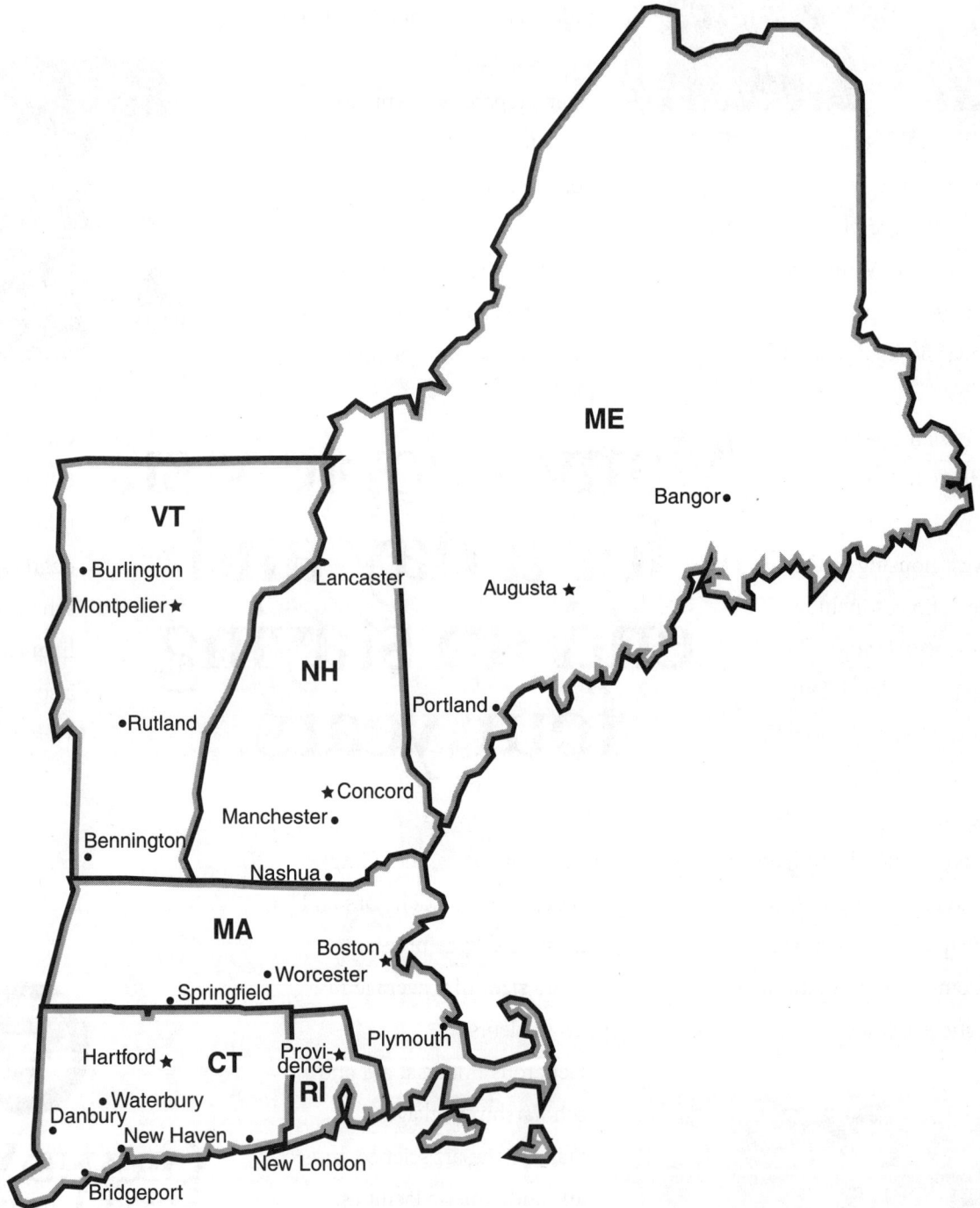

ME

Bangor •

VT

• Burlington

Montpelier ★

Lancaster

Augusta ★

NH

Portland •

•Rutland

★ Concord

Manchester •

Bennington •

Nashua •

MA

Boston ★

• Worcester

Springfield •

Plymouth

Hartford ★ **CT**

Provi-
dence ★

RI

• Waterbury

Danbury •

New Haven •

New London

• Bridgeport

2-yr

Two-Year Colleges

This index includes the names and locations of accredited two-year colleges in the Middle Atlantic and shows responses to Peterson's 2000 Survey of Undergraduate Institutions. The data was collected between November 1999 and May 2000. If an institution submitted incomplete or no data, one or more columns opposite the institution's name is blank.

Y—Yes; N—No; R—Recommended; S—For Some

		Degrees Awarded Transfer Associate (C), Terminal Associate (T), Bachelor's (B), Master's (M), Doctoral (D), First Professional (F)	Undergraduate Enrollment Fall 1999	Percent Attending Part-Time	Percent 25 Years of Age or Older	Percent of Grads Going on to 4-Year Colleges	Open Admissions	High School Equivalency Certificate Accepted	High School Transcript Required	Need-based Aid Available	Part-Time Jobs Available	Career Counseling Available	Job Placement Services Available	College Housing Available	Number of Sports Offered
Connecticut															
Asnuntuck Community College	Enfield	C,T	1,913	90	62		Y	Y	Y	Y	Y	Y	Y	N	
Briarwood College	Southington	C,T	627	45	38	7	N	Y	Y	Y	Y	Y	Y	Y	4
Capital Community College	Hartford	C,T	2,766	85	86		Y	Y	R	Y	Y	Y	Y	N	4
Gateway Community College	New Haven	C,T	4,141	77	46	40	Y	Y	Y		Y	Y	Y	N	1
Gibbs College	Norwalk	T	462	42											
Housatonic Community College	Bridgeport	C,T	3,551	80											
International College of Hospitality Management, Cesar Ritz	Washington	C,T	95	3	23	25	N	Y	Y	Y	Y	Y	Y	Y	4
Manchester Community College	Manchester	C,T	5,252	75	50		Y	Y	Y	Y	Y	Y		N	3
Middlesex Community College	Middletown	C,T	2,317	82	53		Y	Y		Y	Y	Y	Y	N	
Mitchell College	New London	C,T,B	590	19	11	93	N	Y	Y	Y	Y	Y	Y	Y	15
Naugatuck Valley Community College	Waterbury	C,T	4,863	68	46	30	Y	Y	Y	Y	Y	Y	Y	N	3
Northwestern Connecticut Community-Technical Coll	Winsted	C,T	1,848		62	30	Y	Y		Y	Y	Y	Y	N	
Norwalk Community College	Norwalk	C,T	5,220	81	53	41	Y	Y		Y	Y	Y	Y	N	7
Quinebaug Valley Community College	Danielson	C,T	1,281	71	50		Y	Y	R,S	Y	Y	Y		N	2
St. Vincent's College	Bridgeport	C	212												
Three Rivers Community College	Norwich	C,T	3,573	77	60	45	Y	Y	R	Y	Y	Y	Y	N	3
Maine															
Andover College	Portland	T	520	79	63		Y	Y	Y	Y	Y	Y	Y	Y	
Beal College	Bangor	T	368	42	54		Y	Y	Y	Y		Y	Y	N	
Central Maine Medical Center School of Nursing	Lewiston	T	85	14	68		N	Y	Y	Y				Y	
Central Maine Technical College	Auburn	C,T	1,248	57	53	6	N	Y	Y	Y	Y	Y	Y	Y	15
Eastern Maine Technical College	Bangor	C,T	1,277	62	26		N	Y	Y	Y	Y	Y	Y	Y	10
Kennebec Valley Technical College	Fairfield	T	808												
Mid-State College	Auburn	C,T													
New England School of Communications	Bangor	T	145												
Southern Maine Technical College	South Portland	C,T	2,362	56	48	10	N	Y	Y		Y	Y	Y	Y	7
Washington County Technical College	Calais	C,T	390	37	58	4	Y	Y	Y	Y	Y			Y	
York County Technical College	Wells	C,T	703	76			Y	Y	Y	Y	Y	Y		N	
Massachusetts															
Baptist Bible College East	Boston	C,T	115												
Bay State College	Boston	C,T	795	10	12		N	Y	Y	Y	Y	Y	Y	Y	
Berkshire Community College	Pittsfield	C,T	2,428		52	47	Y	Y	Y	Y	Y	Y	Y	N	5
Bristol Community College	Fall River	C,T	6,053	69	49	43	Y	Y	Y	Y	Y	Y	Y	N	
Bunker Hill Community College	Boston	C,T	6,417		53	35	Y	Y	Y	Y	Y	Y	Y	N	6

2-yr

Two-Year Colleges

This index includes the names and locations of accredited two-year colleges in the Middle Atlantic and shows responses to Peterson's 2000 Survey of Undergraduate Institutions. The data was collected between November 1999 and May 2000. If an institution submitted incomplete or no data, one or more columns opposite the institution's name is blank.

		Degrees Awarded Transfer Associate (C), Terminal Associate (T), Bachelor's (B), Master's (M), Doctoral (D), First Professional (F)	Undergraduate Enrollment Fall 1999	Percent Attending Part-Time	Percent 25 Years of Age or Older	Percent of Grads Going on to 4-Year Colleges	Open Admissions	High School Equivalency Certificate Accepted	High School Transcript Required	Need-based Aid Available	Part-Time Jobs Available	Career Counseling Available	Job Placement Services Available	College Housing Available	Number of Sports Offered
Cape Cod Community College	West Barnstable	C,T	3,793	80	57	67	Y	Y	Y	Y	Y	Y	Y	N	10
Dean College	Franklin	C,T	1,313	42	3	90	N	Y	Y	Y	Y	Y	Y	Y	11
Fisher College	Boston	C,T,B	1,577	44	52	50	N	Y	Y	Y	Y	Y	Y	Y	7
Franklin Institute of Boston	Boston	C,T,B	342	3	20	38	N	Y	Y		Y	Y	Y	N	3
Greenfield Community College	Greenfield	C,T	2,240	59											
Holyoke Community College	Holyoke	C,T	5,468												
ITT Technical Institute	Framingham	T													
Katharine Gibbs School	Boston	C,T	535												
Labourlfe College	Boston	C,T	314												
Marian Court College	Swampscott	C	200		45	25	N	Y	Y	Y	Y	Y	Y	N	
Massachusetts Bay Community College	Wellesley Hills	C,T	4,615	56	49		Y	Y		Y	Y	Y	Y	N	7
Massachusetts Communications College	Boston	T	450												
Massasoit Community College	Brockton	C,T	6,472		45	32	Y	Y		Y	Y	Y	Y	N	5
Middlesex Community College	Bedford	C,T	6,933	58	39	48	Y	Y	S	Y	Y	Y	Y	N	3
Mount Wachusett Community College	Gardner	C,T	3,413	63	45	61	Y	Y	Y	Y	Y	Y	Y	N	
Newbury College	Brookline	C,T,B	2,594	70	34	31	N	Y	Y	Y	Y	Y	Y	Y	10
New England College of Finance	Boston	T,B	955		22	50	Y	Y	Y					N	
Northern Essex Community College	Haverhill	C,T	6,375	73	51	40	Y	Y	Y	Y	Y	Y	Y	N	11
North Shore Community College	Danvers	C,T	6,101	64	50	72	Y	Y	S	Y	Y	Y	Y	N	3
Quincy College	Quincy	C,T	3,764		45		Y	Y	Y	Y	Y	Y	Y	N	
Quinsigamond Community College	Worcester	C,T	5,178	65											
Roxbury Community College	Roxbury Crossing	C,T	2,382	57	61		Y	Y	Y	Y	Y	Y	Y	N	5
Springfield Technical Community College	Springfield	C,T	6,474	61	35	81	Y	Y	Y	Y	Y	Y	Y	N	10

New Hampshire

Hesser College	Manchester	C,T,B	3,181	46	25	65	N	Y	Y	Y	Y	Y	Y	Y	8
McIntosh College	Dover	C	863	48											
New Hampshire Comm Tech Coll, Berlin/Laconia	Berlin	C,T	1,345	67			N	Y	Y	Y	Y	Y	Y	N	6
New Hampshire Comm Tech Coll, Manchester/Stratham	Manchester	C,T	2,007												
New Hampshire Comm Tech Coll, Nashua/Claremont	Nashua	C,T	1,282	67	23		N	Y	Y	Y	Y	Y	Y	N	6
New Hampshire Technical Institute	Concord	C	2,655	61	50	18		Y	Y	Y	Y	Y	Y	Y	4

Rhode Island

Community College of Rhode Island	Warwick	C,T	15,610	70	44		Y			Y	Y	Y	Y	N	10
New England Institute of Technology	Warwick	C,T,B	2,537		36		Y	Y	Y	Y	Y	Y	Y	N	

2-yr

Two-Year Colleges

This index includes the names and locations of accredited two-year colleges in the Middle Atlantic and shows responses to Peterson's 2000 Survey of Undergraduate Institutions. The data was collected between November 1999 and May 2000. If an institution submitted incomplete or no data, one or more columns opposite the institution's name is blank.

Y—Yes; N—No; R—Recommended; S—For Some

Vermont

		Degrees Awarded Transfer Associate (C), Terminal Associate (T), Bachelor's (B), Master's (M), Doctoral (D), First Professional (F)	Undergraduate Enrollment Fall 1999	Percent Attending Part-Time	Percent 25 Years of Age or Older	Percent of Grads Going on to 4-Year Colleges	Open Admissions	High School Equivalency Certificate Accepted	High School Transcript Required	Need-based Aid Available	Part-Time Jobs Available	Career Counseling Available	Job Placement Services Available	College Housing Available	Number of Sports Offered
Community College of Vermont	Waterbury	C,T	4,758	88	70		Y	Y		Y	Y	Y		N	
Landmark College	Putney	C,T	341		11	90	N	Y	Y	Y	Y	Y		Y	10
New England Culinary Institute	Montpelier	T,B	626		58	14	N	Y	Y	Y	Y	Y	Y	Y	
Vermont Technical College	Randolph Center	C,T,B	1,145	28	23	18	N	Y	Y	Y	Y	Y	Y	Y	19
Woodbury College	Montpelier	C,T	133	32	87	20	Y	Y	S	Y	Y	Y		N	

4-yr

Four-Year Institutions

This index includes the names and locations of accredited four-year colleges and universities in the Middle Atlantic and shows responses to Peterson's 2000 Survey of Undergraduate Institutions. The data was collected between November 1999 and May 2000. If an institution submitted incomplete or no data, one or more columns opposite the institution's name is blank.

STANDARDIZED TEST SCORE RANGES FOR 1999–2000
% of freshmen scoring within each interval

Degrees Awarded: Associate (A), Bachelor's (B), Master's (M), Doctoral (D), First Professional (P)

Connecticut

Institution	Location	Degrees	Undergrad Enroll. Fall 1999	Computers	ACT 1-5	ACT 6-11	ACT 12-17	ACT 18-23	ACT 24-29	ACT 30-36	SAT-V 200-299	SAT-V 300-399	SAT-V 400-499	SAT-V 500-599	SAT-V 600-699	SAT-V 700-800	SAT-M 200-299	SAT-M 300-399	SAT-M 400-499	SAT-M 500-599	SAT-M 600-699	SAT-M 700-800
Albertus Magnus College	New Haven	A,B,M	1,720	75							1	8	41	35	10	5	0	10	46	35	9	0
Central Connecticut State University	New Britain	B,M	9,264	230							1	11	48	32	7	1	1	12	46	33	6	1
Charter Oak State College	New Britain	A,B	1,429	NR																		
Connecticut College	New London	B,M	1,645	150	0	0	0	19	55	26	0	0	3	24	52	21	0	0	4	23	55	17
Eastern Connecticut State University	Willimantic	A,B,M	4,286	300							1	12	45	35	6	1	2	14	49	29	6	0
Fairfield University	Fairfield	B,M	4,064	140							0	0	16	54	31	4	0	0	12	49	38	5
Hartford College for Women	Hartford	A,B	120	40																		
Holy Apostles College and Seminary	Cromwell	A,B,M,P	13	10																		
Lyme Academy of Fine Arts	Old Lyme	B	75	3									100						100			
Mitchell College	New London	A,B	537	NR							2	28	29	7	2		6	27	25	11	1	
Paier College of Art, Inc.	Hamden	A,B	229	18							0	33	29	25	9	4	4	41	32	22	4	1
Quinnipiac University	Hamden	B,M,P	4,341	140	0	0	9	41	44	6	0	0	33	46	16	5	0	0	28	47	18	7
Sacred Heart University	Fairfield	A,B,M	3,786	NR							0	2	38	47	11	2	0	2	41	45	10	2
Saint Joseph College	West Hartford	B,M	951	150							7	30	56	4	3		0	56	40	4	0	0
Southern Connecticut State University	New Haven	A,B,M	7,445	300																		
Teikyo Post University	Waterbury	A,B	1,289	70							7	30	44	16	1	1	12	35	37	11	4	1
Trinity College	Hartford	B,M	2,112	200	0	0	0	10	70	20	0	0	2	27	53	18	0	0	5	22	55	17
United States Coast Guard Academy	New London	B	838	120	0	0	0	11	78	11	0	0	1	32	57	10	0	0	0	14	69	17
University of Bridgeport	Bridgeport	A,B,M,D,P	1,212	350							2	22	39	25	9	3	4	16	39	21	14	6
University of Connecticut	Storrs	A,B,M,D,P	11,987	1,800							0	1	16	51	26	5	0	0	16	47	31	6
University of Hartford	West Hartford	A,B,M,D	5,030	380	0	0	11	49	35	6	0	4	34	44	16	2	0	3	33	46	17	1
University of New Haven	West Haven	A,B,M,D	2,496	200							0	17	43	29	9	1	0	18	45	26	9	1
Wesleyan University	Middletown	B,M,D	2,734	250					25	75	0	0	2	12	38	48	0	0	2	11	46	41
Western Connecticut State University	Danbury	A,B,M	4,174	300							0	12	48	32	8	0	1	12	49	29	9	0
Yale University	New Haven	B,M,D,P	5,294	350																		

Maine

Institution	Location	Degrees	Undergrad Enroll. Fall 1999	Computers	ACT 1-5	ACT 6-11	ACT 12-17	ACT 18-23	ACT 24-29	ACT 30-36	SAT-V 200-299	SAT-V 300-399	SAT-V 400-499	SAT-V 500-599	SAT-V 600-699	SAT-V 700-800	SAT-M 200-299	SAT-M 300-399	SAT-M 400-499	SAT-M 500-599	SAT-M 600-699	SAT-M 700-800
Bates College	Lewiston	B	1,706	758							0	0	1	9	60	30	0	0	1	7	63	29
Bowdoin College	Brunswick	B	1,600	210							0	0	1	7	48	44	0	0	0	9	53	38
Colby College	Waterville	B	1,764	276	0	0	1	3	63	33	0	0	1	17	59	23	0	0	3	14	57	26
College of the Atlantic	Bar Harbor	B,M	273	42	0	0	0	33	59	8	0	0	0	29	50	21	0	0	10	48	34	8
Husson College	Bangor	A,B,M	1,394	96	0	0	0	92	8	0	0	10	46	39	4	1	1	15	47	33	4	0
Maine College of Art	Portland	B,M	380	40	0	0	20	60	20	0	1	5	2	42	20	4	1	11	44	30	12	2
Maine Maritime Academy	Castine	A,B,M	680	40																		
Saint Joseph's College	Standish	A,B,M	820	71							0	6	41	44	8	1	0	9	43	39	8	1
Thomas College	Waterville	A,B,M	696	60							2	21	49	25	3	0	2	18	41	35	3	1
Unity College	Unity	A,B	512	42							0	4	78	13	5	0	0	5	82	9	4	0
University of Maine	Orono	B,M,D	6,936	250							0	3	28	45	21	3	0	3	29	42	22	4
University of Maine at Augusta	Augusta	A	3,997	88																		
University of Maine at Farmington	Farmington	B	2,262	150							0	5	30	45	16	4	1	6	33	42	12	1
University of Maine at Fort Kent	Fort Kent	A,B	926	100							1	24	49	18	8	0	3	25	47	21	3	1
University of Maine at Machias	Machias	A,B	731	175	0	0	4	58	33	5	1	4	36	48	10	1	1	5	37	47	9	1
University of Maine at Presque Isle	Presque Isle	A,B	1,204	90							1	24	42	30	3	1	2	15	49	26	7	0
University of New England	Biddeford	A,B,M,P	1,473	76							1	4	37	45	12	1	0	9	36	39	15	1
University of Southern Maine	Portland	A,B,M,D,P	6,524	283							0	3	38	49	13	2	0	2	41	47	15	0

4-yr

Four-Year Institutions

This index includes the names and locations of accredited four-year colleges and universities in the Middle Atlantic and shows responses to Peterson's 2000 Survey of Undergraduate Institutions. The data was collected between November 1999 and May 2000. If an institution submitted incomplete or no data, one or more columns opposite the institution's name is blank.

STANDARDIZED TEST SCORE RANGES FOR 1999–2000
% of freshmen scoring within each interval

Massachusetts

Institution	Location	Degrees Awarded	Undergrad Enrollment Fall 1999	Computers	ACT 1-5	6-11	12-17	18-23	24-29	30-36	SATV 200-299	300-399	400-499	500-599	600-699	700-800	SATM 200-299	300-399	400-499	500-599	600-699	700-800
American International College	Springfield	A,B,M,D	1,236	50							1	16	38	33	10	2	1	18	38	41	11	2
Amherst College	Amherst	B	1,664	123	0	0	0	3	39	58	0	0	0	6	39	54	0	0	0	6	40	53
Anna Maria College	Paxton	A,B,M	694	49							1	13	41	32	12	1	0	16	46	33	5	0
The Art Institute of Boston at Lesley	Boston	B	472	25							2	9	36	27	24	2	2	9	45	35	8	1
Assumption College	Worcester	A,B,M	2,352	275	0	0	6	60	34	0	0	1	25	53	20	1	0	1	32	49	17	1
Atlantic Union College	South Lancaster	A,B,M	661		60																	
Babson College	Wellesley	B,M	1,701	350							0	0	8	49	40	3	0	0	1	28	36	15
Bay Path College	Longmeadow	A,B	656	114																		
Becker College	Worcester	A,B	1,010	155																		
Bentley College	Waltham	A,B,M	4,114	3,200	0	0	14	38	42	6	0	4	24	53	18	1	0	0	13	52	30	4
Berklee College of Music	Boston	B	3,012	45																		
Boston Architectural Center	Boston	B,M,P	495	50																		
Boston College	Chestnut Hill	B,M,D,P	9,190	200							0	0	4	24	53	18	0	0	3	18	54	24
Boston Conservatory	Boston	B,M	333	16																		
Boston University	Boston	B,M,D,P	15,469	500	0	0	0	6	67	26	0	0	1	27	53	19	0	0	1	25	55	20
Brandeis University	Waltham	B,M,D	3,040	100							0	0	1	15	54	30	0	0	2	15	50	33
Bridgewater State College	Bridgewater	B,M	6,477	470							0	7	39	43	9	1	0	9	44	39	7	0
Cambridge College	Cambridge	B,M	285	NR																		
Clark University	Worcester	B,M,D	2,013	100	0	0	0	40	51	9	0	1	17	38	37	7	0	1	17	48	30	4
College of Our Lady of the Elms	Chicopee	B,M	724	70							0	13	46	32	9	0	2	16	48	28	6	0
College of the Holy Cross	Worcester	B	2,778	175							0	0	3	26	55	16	0	0	2	25	56	17
Curry College	Milton	B,M	1,894	50							1	20	50	22	6	1	2	31	50	13	2	1
Eastern Nazarene College	Quincy	A,B,M	1,338	70	0	0	14	52	17	17	1	8	29	37	20	5	1	9	34	35	14	7
Emerson College	Boston	B,M,D	3,135	125	0	7	23	38	20	12	0	0	5	41	42	12	0	0	15	53	29	3
Emmanuel College	Boston	B,M	1,303	70	0	0	30	62	8	0	0	6	32	39	20	3	0	11	44	34	10	1
Endicott College	Beverly	A,B,M	1,395	100							0	5	45	44	6	0	0	9	48	36	7	0
Fisher College	Boston	A,B	1,426	112																		
Fitchburg State College	Fitchburg	B,M	2,857	500							1	10	46	34	9	0	1	15	42	34	8	0
Framingham State College	Framingham	B,M	3,599	NR							0	5	41	43	9	2	0	5	46	38	10	1
Franklin Institute of Boston	Boston	B	342	70	38	35	22	5	0	0	20	37	32	8	3	0						
Gordon College	Wenham	B,M	1,487	130	0	0	0	27	73	0	0	0	9	38	42	11	0	0	12	44	37	7
Hampshire College	Amherst	B	1,162	125	0	0	0	1	42	47	0	0	3	18	43	36	0	0	7	41	40	12
Harvard University	Cambridge	B,M,D,P	6,684	NR																		
Hebrew College	Brookline	B,M		4																		
Hellenic College	Brookline	B	51	9								50	50					80	20			
Lasell College	Newton	A,B	706	105							5	10	45	40	5	1	5	10	50	35	5	1
Lesley College	Cambridge	A,B,M,D	571	125							0	6	41	42	10	1	0	7	53	33	6	0
Massachusetts College of Art	Boston	B,M	1,511	250							0	5	15	42	31	7	1	6	19	53	18	3
Massachusetts College of Liberal Arts	North Adams	B,M	1,246	NR							0	4	35	36	22	3	1	5	40	39	14	1
Mass Coll of Pharmacy and Allied Health Sciences	Boston	B,M,D,P	920	60							1	5	37	44	12	1	0	0	26	47	24	3
Massachusetts Institute of Technology	Cambridge	B,M,D	4,292	950	0	0	0	1	21	78	0	0	1	6	35	58	0	0	0	0	12	88
Massachusetts Maritime Academy	Buzzards Bay	B	778	110																		
Merrimack College	North Andover	A,B,M	2,677	175	0	0	1	81	18	0	0	0	6	68	24	2	0	0	7	65	18	5
Montserrat College of Art	Beverly	B	383	60							0	6	30	42	18	4	3	10	52	27	8	0
Mount Holyoke College	South Hadley	B	1,915	245	0	0	0	16	68	16	0	1	5	25	50	20	0	0	6	40	45	9
Mount Ida College	Newton Centre	A,B	1,471	101							5	32	39	19	3	2	3	41	40	14	1	1
Newbury College	Brookline	A,B	2,376	75	0	0	25	50	25	0	2	21	49	23	3	2	3	26	43	22	5	1

4-yr

Four-Year Institutions

This index includes the names and locations of accredited four-year colleges and universities in the Middle Atlantic and shows responses to Peterson's 2000 Survey of Undergraduate Institutions. The data was collected between November 1999 and May 2000. If an institution submitted incomplete or no data, one or more columns opposite the institution's name is blank.

STANDARDIZED TEST SCORE RANGES FOR 1999–2000
% of freshmen scoring within each interval

Name	Location	Degrees Awarded	Undergrad Enrollment Fall 1999	Computers for General Student Use	ACT 1-5	ACT 6-11	ACT 12-17	ACT 18-23	ACT 24-29	ACT 30-36	SAT V 200-299	SAT V 300-399	SAT V 400-499	SAT V 500-599	SAT V 600-699	SAT V 700-800	SAT M 200-299	SAT M 300-399	SAT M 400-499	SAT M 500-599	SAT M 600-699	SAT M 700-800
New England College of Finance	Boston	A,B	955	10																		
New England Conservatory of Music	Boston	B,M,D	398	9																		
Nichols College	Dudley	A,B,M	1,088	850							2	18	55	24	3	0	1	24	42	28	5	0
Northeastern University	Boston	A,B,M,D,P	12,183	1,400	0	0	3	49	42	6	0	2	19	51	26	3	0	1	14	47	32	6
Pine Manor College	Chestnut Hill	A,B,M	323	125	0	0	60	20	20	0	6	28	33	24	9	0	3	37	35	20	5	0
Regis College	Weston	A,B,M	889	151							1	12	31	38	17	1	1	14	40	32	13	0
Saint John's Seminary College of Liberal Arts	Brighton	A,B	31	9																		
Salem State College	Salem	B,M	5,952	150									30	5	1				25	4	1	
School of the Museum of Fine Arts	Boston	B,M	1,095	46																		
Simmons College	Boston	B,M,D	1,235	150							0	3	18	49	26	4	0	4	24	53	18	1
Simon's Rock College of Bard	Great Barrington	A,B	366	25	0	0	0	10	50	40	0	0	8	22	42	28	0	0	8	42	38	12
Smith College	Northampton	B,M,D	2,665	550	0	0	0	11	65	24	0	0	2	17	50	31	0	0	4	30	49	16
Springfield College	Springfield	B,M,D	1,890	95																		
Stonehill College	Easton	B,M	2,360	120							0	0	11	57	29	3	0	0	12	50	35	3
Suffolk University	Boston	A,B,M,D,P	3,160	250							0	8	41	37	14	1	0	14	45	32	8	0
Tufts University	Medford	B,M,D,P	4,950	254	0	0	0	7	54	39	0	0	2	17	50	31	0	0	2	10	47	41
University of Massachusetts Amherst	Amherst	A,B,M,D	18,619	750							0	2	16	48	28	6	0	1	16	46	30	7
University of Massachusetts Boston	Boston	B,M,D	8,575	260							0	5	34	45	14	2	0	4	38	44	13	2
University of Massachusetts Dartmouth	North Dartmouth	B,M,D	5,464	368	0	0	0	73	27	0	0	3	33	47	15	1	0	4	30	48	17	1
University of Massachusetts Lowell	Lowell	A,B,M,D	5,851	1,000							1	6	34	43	14	2	3	32	45	18	2	
Wellesley College	Wellesley	B	2,290	200							0	0	1	11	43	42	0	0	1	10	54	35
Wentworth Institute of Technology	Boston	A,B	3,168	400							1	13	38	37	14	0	1	10	29	38	18	2
Western New England College	Springfield	A,B,M,P	3,288	250							0	3	43	43	11	1	0	2	40	41	15	2
Westfield State College	Westfield	B,M	3,935	180							0	2	44	43	10	1	0	3	40	47	9	1
Wheaton College	Norton	B	1,485	84							0	0	5	36	53	6	0	0	4	47	43	6
Wheelock College	Boston	B,M	604	116							2	12	37	37	11	1	3	14	47	30	5	1
Williams College	Williamstown	B,M	2,052	150							0	0	1	9	34	56	0	0	1	8	32	59
Worcester Polytechnic Institute	Worcester	B,M,D	2,737	1,000							0	1	6	35	45	13	0	0	0	17	54	29
Worcester State College	Worcester	B,M	3,493	250																		

New Hampshire

Name	Location	Degrees Awarded	Undergrad Enrollment Fall 1999	Computers for General Student Use	ACT 1-5	ACT 6-11	ACT 12-17	ACT 18-23	ACT 24-29	ACT 30-36	SAT V 200-299	SAT V 300-399	SAT V 400-499	SAT V 500-599	SAT V 600-699	SAT V 700-800	SAT M 200-299	SAT M 300-399	SAT M 400-499	SAT M 500-599	SAT M 600-699	SAT M 700-800
Colby-Sawyer College	New London	A,B	788	74	0	0	14	67	19	0	0	2	43	47	8	0	0	8	42	43	7	0
Daniel Webster College	Nashua	A,B	918	60							1	6	28	51	12	2	0	5	29	46	18	2
Dartmouth College	Hanover	B,M,D,P	3,998	122							0	0	0	5	30	65	0	0	0	5	29	66
Franklin Pierce College	Rindge	A,B,M	1,350	171	0	0	36	45	19	0	0	9	45	33	8	5	1	11	43	33	10	2
Hesser College	Manchester	A,B	3,181	60																		
Keene State College	Keene	A,B,M	3,820	200	0	0	21	73	6	0	0	6	44	39	10	0	0	8	47	38	7	0
Magdalen College	Warner	B	74	NR	0	0	10	54	36	0	0	10	18	18	36	18	0	10	27	43	10	10
New England College	Henniker	B,M	707	45																		
New Hampshire College	Manchester	A,B,M,D	4,058	250							2	7	46	38	7	0	2	8	45	37	7	1
Notre Dame College	Manchester	A,B,M	685	22							0	16	49	30	5	0	7	16	48	25	4	0
Plymouth State College	Plymouth	A,B,M	3,251	400	0	0	54	38	8	0	0	10	48	35	6	1	1	12	46	33	7	1
Rivier College	Nashua	A,B,M	1,330	93							1	8	53	29	9	0	0	18	50	25	7	0
Saint Anselm College	Manchester	B	1,937	250							0	0	19	53	25	3	0	0	21	52	23	4
Thomas More College of Liberal Arts	Merrimack	B	72	3	0	0	0	0	100	0	0	6	7	25	56	6	0	13	13	49	25	0
University of New Hampshire	Durham	A,B,M,D	10,215	280							0	2	22	51	22	3	0	1	20	49	26	4
University of New Hampshire at Manchester	Manchester	A,B	704	38							0	8	26	55	9	2	0	9	40	37	13	1
University System College for Lifelong Learning	Concord	A,B		128																		
White Pines College	Chester	A,B	100	12																		

Rhode Island

4-yr

Four-Year Institutions

This index includes the names and locations of accredited four-year colleges and universities in the Middle Atlantic and shows responses to Peterson's 2000 Survey of Undergraduate Institutions. The data was collected between November 1999 and May 2000. If an institution submitted incomplete or no data, one or more columns opposite the institution's name is blank.

STANDARDIZED TEST SCORE RANGES FOR 1999–2000 — % of freshmen scoring within each interval

Institution	Location	Degrees Awarded	Undergrad Enrollment Fall 1999	Computers for General Student Use	ACT 1-5	ACT 6-11	ACT 12-17	ACT 18-23	ACT 24-29	ACT 30-36	SAT V 200-299	SAT V 300-399	SAT V 400-499	SAT V 500-599	SAT V 600-699	SAT V 700-800	SAT M 200-299	SAT M 300-399	SAT M 400-499	SAT M 500-599	SAT M 600-699	SAT M 700-800
Brown University	Providence	B,M,D,P	5,868	400	0	0	0	7	43	51	0	0	1	12	32	54	0	0	1	7	38	54
Bryant College	Smithfield	A,B,M	2,812	365	0	0	4	35	58	4	0	2	34	50	12	2	0	0	23	50	24	3
Johnson & Wales University	Providence	A,B,M,D	8,180	340							3	21	43	27	6	0	3	23	44	23	6	1
New England Institute of Technology	Warwick	A,B	2,537	325																		
Providence College	Providence	A,B,M	4,177	130	0	0	3	36	54	7	0	1	7	47	38	7	0	0	8	47	39	6
Rhode Island College	Providence	B,M,D	6,192	350																		
Rhode Island School of Design	Providence	B,M,P	1,861	300							0	4	12	35	39	10	0	1	12	35	43	9
Roger Williams University	Bristol	A,B,M,P	3,375	300							0	1	30	51	16	2	0	1	29	46	23	1
Salve Regina University	Newport	A,B,M,D	1,780	163							0	4	49	39	7	1	0	9	50	36	5	0
University of Rhode Island	Kingston	B,M,D,P	10,223	552							0	3	29	45	18	3	1	3	26	45	22	3

Vermont

Institution	Location	Degrees Awarded	Undergrad Enrollment Fall 1999	Computers for General Student Use	ACT 1-5	ACT 6-11	ACT 12-17	ACT 18-23	ACT 24-29	ACT 30-36	SAT V 200-299	SAT V 300-399	SAT V 400-499	SAT V 500-599	SAT V 600-699	SAT V 700-800	SAT M 200-299	SAT M 300-399	SAT M 400-499	SAT M 500-599	SAT M 600-699	SAT M 700-800
Bennington College	Bennington	B,M	447	60								2	32	56	10				20	49	27	4
Burlington College	Burlington	A,B	163	17																		
Castleton State College	Castleton	A,B,M	1,517	160	0	0	0	100	0	0	2	13	49	29	5	1	3	22	46	25	4	0
Champlain College	Burlington	A,B	2,114	200	0	0	28	60	12	0	1	17	48	28	6	0	1	16	51	25	7	0
College of St. Joseph	Rutland	A,B,M	385	30							5	19	48	26	2	0	2	35	43	13	5	2
Goddard College	Plainfield	B,M	346	20				100				4	18	30	44	4		4	37	44	11	4
Green Mountain College	Poultney	B	641	NR																		
Johnson State College	Johnson	A,B,M	1,345	131							0	8	38	43	10	1	2	13	49	26	11	0
Lyndon State College	Lyndonville	A,B,M	1,098	125							0	13	44	34	8	0	1	14	44	32	7	0
Marlboro College	Marlboro	A,B	283	42							0	0	5	24	47	24	0	0	24	39	29	8
Middlebury College	Middlebury	B,M,D	2,265	200							0	0	1	3	40	56	0	0	1	5	48	46
New England Culinary Institute	Montpelier	A,B	626	14																		
Norwich University	Northfield	B,M	2,098	142							1	7	36	36	18	2	1	7	37	40	14	1
Saint Michael's College	Colchester	B,M	1,939	200							0	0	18	57	22	3	0	0	18	57	23	2
Southern Vermont College	Bennington	A,B	498	33	0	0	25	62	13	0	1	16	44	32	7	0	0	19	36	41	3	1
Sterling College	Craftsbury Common	A,B	90	15			33	67			0	12	40	20	24	4	0	10	46	32	4	8

Degrees Awarded: Associate (A), Bachelor's (B), Master's (M), Doctoral (D), First Professional (P)

HIGH SCHOOL DIPLOMA TEST REQUIREMENTS

CONNECTICUT

Connecticut currently does not require high school students to pass a proficiency test in order to receive a high school diploma.

MAINE

Maine currently does not require high school students to pass a proficiency test in order to receive a high school diploma.

MASSACHUSETTS

All Massachusetts public school students in grades 4, 8, and 10 are required to take the Massachusetts Comprehensive Assessment System (MCAS) to measure performance based on the Massachusetts Curriculum Framework learning standards report on performance of individual students, schools, and districts. Beginning in the year 2001, students will be required to pass the tenth grade test (besides completing all of your school's requirements) to get a diploma. The test covers English language arts, mathematics, science and technology, history, and social science (grades 8 and 10). In the future, MCAS will also test learning standards in the Foreign Languages Curriculum Framework, though there will be no consequences until the class of 2004 pending legislative action. For more information, visit the Massachusetts Department of Education Web site at www.doe.mass.edu or call 781-338-3000.

NEW HAMPSHIRE

New Hampshire currently does not require high school students to pass a proficiency test in order to receive a high school diploma.

RHODE ISLAND

Rhode Island currently does not require high school students to pass a proficiency test in order to receive a high school diploma.

VERMONT

Vermont currently does not require high school students to pass a proficiency test in order to receive a high school diploma.

SPECIAL MESSAGES FROM REGIONAL COLLEGES AND UNIVERSITIES

ALBERTUS MAGNUS COLLEGE

New Haven, Connecticut

Social Life

One of Albertus Magnus College's chief attractions is its comfortable size. Every student's name, face, and aspirations are known by everyone from the President on down. At Albertus, no student is just another number in a large lecture hall; Albertus simply doesn't have any lecture halls. Resident students enjoy a degree of comfort found on few other campuses: most of the residence halls are mansions dating from the turn of the century. One in 4 students participates in varsity athletics. Albertus is a member of NCAA Division III. Students participate in a wide variety of campus clubs and organizations as well as a comprehensive, professional theater program.

Academic Highlights

Albertus Magnus awards the Bachelor of Arts, Bachelor of Science, Bachelor of Fine Arts, Associate of Arts, Master of Arts in Liberal Studies, and Master of Science Management degrees. In 1997, Albertus became the first and only college in Connecticut to offer the Master of Arts in Art Therapy degree. Major courses of study for the bachelor's degree programs are offered through twelve academic departments. Within these majors are fifty-three concentrations. The College supports a large continuing education program that supplements the traditional day student population. Other highlights include the Office of Career Services for internships and job placement after graduation.

Interviews and Campus Visits

Campus visits are strongly encouraged and prove very valuable in making informed decisions. Weekday visits are suggested, but weekend visits are available for most of the calendar year. Also open to prospective students are overnight stays Monday through Thursday evenings and opportunities to sit in on active classroom situations. For more information about campus visits, students should call the Office of Admission at 203-773-8501 or 800-578-9160 (toll-free).

For Further Information

Write to Richard Lolatte
Dean of Admission
Albertus Magnus College
700 Prospect Street
New Haven, CT 06511
Web site: http://www.albertus.edu

AMERICAN INTERNATIONAL COLLEGE

Springfield, Massachusetts

Social Life

Approximately 65 percent of AIC's students live on campus in five residence halls: two coed, two male, and one female. There are more than three dozen student-run clubs and organizations to become involved with on campus, including the Garrett Players, the student drama group; some students choose to become involved with the very active student government. There are clubs for skiers, singers, language enthusiasts, and equestrians, to name a few. In addition, AIC boasts a premier Division II athletic program that includes many sports that are regularly ranked on the national level.

Academic Highlights

At AIC, students find a wide range of academic programs offered in the Schools of Arts and Sciences, Business Administration, Psychology and Education, and Health Science, which offers majors in nursing, physical therapy, and occupational therapy. AIC graduates are especially well suited to becoming the leaders and problem-solvers of the twenty-first century for a variety of reasons, including the fact that all students at AIC have the opportunity to study directly in their chosen field through the internship program. An 8:1 student-faculty ratio and above average first-time board passing ratios highlight the Bachelor of Science in Nursing degree program. The nearly 100 percent placement of accounting grads strengthens that competitive program. A semester of study in Washington, D.C., is open to all students, especially benefitting those involved in political science and prelaw. Students may choose to study abroad or intern in their own home area.

Interviews and Campus Visits

Although interviews are not required, they are highly recommended. Students should plan to spend as much time on campus as necessary in order to really feel comfortable at AIC. This may include a traditional visit to the Office of Admissions for an informative, personal interview; a tour of the campus with a current student; sitting in on a class or two; meeting one-on-one with a professor or coach; and even spending a night in the dorm. The Office of Admissions coordinates any or all of the above for interested students weekdays from 9 a.m. to 4 p.m. and Saturday mornings, by appointment, from 9 a.m. to noon. Throughout the year, Open Houses and receptions are also held. For more information about appointments and campus visits, students should call the admissions office at 800-242-3142 (toll-free). The office is located in the D.A.R. building.

For Further Information

Write to the Office of Admissions
American International College
1000 State Street
Springfield, MA 01109

DANIEL WEBSTER COLLEGE

Nashua, New Hampshire

Social Life

Daniel Webster College (DWC) is primarily a residential campus that offers a wide range of student activities to complement the educational experience. An active on-campus club life is offered, as is a strong NCAA Division III athletics program for both men and women. Together with a student activities board, the College presents a lively calendar of diverse events, including the DWC Film Series, visiting speakers, well-known performing artists, and a variety of seasonal activities, such as Ski Day.

Academic Highlights

The Eaton-Richmond Center provides students with access to the most up-to-date personal computers and hardware that support multiple users. The library contains an ever-expanding collection of more than 32,000 volumes and 300 periodical titles in either hard copy or microform. Special programs include customized internships, study abroad, and a unique arrangement for off-campus study with the eleven other members of the New Hampshire College and University Council.

Interviews and Campus Visits

A personal visit to campus and an individual interview are highly recommended for a student to learn the most about Daniel Webster College. Students get a personalized, comprehensive tour from a knowledgeable student guide who can provide insights on student life at DWC. In addition, visiting students receive a Boarding Pass to return for the ultimate campus tour, at 1,000 feet above the ground, in DWC's Eagle Express plane. Special attractions on the campus tour include the Anne Bridge Baddour Learning Center, which houses the College library and computer labs; the new Eaton-Richmond Center, with state-of-the-art computer and A/V facilities and a 350-seat auditorium; and the Tamposi Aviation Center at the edge of Nashua Airport. At the aviation center, visitors can watch DWC student pilots practicing in the College's new Cessna 172s, Mooney 201s, Cessna multi-engine Crusaders, Grob motorgliders, and CAP-10 aerobatic aircraft. Classrooms, residential living areas, the College Center, and recreational facilities are also included in the tour. For information about appointments and campus visits, students should call the Admissions Office at 603-577-6600 or 800-325-6876 (toll-free), Monday through Saturday, 9 a.m. to 5 p.m.

For Further Information

Write to the Director of Admissions
Daniel Webster College
20 University Drive
Nashua, NH 03063-1300
E-mail: admissions@dwc.edu
Web site: http://www.dwc.edu

EMERSON COLLEGE

Boston, Massachusetts

Social Life

There are more than fifty student organizations and performance groups, ten NCAA Division III intercollegiate teams, student publications, and honor societies at Emerson College. Located on Boston Common in the heart of the city's Theatre District, the campus is within walking distance of the Massachusetts State House, historic Freedom Trail, Newbury Street shops, financial district, and numerous restaurants and museums.

Academic Highlights

Emerson is one of the premier colleges in the United States for the study of communication and the performing arts. Students may choose from more than twenty undergraduate majors and twelve graduate programs supported by state-of-the-art facilities and a nationally renowned faculty. The campus is home to WERS 88.9 FM, the oldest non-commercial radio station in New England; the 850-seat Emerson Majestic Theatre; and *Ploughshares*, the journal for new writing. The College also sponsors programs in Los Angeles, Kasteel Well (The Netherlands), summer film programs in Prague, and course cross-registration with the six-member Boston Pro-Arts Consortium.

Interviews and Campus Visits

Student-guided tours are conducted on most weekdays and some Saturdays during the academic year. (weekdays only, during the summer.) Students should contact the Admission Office for the current schedule and availability. Tours generally follow an information session led by a member of the admission staff. Interviews are not required for admission to most programs at Emerson and are informational in nature. Students who wish to discuss pertinent issues related to the admission process are encouraged to contact the Admission Office at 617-824-8600 to arrange for an individual appointment. The fax number is 617-824-8906.

For Further Information

Write to the Office of Undergraduate Admission
Emerson College
120 Boylston Street
Boston, MA 02116-4624
E-mail: admission@emerson.edu
Web site: http://www.emerson.edu

EMMANUEL COLLEGE

Boston, Massachusetts

Social Life

The campus sports a wide variety of academic clubs, honor societies, performance groups, and other activities. NCAA Division III athletics include women's basketball, cross-country, indoor track and field, soccer, softball, tennis, and volleyball and men's basketball, cross-country, indoor track and field, soccer, and volleyball.

Academic Highlights

Emmanuel's liberal arts curriculum allows students to explore widely in the arts and sciences, preparing them for success after college. Students may choose from a variety of offered majors and minors. Students with multiple interests or talents may design their own major through an individualized major program. Through this program, students may combine two or three subjects to create one major. Internships provide opportunities for career exploration and the acquisition of professional skills. The honors program provides highly qualified students with opportunities for additional intellectual challenge. Emmanuel is a member of the Colleges of the Fenway consortium, which Massachusetts College of Art, Massachusetts College of Pharmacy and Health Sciences, Simmons College, Wentworth Institute of Technology, and Wheelock College. Through the Consortium, students may take academic classes at the member institutions, as well as take part in many social activities.

Interviews and Campus Visits

Personal Interviews and Campus Visits are encouraged for all applicants. Visitors can meet admissions representatives, current students, faculty members and coaches, as well as sit in on classes and tour the campus. To arrange an interview or a campus visit, students should call the Office of Admissions at 617-735-9715. The fax number is 617-735-9801.

For Further Information

Write to Sandra Robbins
Dean of Admissions
Emmanuel College
Offices of Admissions
400 The Fenway
Boston, MA 02115
E-mail: enroll@emmanuel.edu
Web site: http://www.emmanuel.edu

INTERNATIONAL COLLEGE OF HOSPITALITY MANAGEMENT, CÉSAR RITZ

Washington, Connecticut

Social Life

The location of the International College of Hospitality Management, midway between New York City and Boston, with easy access to

Hartford and Danbury, enables students to participate in a variety of activities in major cities and to enjoy an assortment of outdoor activities in the surrounding area of northwestern Connecticut. The College offers a social life both on and off campus, including membership in student clubs and organizations, involvement in major campus social events, off-campus trips, special weekend excursions, campus competitions and tournaments in sports, and other recreational programs.

Academic Highlights

The International College of Hospitality Management, located in Washington, Connecticut, is the only Swiss college of hospitality management in the United States. It is one of four internationally acclaimed Hötelcönsult César Ritz Colleges, with affiliate campuses located in Le Bouveret and Brig, Switzerland, and Sydney, Australia. Students are prepared for successful careers in the hospitality industry around the world through a combination of the renowned Swiss art of hospitality with American management techniques. The academic program and practical experience offered at the College are reinforced by two 800-hour paid internships at prestigious hotels, restaurants, resorts, and hospitality-related businesses in the United States and abroad. The College organizes career fairs twice a year, wherein students and alumni are selected for 800-hour paid internships and positions of longer duration. The fairs are attended by recruiters from approximately thirty leading hotel and resort properties, typically five-star hospitality establishments. Students receive a thorough foundation in hotel, resort, and country club management; travel and tourism; and casino and ski resort operations management. Graduates have a career placement rate of 100 percent. The College offers a two-year Associate of Science degree in hospitality management, a one-year certificate program in hospitality management, and the opportunity to pursue a Bachelor of Arts degree in hotel and restaurant administration, awarded by Washington State University, at the campus in Brig, Switzerland. Transfer to a college or university within the United States for completion of the bachelor's degree is another option available to students.

Interviews and Campus Visits

Due to the unique nature of the College, students are strongly encouraged to visit the International College of Hospitality Management. The campus interview and tour offer prospective students the opportunity to meet with members of the admission staff and faculty and students. The Visitor Information Program (VIP) is available to prospective students for a complimentary campus stay of up to two nights to experience all that the College has to offer. To arrange for a campus visit, students should call the Office of Admissions at 860-868-9555 or 800-955-0809 (toll-free), Monday through Friday, 8 a.m. to 5 p.m. The fax number is 860-868-2114.

For Further Information

Write to Office of Admissions
International College of Hospitality Management
101 Wykeham Road
Washington, CT 06793
E-mail: admissions@ichm.cc.ct.us
Web site: http://www.ichm.cc.ct.us

MASSACHUSETTS COLLEGE OF PHARMACY AND HEALTH SCIENCES

Boston, Massachusetts

Social Life

There are five professional fraternities on campus: two all female, two all male, and one coed. The MCPHS Cardinals field varsity intercollegiate teams in men's and women's soccer, basketball, golf, and cross-country track as well as men's baseball and women's softball and volleyball. Students also participate in a variety of intramural sports. Additional organizations on campus include the Academy of Students of Pharmacy, Black Student Union, Indian Student Organization, International Student Association, Multicultural Student Association, Republic of China Student Association, Vietnamese Student Association, yearbook, and *The Dispenser* (College newspaper).

Academic Highlights

In early 1996, the College completed construction of an eight-story, 230,000-square-foot mixed-use facility. Connected to the existing George Robert White Building by a sky-lighted atrium, the new building includes sophisticated research facilities, modern laboratories, faculty offices, classrooms, a 160-student residence hall, and dining commons. A portion of the facility's research space has been leased to the Brigham and Women's Hospital, solidifying the College's nearly half-century-old education union with that distinguished institution. Of the full-time faculty members at the College, 61 percent hold earned doctoral degrees. There are two computer labs on campus. Free tutoring is available. Related part-time employment is available through College affiliates, and extensive listings of internship and externship sites are available. Pharmacy students are directly enrolled in the six-year Doctor of Pharmacy degree program. The College recently increased its program offerings in allied health sciences, with an innovative six-year Master of Physician Assistant Studies program as well as a Bachelor of Science degree program in radiologic sciences, with concentrations available in radiation therapy, nuclear medicine technology, and radiography. Other recent introductions include B.S. degrees in pharmaceutical sciences and in premed and health studies.

Interviews and Campus Visits

Priding itself on the personal approach, the College encourages each student to have an interview. These interviews are strictly informational and are primarily for the student's benefit. Visiting students should take special note of the number and proximity of hospitals and research facilities surrounding the College. Students intern and work part-time at these sites. The College recognizes the importance of experiential programs and is proud of its participation in the world-renowned Boston Longwood Medical Area. For information about appointments and campus visits, students should call the Admissions Office at 617-732-2850 or 800-225-5506 (toll-free except 617 area code), Monday through Friday, 8:30 a.m. to 4:30 p.m.

For Further Information

Write to the Office of Admission
Massachusetts College of Pharmacy and Health Sciences
179 Longwood Avenue
Boston, MA 02115
E-mail: admissions@mcp.edu
Web site: http://www.mcp.edu

MERRIMACK COLLEGE

North Andover, Massachusetts

Social Life

Merrimack's 2,000 students, 80 percent of whom are resident students, find an active campus life with social, cultural, athletic, and volunteer offerings. In January 2001, a new Campus Center that houses numerous dining options, student clubs and organizations, lounges, a bookstore, and a post office was completed. A recreation center with an indoor track, aerobic and weight rooms, and an all-pur-

pose field house also will be completed. With more than sixty clubs and organizations, numerous intramural offerings, and sixteen Division II and Division I varsity sports, there are plenty of activities to accommodate every student.

Academic Highlights

Two new majors, communication studies and digital media/graphic design, enhance an already wide array of academic offerings in the Liberal Arts, Business, Science, and Engineering Schools. Students work alongside faculty members and have opportunities that are sometimes only available to students at the graduate level. Merrimack also offers its students the opportunity to gain relevant work experience and explore career choices through the Cooperative Education Program. This four- or five-year program is available to academically strong students in all majors. Study-abroad programs and national opportunities, such as the American University semester internship, further enhance the learning experience at Merrimack. The student-faculty ratio at Merrimack is 14:1.

Interviews and Campus Visits

Merrimack welcomes visits to the campus year-round. Although not required, the interview can offer a prospective student the opportunity to meet with students and counselors to learn about the Merrimack community. Tours are conducted by the President's ambassadors twice a day, Monday through Friday and on select weekends. Information sessions are held on numerous weekends throughout the year. Merrimack College's campus extends over 220 beautifully landscaped acres. At the center is McQuade Library, housing the Computer Center, Media Center, television studio, and Academic Support Services. The Volpe Athletic Center features a 3,600-seat hockey arena, a 1,700-seat gymnasium, and fitness and aerobic rooms. Renovations to this complex and the athletic fields are underway and ongoing for the next year. The Mendel Center for the Sciences is the newest of the academic buildings and houses state-of-the-art labs and computer and instructional facilities, along with the finest astronomy dome and telescope north of Boston. Deegan Hall and Ash Center house the freshmen in an integrated social and academic environment that allows all freshmen an opportunity to strengthen their skills upon entering Merrimack to better ensure success. Both of these recently built residence halls have been tremendously received by the students. For information about appointments and campus visits, students should call the Admission Office at 978-837-5100, Monday through Friday, 8:30 a.m. to 4:30 p.m.

For Further Information

Write to Mary Lou Retelle
Dean of Admission and Financial Aid
Austin Hall
Merrimack College
North Andover, MA 01845
Web site: http://www.Merrimack.edu

MITCHELL COLLEGE

New London, Connecticut

Social Life

Ninety percent of Mitchell College's students live on campus, making Social Life an important part of the college experience. Residence hall and campuswide events include dances, movies, recreational and cultural outings to Boston and New York, varsity and intramural sports, student clubs and organizations, and professional entertainers.

Academic Highlights

Mitchell College offers a wide array of four- and two-year degrees to accommodate all students' interests. Every student is capable of learning, developing, and being academically successful. Mitchell is particularly known for working with students who have yet to realize their full potential and students who have a diagnosed learning disability.

Interviews and Campus Visits

Student interviews are a requirement of the application process. Open Houses are conducted in October, February, and April. To schedule a campus visit, students should call the Admission Office, located in Henry Hall, at 800-443-2811 (toll-free), Monday through Friday, 8:30 a.m. to 5 p.m.

For Further Information

Write to Kevin Mayne
Vice President for Enrollment Management and Marketing
Mitchell College
437 Pequot Avenue
New London, CT 06320
E-mail: admissions@mitchell.edu

NORWICH UNIVERSITY

Northfield, Vermont

Social Life

The Corps of Cadets, sixteen Division III athletic teams, a regimental band, Mountain Cold Weather, rugby, Leadership Development, and over 60 other clubs and social activities are available to students. A season's pass to two of the best ski areas in the East, at a great student discount, makes students fans of Vermont winters. Indoor activities include working out in the University's exceptional fitness facilities and relaxing with friends in the Student Union.

Academic Highlights

Norwich University offers its students the special opportunity of attending one university with two distinct student bodies: the Corps of Cadets and traditional civilian students. Norwich is the home of the oldest private military college, with the second-oldest Corps of Cadets, in the country. Offering twenty-nine academic majors, Norwich has created much enthusiasm with its five-year architecture program, a math/science and engineering complex, and its outstanding criminal justice, nursing, business, and engineering programs.

Interviews and Campus Visits

All interested students are encouraged to visit, either during an Open House or for a personal interview and tour. Overnight visits are also strongly encouraged for all applicants. These visits include spending an evening with current students in the dorms, attending classes, and meeting with faculty and staff members. For information about appointments and campus visits, students should call the Admissions Office at 800-468-6679 (toll-free), Monday through Friday, 8 a.m. to 5 p.m. The Admissions Office is located in Roberts Hall on our main campus.

For Further Information

Write to Ms. Karen McGrath
Dean of Enrollment Management
Norwich University
158 Harmon Drive
Northfield, VT 05663
E-mail: nuadm@norwich.edu
Web site: http://www.norwich.edu

QUINNIPIAC UNIVERSITY

Hamden, Connecticut

Social Life

Quinnipiac has more than sixty-five special interest and multicultural clubs for student participation. Student government, the newspaper, the yearbook, and the student-run radio station are popular, as is a large intramural sports program. About 15 percent of the students are active in fraternities and sororities. Quinnipiac is primarily residential and has no religious affiliation.

Academic Highlights

Academic life focuses on the Bernhard Library building with automated library systems and more than 100 personal computer workstations, which provides access to extensive electronic resources as well as the University's own print collections. A $7-million state-of-the-art School of Business Center contains computer-equipped classrooms, satellite downlinks for national and international programming, and case-study seminar rooms that make this one of the most comprehensive business education facilities in the Northeast. The Center also houses technologically up-to-date television, radio, video-editing, and desktop-publishing studios and a news technology center for the School of Communications.

Interviews and Campus Visits

Interviews are strongly recommended but not required. The interview, which is combined with a campus tour led by a student guide, is viewed largely as an opportunity to exchange information. There is also opportunity for discussion with faculty and staff members, including coaches. There are three fall Open House programs and one spring Open House especially for high school juniors and sophomores. The Admissions Office invites accepted students to plan an overnight visit or attend one of two Admitted Student Day programs. Residence halls of different styles, including suites, apartments, and town houses, highlight a visit to the Quinnipiac campus. The beauty of the campus is enhanced by Sleeping Giant Mountain, a 1,700-acre state park that borders the school, providing hiking and picnicking within walking distance. The $3-million campus center serves all students, while the gymnasium, with its 28,000-square-foot, $1.4-million addition and surrounding fields, supplies all the essentials for Division I athletics, intramurals, and fitness, including a combination large weight room and exercise center and two multipurpose dance/aerobic studios. For information about appointments and campus visits, students should call the Admissions Office at 203-582-8600 or 800-462-1944 (toll-free), Monday through Friday, 8 a.m. to 5 p.m. The office is located on campus.

For Further Information

Write to Mrs. Joan Isaac Mohr
Vice President and Dean of Admissions
Quinnipiac University
275 Mt. Carmel Avenue
Hamden, CT 06518

REGIS COLLEGE

Weston, Massachusetts

Social Life

Regis College offers the best of two worlds—a suburban setting with easy access to the cultural and social activities of Boston. Students also have opportunities to become involved in campus life through more than twenty-five organizations, including student government, the service corps, the theater company, the glee club, and campus ministry. NCAA Division III athletic teams include basketball, crew, cross-country, field hockey, soccer, softball, swimming/diving, tennis, track and field, and volleyball.

Academic Highlights

Regis College offers challenging academic programs that focus on the total development of the student. In addition to the twenty-one major areas of study, students are encouraged to pursue the various special programs available, including study abroad; a semester in Washington, D.C.; a semester exchange with other Sisters of St. Joseph colleges throughout the United States; cross-registration opportunities with Bentley, Babson, and Boston colleges; and individually designed majors. These opportunities, combined with the on-campus radio station, graphic design studio, language laboratories, and other modern facilities, provide an environment in which students are able to develop the skills and knowledge necessary to participate fully in the twenty-first century. Regis College sponsors a comprehensive merit scholarship program for academically talented students. These scholarships are distributed on a competitive basis. All applicants for admission are considered.

Interviews and Campus Visits

Prospective students are encouraged to visit the campus early in their junior or senior year and may choose from fall and summer Open Houses, Overnight Programs, and Academic Days. Each visit includes a personal, student-guided tour of campus followed by an informational interview with a member of the admission staff. During the informational interview, the admission and financial aid process is explained, as are the advantages of a women's college education. Visitors to the campus tour the state-of-the-art Fine Arts Center, which features a 650-seat theater, an open art gallery, soundproof music rooms, a graphic arts studio, and a black box theater. The Regis College athletic complex offers a competition-sized swimming pool; jacuzzi; sauna; dance and exercise studio; weight training room with Nautilus, Stairmaster, and Eagle equipment; and indoor tennis, squash, and basketball courts. For information about appointments and campus visits, students should call the Admissions Office at 800-456-1820 (toll-free), Monday through Saturday, 9 a.m. to 4:30 p.m. The office is located on campus.

For Further Information

Write to the Director of Admission
Regis College
235 Wellesley Street
Weston, MA 02493-1571
E-mail: admission@regiscollege.edu
Web site: http://www.regiscollege.edu

RHODE ISLAND COLLEGE

Providence, Rhode Island

Social Life

There are five residence halls on campus that provide a close "community within a community" for 830 students. Commuters and residents alike may join any of nearly eighty student organizations, including a completely student-run FM radio station, a student newspaper, service and departmental clubs, multicultural organizations, and more. The College's Division III athletics program fields nine varsity sports for women and eight for men. Student Activities and the various residence organizations plan monthly events and programs. The College's 170-acre suburban campus is just minutes from downtown Providence, Rhode Island's revitalized capital city.

Academic Highlights

The College is well-known for its numerous programs in education,

nursing, management, social work, technology, and the fine and performing arts. The curriculum choice of undergraduates is as follows: 32 percent in the arts and sciences, 32 percent in education, 12 percent in management and technology, 11 percent in nursing, and 4 percent in social work. The top five most popular academic majors are psychology, communications, English, biology, and justice studies. The average class size is 28, and all classes are taught by faculty members rather than graduate or teaching assistants. The College Honors Program provides exceptional educational opportunities for academically superior students, with smaller class size for even greater faculty-student interaction. Study abroad is encouraged, and the College has various affiliations and programs available. The Ridgway F. Shinn Study Abroad Fund helps students subsidize international study. Students have easy access to state-of-the-art computer facilities, including a new Technology Center. A new performing arts classroom facility is expected to be completed by January 2000.

Interviews and Campus Visits

Interviews are not required, but candidates are encouraged to attend an information session or meet with a staff member during their senior year. These sessions provide students with information about the College and the admissions process and provide an opportunity to tour the campus. Student-guided tours of the campus are available by appointment. An annual Open House is held each November, which offers students and their families a chance to meet RIC faculty and staff members and students and tour the campus. Prospective students may also take a virtual tour of the campus via the Web site listed below. For further information, students should call the Office of Undergraduate Admissions at 800-669-5760 (toll-free, voice or TDD), Monday through Friday, 8:30 a.m. to 4:30 p.m. The office is located in the Forman Center.

For Further Information

Write to Dr. Holly L. Shadoian, Director of Admissions
The Forman Center
Rhode Island College
600 Mt. Pleasant Avenue
Providence, RI 02908
E-mail: admissions@ric.edu
Web site: http://www.ric.edu

ROGER WILLIAMS UNIVERSITY

Bristol, Rhode Island

Social Life

The residential nonsectarian Roger Williams University attracts nearly 90 percent of its students from out-of-state. Campus events, departmental honors/academic societies, clubs, organizations, and intercollegiate (Division III), intramural, and recreational athletics highlight an informal social atmosphere. The 140-acre waterfront campus in historic Bristol, near Newport and Providence, is central to many New England locations. The University features the Feinstein Enriching America Program.

Academic Highlights

Undergraduate academic programs combine a traditional liberal arts education with preparation for the professions. All students complete an interdisciplinary core curriculum, a major, and a liberal arts concentration/minor. Students select their majors from the following disciplines: accounting, American studies, anthropology/sociology, architecture, art and architectural history, biology, business management, chemistry, communications, computer engineering, computer information systems, computer science, construction management, creative writing, criminal justice, dance performance, elementary and secondary education, engineering, English literature, environmental engineering, environmental science, financial services, foreign languages, heritage resource studies, historic preservation, history, international business, marine biology, marketing, mathematics, paralegal studies, philosophy, political science, psychology, theater, and visual arts studies. Students may also enter the University within one of the Colleges and Schools with an undeclared major. Other programs include an undergraduate honors program, prelaw, premedicine, preveterinary studies, and the 3+3 program, (bachelor's and Juris Doctor degrees). Students can also study English as a second language, and they may participate in study-abroad programs in Italy, England, and other sites.

Interviews and Campus Visits

Roger Williams encourages prospective students to visit the University for an interview and tour. Interviews are informational in nature; students learn about academic and social life on campus, while the University hopes to hear about students' interests and ambitions. The University also sponsors open houses, Discovery Days, Transfer Days, Junior Jumpstart, and Accepted Students' Days. For more information about appointments and campus visits, students should call the Office of Admissions at 401-254-3500 or 800-458-7144 Ext. 3500 (toll-free out-of-state).

For Further Information

Write to Ms. Lynn Fawthrop, Dean of Enrollment Management,
Roger Williams University
One Old Ferry Road
Bristol, RI 02809-2921
E-mail: admit@alpha.rwu.edu.

SCHOOL OF THE MUSEUM OF FINE ARTS

Boston, Massachusetts

Social Life

Boston is home to more educational and cultural institutions than any other U.S. city. SMFA is a vital member of the art community, presenting a dynamic schedule of exhibitions, lectures, and panel discussions throughout the year. The School's Grossman Gallery provides exhibition spaces for students, faculty members, and visiting artists. Shows change weekly or biweekly. A variety of social events and activities are also scheduled, including frequent trips to New York City.

Academic Highlights

SMFA is the only art school that offers students the opportunity to design their own individualized course of study. The focus is on creative investigation, risk-taking, and the exploration of individual vision. Options for study include the all-studio Diploma, Fifth Year Certificate, and Post-Baccalaureate Certificate. In affiliation with Tufts University, the Museum School offers B.F.A., B.F.A. in art education, Five-Year Combined B.A./B.S. and B.F.A., M.F.A., and M.F.A. in art education degrees. Many cross-registration opportunities are offered through the Boston Pro Arts Consortium and the Association of Independent Colleges of Art and Design.

Interviews and Campus Visits

Prospective students are encouraged to visit the School for a tour and interview. Students visiting the School can spend time in studio classes and talk to faculty members and students, observing firsthand the diversity of the population and the work being created. Studios, ranging from painting to video, from film and animation to photography, stained glass, and welding, are viewed on a tour of the School. Prospective students may also visit Boston's Museum of Fine Arts. For

information about appointments and campus visits, students should call the Admissions Office at 617-369-3626 or 800-643-6078 (toll-free), Monday through Friday, 9 a.m. to 5 p.m. The office is located on campus.

For Further Information

Write to John Williamson, Director of Enrollment
School of the Museum of Fine Arts
230 The Fenway
Boston, MA 02115
E-mail: admissions@smfa.edu
Web site: http://www.smfa.edu

SOUTHERN VERMONT COLLEGE

Bennington, Vermont

Social Life

SVC's Student Association is very active, planning many events for students. These activities range from movies to karaoke groups, from cultural programs to dances. They are designed to encourage student interaction, a spirit of cooperation, and a vital, close-knit campus environment. Sports on the NCAA III level, as well as intramural, are very popular.

Academic Highlights

Every student is required to participate in SVC's internship program. This program allows students to apply classroom knowledge to everyday, practical work situations. Students may design an individualized major with the help of their faculty advisers. Students with learning disabilities benefit from an excellent program at SVC, receiving extensive tutoring and assistance from support services in order to help them succeed. Career planning services are available to all students.

Interviews and Campus Visits

The best way to learn about Southern Vermont College and experience the personalized nature of its learning environment is to visit the campus. An interview with an admission professional is strongly encouraged. This is the best way of revealing the individual motivation a student can bring to the College. Campus visits may be arranged year-round, Monday through Friday. For information about campus visits, students should call the Admissions Office at 802-447-6304 or 800-378-2782 (toll-free), Monday through Friday, 8:30 a.m. to 5 p.m.

For Further Information

Write to Ms. Elizabeth Gatti, Director of Admissions
Southern Vermont College
982 Mansion Drive
Bennington, VT 05201
E-mail: admis@svc.edu

SAINT JOSEPH COLLEGE

West Hartford, Connecticut

Social Life

Saint Joseph College (SJC) is a diverse, tightly knit community where faculty members and students know one another by name. On-campus activities, including concerts, performances, multicultural events, dances, and NCAA Division III sports, draw guests from nearby Trinity College, the University of Hartford, and the Coast Guard Academy. Students also attend events on those campuses and in Hartford's arts and entertainment district, which features galleries, coffee bars, theaters, concert venues, and professional sports teams. Community service, leadership development, and campus ministry are integral to campus life. There are several clubs in which to participate, and most have outreach components. Themed weekend programs are very popular.

Academic Highlights

The number one reason students choose SJC is academic excellence. More than twenty-five majors offer diverse internships and field placements both locally and abroad. Success in every program springs from the combination of SJC's liberal arts and sciences curriculum and active mentorship by faculty members, advisers, and alumnae. This combination gives students the critical thinking and communication skills and professional support network necessary to compete in tomorrow's marketplace. Study abroad, an honors program, and cross-registration with area colleges are available. An excellent system of academic advising and tutoring is provided. The College's writing portfolio program has received national acclaim. Students work with faculty members on scholarly research and serve with faculty members and administrators on major committees. Qualified students may pursue double and even triple majors.

Interviews and Campus Visits

An interview with an admissions counselor is strongly recommended and easily arranged. A campus visit is vital to become better acquainted with SJC, and numerous visitation opportunities are planned throughout the year. During campus visits, prospective students and their families can take student-conducted tours of the 84-acre campus, attend classes, meet with faculty members and academic advisers, and learn about financial aid. Visitors are encouraged to explore SJC's laboratory schools, The School for Young Children and The Gengras Center; the athletic center; the state-of-the-art science labs, 80 percent of which have been updated in the last one to five years; the art gallery; the library; the residence halls; and The Carol Autorino Center for the Arts and Humanities, which opened in 2000. Special van tours of West Hartford and the capital city of Hartford are also offered. The College is located midway between Boston and New York City. For more information and to schedule Interviews and Campus Visits, students should call the Office of Admissions at 860-231-5216 or 800-285-6565 (toll-free).

For Further Information

Write to Ms. Kelly Getman Crowley, Director of Admissions
Saint Joseph College
1678 Asylum Avenue
West Hartford, CT 06117
E-mail: admissions@mercy.sjc.edu
Web site: http://www.sjc.edu

UNIVERSITY OF BRIDGEPORT

Bridgeport, Connecticut

Social Life

The University supports a wide range of student clubs and organizations to expand and cultivate the academic, professional, and cultural interests of its students. Students are involved in a wide range of volunteer activities, including assistance with admissions and orientation programs and programs for students seeking volunteer opportunities in the community.

Academic Highlights

The University of Bridgeport (UB) recently added a martial arts track to its elective studies program and new programs in world religions and international political economy and diplomacy. Many students wishing to pursue graduate programs in chiropractic and natur-

opathic medicine attend UB for prechiropractic and prenaturopathic medicine. To enhance their classroom education, students can take advantage of a variety of internship and co-op opportunities with such corporations as IBM, General Motors, Bristol Myers-Squibb, Price Waterhouse Coopers, and Lucent Technologies. UB offers a variety of scholarship opportunities, ranging from $3000 up to full tuition and room and board for qualified students.

Interviews and Campus Visits

Interviews and campus visits help students know the UB campus and students. There are numerous visitation opportunities planned throughout the year, including open houses in the fall and spring and campus tours scheduled every Wednesday at 10:30 a.m. and 2:30 p.m. or by appointment. Campus visit days are held on select Saturdays every month at 10:30 a.m. Students can tour the campus and meet faculty members and fellow students during these events. For more information or to schedule Interviews and Campus Visits, students should call UB toll-free at 800-EXCEL-UB or 203-576-4560.

For Further Information

Write to Joseph Marrone, Associate Dean of Admissions
University of Bridgeport
126 Park Avenue
Bridgeport, CT 06601
E-mail: jmarrone@bridgeport.edu
Web site: http://www.bridgeport.edu

UNIVERSITY OF MAINE AT FARMINGTON

Farmington, Maine

Social Life

With more than fifty student organizations; varsity, club, and intramural sports; musical, dance, and theatrical groups; and a wealth of outdoor activities, including nearby world-class skiing, hiking, canoeing, kayaking, and mountain biking, there is always something to do and someplace to go.

Academic Highlights

A strong liberal arts core creates the foundation for UMF's excellent academic programs in the arts and sciences, education, and human services programs. The quality of programs, small classes, 15:1 student-faculty ratio, student selectivity, and other factors earned UMF the top Public Liberal Arts College in the Northern U.S. rating by *U.S. News & World Report* for the last three years. *Kiplinger's Personal Finance* identified UMF as one of the nation's 100 Best Public University Values and one where the faculty knows students' names. UMF's teacher education programs are nationally accredited by NCATE. Learning centers and computer labs offer support for students and jobs for those with an academic area of strength. The Honors Program provides an intellectual challenge for academically gifted students. Exchange programs and study-tour courses use the entire world to enhance the curriculum. Internships, practicums, and the work initiative program allow students to begin building their resume with academically focused, real-world experience. The campus is wired, with online residence hall rooms, Ethernet access, free e-mail, multiple computer labs open 24 hours, 7 days, and a library with online resources.

Interviews and Campus Visits

Residence halls, academic and administrative buildings, the library, the computer center, and student center are locate on a traditional New England college campus, which is just a 3 minute walk from downtown Farmington. Campus visits, tours, and interviews are encouraged. Fall Open Houses and Spring Visit Days are an excellent way to meet faculty members and students and learn more about the college. Tours and interviews are generally available Monday through Friday from 8:30 a.m to 4:30 p.m. Students should call, fax, or e-mail the office to schedule. Phone: 207-778-7050 Fax: 207-778-2D8182

For Further Information

Write to the Admission Office
University of Maine at Farmington
246 Main Street
Farmington, ME 04938
E-mail: umfadmit@maine.edu
Web site: http://www.umf.maine.edu

University of Massachusetts Lowell

Lowell, Massachusetts

Social Life

There are more than 100 campus organizations to choose from, including academic, recreational, social, and special interest groups; musical ensembles; the student newspaper; an FM radio station; and The Off-Broadway Players. Campuswide events include University Week and Spring Carnival, and residence hall associations regularly sponsor social and recreational events. Students are involved in a wide variety of community service activities, the twenty-two intercollegiate sports teams, and a lively recreational sports program.

Academic Highlights

UMass Lowell offers eighty-two different undergraduate concentrations in five colleges, including recent popular choices like meteorology, sound recording technology, exercise physiology, criminal justice, and plastics engineering. Most courses incorporate some kind of practical component that gives students hands-on experience in their field. A wide range of resources, including a University-wide honors program, multimedia computer labs, and an active peer tutoring program, ensure that all students have access to the programs and services that support their success.

Interviews and Campus Visits

Individual interviews are recommended but not required. Students desiring interviews are asked to call the Office of Undergraduate Admissions to schedule appointments and to arrange a tour. Special high school days are conducted in fall and late winter by individual colleges within the University. High school counselors are advised of dates, and any students who have sent inquiries are invited. Students should visit the University's campuses, which cover more than 100 acres on both sides of the beautiful Merrimack River. Some fifty buildings house the residential, administration, and instructional centers, which contain modern laboratory facilities and equipment and several comprehensive computer centers. In 1998, the campus opened a nearby hockey arena and an on-campus baseball stadium, both built in partnership with the city of Lowell and shared by University and professional teams. In the next few years, students will be using a new campus center that will provide expanded recreational and social areas. Lowell is an exciting place in which to live. The National Historical Park was established to illustrate the importance of Lowell as the birthplace of the Industrial Revolution in America. Efforts to preserve and adapt many of Lowell's historic buildings are under way. For information about appointments and campus visits, students should call the Office of Admissions at 508-934-3931 or 800-410-4607 (toll-free), Monday and Tuesday, 8:30 a.m. to 7 p.m., and Wednesday, Thursday, and Friday, 8:30 a.m. to 5 p.m. The office is located in Dugan Hall on South Campus.

For Further Information

Write to the Office of Undergraduate Admissions

University of Massachusetts Lowell
883 Broadway Street-Room 110
Lowell, MA 01854-5104

Vermont Technical College

Randolph Center, Vermont

Social Life

With a scenic hilltop campus in a picturesque New England village, Vermont Technical College (VTC) combines a high-tech academic focus with small-college charm. Most students reside in the residence halls, which are fully wired for the information age. Students with their own computers have full LAN and Internet access from their rooms as well as phone service, voice mail, and cable TV. Students have ample opportunity to participate in campus activities, ranging from athletics to student government to clubs and social events.

Academic Highlights

Vermont Tech equips students with the technical, communication, and problem-solving skills needed to excel in today's high-tech world. Extensive laboratory facilities support two- and four-year programs ranging from architecture and building to electrical, civil, and mechanical engineering technology and from biotechnology to veterinary technology. The College has an extensive campuswide computer network and four separate computer-aided design and drafting (CADD) labs. Two-year programs in e-commerce technology and three-year options in selected engineering technology programs are new programs being offered.

Interviews and Campus Visits

Personal interviews are recommended for most programs and are required for veterinary technology. Spending a day on campus is strongly recommended as the best way to get a feel for the VTC experience. To arrange a tour and interview, students should call the Office of Admissions weekdays between 8 a.m. and 4:30 p.m. at 802-728-1000 (voice and TDD) or 800-442-8821 (toll-free, voice, and TDD).

For Further Information

Write to Ms. Rosemary Distel, Director of Admissions
Vermont Technical College
P.O. Box 500
Randolph Center, VT 05061
E-mail: admissions@vtc.vsc.edu
Web site: http://www.vtc.vsc.edu

Wentworth Institute of Technology

Boston, Massachusetts

Social Life

Wentworth's active Student Government serves as the official representative of the student body. Student activities include chapters of professional associations, hobby and social clubs, and club, intramural, and varsity sports. An extensive calendar of events is coordinated each semester. Fraternities and sororities are not available at Wentworth. Approximately half of all full-time students live on campus. Wentworth does not maintain any religious affiliations.

Academic Highlights

Wentworth's degree programs specialize in architecture, computer science, design, engineering, engineering technology, and management of technology. The curriculum combines theory learned in the classroom, laboratory training, and on-the-job experience received through the cooperative education program, the largest of its kind in the Northeast. Majors are offered in sixteen technical disciplines. Wentworth is recognized by business, industry, and academic leaders as an innovator in the training of engineering technologists.

Interviews and Campus Visits

Interviews are encouraged, and prospective students are invited to visit Wentworth and meet with a member of the admissions staff. Tours of the facilities, including classrooms, residence halls, studios, and laboratories, are available. Appointments for interviews and tours are requested. Overnight visits may be arranged by contacting an admissions counselor. While on campus, visitors can see Wentworth's varied educational resources, including state-of-the-art laboratories and design studios, the Alumni Library, and the Computer Center. Also of interest are Wentworth's athletic, recreational, and residential facilities. For information about appointments and campus visits, students should call the Office of Admissions at 617-989-4000 or 800-556-0610 (toll-free), Monday through Friday, 8:15 a.m. to 4:45 p.m. The office is located in Wentworth Hall, the main administration building.

For Further Information

Write to Ms. Keiko S. Broomhead, Director of Admissions
Wentworth Institute of Technology
550 Huntington Avenue
Boston, MA 02115-5998
E-mail: admissions@wit.edu
Web site: http://www.wit.edu

WESTERN CONNECTICUT STATE UNIVERSITY

Danbury, Connecticut

Social Life

There are five residence halls on campus. Students run academic and fraternal organizations, publish a newspaper and yearbook, run a radio station, and administer their own campus government association. There are a variety of NCAA III men's and women's sports, intramural sports, and a recreation center that includes a swimming pool, indoor track, and weight lifting machines.

Academic Highlights

The faculty has 354 members; 83 percent of full-time faculty members have doctoral, terminal, or first professional degrees. The student-faculty ratio is 15:1. The library holds 175,294 volumes and more than 7,179 serials. Special programs include services for learning-disabled students, study abroad, and the Jane Goodall Institute for environmental studies. The most popular majors include communications and theater arts, education, business, justice and law administration, and music education. Western offers excellent undergraduate educational programs through four academic units: the Ancell School of Business, the School of Arts and Sciences, the School of Professional Studies, and the Division of Graduate and Continuing Education.

Interviews and Campus Visits

Interviews are not required, but candidates are encouraged to attend an information session before they enroll. These sessions provide stu-

dents with information about the University and the admissions process and offer an important opportunity to assess how the University can help students meet their long-term educational goals. It also affords students the opportunity to meet with professors, other potential students, and current students. Student-guided tours are also available. While on tour, students are able to visit the library, the residence hall, science and computer laboratories, the newly remodeled student center, and the recreation center. For information about appointments and campus visits, call the Office of Admissions at 203-837-9000 or 877-837-WCSU (toll-free).

For Further Information

Write to Mr. William Hawkins, Enrollment Management Officer
Western Connecticut State University
181 White Street
Danbury, CT 06810
E-mail: hawkinsw@wcsu.edu

WESTERN NEW ENGLAND COLLEGE

Springfield, Massachusetts

Social Life

Most students are involved in the fifty clubs, the active intramural program, or the nineteen varsity athletic teams. The state-of-the-art Alumni Healthful Living Center is the focal point for many recreational and athletic activities. The College is primarily residential with a variety of housing options, including traditional dormitories, suites, apartments, and town houses.

Academic Highlights

There are no large lecture classes at Western New England College, and instruction is provided by faculty members, not graduate students. The typical classroom contains only thirty-six chairs, and the average class size is 20. These factors encourage student-faculty member interaction and personal attention. Freshman students take a First Year Seminar course that addresses academic and social issues and assists in the transition to college. Internships and engineering senior projects provide students valuable experiences to enhance their classroom education. The College's 3 + 3 Law Program offers eligible students an opportunity to earn their bachelor's degree and a Juris Doctor degree from Western New England College School of Law in six years instead of seven.

Interviews and Campus Visits

Students are strongly encouraged to visit the beautiful campus to learn more about the College. Interviews are informational rather than required as a criterion for acceptance. Visits can be arranged weekdays from 9 a.m. to 3 p.m., most Saturday mornings, or during one of the College's many Open House programs. For information, students should call 413-782-1321 or 800-325-1122 Ext. 1321 (toll-free).

For Further Information

Write to Admissions
Western New England College
1215 Wilbraham Road
Springfield, MA 01119

CAREER AND VOCATIONAL SCHOOLS

The data presented in this section was collected from two sources: Peterson's/Career College Association 2000 Survey of Career Colleges and Peterson's 1998 Survey of Vocational Schools.

CONNECTICUT

Baran Institute of Technology
611 Day Hill Road
Windsor, CT 06095
860-688-3353

Boston Bartenders School of America
614 Asylum Avenue
Hartford, CT 06105
203-522-1999

Connecticut Business Institute
605 Broad Street
Stratford, CT 06497
203-377-1775

Connecticut Center for Massage Therapy
25 Sylvan Road South
Westport, CT 06880
877-292-2268

Connecticut Center for Massage Therapy
75 Kitts Lane
Newington, CT 06111-3954
877-282-2268

Connecticut Institute of Art
581 West Putnam Avenue
U.S. Route 1
Greenwich, CT 06830-6005
800-278-7246

Katherine Gibbs College
148 East Avenue
Norwalk, CT 06851
203-838-4173 Ext. 301

Ridley-Lowell Business and Technical Institute
470 Bank Street
New London, CT 06320
860-443-7441

MAINE

International Film and Television Workshops
2 Central Street
PO Box 200
Rockport, ME 04856
207-236-8581

New England School of Communications
One College Circle
Bangor, ME 04401-2999
207-941-7176 Ext. 1090

Washington County Technical College
RR1, PO Box 22C
Calais, ME 04619
207-454-1000

MASSACHUSETTS

Bancroft School of Massage Therapy
333 Shrewsbury Street
Worcester, MA 01604
508-757-7923

Blaine! The Beauty Career Schools
314 Moody Street
Waltham, MA 02154
781-899-1500

Bryman Institute
1505 Commonwealth Avenue
Brighton, MA 02135
617-783-9955

Computer Learning Centers, Inc.
5 Middlesex Avenue
Somerville, MA 02145-9924
617-776-3509 Ext. 250

Computer Learning Centers, Inc.
211 Plain Street
Lowell, MA 01852
978-458-4800 Ext. 202

Hallmark Institute of Photography
PO Box 308
Turners Falls, MA 01376-0308
413-863-2478

ITT Technical Institute
10 Forbes Road
Woburn, MA 01801
781-937-8324

ITT Technical Institute
333 Providence Highway
Norwood, MA 02062
781-278-7200

Katharine Gibbs School
126 Newbury Street
Boston, MA 02116
617-578-7100

Lee Institute
310 Harvard Street
Brookline, MA 02146
617-734-3211

Lincoln Institute of Land Policy
113 Brattle St.
Cambridge, MA 02138
617-661-3016

Massachusetts Communications College
10 Brookline Place West
Brookline, MA 02445
617-739-1700

Massachusetts Communications College
142 Berkeley Street
Boston, MA 02116
617-267-7910

Middlesex Community College
Springs Road
Bedford, MA 01730
978-656-3200

Mildred Elley
505 East Street
St. Luke's Square
Pittsfield, MA 01201
413-499-8618 Ext. 227

Mount Wachusett Community College
444 Green Street
Gardner, MA 01440
508-632-6600

North Shore Community College
1 Ferncroft Road
Danvers, MA 01923
978-762-4000

Porter and Chester Institute
134 Dulong Circle
Chicopee, MA 01022
413-593-3339

Printing Institute of New England
Incorporated
10 Tech Circle
Natick, MA 01760
508-655-8700

RETS Electronic Schools
965 Commonwealth Avenue
Boston, MA 02215
617-783-1197

Ultrasound Diagnostic School
365 Cadwell Drive
Springfield, MA 01104-1739
413-739-4700

Worcester Technical Institute
251 Belmont Street
Worcester, MA 01605
508-799-1945

New Hampshire

Hesser College
3 Sundial Avenue
Manchester, NH 03103
603-668-6660 Ext. 2102

McIntosh College
23 Cataract Avenue
Dover, NH 03820-3990
800-624-6867

Rhode Island

Johnson & Wales University
8 Abbott Park Place
Providence, RI 02903-3703
401-598-2310

Katharine Gibbs School
178 Butler Avenue
Providence, RI 02906
401-861-1420

Motoring Technical Training Institute
54 Water Street
East Providence, RI 02914
401-434-4840

Nasson Institute
286 Main Street
Pawtucket, RI 02860
401-728-1570

New England Institute of Technology
2500 Post Road
Warwick, RI 02886-2266
401-739-5000 Ext. 3308

Vermont

Champlain College
163 South Willard Street
Burlington, VT 05402-0670
802-860-2700

Distance Learning International, Inc.
80 North Main Street
Saint Albans, VT 05478
802-524-2223

New England Culinary Institute
250 Main Street
Montpelier, VT 05602-9720
802-223-6324

SCHOLARSHIPS AND FINANCIAL AID PROGRAMS

THE DATA PRESENTED IN THIS APPENDIX WAS COLLECTED IN PETERSON'S 2000 SURVEY OF PRIVATE AID. (THIS DATA WAS COLLECTED BETWEEN DECEMBER 1999 AND APRIL 2000)

CONNECTICUT

Aid for Public College Students Grant Program/Connecticut
Award for students at Connecticut public institutions. Must be state residents and enrolled at least half-time. Renewable award based on financial need and academic progress. Application deadlines vary by institution.
Award: Grant for use in any year; renewable.
Eligibility Requirements: Applicant must be a resident of Connecticut and enrolled at a two-year or four-year institution in Connecticut.
Application Requirements: Application, financial need analysis, transcript.
Contact: John Siegrist, Financial Aid Office, Connecticut Department of Higher Education, 61 Woodland Street, Hartford, CT 06105-2326; **Phone:** 860-947-1855; **Fax:** 860-947-1311

Capitol Scholarship Program
Award for Connecticut residents attending eligible institutions in Connecticut or in a state with reciprocity with Connecticut (Delaware, Maine, Massachusetts, New Hampshire, Pennsylvania, Rhode Island, and Vermont), or in Washington, D.C. Must rank in top twenty percent of class or score at least 1200 on SAT and show financial need.
Award: Scholarship for use in any year; renewable.
Amount: $300–$2000.

Eligibility Requirements: Applicant must be a resident of Connecticut and enrolled at a two-year or four-year institution or university in Connecticut, Delaware, the District of Columbia, Maine, Massachusetts, New Hampshire, Pennsylvania, Rhode Island, or Vermont. Applicant must have 3.5 GPA or higher.
Application Requirements: Application, financial need analysis, test scores. **Application deadline:** February 15.
Contact: John Siegrist, Financial Aid Office, Connecticut Department of Higher Education, 61 Woodland Street, Hartford, CT 06105-2326; **Phone:** 860-947-1855; **Fax:** 860-947-1311

Connecticut Independent College Student Grants
Award for Connecticut residents attending an independent college or university within the state on at least a half-time basis. Renewable awards based on financial need. Application deadline varies by institution.
Award: Grant for use in any year; renewable.
Amount: Up to $7777.
Eligibility Requirements: Applicant must be a resident of Connecticut and enrolled at a two-year or four-year institution or university in Connecticut.
Application Requirements: Application, financial need analysis, transcript.
Contact: John Siegrist, Financial Aid Office, Connecticut Department of Higher Education, 61 Woodland Street, Hartford, CT 06105-2326; **Phone:** 860-947-1855; **Fax:** 860-947-1311

Connecticut Tuition Waiver for Senior Citizens
Renewable tuition waiver for a Connecticut senior citizen to use at an accredited two- or four-year institution in Connecticut. Must show financial need and prove senior citizen status. Award for undergraduate study only.
Award: Grant for use in freshman, sophomore, junior, or senior years; renewable.
Eligibility Requirements: Applicant must be a resident of Connecticut and enrolled at a two-year or four-year institution in Connecticut.
Application Requirements: Application, financial need analysis.
Application deadline: Continuous.
Contact: John Siegrist, Financial Aid Office, Connecticut Department of Higher Education, 61 Woodland Street, Hartford, CT 06105-2326; **Phone:** 860-947-1855; **Fax:** 860-947-1311

Robert C. Byrd Honors Scholarship—Connecticut
Renewable scholarship for Connecticut high school seniors in the top 2% of their class or scoring 1400 or above on the SAT. Acceptance letter from college required.
Award: Scholarship for use in freshman, sophomore, junior, or senior years; renewable. **Amount:** Up to $1500.
Eligibility Requirements: Applicant must be a high school student, a resident of Connecticut, and enrolled at a two-year or four-year institution. Applicant must have 3.5 GPA or higher. Restricted to U.S. citizens.
Application Requirements: Application, test scores.
Application deadline: Continuous.
Contact: John Siegrist, Financial Aid Office, Connecticut Department of Higher Education, 61 Woodland Street, Hartford, CT 06105-2326; **Phone:** 860-947-1855; **Fax:** 860-947-1311

MAINE

Maine Student Incentive Scholarship Program

Scholarships for residents of Maine attending an eligible school, full-time, in Alaska, Connecticut, Delaware, the District of Columbia, Maine, Maryland, Massachusetts, New Hampshire, Pennsylvania, Rhode Island, or Vermont. Award based on need. Must reapply annually. Complete Free Application For Federal Student Aid to apply. One-time award of $500–$1000 for undergraduate study.

Award: Grant for use in freshman, sophomore, junior, or senior years; not renewable. **Number:** 8900–12,500. **Amount:** $500–$1000.

Eligibility Requirements: Applicant must be a resident of Maine and enrolled at a two-year, four-year, or technical institution or university in Alaska, Connecticut, Delaware, the District of Columbia, Maine, Maryland, Massachusetts, New Hampshire, Pennsylvania, Rhode Island, or Vermont.

Application Requirements: Application, financial need analysis.

Application deadline: May 1.

Contact: Rochelle Bridgham, Program Officer, Finance Authority of Maine, 5 Community Drive, Augusta, ME 04332-0949; **Phone:** 800-228-3734 (toll-free); **Fax:** 207-623-0095; **E-mail:** rochelle@famemaine.com

Veterans Dependents Educational Benefits— Maine

Award for dependents or spouses of veterans who were prisoners-of-war, missing in action, or permanently disabled as a result of service. Veteran must have been a Maine resident at service entry for five years preceding application. For use at Maine institutions. Must be high school graduate. Must submit birth certificate. Award renewable for eight semesters for those under 22 years of age.

Award: Scholarship for use in any year; renewable.

Eligibility Requirements: Applicant must be age 21 or under, a resident of Maine, and enrolled at an accredited university in Maine. Applicant or parent must meet one or more of the following requirements: general military experience, retired from active duty, disabled or killed as a result of military service, prisoner of war, or missing in action.

Application Requirements: Application. **Application deadline:** Continuous.

Contact: Leslie Breton, Administrator, Maine Division of Veterans Services, State House Station 117, Augusta, ME 04333-0117; **Phone:** 207-626-4464; **Fax:** 207-626-4471; **E-mail:** mvs@me-arng.ngb.army.mil

MASSACHUSETTS

Christian A. Herter Memorial Scholarship

Renewable award for Massachusetts residents who are in the tenth or eleventh grades. Must exhibit severe personal or family-related difficulties or medical problems or have overcome a personal obstacle. Provides up to 50% of the student's calculated need, as determined by federal methodology, at the college of their choice within the continental U.S.

Award: Scholarship for use in freshman, sophomore, junior, or senior years; renewable. **Number:** 100–200. **Amount:** $2500–$6500.

Eligibility Requirements: Applicant must be a high

school student, a resident of Massachusetts, and enrolled at a two-year or four-year institution or university. Applicant must have 2.5 GPA or higher.

Application Requirements: Application, essay, financial need analysis, interview, transcript. **Application deadline:** March 31.

Contact: Cynthia Gray, Assistant Director, Massachusetts Office of Student Financial Assistance, 330 Stuart Street, Boston, MA 02116

Gilbert Grant

Must be permanent Massachusetts resident for at least one year, attending an independent, regionally accredited Massachusetts school full-time. File the Free Application for Federal Student Aid after January 1. Contact college financial aid office for complete details.

Award: Grant for use in freshman, sophomore, junior, or senior years; not renewable. **Amount:** $200–$2500.

Eligibility Requirements: Applicant must be a resident of Massachusetts and enrolled at a two-year or four-year institution or university in Massachusetts.

Application Requirements: Application, financial need analysis.

Contact: Scholarship Information, Massachusetts Office of Student Financial Assistance, 330 Stuart Street, Boston, MA 02116

Higher Education Coordinating Council— Tuition Waiver Program

Renewable award is tuition exemption for up to four years. Available to active members of the Air Force, Army, Navy, Marines, or Coast Guard who are residents of Massachusetts. For use at a Massachusetts college or university. Deadlines vary. Contact veterans coordinator at college.

Award: Scholarship for use in freshman, sophomore, junior, or senior years; renewable.

Eligibility Requirements: Applicant must be a resident of Massachusetts and enrolled at a two-year or four-year institution or university in Massachusetts. Applicant must have served in the Air Force, Army, Coast Guard, Marine Corp, or Navy.

Application Requirements: Application, financial need analysis.

Contact: Scholarship Director, Massachusetts Office of Student Financial Assistance, 330 Stuart Street, Boston, MA 02116

Massachusetts Grant

Renewable award upon reapplication and eligibility for Massachusetts residents to attend undergraduate postsecondary institutions in Connecticut, Maine, Maryland, Massachusetts, New Jersey, Pennsylvania, Rhode Island, Vermont, and the District of Columbia. High school seniors may apply. Need-based award.

Award: Grant for use in freshman, sophomore, junior, or senior years; not renewable. **Number:** 32,000–35,000. **Amount:** $200–$2500.

Eligibility Requirements: Applicant must be a resident of Massachusetts and enrolled at a two-year, four-year, or technical institution or university in Connecticut, the District of Columbia, Maine, Maryland, Massachusetts, New Jersey, Pennsylvania, Rhode Island, or Vermont.

Application Requirements: Application, financial need analysis.

Application deadline: May 1.

Contact: Scholarship Director, Massachusetts Office of Student Financial Assistance, 330 Stuart Street, Boston, MA 02116

Public Service Scholarship—Massachusetts

Scholarships for children and/or spouses of deceased members of fire, police, and corrections departments who were killed in the line of duty. Award also available to children of deceased veterans whose death was service-related or who were prisoners-of-war or missing in action. For Massachusetts residents attending Massachusetts institutions.

Award: Scholarship for use in freshman, sophomore, junior, or senior years; renewable. **Amount:** $918–$1904.

Eligibility Requirements: Applicant must be a resident of Massachusetts and enrolled at a two-year or four-year institution or university in Massachusetts and must have employment experience in police/firefighting. Applicant or parent must meet one or more of the following requirements: general military experience, retired from active duty, disabled or killed as a result of military service, prisoner of war, or missing in action.

Application Requirements: Application. **Application deadline:** May 1.

Contact: Jill McTague, Senior Counselor, Massachusetts Office of Student Financial Assistance, 330 Stuart Street, Boston, MA 02116

Tomorrow's Teachers Scholarship Program

Tuition waiver for graduating high school senior ranking in top 25% of class. Must be a resident of Massachusetts and pursue a bachelor's degree at a public college or university in the Commonwealth. Must commit to teach for four years in a Massachusetts public school. Must maintain a 3.0 GPA.

Award: Scholarship for use in freshman, sophomore, junior, or senior years; renewable.

Eligibility Requirements: Applicant must be a high school student, a resident of Massachusetts, and enrolled at a four-year institution or university in Massachusetts.

Application Requirements: Application.

Contact: Scholarship Director, Massachusetts Office of Student Financial Assistance, 330 Stuart Street, Suite 304, Boston, MA 02116; **Phone:** 617-727-9420; **Fax:** 617-727-0667

Tuition Waiver (General)—Massachusetts

Need-based tuition waiver for full-time students. Must attend a Massachusetts public institution of higher education and be a permanent Massachusetts resident. File the Free Application For Federal Student Aid after January 1. Award is for undergraduate use.

Award: Scholarship for use in freshman, sophomore, junior, or senior years; renewable.

Eligibility Requirements: Applicant must be a resident of Massachusetts and enrolled at a two-year or four-year institution or university in Massachusetts.

Application Requirements: Application, financial need analysis.

Application deadline: May 1.

Contact: School Financial Aid Office, Massachusetts Office of Student Financial Assistance, 330 Stuart Street, Boston, MA 02116

NEW HAMPSHIRE

New Hampshire Incentive Program (NHIP)

Renewable grants for New Hampshire residents attending school in New Hampshire, Connecticut, Maine, Massachusetts, Rhode Island, or Vermont. Must be a full-time student with financial need.

Deadline is May 1. Complete Free Application for Federal Student Aid.
Award: Grant for use in freshman, sophomore, junior, or senior years; not renewable. **Number:** 2500–3000. **Amount:** $450–$1000.
Eligibility Requirements: Applicant must be a resident of New Hampshire and enrolled at a two-year, four-year, or technical institution or university in Connecticut, Maine, Massachusetts, New Hampshire, Rhode Island, or Vermont.
Application Requirements: Application, financial need analysis.
Application deadline: May 1.
Contact: Judith Knapp, Student Financial Assistant Coordinator, New Hampshire Postsecondary Education Commission, Two Industrial Park Drive, Concord, NH 03301-8512; **Phone:** 603-271-2555; **Fax:** 603-271-2696; **E-mail:** jknapp@nhsa.state.nh.us

Scholarships for Orphans of Veterans—New Hampshire

Awards for New Hampshire residents whose parent died as a result of service in WWI, WWII, the Korean Conflict, or the Southeast Asian Conflict. Possible full tuition and $1000 per year with automatic renewal on reapplication. Contact department for application deadlines. Must be under 26. Must include proof of eligibility and proof of parent's death.
Award: Grant for use in any year; renewable.
Number: 1–10. **Amount:** $1000.
Eligibility Requirements: Applicant must be age 26, a resident of New Hampshire, and enrolled at a two-year or four-year institution or university. Restricted to U.S. citizens. Applicant or parent must meet one or more of the following requirements: general military experience, retired from active duty, disabled or killed as a result of military service, prisoner of war, or missing in action.
Application Requirements: Application.
Contact: Patti Edes, Student Financial Assistant Coordinator, New Hampshire Postsecondary Education Commission, Two Industrial Park Drive, Concord, NH 03301-8512; **Phone:** 603-271-2555; **Fax:** 603-271-2696; **E-mail:** pedes@nhsa.state.nh.us

RHODE ISLAND

Burns and Haynes Textile Scholarship Fund

Award to benefit students studying textile technology. Preference given to children of members of National Association of Textile Supervisors.
Award: Scholarship for use in any year; renewable.
Number: 1. **Amount:** $500.
Eligibility Requirements: Applicant must be enrolled at a four-year institution and must have an interest in designated field specified by sponsor.
Application deadline: September.
Contact: John Beardon, Rhode Island Foundation, PO Box 325 Village Station, Medway, MA 02053

Rhode Island Higher Education Grant Program

Grants for residents of Rhode Island attending an approved school in U.S., Canada, or Mexico. Based on need. Renewable for up to four years if in good academic standing. Applications accepted January 1 through March 1. Several awards of variable amounts.
Award: Grant for use in freshman, sophomore, junior, or senior years; renewable.
Number: 10,000–12,000. **Amount:** $250–$750.
Eligibility Requirements: Applicant must be a resident

of Rhode Island and enrolled at a two-year, four-year, or technical institution or university. Restricted to U.S. citizens.
Application Requirements: Application, financial need analysis.
Application deadline: March 1.
Contact: Mary Ann Welch, Director of Program Administration, Rhode Island Higher Education Assistance Authority, 560 Jefferson Boulevard, 222 21st. Avenue South, Warwick, RI 02886; **Phone:** 401-736-1100; **Fax:** 401-732-3541

VERMONT

Vermont Non-Degree Student Grant Program

Renewable grants for Vermont residents enrolled in non-degree programs at colleges, vocational centers, and high school adult courses. May receive funds for two enrollment periods per year, up to $380 per course, per semester. Award based upon financial need.
Award: Grant for use in any year; renewable.
Amount: Up to $380.
Eligibility Requirements: Applicant must be a resident of Vermont and enrolled at an accredited university.
Application Requirements: Application, financial need analysis.
Application deadline: Continuous.
Contact: Grant Program, Vermont Student Assistance Corporation, PO Box 2000, Winooski, VT 05404-2000; **Phone:** 802-655-9602; **Fax:** 802-654-3765

Vermont Part-Time Student Grants

For undergraduates carrying less than twelve credits per semester who have not received a bachelor's degree. Must be Vermont resident. Based on financial need. Complete Vermont Financial Aid Packet to apply. May be used at any approved postsecondary institution.
Award: Grant for use in freshman, sophomore, junior, or senior years; renewable. **Amount:** $250–$5100.
Eligibility Requirements: Applicant must be a resident of Vermont and enrolled at an accredited university.
Application Requirements: Application, financial need analysis.
Application deadline: Continuous.
Contact: Grant Program, Vermont Student Assistance Corporation, PO Box 2000, Winooski, VT 05404-2000; **Phone:** 802-655-9602; **Fax:** 802-654-3765

SCHOOL-TO-WORK PROGRAMS

THIS LISTING OF SCHOOL-TO-WORK PROGRAMS WAS COLLECTED FROM INDIVIDUAL STATE DEPARTMENT WEB SITES AND INTERVIEWS WITH STATE-TO-WORK PROGRAM ADMINISTRATORS.

CONNECTICUT

Connecticut's School-to-Career

(STC) system is organized around eight industry-developed career clusters: arts and media; business and finance; construction technologies and design; environmental and natural resources and agriculture; government, education, and human services; health and biosciences; retail, tourism, recreation, and entrepreneurship; and technologies: manufacturing, communications, and repair. Participating students have the opportunity to select a career cluster and receive school-based instruction focused on academic, employability, and technical skills as well as structured workplace experiences coordinated with classroom instruction. Students also receive comprehensive career guidance. They outline their interests with career portfolios in middle school and participate in job shadowing, mentoring, internships, service learning, and paid work experience during grades 10–12.

Connecticut has eight designated STC regions, with the Community Technical College System serving as one of the regional Tri-Conveners with the regional workforce development boards and regional educational service centers. The Department of Higher Education and the Community Technical College System are aligning existing curricula with advanced skill standards with the determination of assessing the academic, employability, and technical skills at the postsecondary level. For more information about Connecticut's STW programs, contact the state director, George A. Coleman, at 860-807-2005 or visit the Connecticut State Department of Education Web site at www.state.ct.us/sde.

MAINE

Maine's statewide school-to-work program is called Career Opportunities 2000, or CO2. There are six distinct components or dimensions of Maine's original

Career Opportunities 2000 statewide school-to-work opportunities system concept: 1) universal high-performance education (UHPE), K–10, which culminated in the award of a Certificate of Core Mastery; 2) Comprehensive Career Development Services, K–Adult, which featured Individual Opportunity Plans for all students; 3) seven clearly articulated Career/Life Pathways for grades 11–13+; 4) Comprehensive Student Support/Safety Net Programs and a youth corrections-to-work program; 5) a statewide network of STW-based Dropout Recovery Centers and a youth corrections-to-work program; and 6) an automated student follow-up and accountability system, which is currently being developed by the Center for Labor Market Studies at Northeastern University. For more information on these programs, contact the state director, Chris Lyons, at 207-287-5854 or via e-mail at chris.lyons@state.me.us. In addition, you can visit the following Web sites for more information: State of Maine Department of Education (janus.state.me.us/education/home-page.htm); Jobs for Maine's Graduates (www.jmg.org); Maine Technical College System (www.mtcs.net).

MASSACHUSETTS

Massachusetts, one of the first eight school-to-work (STW) implementation states, is in the final year of its federal grant. Along with diminishing federal funds, the initiative now relies on state and local funds to support school-to-career activities as well as specific support for more than 100 professionals who broker and structure work-based learning opportunities.

More than one third of all secondary schools in Massachusetts are offering career pathways to students. Seventy-five job coaches work throughout the state to secure meaningful internships for students and to establish strong connections between the workplace and the school. Massachusetts's Summer of Work and Learning program targets summer job activities for teams of students and teachers to work with one another on specific projects on job sites and in the classroom. At present, more than 10,000 employers provide work-based learning opportunities for students, and more than 22,000 students are participating in paid and unpaid workplace internships that are connected with classroom activities. For more information on programs in Massachusetts, contact the state director, Keith Westrich, at 781-388-3300, ext. 311, or via e-mail at kwestrich@doe.mass.edu. Additional information can be found on the State of Massachusetts School-to-Work Programs' Web site (www.doe.mass.edu/stw).

NEW HAMPSHIRE

New Hampshire's school-to-work programs are implemented by five regional partnerships throughout the state representing five career pathways: travel and tourism, biotechnology, manufacturing/engineering, information systems, and finance. Registered Youth Apprenticeships are available to students throughout the state. For more information, contact the state director, Justina Hale-List, at 603-271-3729 or via e-mail at Thalelist@ed.state.nh.us. Additional information can be found on the State of New Hampshire Department of Education's Web site (www.state.nh.us/doe).

RHODE ISLAND

Ninth and tenth graders begin exploring career majors, and in the last two years of high school, students connect interest in a career major with work-based learning. To demonstrate a student's mastery of high academic standards and workplace competencies, Certificates of Initial and Advanced Mastery are awarded. Students are also encouraged to seek education and training after graduation. The Community College of Rhode Island, Rhode Island College, and the University of Rhode Island are active School-to-Career partners. There is strong employer participation, and Rhode Island's size provides easy access to a range of resources. Rhode Island's STC Transition effort is distinguished by the inclusion of family involvement. A parent advocacy group is to be formed at the state level and local partnerships are required to include families.

Rhode Island is creating a gateway for students, such as the Certificate of Initial Mastery, which incorporates elements of the Common Core and mathematics, science, and language arts, followed by a Certificate of Advanced Mastery or industry-recognized certificate that leads to postsecondary options. Student accomplishments are benchmarked at grades 4, 8, and 10. Currently nine school districts in Rhode Island are piloting the Certificate of Initial Mastery. The Rhode Island Department of Labor and Training has taken the lead in organizing and initiating a statewide pilot of Jobs for America's Graduates (JAG). Currently, Jobs for Ocean State Graduates is successfully operating in ten high schools. The state plans to create a state level Job

Bank to connect schools and employers; employer database implementation is underway.

Much effort is being made by the Chambers of Commerce and community-based organizations to connect dropouts with STC, including providing GED preparation, and alternative learning environments. Rhode Island stresses that STC is for "all kids," with special programs that educate profoundly disabled students for work. For more information on all of these programs, contact Rhode Island State Director Linda Soderberg at 401-222-4922 or via e-mail at Lsoderberg@dlt.state.ri.us. In additional, information can be found on the following Web sites: Rhode Island State Department of Education (www.ridoe.net); Rhode Island School-to-Career (www.det.state.ri.us/webdev/stc/index.htm).

VERMONT

Vermont's local school-to-work activities are developed and directed by fourteen regional partnerships, which have been developed around job market regions. Work-based learning experiences are provided primarily by small business, which make up 80 percent of all employers in Vermont. Vermont students begin to participate in school-to-work activities early on, assuming increasing responsibility for choosing learning options as they progress through secondary school. Career portfolios and eleventh- and twelfth-grade career pathways provide a context for organizing study and facilitate postsecondary options, if desired. Students can participate in a wide variety of school-to-work experiences, including classroom-based learning, job shadowing, applied learning, co-ops,

apprenticeships, and service opportunities. Certification of student learning is based on high standards of performance.

An example of Vermont's school-to-work program is the relationship between Bellow Falls Union High School and Fall Mountain Motors, an automobile dealership. Students participate in an unpaid, work-based learning program two hours a day, five days a week for two months as part of the Intensive Studies Work Experience program, which rotates students through several job placements.

For more information about Vermont's school-to-work programs, contact the state director, Jeanie Crosby, at 802-828-5403 or via e-mail at jcrosby@gvr.state.vt.us. You can also visit the following Web sites for additional information: State of Vermont Department of Education (www.state.vt.us/educ); Vermont School-to-Work Program (www.state.vt.us/stw).

INTERNSHIPS

DATA PRESENTED IN THIS APPENDIX WAS COLLECTED IN PETERSON'S 2000 SURVEY OF INTERNSHIPS. (THIS DATA WAS COLLECTED BETWEEN DECEMBER 1999 AND APRIL 2000)

CONNECTICUT

Automotive Restoration, Inc. and Vintage Racing Services, Inc.
General Information: Antique and classic automobile restoration shop that performs panel fabrication, woodwork, upholstery, body, paint, and mechanical work; also includes management, appraisal, and evaluation.
Contact: Kent Bain, President, 1785 Barnum Avenue, Stratford, CT 06614; **Phone:** 203-377-6745; **Fax:** 203-386-0486; **E-mail:** bainks@msn.com; **Web site:** www.automotiverestorationinc.org

Big Brothers/Big Sisters of Meriden/Wallingford
General Information: Nonprofit agency designed to improve the lives of children by providing them with a one-to-one mentoring experience with a

professionally screened and supervised volunteer.
Contact: Liz Davis, Executive Director, 6 Fairfield Boulevard, Wallingford, CT 06492; **Phone:** 203-269-8200

Connecticut Opera Association, Inc.
General Information: 57-year-old regional opera company offering quality productions, guest artists from both American and international companies, and a resident ensemble.
Contact: Maria Levy, Managing Director, 226 Farmington Avenue, Hartford, CT 06105; B]**Fax:** 860-293-1715; **E-mail:** marialevyct@aol.com; **Web site:** www.connecticutopera.org

Kid Protection Network
General Information: Nonprofit organization that campaigns to keep streets safe for all children.
Contact: Michael Cluney, President, PO Box 516, Middlefield, CT 06455; **Phone:** 860-349-5614; **Fax:** 860-685-2411; **E-mail:** mcluney@wesleyan.edu; **Web site:** www.kidprotectionnetwork.org

The Maritime Aquarium at Norwalk
General Information: An aquarium, maritime museum, and educational center that encourages and excites appreciation of science and the interrelationship of global ecology and natural and cultural events as they relate to Long Island Sound.
Contact: Holly Turner, Intern Coordinator, 10 North Water Street, Norwalk, CT 06854; **Fax:** 203-838-5416; **E-mail:** intern.coor@aol.com; **Web site:** maritimeaquarium.org

Westport Country Playhouse
General Information: Professional summer theater in an historic building.
Contact: Julie A. Monahan, General Manager, 25 Powers Court, Westport, CT 06880; B]**Phone:** 203-227-5137; **Fax:** 203-221-7482; **E-mail:** westportplay@mindspring.com; **Web site:** www.westportplayhouse.org

MASSACHUSETTS

Boston YWCA
General Information: Organization that raises public awareness of economic security, child care, the health of the young, and world peace.
Contact: Pat Creary, Human Resources Manager, 140 Clarendon Street, Boston, MA 02116; **Phone:** 617-351-7642; **Fax:** 617-351-7615

Boys and Girls Club of Plymouth, Inc.
General Information: Organization that provides area youth with activities designed to build self-esteem, develop leadership skills, and promote positive life choices.
Contact: Ron Randall, Executive Director, PO Box 3479, Plymouth, MA 02361; **Phone:** 508-746-6070; **Fax:** 508-746-5953

C. Paul Luongo Company, Public Relations and Marketing
General Information: Public relations firm and marketing agency that offers corporate, product, and financial publicity consulting and marketing communications services throughout the U.S. and Canada.
Contact: C. Paul Luongo, President, 441 Stuart Street, Boston, MA 02116; **Phone:** 617-266-4210

Center for Campus Organizing

General Information: National clearinghouse that promotes progressive activism and investigative journalism on campuses.
Contact: Bill Capowski, Executive Director, 165 Friend Street #1, Boston, MA 02114; **Phone:** 617-725-2886; **Fax:** 617-725-2873; **E-mail:** cco@igc.org; **Web site:** www.cco.org

Citizens for Participation in Political Action (CPPAX)

General Information: Multi-issue, progressive grassroots political organization with a current focus on economic democracy, including fair taxes, adequate human services, cuts in military budget, economic and labor rights issues, and campaign finance reform.
Contact: Debbie Nichelson, Administrative Director, 25 West Street, 4th Floor, Boston, MA 02111; **Phone:** 617-426-3040; **Fax:** 617-426-8389; **E-mail:** cppax@cppax.org; **Web site:** www.cppax.com

College Light Opera Company

General Information: Summer stock music theater serving as training ground for all aspects of theater performance and management.
Contact: Robert A. Haslun, Producer, Highfield Theatre, PO Drawer 906, Falmouth, MA 02541; **Phone:** 440-774-8485; **Fax:** 440-775-8642; **E-mail:** bob.haslun@oberlin.edu; **Web site:** www.capecod.net/cloc

Girls Incorporated of Greater Lowell

General Information: Nonprofit organization that provides after-school programs for girls ages 6–18 in the greater Lowell area.
Contact: Carol S. Duncan, 220 Worthen Street, Lowell, MA 01852; **Phone:** 978-458-6529; **E-mail:** ggrlowell@aol.com

INFACT

General Information: National grassroots nonprofit organization whose purpose is to stop life-threatening abuses of transnational corporations and increase their accountability to people around the world.
Contact: Larisa Ruoff, Internship Coordinator, 46 Plympton Street, Boston, MA 02118; **Phone:** 617-695-2525; **Fax:** 617-695-2626; **E-mail:** infact@igc.org; **Web site:** www.infact.org

Massachusetts Society of Prevention of Cruelty to Children–Cape Cod

General Information: Child welfare agency that focuses on the prevention of child abuse and neglect.
Contact: Nancy Roberts, Good Start Director, 206 Breed's Hill Road, Hyannis, MA 02601; **Phone:** 800-272-9722 (toll-free); **Fax:** 508-790-3988

Merrimack Repertory Theatre

General Information: Professional theater producing seven quality productions from September through May.
Contact: Linda Trudel, Administrative Assistant, 50 East Merrimack Street, Lowell, MA 01852; **Phone:** 978-454-6324, Ext. 224; **Fax:** 978-934-0166; **E-mail:** mrtlowell@aol.com; **Web site:** www.mrtlowell.com

The Salvation Army Massachusetts Division

General Information: A worldwide evangelical Christian church, human service agency, and non-profit corporation.
Contact: Dorine Foreman, Personnel Secretary, 147 Berkeley Street, Boston, MA 02116; **Phone:** 617-542-5420, Ext. 170; **Fax:** 617-338-7990

Truro Center for the Arts at Castle Hill

General Information: Summer art school offering a wide range of workshops in painting, printmaking, drawing, sculpture, writing, photography, book arts, metal, and clay taught by well-established artists and craftspeople.
Contact: Mary Stackhouse, Director, PO Box 756, Truro, MA 02666; **Phone:** 508-349-7511; **Fax:** 508-349-7513; **E-mail:** castlehill@capecod.net; **Web site:** www.castlehill.org

U.S. Fish and Wildlife Service

General Information: Federal agency conserving the nation's natural resources.
Contact: Janice Rowan, Coordinator, 103 East Plumtree Road, Sunderland, MA 01375; **Phone:** 413-548-9138; **Fax:** 413-548-9622; **E-mail:** jan_rowan@fws.gov; **Web site:** www.fws.gov/r5crc

Williamstown Theater Festival

General Information: Summer theater, which presents productions of revivals of classics and new works by new and established playwrights.
Contact: Anne Lowrie, Company Manager, 1000 Main Street, PO Box 517, Williamstown, MA 01267; **Phone:** 212-228-2286; **Fax:** 212-228-9091; **E-mail:** alowrie@wtfestival.org; **Web site:** www.wtfestival.org

MAINE

H.O.M.E. Inc.

General Information: Corporation dedicated to "helping people to help themselves" by providing education, an outlet for the sale of crafts, and health care to low-income individuals in addition to job training and housing.
Contact: Randy Eldridge, Volunteer Coordinator, PO Box 10, Orland, ME 04472; **Phone:** 207-469-7961; **E-mail:** padre@acadia.net; **Web site:** www.h.o.m.e.coop.net

Penobscot Bay Press

General Information: Publisher of books, computer graphics, and three weekly newspapers.
Contact: Nat Barrows, Publisher, PO Box 36, Stonington, ME 04681; **Fax:** 207-367-6397; **E-mail:** pbp@acadia.net

Waterville Area Boys and Girls Club

General Information: Nonprofit youth agency that provides social, educational, and recreational activities to persons ages 6–20.
Contact: Stephen Crate, Volunteer Coordinator, 126 North Street, Waterville, ME 04901; **Phone:** 207-873-0684; **Fax:** 207-861-8016; **E-mail:** scrate@mint.net; **Web site:** www.aplaceforkidstogo.com

RHODE ISLAND

Rhode Island State Government Intern Program

General Information: Program that places college, graduate, and law students in Rhode Island's government agencies for internships.
Contact: Robert W. Gemma, Executive Director, Room 8AA, State House Building, Providence, RI 02903; **Phone:** 401-222-6782; **Fax:** 401-222-6142; **E-mail:** rgemma@rilin.state.ri.us; **Web site:** www.rilin.state.ri.us

University of Rhode Island, Environmental Education Center

General Information: Organization dedicated to educating school-age children about the environment, ecology, cultural history, farming, and group building.
Contact: John Jacques, Manager, W. Alton Jones Campus, 401 Victory Highway, West Greenwich, RI 02817; **Phone:** 401-397-3304, Ext. 6043; **Fax:** 401-397-3293; **E-mail:** urieec@etal.uri.edu; **Web site:** www.uri.edu/ajc

VERMONT

Explorations in Travel, Inc.

General Information: Organization that provides travel opportunities and volunteer placements for students and adults.
Contact: John Lee, Volunteer Coordinator, 1922 River Road, Guilford, VT 05301; **Phone:** 802-257-0152; **Fax:** 802-257-2784; **E-mail:** explore@sover.net; **Web site:** www.exploretravel.com

Merck Forest and Farmland Center

General Information: Center that teaches about land stewardship and sustainability by providing programs, access, and demonstrations on more than 3,130 acres of working farm and forest land.
Contact: Ellen Rathbone, Program Director, Box 86, Route 315, Rupert, VT 05768; **Phone:** 802-394-7836; **Fax:** 802-394-2519; **E-mail:** merck@vermontel.com; **Web site:** www.merckforest.org

SUMMER OPPORTUNITIES

DATA PRESENTED IN THIS APPENDIX WAS COLLECTED IN PETERSON'S 2000 SURVEY OF SUMMER OPPORTUNITIES. (THIS DATA WAS COLLECTED BETWEEN MAY THROUGH AUGUST 2000)

CONNECTICUT

Academy One

Windsor, CT
General Information: Coed residential and day sports program.
Contact: Dr. Joseph Machnik, Director, PO Box 389, 916 Palm Boulevard, Isle of Palms, SC 29451; **Phone:** 800-622-4645 (toll-free) or 843-886-0885; **E-mail:** info@no1soccercamps.com; **Web site:** www.no1soccercamps.com

AIM—Academy Introduction Mission—United States Coast Guard Academy

New London, CT
General Information: Coed residential academic program established in 1955.
Contact: Lt. J.G. Jennifer Becher, AIM Project Officer, 31 Mohegan Avenue, New London, CT 06320-8103; **Phone:** 860-701-6781 or 860-701-6700; **E-mail:** admissions@cga.uscg.mil; **Web site:** www.cga.edu/admiss

American Computer Experience—Summer Computer Camp—University of Hartford

West Hartford, CT

General Information: Coed residential and day academic program.

Contact: Director, PO Box 15367, Atlanta, GA 30333; **Phone:** 800-386-4223 (toll-free); **E-mail:** ace@computercamp.com; **Web site:** www. aceplanet.com

Arts/Theatre Week at Camp Washington

Lakeside, CT

General Information: Coed residential arts program established in 1985.

Contact: Elia Vecchitto, Camp Director, 190 Kenyon Road, Lakeside, CT 06758; **Phone:** 860-567-9623 or 860-567-3037; **E-mail:** elia_v@hotmail.com; **Web site:** www.campwashington.org

Brookfield Craft Center Summer Workshops

Brookfield, CT

General Information: Coed day arts program established in 1954.

Contact: Dee Wagner, Registrar, PO Box 122, Route 25, Brookfield, CT 06804-0122, **Phone:** 203-775-4526 or 203-740-7815; **E-mail:** brkfldcrft@aol.com; **Web site:** www. brookfieldcraftcenter.org

Camp Washington

Lakeside, CT

General Information: Coed residential outdoor/wilderness program established in 1917.

Contact: Elia Vecchitto, Camp Director, 190 Kenyon Road, Lakeside, CT 06758; **Phone:** 860-567-9623 or 860-567-3037; **E-mail:** elia_v@ hotmail.com; **Web site:** www.campwashington.org

Center for Creative Youth

Middletown, CT

General Information: Coed residential arts program established in 1977.

Contact: Nancy Wolfe, Managing Director, 350 High Street, Middletown, CT 06459; **Phone:** 860-685-3307 or 860-685-3311; **E-mail:** ccy@wesleyan.edu; **Web site:** www.wesleyan.edu/CCY

Cheshire Academy Summer Academic Programs

Cheshire, CT

General Information: Coed residential and day academic program established in 1911.

Contact: Joseph C. Hanrahan, Director of Summer Programs, 10 Main Street, Cheshire, CT 06410, **Phone:** 203-272-5396 or 203-250-7209; **E-mail:** summer@cheshacad.pvt.k12.ct.us; **Web site:** www.cheshireacademy.org

Cheshire Academy Summer Arts Program

Cheshire, CT

General Information: Coed residential and day arts program.

Contact: Joseph C. Hanrahan, Director of Summer Programs, 10 Main Street, Cheshire, CT 06410; **Phone:** 203-272-5396 or 203-250-7209; **E-mail:** summer@cheshacad.pvt.k12.ct.us; **Web site:** www.cheshireacademy.org

Cheshire Academy Summer Athletics Program

Cheshire, CT

General Information: Coed residential and day sports program.

Contact: Joseph C. Hanrahan, Director of Summer Programs, 10 Main Street, Cheshire, CT 06410; **Phone:** 203-272-5396 or 203-250-7209; **E-mail:** summer@cheshacad.pvt.k12.ct.us; **Web site:** www.cheshireacademy.org

Choate Rosemary Hall English Language Institute/Focus Program

Wallingford, CT

General Information: Coed residential and day academic program established in 1999.

Contact: Ms. Nancy Miller, Director of Admission, 333 Christian Street, Wallingford, CT 06492; **Phone:** 203-697-2365 or 203-697-2519; **E-mail:** nmiller@choate.edu; **Web site:** www.choate.edu/summer

Choate Rosemary Hall Focus Program

Wallingford, CT

General Information: Coed residential and day academic program established in 1998.

Contact: Ms. Nancy Miller, Director of Admissions, 333 Christian Street, Wallingford, CT 06492; **Phone:** 203-697-2365 or 203-697-2519; **E-mail:** nmiller@choate.edu; **Web site:** www.choate.edu/summer

Choate Rosemary Hall Full Year Credit Program

Wallingford, CT

General Information: Coed residential and day academic program established in 1999.

Contact: Ms. Nancy Miller, Director of Admission, 333 Christian Street, Wallingford, CT 06492; **Phone:** 203-697-2365 or 203-697-2519; **E-mail:** nmiller@choate.edu; **Web site:** www.choate.edu/summer

Choate Rosemary Hall John F. Kennedy Institute in Government

Wallingford, CT

General Information: Coed residential and day academic program established in 1985.

Contact: Ms. Nancy Miller, Director of Admission, 333 Christian Street, Wallingford, CT 06492; **Phone:** 203-697-2365 or 203-697-2519; **E-mail:** nmiller@choate.edu; **Web site:** www.choate.edu/summer

Choate Rosemary Hall Math/Science Institute for Girls

Wallingford, CT

General Information: Girls residential and day academic program established in 1995.

Contact: Ms. Nancy Miller, Director of Admission, 333 Christian Street, Wallingford, CT 06492; **Phone:** 203-697-2365 or 203-697-2519; **E-mail:** nmiller@choate.edu; **Web site:** www.choate.edu/summer

Choate Rosemary Hall Summer Arts Conservatory—Playwriting

Wallingford, CT

General Information: Coed residential and day arts program established in 1982.

Contact: Mr. Paul J. Tines, Director, Arts Conservatory, Paul Mellon Arts Center, 333 Christian Street, Wallingford, CT 06492; **Phone:** 203-697-2488 or 203-697-2396; **E-mail:** ptines@choate.edu; **Web site:** www.choate.edu

Choate Rosemary Hall Summer Arts Conservatory—Strings Program

Wallingford, CT

General Information: Coed residential and day arts program established in 1982.

Contact: Mr. Paul J. Tines, Director, Arts Conservatory, Paul Mellon Arts Center, 333 Christian Street, Wallingford, CT 06492; **Phone:** 203-697-2488 or 203-697-2396; **E-mail:** ptines@choate.edu; **Web site:** www.choate.edu

Choate Rosemary Hall Summer Arts Conservatory—Theater

Wallingford, CT

General Information: Coed residential and day arts program established in 1982.

Contact: Mr. Paul J. Tines, Director, Arts Conservatory, Paul Mellon Arts Center, 333 Christian Street, Wallingford, CT 06492; **Phone:** 203-697-2488 or 203-697-2396; **E-mail:** ptines@choate.edu; **Web site:** www.choate.edu/ summer

Choate Rosemary Hall Summer Arts Conservatory—Visual Arts Program

Wallingford, CT

General Information: Coed residential and day arts program established in 1982.

Contact: Mr. Paul J. Tines, Director, Arts Conservatory, Paul Mellon Arts Center, 333 Christian Street, Wallingford, CT 06492; **Phone:** 203-697-2488 or 203-697-2396; **E-mail:** ptines@choate.edu; **Web site:** www.choate.edu

Choate Rosemary Hall Summer Session

Wallingford, CT

General Information: Coed residential and day academic program established in 1916.

Contact: Ms. Nancy Miller, Director of Admission for Summer Programs, 333 Christian Street, Wallingford, CT 06492; **Phone:** 203-697-2365 or 203-697-2519; **E-mail:** nmiller@choate.edu; **Web site:** www.choate.edu/summer

Choate Rosemary Hall Young Writers Workshop

Wallingford, CT

General Information: Coed residential and day academic program established in 1997.

Contact: Nancy Miller, Director of Admissions, 333 Christian Street, Wallingford, CT 06492; **Phone:** 203-697-2365 or 203-697-2519; **E-mail:** nmiller@choate.edu; **Web site:** www.choate.edu/summer

Community Outreach Program

Lakeside, CT

General Information: Coed residential community service program established in 1999.

Contact: Elia Vecchitto, Camp Director, 190 Kenyon Road, Lakeside, CT 06758; **Phone:** 860-567-9623 or 860-567-3037; **E-mail:** elia_v@ hotmail.com; **Web site:** www.campwashington.org

Exploration Senior Program at Yale University

New Haven, CT

General Information: Coed residential and day academic program established in 1977.

Contact: Ms. Diane Scott, Head of Program, Yale University, New Haven, CT 06520; **Web site:** www.explo.org

Hyde School Summer Challenge Program

Woodstock, CT

General Information: Coed residential academic program.

Contact: Robert Felt, Director of Admissions, PO Box 237, Woodstock, CT 06281-0237, **Phone:** 860-963-9096; **E-mail:** admissionswoodstock@hyde.edu; **Web site:** www.hyde.edu

iD Tech Camps—University of Connecticut

Hartford, CT

General Information: Coed residential and day academic program established in 1999.

Contact: Mr. Pete Ingram-Cauchi, President, 2103 South Bascom Avenue, Campbell, CA 95008; **Phone:** 888-709-TECH (toll-free) or 408-626-9505; **E-mail:** info@internaldrive.com; **Web site:** www.internaldrive.com

Kent School Summer Camp for Creative Writing

Kent, CT

General Information: Coed residential and day academic program established in 1995.

Contact: Mr. Todd Marble, Summer Camp Director, Route 341, Kent, CT 06757; **Phone:** 860-927-6038 or 860-927-6039; **E-mail:** marblet@kent-school.edu; **Web site:** www.kent-school.edu

Landmark Volunteers—Connecticut

General Information: Coed residential community service program established in 1992.

Contact: Ann Barrett, Executive Director, PO Box 455, Sheffield, MA 01257; **Phone:** 413-229-0255 or 413-229-2050; **E-mail:** landmark@volunteers.com; **Web site:** www.volunteers.com

Litchfield Jazz Festival Summer Music School Program

Litchfield, CT

General Information: Coed residential arts program.

Contact: Mitchell Alan Goldfield, Program Director, PO Box 69, Litchfield, CT 06759; **Phone:** 860-567-4162 or 860-567-3592; **E-mail:** magi@ix.netcom.com; **Web site:** www.litchfieldjazzfest.com

Marvelwood Summer

Kent, CT

General Information: Coed residential and day academic program established in 1964.

Contact: Ms. Beth Wirsul, Assistant Director of Admissions, 476 Skiff Mountain Road, PO Box 3001, Kent, CT 06757, **Phone:** 860-927-0047 or 860-927-5325; **E-mail:** marvelwood.school@snet.net; **Web site:** www.themarvelwoodschool.com

Miss Porter's School Summer Challenge and American Experience

Farmington, CT

General Information: Girls residential academic program.

Contact: Christopher Hampton, Director of Summer Programs, 60 Main Street, Farmington, CT 06032; **Phone:** 860-409-3692; **E-mail:** christopher_hampton@missporters.org; **Web site:** www.missporters.org

Music/Choir Program at Camp Washington

Lakeside, CT

General Information: Coed residential arts program established in 1985.

Contact: Elia Vecchitto, Camp Director, 190 Kenyon Road, Lakeside, CT 06758; **Phone:** 860-567-9623 or 860-567-3037; **E-mail:** elia_v@hotmail.com; **Web site:** www.campwashington.org

National Computer Camps at Sacred Heart University

Fairfield, CT

General Information: Coed residential and day academic program established in 1977.

Contact: Dr. Michael Zabinski, President, PO Box 585, Orange, CT 06477; **Phone:** 203-795-9667; **E-mail:** info@nccamp.com; **Web site:** www.nccamp.com

National Guitar Workshop

New Milford, CT

General Information: Coed residential and day arts program established in 1984.

Contact: Ms. Paula Dutton, Director, Connecticut Campus, PO Box 222, Lakeside, CT 06758; **Phone:** 860-567-3736 ext. 103 or 860-567-0374; **E-mail:** paula@guitarworkshop.com; **Web site:** www.guitarworkshop.com

NIKE Advanced Player School

New Haven, CT

General Information: Boys residential and day sports program.

Contact: Jason West, Director of Marketing, 919 Sir Francis Drake Boulevard, Kentfield, CA 94904; **Phone:** 415-459-0459 or 415-459-1453; **E-mail:** jwest@us-sportscamps.com; **Web site:** www.ecamps.com

NIKE Junior Resident Camp

Windsor, CT

General Information: Coed residential and day sports program.

Contact: Jason West, Director of Marketing, 919 Sir Francis Drake Boulevard, Kentfield, CA 94904; **Phone:** 415-459-0459 or 415-459-1453; **E-mail:** jwest@us-sportscamps.coml; **Web site:** www.ecamps.com

No. 1 College Prep Academy

Windsor, CT

General Information: Coed residential and day sports program.

Contact: Dr. Jospeh Machnik, Director, PO Box 389, 916 Palm Boulevard, Isle of Palms, SC 29451; **Phone:** 800-622-4645 (toll-free) or 843-886-0885; **E-mail:** info@no1soccercamps.com; **Web site:** www.no1soccercamps.com

No. 1 Goalkeeper Camp, No. 1 Striker Camp

Pomfret, CT

General Information: Coed residential and day sports program established in 1977.

Contact: Dr. Joseph Machnik, Director, P O Box 389, 916 Palm Boulevard, Isle of Palms, SC 29451; **Phone:** 800-622-4645 (toll-free) or 843-886-0885; **E-mail:** info@no1soccercamps.com; **Web site:** www.no1soccercamps.com

No. 1 Goalkeeper Camp, No. 1 Striker Camp

Windsor, CT

General Information: Coed residential and day sports program established in 1977.

Contact: Dr. Joseph Machnik, Director, P O Box 389, 916 Palm Boulevard, Isle of Palms, SC 29451; **Phone:** 800-622-4645 (toll-free) or 843-886-0885; **E-mail:** info@no1soccercamp.com; **Web site:** www.no1soccercamps.com

Rectory School Summer Session

Pomfret, CT

General Information: Coed residential and day aca-

demic program established in 1950.

Contact: Stephen A. DiPaolo, Director of Admissions, PO Box 68, 528 Pomfret Street, Pomfret, CT 06258; **Phone:** 860-928-1328 or 860-963-2355; **E-mail:** recadmit@neca.com; **Web site:** www.neca.com/~librslo1/rectory.htm

Rumsey Hall School Summer Session

Washington Depot, CT

General Information: Coed residential and day academic program established in 1975.

Contact: Matthew S. Hoeniger, 201 Romford Road, Washington Depot, CT 06794; **Phone:** 860-868-0535 or 860-868-7907; **E-mail:** rhsadm@wtco.net; **Web site:** www.rumsey.pvt.k12.ct.us

Salisbury Summer School of Reading and English

Salisbury, CT

General Information: Coed residential academic program established in 1946.

Contact: Summer School Office, 251 Canaan Road, Salisbury, CT 06068; **Phone:** 860-435-5751 or 860-435-5750; **Web site:** www.salisburyschool.org

SJ Ranch

Ellington, CT

General Information: Girls residential and day sports program established in 1956.

Contact: Pat Haines, Director, 130 Sandy Beach Road, Ellington, CT 06029; **Phone:** 860-872-4742 or 860-870-4914; **E-mail:** sjranch@erols.com

Summer WISE Camp

Middlebury, CT

General Information: Girls residential academic program established in 1998.

Contact: Carol R. Santos, Director of Summer WISE, PO Box 847, Middlebury, CT 06762; **Phone:** 203-577-4503 or 203-577-4588; **E-mail:** csantos@westoverschool.org; **Web site:** www.westoverschool.org

Taft Summer School

Watertown, CT

General Information: Coed residential and day academic program established in 1982.

Contact: Penny Townsend, Director, 110 Woodbury Road, Watertown, CT 06795; **Phone:** 860-945-7961 or 860-945-7859; **E-mail:** summerschool@taftschool.org; **Web site:** www.taftschool.org

The Loomis Chaffee Summer Programs

Windsor, CT

General Information: Coed residential and day academic program established in 1990.

Contact: Joseph McCarthy, Director, Summer Programs, Windsor, CT 06095; **Phone:** 860-687-6117 or 860-687-6141; **E-mail:** lcsp@loomis.org; **Web site:** loomis.org/site_home.htm

The Summer Academy at Suffield

Suffield, CT

General Information: Coed residential and day academic and arts program established in 1995.

Contact: Amparo Adib-Samii, Summer Academy Office, 185 North Main Street, Suffield, CT 06078; **Phone:** 860-386-4475 or 860-386-4476; **E-mail:** summer@suffieldacademy.org; **Web site:** www.suffieldacademy.org/summacad/index.htm

The Woodhall School Summer Session
Bethlehem, CT
General Information: Boys residential and day academic program established in 1983.
Contact: Ms. Sally Campbell Woodhall, Head of School, PO Box 550, Bethlehem, CT 06751; **Phone:** 203-266-7788 or 203-266-5896

University of Connecticut Mentor Connection
Storrs, CT
General Information: Coed residential academic program.
Contact: Heather Spottiswoode, Program Coordinator, 2131 Hillside Road, U7, Storrs, CT 06269-3007; **Phone:** 860-486-0283 or 860-486-2900; **E-mail:** heather.spottiswoode@uconn.edu; **Web site:** www.gifted.uconn.edu/

MAINE

American Computer Experience—Summer Computer Camp—University of New England
Portland, ME
General Information: Coed residential and day academic program.
Contact: Director, PO Box 15367, Atlanta, GA 30333; **Phone:** 800-386-4223 (toll-free); **E-mail:** ace@computercamp.com; **Web site:** www.aceplanet.com

Camp Chewonki for Girls
Wiscasset, ME
General Information: Girls residential adventure program established in 2000.
Contact: Dick Thomas, Camp Director, 485 Chewonki Neck Road, Wiscasset, ME 04578; **Phone:** 207-882-7323 or 207-882-4074; **E-mail:** camp@chewonki.org; **Web site:** www.chewonki.org

Camp Chewonki Wilderness Expeditions
Wiscasset, ME
General Information: Coed residential adventure and outdoor/wilderness program established in 1915.
Contact: Dick Thomas, Camp Director, 485 Chewonki Neck Road, Wiscasset, ME 04578; **Phone:** 207-882-7323 or 207-882-4074; **E-mail:** camp@chewonki.org; **Web site:** www.chewonki.org

Camp Hawthorne Creative Arts Camp
Raymond, ME
General Information: Coed residential arts program established in 1987.
Contact: Ronald Furst, Director, 10 Scotland Bridge Road, York, ME 03909; **Phone:** 207-363-1773; **E-mail:** camphaw@nh.ultranet.com

Hidden Valley Camp
Freedom, ME
General Information: Coed residential arts program established in 1946.
Contact: Meg Kassen, Co-Owner/Director, RR 1, Box 2360, Freedom, ME 04941; **Phone:** 207-342-5177 or 207-342-5685; **E-mail:** summer@hiddenvalleycamp.com; **Web site:** www.hiddenvalleycamp.com

Hyde School Summer Challenge Program
Bath, ME
General Information: Coed residential academic program established in 1966.
Contact: Robert C. Felt, Director of Admissions, 616 High Street, Bath, ME 04530-5002; **Phone:** 207-443-5584 or 207-442-9346; **E-mail:** admissions-bath@hyde.edu; **Web site:** www.hyde.edu

Landmark Volunteers: Maine
General Information: Coed residential community service program established in 1992.
Contact: Ann Barrett, Executive Director, PO Box 455, Sheffield, MA 01257; **Phone:** 413-229-0255 or 413-229-2050; **E-mail:** landmark@volunteers.com; **Web site:** www.volunteers.com

Maine College of Art Early College Program
Portland, ME
General Information: Coed residential and day academic and arts program established in 1973.
Contact: Cindy Meyers, Director of Special Programs, 97 Spring Street, Portland, ME 04101; **Phone:** 207-775-3052 ext. 231 or 207-772-5069; **E-mail:** earlycollege@meca.edu; **Web site:** www.meca.edu/

The Festival of Creative Youth
Portland, ME
General Information: Coed day academic and arts program established in 1980.
Contact: John Glynn, Academic Director, PO Box 4353, Portland, ME 04101; **Phone:** 207-799-1950

MASSACHUSETTS

Academic Study Associates–ASA at the University of Massachusetts Amherst
Amherst, MA
General Information: Coed residential and day academic program established in 1987.
Contact: Marcia Evans, Director, 355 Main Street, PO Box 800, Armonk, NY 10504-0800; **Phone:** 914-273-2250 or 914-273-5430; **E-mail:** summer@asaprograms.com; **Web site:** www.asaprograms.com

AIFS Summer Institute for the Gifted—Amherst College
Amherst, MA
General Information: Coed residential academic program.
Contact: Barbara Wilson, Admissions Counselor, American Institute for Foreign Study (UK); 37 Queen's Gate, London, SW7 5HR; **Phone:** 44 207 581 7357 or 44 207 581 7355; **Web site:** www.aifs.com/studyusa

American Computer Experience—Summer Computer Camp—Amherst College
Amherst, MA
General Information: Coed residential and day academic program.
Contact: Director, PO Box 15367, Atlanta, GA 30333; **Phone:** 800-386-4223 (toll-free); **E-mail:** ace@computercamp.com; **Web site:** www.aceplanet.com

American Computer Experience—Summer Computer Camp—Babson College
Boston, MA
General Information: Coed day academic program.
Contact: Director, PO Box 15367, Atlanta, GA 30333; **Phone:** 800-386-4223 (toll-free); **E-mail:** ace@computercamp.com; **Web site:** www.aceplanet.com

American Computer Experience—Summer Computer Camp—Endicott College
Beverly, MA
General Information: Coed residential and day academic program.

Contact: Director, PO Box 15367, Atlanta, GA 30333; **Phone:** 800-386-4223 (toll-free); **E-mail:** ace@computercamp.com; **Web site:** www.aceplanet.com

American Computer Experience—Summer Computer Camp—Merrimack College
North Andover, MA
General Information: Coed residential and day academic program.
Contact: Director, PO Box 15367, Atlanta, GA 30333; **Phone:** 800-386-4223 (toll-free); **E-mail:** ace@computercamp.com; **Web site:** www.aceplanet.com

American Computer Experience—Summer Computer Camp—Northeastern University
Boston, MA
General Information: Coed residential and day academic program.
Contact: Director, PO Box 15367, Atlanta, GA 30333; **Phone:** 800-386-4223 (toll-free); **E-mail:** ace@computercamp.com; **Web site:** www.aceplanet.com

Bonnie Castle Riding Camp
Greenfield, MA
General Information: Girls residential and day sports program established in 1982.
Contact: Mina Payne Cooper, Director of Riding Program, 574 Bernardston Road, Greenfield, MA 01301; **Phone:** 413-774-2711 or 413-772-2602; **Web site:** www.sbschool.org

Boston College Experience
Chestnut Hill, MA
General Information: Coed residential and day academic program established in 1984.
Contact: Ms. Dova Romelus, Coordinator, The Boston College Experience, McGuinn Hall, Room 100, Chestnut Hill, MA 02467; **Phone:** 617-552-3900 or 617-552-3199; **E-mail:** romelus@bc.edu; **Web site:** www.bc.edu/bce

Boston University High School Honors Program
Boston, MA
General Information: Coed residential academic program established in 1977.
Contact: Jeremy Ryan, Director, High School Honors Program, Boston University Summer Term, 755 Commonwealth Avenue, Room B4A, Boston, MA 02215; **Phone:** 617-353-1378 or 617-353-7120; **Web site:** www.bu.edu

Boston University Promys Program
Boston, MA
General Information: Coed residential academic program established in 1989.
Contact: Mr. Thomas Harms, Promys Administrative Coordinator, Department of Math, 111 Cummington Street, Boston, MA 02215; **Phone:** 617-353-2563 or 617-353-8100; **E-mail:** promys@math.bu.edu; **Web site:** www.promys.org

Brandeis Summer Odyssey
Waltham, MA
General Information: Coed residential and day academic program established in 1988.
Contact: Monica Fairbairn, Director, Summer Odyssey, MS-085, Waltham, MA 02254-9110; **Phone:** 781-736-2111 or 781-736-2122; **E-mail:** odyssey@brandeis.edu; **Web site:** www.brandeis.edu/sumsch/odyssey

Camp $tart-Up

Wellesley, MA

General Information: Girls residential academic program established in 1994.

Contact: Valjeanne Estes, Camp Director, 126 Powers Avenue, Santa Barbara, CA 93103; **Phone:** 800-350-1816 (toll-free) or 805-965-3148; **E-mail:** vestes@independentmeans.com; **Web site:** www.independentmeans.com

Camp Burgess for Boys/Camp Hayward for Girls

Sandwich, MA

General Information: Coed residential adventure program established in 1928.

Contact: Lloyd Ewart, Camp Director, 75 Stowe Road, Sandwich, MA 02563; **Phone:** 508-428-2571 or 508-420-3545; **E-mail:** camp@ssymca.org; **Web site:** www.ssymca.org

Chris Slade Football Camp/Sports International

Bridgewater, MA

General Information: Coed residential and day sports program established in 1983.

Contact: Mr. Chuck Bollweg, President, 12061 Tech Road, Silver Spring, MD 20904; **Phone:** 800-555-0801 (toll-free) or 301-625-7723; **Web site:** www.footballcamps.com

Computer-Ed High-Tech Camp

Woburn, MA

General Information: Coed residential and day academic program established in 1982.

Contact: Ms. Francesca Foti, Director, Trade Center Park, 100 Sylvan Road G500, Woburn, MA 01801; **Phone:** 781-933-7681 or 781-938-0741; **E-mail:** camp@computered.com; **Web site:** www.computer-edcamps.com

Cushing Academy Summer Session

Ashburnham, MA

General Information: Coed residential and day arts program established in 1976.

Contact: Ms. Deborah A. Gustafson, Associate Director of the Summer Session, 39 School Street, P O Box 8000, Ashburnham, MA 01430-8000; **Phone:** 978-827-7700 or 978-827-6927; **E-mail:** summersession@cushing.org; **Web site:** www.cushing.org

Cybercamps—Babson College

Babson Park, MA

General Information: Coed residential and day academic program established in 1996.

Contact: Information Office, 12131 113th Avenue NE, Suite 102, Kirkland, WA 98034; **Phone:** 888-904-CAMP (toll-free) or 425-825-4601; **E-mail:** info@cybercamps.com; **Web site:** www.cybercamps.com

Cybercamps—Bentley College

Waltham, MA

General Information: Coed residential and day academic program established in 1996.

Contact: Information Office, 12131 113th Avenue NE, Suite 102, Kirkland, WA 98034; **Phone:** 888-904-CAMP (toll-free) or 425-825-4601; **E-mail:** info@cybercamps.com; **Web site:** www.cybercamps.com

Cybercamps—Curry College

Milton, MA

General Information: Coed residential and day academic program established in 1996.

Contact: Information Office, 12131 113th Avenue NE, Suite 102, Kirkland, WA 98034; **Phone:** 888-904-CAMP (toll-free) or 425-825-4601; **E-mail:** info@cybercamps.com; **Web site:** www.cybercamps.com

Cybercamps—Emmanuel College

Boston, MA

General Information: Coed residential and day academic program established in 1996.

Contact: Information Office, 12131 113th Avenue NE, Suite 102, Kirkland, WA 98034; **Phone:** 888-904-CAMP (toll-free) or 425-825-4601; **E-mail:** info@cybercamps.com; **Web site:** www.cybercamps.com

Eaglebrook Summer Semester

Deerfield, MA

General Information: Coed residential academic program established in 1996.

Contact: Mr. Karl J. Koenigsbauer, Director, Deerfield, MA 01342; **Phone:** 413-774-7411 or 413-772-2394; **Web site:** www.eaglebrook.org

Excel at Amherst College and Williams College

General Information: Coed residential academic and arts program established in 1992.

Contact: Tim Weed, Director, 345 Hickory Ridge Road, Putney, VT 05346; **Phone:** 802-387-5885 or 802-387-4276; **E-mail:** excel@goputney.com; **Web site:** www.goputney.com

Exploration Intermediate Program at Wellesley College

Wellesley, MA

General Information: Coed residential and day academic program established in 1983.

Contact: Head of Program, PO Box 368, 470 Washington Street, Norwood, MA 02062; **Web site:** www.explo.org

Exploration Junior Program at St. Mark's School

Southborough, MA

General Information: Coed residential and day academic program established in 1994.

Contact: Ms. Moira Kelly, Head of Program, St. Mark's School, Southborough, MA 01772; **Phone:** 508-786-1350 or 508-786-1360; **Web site:** www.explo.org

Frontiers/Strive Pre-College Summer Programs

Worcester, MA

General Information: Coed residential academic program.

Contact: Frontiers/Strive Summer Program, 100 Institute Road, Worcester, MA 01609-2280; **Phone:** 508-831-5796 or 508-831-5818; **E-mail:** outreach@wpi.edu; **Web site:** www.wpi.edu/+outreach

Go Girls Summer Discovery Program

Longmeadow, MA

General Information: Girls day arts program established in 1999.

Contact: Steven Smith, Director of Athletics, 588 Longmeadow Street, Longmeadow, MA 01106; **Phone:** 413-565-1244; **E-mail:** ssmith@baypath.edu; **Web site:** www.baypath.edu

Harvard University Summer School: Secondary School Program

Cambridge, MA

General Information: Coed residential and day academic program established in 1871.

Contact: Secondary School Program, 51 Brattle Street, Cambridge, MA 02138; **Phone:** 617-495-3192 or 617-495-9176; **E-mail:** hewitt@hudce.harvard.edu; **Web site:** www.ssp.harvard.edu

iD Tech Camps—MIT

Cambridge, MA

General Information: Coed residential and day academic program established in 1999.

Contact: Mr. Pete Ingram-Cauchi, President, 2103 South Bascom Avenue, Campbell, CA 95008; **Phone:** 888-709-TECH (toll-free) or 408-626-9505; **E-mail:** info@internaldrive.com; **Web site:** www.internaldrive.com

Institute for Television, Film, and Radio Production

Boston, MA

General Information: Coed residential academic program established in 1989.

Contact: Mary Ferreira, Senior Program Coordinator, 640 Commonwealth Avenue, Boston, MA 02215; **Phone:** 617-353-5015 or 617-353-3405; **E-mail:** itrp@bu.edu; **Web site:** www.bu.edu/com/itrp

Kayak Adventures Unlimited

General Information: Coed residential and day adventure program established in 1981.

Contact: Taylor Cook, Director, 499 Loomis Street, Westfield, MA 01085; **Phone:** 413-562-7431 or 413-562-7431; **E-mail:** adventures@weu.com; **Web site:** www.weu.com

Landmark School Summer Academic Program

Prides Crossing, MA

General Information: Coed residential and day academic program established in 1971.

Contact: Veronica Kenney, Director of Admission, PO Box 227, Prides Crossing, MA 01965-0227; **Phone:** 978-236-3000 or 978-927-7268; **E-mail:** vkenney@landmarkschool.org; **Web site:** www.landmarkschool.org

Landmark School Summer Adventure Ropes Program

Prides Crossing, MA

General Information: Coed residential and day academic program established in 2000.

Contact: Veronica Kenney, Director of Admission, PO Box 227, Prides Crossing, MA 01965-0227; **Phone:** 978-236-3000 or 978-927-7268; **E-mail:** vkenney@landmarkschool.org; **Web site:** www.landmarkschool.org

Landmark School Summer Marine Science Program

Prides Crossing, MA

General Information: Coed residential and day academic program established in 1987.

Contact: Veronica Kenney, Director of Admission, PO Box 227, Prides Crossing, MA 01965-0227; **Phone:** 978-236-3000 or 978-927-7268; **E-mail:** vkenney@landmarkschool.org; **Web site:** www.landmarkschool.org

Landmark School Summer Seamanship Program

Prides Crossing, MA

General Information: Coed residential and day academic program established in 1978.

Contact: Veronica Kenney, Director of Admission, PO Box 227, Prides Crossing, MA 01965-0227; **Phone:** 978-236-3000 or 978-927-7266; **E-mail:** vkenney@landmarkschool.org; **Web site:** www.landmarkschool.org

Landmark Volunteers: Massachusetts

General Information: Coed residential community service program established in 1992.

Contact: Ann Barrett, Executive Director, PO Box 455, Sheffield, MA 01257; **Phone:** 413-229-0255 or 413-229-2050; **E-mail:** landmark@volunteers.com; **Web site:** www.volunteers.com

Lawrence Academy Classical Acting Workshop

Groton, MA

General Information: Coed day arts program established in 2000.

Contact: Mr. David F. Smith, Director of Coordinate Programs, PO Box 992, Groton, MA 01450; **Phone:** 978-448-6535 or 978-448-9208; **E-mail:** dsmith@lacademy.edu; **Web site:** www.lacademy.edu

Lawrence Academy Environmental Field Study

Groton, MA

General Information: Coed day academic program established in 2000.

Contact: Mr. David F. Smith, Director of Coordinate Programs, PO Box 992, Groton, MA 01450; **Phone:** 978-448-6535 or 978-448-9208; **E-mail:** dsmith@lacademy.edu; **Web site:** www.lacademy.edu

Lawrence Academy International Summer School

Groton, MA

General Information: Coed residential academic program established in 1993.

Contact: Ms. Maria Graceffa-Rivera, Director, Lawrence Academy International School, PO Box 992, Groton, MA 01450; **Phone:** 978-448-6535 or 978-448-9208; **Web site:** www.lacademy.edu

Lawrence Academy Summer Arts Camp

Groton, MA

General Information: Coed day arts program established in 1993.

Contact: Mr. David F. Smith, Director of Coordinate Programs, PO Box 992, Groton, MA 01450; **Phone:** 978-448-6535 or 978-448-9208; **E-mail:** dsmith@lacademy.edu; **Web site:** www.lacademy.edu

Linden Hill Summer Program

Northfield, MA

General Information: Coed residential academic program established in 1998.

Contact: Michael P. Holland, Executive Director, 154 South Mountain Road, Northfield, MA 01360-9681; **Phone:** 888-254-6336 (toll-free) or 413-498-2908; **E-mail:** admissions@lindenhs.org; **Web site:** www.lindenhs.org

Massachusetts College of Art/August Studios in Art & Design

Boston, MA

General Information: Coed residential and day arts program established in 1990.

Contact: Suzanne Stokes, K-12 Outreach Coordinator, 621 Huntington Avenue, Boston, MA 02115; **Phone:** 617-232-1555 ext. 595 or 617-975-2098; **E-mail:** sstokes@massart.edu; **Web site:** www.massart.edu

Massachusetts College of Art/Creative Vacation

Boston, MA

General Information: Coed day arts program established in 1994.

Contact: Suzanne Stokes, K–12 Outreach Coordinator, 621 Huntington Avenue, Boston, MA 02115; **Phone:** 617-232-1555 ext. 595 or 617-975-2098; **Web site:** www.massart.edu/

Massachusetts College of Art/Saturday Studios

Boston, MA

General Information: Coed day arts program established in 1931.

Contact: Suzanne Stokes, K-12 Outreach Coordinator, 621 Huntington Avenue, Boston, MA 02115; **Phone:** 617-232-1555 ext. 595 or 617-975-2098; **Web site:** www.massart.edu/

NIKE Junior Resident Camp

Williamstown, MA

General Information: Coed residential and day sports program.

Contact: Jason West, Director of Marketing, 919 Sir Francis Drake Boulevard, Kentfield, CA 94904; **Phone:** 415-459-0459 or 415-459-1453; **E-mail:** jwest@us-sportscamps.com; **Web site:** www.ecamps.com

Northfield Mount Hermon Summer School

Northfield, MA

General Information: Coed residential and day academic program established in 1961.

Contact: Tomas P. Pratt, Director, 206 Main Street, Northfield, MA 01360; **Phone:** 413-498-3290 or 413-498-3112; **E-mail:** summer_school@nmhschool.org; **Web site:** www.nmh.northfield.ma.us/summer/

Phillips Academy Summer Session

Andover, MA

General Information: Coed residential and day academic program established in 1942.

Contact: Maxine S. Grogan, Dean of Admission, 180 Main Street, Andover, MA 01810; **Phone:** 978-749-4400 or 978-749-4414; **E-mail:** summersession@andover.edu; **Web site:** www.andover.edu

Quest Scholars Program at Harvard

Cambridge, MA

General Information: Coed residential academic and community service program established in 1999.

Contact: Ms. Dana Gavrieli, Director, Phillips Brooks House, Harvard Yard, Cambridge, MA 02138; **Phone:** 617-495-7671 or 801-729-2308; **E-mail:** quest@fas.harvard.edu; **Web site:** www.questscholars.org

Simon's Rock College of Bard Young Writers Workshop

Great Barrington, MA

General Information: Coed residential academic program established in 1983.

Contact: Dr. Jamie Hutchinson, Program Director, Young Writers Workshop, Great Barrington, MA 01230; **Phone:** 413-528-7231 or 413-528-7365; **E-mail:** jamieh@simons-rock.edu; **Web site:** www.simons-rock.edu

Smith College Summer Science Program

Northampton, MA

General Information: Girls residential academic program established in 1990.

Contact: Dr. Gail E. Scordilis, Director, Clark Science Center, Northampton, MA 01063; **Phone:** 413-585-3879 or 413-585-3068; **E-mail:** gscordil@science.smith.edu; **Web site:** www.smith.edu/summerprograms/SSSP/

Springfield College Allied Health Career Exploration Program

Springfield, MA

General Information: Coed residential academic program established in 1998.

Contact: Diane Erickson, Director of Continuing Education, 263 Alden Street, Springfield, MA 01108; **Phone:** 413-748-3111 or 413-748-3552; **E-mail:** conteduc@spfldcol.edu; **Web site:** www.spfldcol.edu

Springfield College Athletic Trainer Workshop

Springfield, MA

General Information: Coed residential academic program established in 1990.

Contact: Diane Erickson, Director of Continuing Education, 263 Alden Street, Springfield, MA 01108; **Phone:** 413-748-3111 or 413-748-3552; **E-mail:** conteduc@spfldcol.edu; **Web site:** www.spfldcol.edu

Springfield College Sports Management Career Exploration Program

Springfield, MA

General Information: Coed residential academic program established in 2000.

Contact: Diane Erickson, Director of Continuing Education, 263 Alden Street, Springfield, MA 01108; **Phone:** 413-748-3111 or 413-748-3552; **E-mail:** conteduc@spfldcol.edu; **Web site:** www.spfldcol.edu

Stoneleigh—Burnham School Softball Camp

Greenfield, MA

General Information: Girls residential sports program established in 1990.

Contact: Dr. Paul C. Bassett, Camp Director, 574 Bernardston Road, Greenfield, MA 01301; **Phone:** 413-774-2711 or 413-772-2602; **Web site:** www.sbschool.org

Stoneleigh—Burnham School Summer Dance Camp

Greenfield, MA

General Information: Girls residential arts program established in 1997.

Contact: Ms. Ann Sorvino, Director, 574 Bernardston Road, Greenfield, MA 01301; **Phone:** 413-774-2711 or 413-772-2602; **E-mail:** asorvino@sbschool.org; **Web site:** www.sbschool.org

Stoneleigh–Burnham School: A Voice of Her Own

Greenfield, MA

General Information: Girls residential academic program established in 1998.
Contact: Dr. Paul C. Bassett, Camp Director, 574 Bernardston Road, Greenfield, MA 01301; **Phone:** 413-774-2711 or 413-772-2602; **Web site:** www.sbschool.org

Summer $tock
Wellesley, MA
General Information: Girls residential academic program established in 2000.
Contact: Barbara Dowd, Director of Programs, 12 Merrill Street, Newburyport, MA 01950; **Phone:** 978-463-0259 or 978-465-8598; **E-mail:** bdowd1@independentmeans.com; **Web site:** www.independentmeans.com

Summer Fenn Day Camp
Concord, MA
General Information: Coed day arts program.
Contact: Mr. David A. Platt, Director of Summer Programs, 516 Monument Street, Concord, MA 01742-1894; **Phone:** 978-318-3614 or 978-371-7520; **E-mail:** summercamp@fenn.org; **Web site:** www.fenn.org

SuperCamp—Hampshire College
Amherst, MA
General Information: Coed residential academic program established in 1981.
Contact: Ms. Jan Miner, Enrollment Coordinator, 1725 South Coast Highway, Oceanside, CA 92054; **Phone:** 800-285-3276 (toll-free) or 760-722-3507; **E-mail:** info@supercamp.com; **Web site:** www.super-camp.com

Tabor Academy Summer Program
Marion, MA
General Information: Coed residential and day academic program established in 1917.
Contact: Donn A. Tyler, Director, 66 Spring Street, Marion, MA 02738; **Phone:** 508-748-2000 or 508-291-8392; **E-mail:** dtyler@tabor.pvt.k12.ma.us; **Web site:** www.taboracademy.org

The Art Institute of Boston Pre-College Program
Boston, MA
General Information: Coed day arts program established in 1912.
Contact: Diana Arcadipone, Dean of Professional and Continuing Education, 700 Beacon Street Boston, MA 02215-2598; **Phone:** 617-262-1223 ext. 304 or 617-437-1226; **Web site:** www.aiboston.edu/cur_on.html

The Boston Conservatory Summer Dance
Boston, MA
General Information: Coed residential and day arts program established in 1998.
Contact: Ms. Emiko Tokunaga, Artistic Director Summer Dance, Dance Division, 8 The Fenway, Boston, MA 02215; **Phone:** 617-912-9157 or 617-912-9138; **E-mail:** etokunaga@bostonconservatory.edu; **Web site:** www.bostonconservatory.edu

The New York Film Academy at the Harvard Faculty Club
Cambridge, MA
General Information: Coed residential arts program established in 1992.
Contact: Elli Ventouras, 100 East 17th Street, New York, NY 10003; **Phone:** 212-674-4300 or 212-477-1414; **E-mail:** film@nyfa.com; **Web site:** www.nyfa.com

The Winchendon School Summer Session
Winchendon, MA
General Information: Coed residential academic program established in 1985.
Contact: Mr. J. William LaBelle, Headmaster, 172 Ash Street, Winchendon, MA 01475; **Phone:** 978-297-1223 or 978-297-0911; **E-mail:** admissions@winchendon.org; **Web site:** www.winchendon.org

Tufts Summer Study
Medford, MA
General Information: Coed day academic program established in 1984.
Contact: Sharon Freeman, Manager, Tufts University Summer Session, 108 Packard Avenue, Medford, MA 02155; **Phone:** 617-627-3454 or 617-627-3295; **E-mail:** highschool@tufts.edu; **Web site:** ase.tufts.edu/summer

Walnut Hill Summer Theater School
Natick, MA
General Information: Coed residential and day arts program established in 1976.
Contact: Joe Cabral, Director, 12 Highland Street, Natick, MA 01760; **Phone:** 617-893-5622 or 508-653-9593; **Web site:** www.walnuthillarts.org

Wilderness Experiences Unlimited
General Information: Coed residential and day adventure and outdoor/wilderness program established in 1981.
Contact: Taylor Scott Cook, Executive Director, 499 Loomis Street, Westfield, MA 01085; **Phone:** 413-562-7431 or 413-569-6445; **E-mail:** adventures@weu.com; **Web site:** www.weu.com

New Hampshire

American Computer Experience–Summer Computer Camp–University of New Hampshire–Durham
General Information: Coed residential and day academic program.
Contact: Director, PO Box 15367, Atlanta, GA 30333; **Phone:** 800-386-4223 (toll-free); **E-mail:** ace@computercamp.com; **Web site:** www.aceplanet.com

American Youth Foundation—Camp Merrowvista
Center Tuftonboro, NH
General Information: Coed residential outdoor/wilderness program established in 1925.
Contact: Lisa Boucher, Merrowvista Registrar, 147 Canaan Road, Center Tuftonboro, NH 03816; **Phone:** 603-539-6607 or 603-539-7504; **E-mail:** merrowvist@aol.com; **Web site:** www.ayf.com

Brewster Academy Summer Session
Wolfeboro, NH
General Information: Coed residential and day academic program established in 1994.
Contact: Everett Logan, Admissions Associate, 80 Academy Drive, Wolfeboro, NH 03894; **Phone:** 603-569-7184 or 603-569-7272; **E-mail:** everett_logan@brewsternet.com; **Web site:** www.brewsternet.com/Pages/Students/summer_session.html

INTERLOCKEN: Leaders in Action
Hillsboro, NH

General Information: Coed residential community service program established in 1967.
Contact: Richard Herman, Director, RR2, Box 165, Hillsboro, NH 03244; **Phone:** 800-862-7762 (toll-free) or 603-478-5260; **E-mail:** mail@interlocken. org; **Web site:** www.interlocken.org

INTERLOCKEN: Random Acts of Kindness
Hillsboro, NH
General Information: Coed residential community service program established in 1967.
Contact: Richard Herman, Director, RR2, Box 165, Hillsboro, NH 03244; **Phone:** 603-478-3166 or 603-478-5260; **E-mail:** mail@interlocken.org; **Web site:** www.interlocken.org

Landmark Volunteers: New Hampshire
General Information: Coed residential community service and outdoor/wilderness program established in 1992.
Contact: Ann Barrett, Executive Director, PO Box 455, Sheffield, MA 01257; **Phone:** 413-229-0255 or 413-229-2050; **E-mail:** landmark@volunteers. com; **Web site:** www.volunteers.com

Performance Plus—Positive Learning Using the Stage
New Hampton, NH
General Information: Coed residential and day arts program established in 2000.
Contact: Ms. Lori Murphy, Associate Director, PO Box 579, New Hampton, NH 03256; **Phone:** 603-744-5401 ext. 101 or 603-744-3433; **E-mail:** lmurphy@performplus.org; **Web site:** www.performplus.org

Summer Program for Young Musicians
Dublin, NH
General Information: Coed residential arts program established in 1972.
Contact: Mr. Seth Brenzel, Associate Director, PO Box 320553, San Francisco, CA 94132-0553; **Phone:** 800-323-8653 (toll-free); **E-mail:** sbrenzel@waldenschool.org; **Web site:** www.waldenschool.org

The Cardigan Mountain School Summer Session
Canaan, NH
General Information: Coed residential and day academic program established in 1951.
Contact: T. Jeffrey Driscoll, Director of Admissions and Financial Aid, RR 2, Box 58, Canaan, NH 03741-9307; **Phone:** 603-523-3528 or 603-523-3565; **E-mail:** jdriscol@cardigan.org; **Web site:** www.cardigan.org

Rhode Island

American Computer Experience—Summer Computer Camp—Roger Williams University
Bristol, RI
General Information: Coed residential and day academic program.
Contact: Director, PO Box 15367, Atlanta, GA 30333; **Phone:** 800-386-4223 (toll-free); **E-mail:** ace@computercamp.com; **Web site:** www.aceplanet.com

Brown University Summer Programs—Pre-College Program
Providence, RI
General Information: Coed residential and day academic program established in 1982.

Contact: Ms. Karen H. Sibley, Dean of Summer Studies, 133 Waterman Street, Box T, Providence, RI 02912-9120; **Phone:** 401-863-7900 or 401-863-7908; **E-mail:** summer@brown.edu; **Web site:** www.brown.edu/Administration/Summer_Studies

Cybercamps—Brown University
Providence, RI

General Information: Coed residential and day academic program established in 1996.
Contact: Information Office, 12131 113th Avenue NE, Suite 102, Kirkland, WA 98034; **Phone:** 888-904-CAMP (toll-free) or 425-825-4601; **E-mail:** info@cybercamps.com; **Web site:** www.cybercamps.com

Rhode Island School of Design Pre-College Summer Foundation Program
Providence, RI

General Information: Coed residential and day arts program established in 1970.
Contact: Continuing Education Office/Summer Programs, 2 College Street, Providence, RI 02903-2787; **Phone:** 401-454-6200 or 401-454-6218; **E-mail:** summer@risd.edu; **Web site:** www.risd.edu/summer.cfm

St. George's Summer Session
Newport, RI

General Information: Coed residential and day academic program established in 1944.
Contact: Robert C. Weston, Director of Summer Session, PO Box 1910, Newport, RI 02840-0190; **Phone:** 401-842-6712 or 401-842-6763; **E-mail:** robert_weston@stgeorges.edu; **Web site:** www.stgeorges.edu

Teen Expeditions
West Greenwich, RI

General Information: Coed residential adventure program established in 1963.
Contact: John Jacques, Manager, W. Alton Jones Campus, 401 Victory Highway, West Greenwich; RI 02817, **Phone:** 401-397-3304 ext. 6043 or 401-397-3293; **E-mail:** urieec@etal.uri.edu; **Web site:** www.uri.edu/ajc

VERMONT

American Computer Experience—Summer Computer Camp—University of Vermont
Burlington, VT

General Information: Coed residential and day academic program.
Contact: Director, PO Box 15367, Atlanta, GA 30333; **Phone:** 800-386-4223 (toll-free); **E-mail:** ace@computercamp.com; **Web site:** www.aceplanet.com

Audubon Journeys
Brandon, VT

General Information: Coed residential adventure program established in 1999.
Contact: Mr. Larry Berrin, Director, 65 Millet Street, Richmond, VT 05477; **Phone:** 802-434-4300 or 802-434-4891; **E-mail:** vermont@audubon.org; **Web site:** www.audubon.org

Bennington College July Program
Bennington, VT

General Information: Coed residential academic program established in 1979.
Contact: Ms. Adrienne Marcus, Director,

Bennington College July Program, Bennington, VT 05201; **Phone:** 802-440-4418 or 802-440-4424; **E-mail:** july_program@bennington.edu; **Web site:** www.bennington.edu/julyp/index.htm

Burklyn Ballet Theatre
Johnson, VT

General Information: Coed residential and day arts program established in 1976.
Contact: Angela E. Whitehill, Artistic Director, PO Box 302, Johnson, VT 05656-0302; **Phone:** 802-635-1390; **E-mail:** burklyn@aol.com; **Web site:** www.burklynballet.com

Burklyn Ballet Theatre II, The Intermediate Program
Johnson, VT

General Information: Coed residential arts program established in 1995.
Contact: Angela Whitehill, Director, PO Box 302, Johnson, VT 05656-0302; **Phone:** 802-635-1390; **E-mail:** Burklyn@aol.com; **Web site:** www.burklynballet.com

Craftsbury Running Camps
Craftsbury Common, VT

General Information: Coed residential sports program established in 1976.
Contact: Craftsbury Running Camp, PO Box 31, Craftsbury Common, VT 05827; **Phone:** 800-729-7751 (toll-free) or 802-586-7768; **E-mail:** crafts@sover.net; **Web site:** www.craftsbury.com

Craftsbury Sculling Camp
Craftsbury Common, VT

General Information: Coed residential sports program established in 1977.
Contact: Craftsbury Sculling Camp, PO Box 31, Craftsbury Common, VT 05827; **Phone:** 802-586-7767 or 802-586-7768; **E-mail:** crafts@sover.net; **Web site:** www.craftsbury.com

Farm and Wilderness Camps—Flying Cloud
Plymouth, VT

General Information: Boys residential outdoor/wilderness program established in 1965.
Contact: Mr. Robert J. Schultz, Executive Director, 263 Farm and Wilderness Road, Plymouth, VT 05056; **Phone:** 802-422-3761 or 802-422-8660; **E-mail:** fandw@fandw.org; **Web site:** www.fandw.org

Farm and Wilderness Camps—Indian Brook
Plymouth, VT

General Information: Girls residential outdoor/wilderness program established in 1940.
Contact: Mr. Robert J. Schultz, Executive Director, 263 Farm and Wilderness Road, Plymouth, VT 05056; **Phone:** 802-422-3761 or 802-422-8660; **E-mail:** fandw@fandw.org; **Web site:** www.fandw.org

Farm and Wilderness Camps—Saltash Mountain
Plymouth, VT

General Information: Coed residential outdoor/wilderness program established in 1962.
Contact: Mr. Robert J. Schultz, Executive Director, 263 Farm and Wilderness Road, Plymouth, VT 05056; **Phone:** 802-422-3761 or 802-422-8660; **E-mail:** fandw@fandw.org; **Web site:** www.fandw.org

Farm and Wilderness Camps—Tamarack Farm
Plymouth, VT

General Information: Coed residential community service program established in 1951.

Contact: Mr. Robert J. Schultz, Executive Director, 263 Farm and Wilderness Road, Plymouth, VT 05056; **Phone:** 802-422-3761 or 802-422-8660; **E-mail:** fandw@fandw.org; **Web site:** www.fandw.org

Farm and Wilderness Camps—Timberlake
Plymouth, VT

General Information: Boys residential outdoor/wilderness program established in 1939.
Contact: Mr. Robert J. Schultz, Executive Director, 263 Farm and Wilderness Road, Plymouth, VT 05056; **Phone:** 802-422-3761 or 802-422-8660; **E-mail:** fandw@fandw.org; **Web site:** www.fandw.org

Landmark Volunteers—Vermont
General Information: Coed residential community service program established in 1992.
Contact: Ann Barrett, Executive Director, PO Box 455, Sheffield, MA 01257; **Phone:** 413-229-0255 or 413-229-2050; **E-mail:** landmark@volunteers.com; **Web site:** www.volunteers.com

Mud City Adventures
Stowe, VT

General Information: Coed residential and day adventure program established in 1994.
Contact: Ms. Christine A. Colengeli, Director, PO Box 535, Stowe, VT 05672; **Phone:** 802-253-8890; **E-mail:** mudcity@stowe.nu; **Web site:** www.mudcityadventures.com

NIKE Junior Resident Camp
Stowe, VT

General Information: Coed residential and day sports program.
Contact: Jason West, Director of Marketing, 919 Sir Francis Drake Boulevard, Kentfield, CA 94904; **Phone:** 415-459-0459 or 415-459-1453; **E-mail:** jwest@us-sportscamps.com; **Web site:** www.ecamps.com

NIKE Parent/Child Golf School
Stratton, VT

General Information: Coed day sports program.
Contact: Jason West, Director of Marketing, 919 Sir Francis Drake Boulevard, Kentfield, CA 94904; **Phone:** 415-459-0459 or 415-459-1453; **E-mail:** jwest@us-sportscamps.com; **Web site:** www.ecamps.com

Norwich Future Leader Program
Northfield, VT

General Information: Coed residential academic program established in 1998.
Contact: Patrick van Rooyen, Director, 158 Harmon Drive, Northfield, VT 05663; **Phone:** 802-485-2531 or 802-485-2032; **E-mail:** jrleader@norwich.edu; **Web site:** www.norwich.edu/flp/index.htm

Putney School Summer Arts Workshop
Putney, VT

General Information: Coed residential and day arts program established in 1987.
Contact: Nicole Veilleux, Assistant Director, Elm Lea Farm, Putney, VT 05346; **Phone:** 802-387-6297 or 802-387-6216; **E-mail:** summer@putney.com; **Web site:** www.putney.com

Putney School Summer Program for International Education
Putney, VT

General Information: Coed residential and day aca-

demic program established in 1990.
Contact: Ms. Nicole Veilleux, Assistant Director, Elm Lea Farm, Putney, VT 05346; **Phone:** 802-387-6294 or 802-387-6216; **E-mail:** summer@putney.com; **Web site:** www.putney.com

Putney School Summer Writing Program
Putney, VT
General Information: Coed residential and day academic and arts program established in 1997.
Contact: Ms. Nicole Veilleux, Assistant Director, Elm Lea Farm, Putney, VT 05346; **Phone:** 802-387-6297 or 802-387-6216; **E-mail:** summer@putney.com; **Web site:** www.putney.com

Summer Discovery at Vermont
Burlington, VT
General Information: Coed residential academic program established in 1990.
Contact: The Musiker Family, Director, 1326 Old Northern Boulevard, Roslyn Village, NY 11576; **Phone:** 516-621-3939 or 516-625-3438; **E-mail:** discovery@summerfun.com; **Web site:** www.summerfun.com

Summer Sports Camps—Basketball (Boys)
Bennington, VT
General Information: Boys day sports program established in 1993.
Contact: Scott Kilgallon, Athletic Director, 982 Mansion Drive, Bennington, VT 05201; **Phone:** 802-447-4660 or 802-447-4652; **Web site:** www.svc.edu

Summer Sports Camps—Basketball (Girls)
Bennington, VT
General Information: Girls day sports program established in 1993.
Contact: Scott Kilgallon, Athletic Director, 982 Mansion Drive, Bennington, VT 05201; **Phone:** 802-447-4660 or 802-447-4652; **Web site:** www.svc.edu

Summer Sports Camps—Soccer
Bennington, VT
General Information: Coed day sports program established in 1993.
Contact: Scott Kilgallon, Athletic Director, 982 Mansion Drive, Bennington, VT 05201; **Phone:** 802-447-4660 or 802-447-4652; **Web site:** www.svc.edu

The Putney Chamber Music Intensive
Putney, VT
General Information: Coed residential and day arts program.
Contact: Ms. Nicole Veilleux, Assistant Director, Elm Lea Farm, Putney, VT 05346; **Phone:** 802-387-6297 or 802-387-6216; **E-mail:** summer@putney.com; **Web site:** www.putney.com

University of Vermont Summer Program for High School Students in Engineering, Computers, and Math
Burlington, VT
General Information: Coed residential academic program established in 1992.
Contact: Dawn Densmore, Program Manager, Office of the Dean, 109 Votey Building, Burlington, VT 05405; **Phone:** 802-656-8748 or 802-656-8802; **Web site:** www.uvm.edu

Windridge Tennis Camp at Craftsbury Common
Craftsbury Common, VT

General Information: Coed residential sports program established in 1973.
Contact: Charles Witherell, Director, PO Box 27, Craftsbury Common, VT 05827; **Phone:** 802-586-9646 or 802-586-7785; **E-mail:** wcampcc@aol.com; **Web site:** www.windridgetw.com

Windridge Tennis Camp at Teela-Wooket, Vermont
Roxbury, VT
General Information: Coed residential sports program established in 1986.
Contact: Deb Fennell, Director, 1215 Roxbury Road, Roxbury, VT 05669; **Phone:** 802-485-5400 or 802-485-8092; **E-mail:** wcamps@aol.com; **Web site:** www.windridgetw.com

BIBLIOGRAPHY

Articles
"1998–1999 Almanac," *The Chronicle of Higher Education,* August 28, 1998.

"America's Best Colleges." Washington, D.C.: *U.S. News & World Report,* 1996.

"The Job Search and Making It," *Hispanic Times Magazine,* March 1996.

"Six Basic Skills Apply in Workplace, Everyday Life," *Nashville Business Journal,* January 1996.

Books
Adams, Jenni. *Stress, A New Positive Approach.* London: David & Charles, 1989.

Aveizer, K. Patricia. *Game Plan for Getting Into College.* Princeton: Peterson's, 2000.

Bingham, Mindy, and Sandy Stryker. *Career Choices.* Santa Barbara: Academic Innovations, 1990.

Bloch, Deborah P. *How to Have a Winning Job Interview.* Lincolnwood, Illinois: VGM Career Horizons, 1991.

Blonna, Richard. *Coping With Stress in a Changing World.* St. Louis: Mosby, 1996.

Boyer, Ernest L., and Paul Boyer. *Smart Parents, Guide to College.* Princeton: Peterson's, 1996.

Carter, Carol. *Majoring in the Rest of Your Life.* New York: The Noonday Press, 1990.

Deutschman, Alan. *Winning Money for College.* Princeton: Peterson's, 1997

Eberts, Marjorie, and Margaret Gisler. *How to Prepare for College.* Lincolnwood, Illinois: VGM Career Horizons, 1994.

Golden, M., L. Kilb, and A. Mayerson. *Explanation of the Contents of the Americans with Disabilities Act of 1990.* Washington, D. C.: Disability Rights Education and Defense Fund, 1992.

Hayden, Thomas C. *Handbook for College Admissions.* Princeton: Peterson's, 1995.
Kowadlo, Bonnie F., and Madelyn Schulman. *Working Smart.* Cincinnati: South-Western Publishing Co., 1995.

Kropp, Paul. *Raising A Reader.* New York: Doubleday, 1993.

Marler, Patty, and Jan Bailey. *Resumes Made Easy.* Lincolnwood, Illinois: VGM Career Horizons, 1995.

Miller, Lyle H., and Alma Dell Smith. *The Stress Solution.* New York: Pocket Books, 1993.

O'Brien, Jack. *Kiplinger's Career Starter.* Washington, D.C.: Kiplinger Books, 1993.

O'Brien, Linda. *An Instruction Booklet for the Parents of College Bound Students.* Dayton, Ohio: Woodburn Press, 1996.

Pedersen, Laura. *Street-Smart Career Guide: A Step-by-Step Program for Your Career Development.* New York: Crown Trade Paperbacks, 1993.

Schmidt, Peggy. *The New 90-Minute Resume.* Princeton: Peterson's, 1996.

Schmidt, Peggy. *The 90-Minute Interview Prep Book.* Princeton: Peterson's, 1996.

Reference Material
College Board Guide to 150 Popular College Majors. New York: College Entrance Examination Board, 1992.

College Money Handbook 2001. Princeton: Peterson's, 2000.

Colleges for Students with Learning Disabilities and Attention Deficit Disorder. Princeton: Peterson's, 2001.

Counselor's Guide to Ohio Independent Colleges & Universities. Columbus: The Association of Independent Colleges and Universities of Ohio and The Ohio Association of Private College Admission Counselors, 1996.

Culinary Schools 2001. Princeton: Peterson's, 2000.

Directory of College Scholarships and Loans. The Dayton-Montgomery County Scholarship Program. The Dayton Postsecondary Education Demonstration Laboratory, and The Dayton Foundation. Dayton, Ohio: 1992.

How to Get Into College. Livingston, New Jersey: Newsweek, Inc. and Kaplan Educational Centers, 1997.
Peterson's College and University Almanac 2001. Princeton: Peterson's, 2000.

Peterson's Competitive Colleges 2000–2001. Princeton: Peterson's, 2000.

Peterson's Four-Year Colleges–2001. Princeton: Peterson's, 1999.

Peterson's Sports Scholarships and Athletic Programs. Princeton: Peterson's, 1999.

Peterson's Vocational Schools. Princeton: Peterson's, 1999.

Scholarships, Grants and Prizes. Princeton: Peterson's, 2000.

Study Abroad. Princeton: Peterson's, 2000.

Summer Jobs for Students. Princeton: Peterson's, 2000.

Summer Opportunities for Kids and Teenagers. Princeton: Peterson's, 2000."

1998–2008 Employment Projections," Occupational Outlook Program, U.S. Bureau of Labor Statistics.

Brochures/Literature

"1998–2008 Employment Projections," Occupational Outlook Program, U.S. Bureau of Labor Statistics.

"1999 College Freshman with Disabilities Report," HEATH Resource Center, American Council on Education.

"1999 Current Population Report," U.S. Bureau of Census.

"ACT College Planning Guide," American College Testing, P.O. Box 168, Iowa City, Iowa 52243.

"ADA Handbook," Equal Employment Opportunity Commission and U.S. Department of Justice, Washington, D.C. (EEOC-BK 19), October 1991.

"ASVAB Student & Parent Guide," Department of Defense, 2500 Green Bay Road, North Chicago, Illinois 60064-3094.

"Adult Vocational Education," Ohio Department of Education, Division of Vocational and Career Education, 65 South Front Street, Room 907, Columbus, Ohio 43266-0308.

"The Americans with Disabilities Act," Heath Resource Center, American Council on Education, One Dupont Circle, Suite 800, Washington, D.C. 20036-1193.

"Answering the Challenge," Ohio Department of Education, Division of Vocational and Career Education, 65 South Front Street, Room 907, Columbus, Ohio 43266-0308.

"Associate Degree Preferred," Ohio Association of Two-Year College Admission Officers, Edison Community College, Piqua, Ohio 45356.

"Audition and Portfolio Information," Otterbein College, Westerville, Ohio 43081.

"Bulletin for the SAT Programs," College Board SAT Program, P.O. Box 6200, Princeton, New Jersey 08541-6200.

"A Call to College," Newark High School, 314 Granville Street, Newark, Ohio 43055.

"Camp Attracting Prospective Educators," Bowling Green State University, 444 Education Building, Bowling Green, Ohio 43403.

"Career Skills Checklist," Vocational Instructional Materials Laboratory, The Ohio State University, 1900 Kenny Road, Columbus, Ohio 43210-1090.

"Changing Lives," Student Loan Funding Corporation, One West Fourth Street, Suite 200, Cincinnati, Ohio 45202.

"Charting Your Future," VIESA Career Guidebook, The American College Testing Services, P.O. Box 168, Iowa City, Iowa 52243.

"College Planning Timeline," I Know I Can, 270 East State Street, Columbus, Ohio 43215.

"Cool Stuff," Otterbein College, Office of Continuing Studies, Westerville, Ohio 43081.

"The Dayton-Montgomery County Scholarship Program," The Dayton-Montgomery County Scholarship Program, 348 West First Street, Dayton, Ohio 45402.

"Definition of Disability: Outline," Disability Rights Education and Defense Fund, Washington, D.C., 1992.

"Department of Theatre & Dance," Otterbein College, Westerville, Ohio 43081.

"Discover Card Tribute Award Program," American Association of School Administrators, P.O. Box 9338, Arlington, Virginia 22219.

"Education In America: Historic Forces and Current Counterforces," Cleveland Commission on Higher Education, 1422 Euclid Avenue, Hanna Building, Suite 1162, Cleveland, Ohio 44115.

"The Employee Handbook of New Work Habits For a Radically Changing World," Pritchett & Associates, P.O. Box 802889, Dallas, Texas 75380-9609.

"Fraternity Friends Forever," National Interfraternity Council, 3901 West 86th, Suite 390, Indianapolis, Indiana 46268-1791.

"General Educational Development (GED) Test," State GED Office, Ohio Department of Education, 65 South Front Street, Room 812, Columbus, Ohio 43266-0308.

"Get Set for College," American College Testing, P.O. Box 168, Iowa City, Iowa 52243.

"Get the Answers to Your Questions at the College Information Center," Cincinnati Youth Collaborative, 699 Race Street, Cincinnati, Ohio 45202.

"Going to College?" The College Board, P.O. Box 6200, Princeton, New Jersey 08541-6200.

"A Guide to the College Admission Process," National Association of College Admission Counselors, 1631 Prince Street, Alexandria, Virginia 22314-2818.

"Guide for Parents," National Association of College Admission Counselors, 1800 Diagonal Road, Suite 430, Alexandria, Virginia 22314.

"Happiness is Having a Job," Hilliard High School Business Education Department, 5100 Davidson Road, Hilliard, Ohio 43026.

"I Know I Can," I Know I Can, c/o Columbus City School District, 270 East State Street, Columbus, Ohio 43215.

"Kids In College," Columbus State Community College, P.O. Box 1609, 550 East Spring Street, Columbus, Ohio 43216-1609.

"Making Sure You Are Eligible to Participate in College Sports," NCAA Initial-Eligibility Clearinghouse, P.O. Box 4043, Iowa City, Iowa 52243-4043.

"Midwest Talent Search," Northwestern University, Center for Talent Development, 617 Dartmouth Place, Evanston, Illinois 60208-4175.

"Midwestern SAT Program," The College Board, P.O. Box 6200, Princeton, New Jersey 08541-6200.

"Music at Otterbein," Otterbein College, Westerville, Ohio 43081.

"Need Something To Do This Summer?" The Dayton-Montgomery County Scholarship Program, 348 West First Street, Dayton, Ohio 45402.

"Occupational Trends," The Ohio Bureau of Employment Services, 145 South Front Street, P.O. Box 1618, Columbus, Ohio 43216-1618.

"Outstanding Fiction for the College Bound," American Library Association, 50 East Huron Street, Chicago, Illinois 60611.

"Parent and Student Guide," Dayton-Montgomery County Scholarship Program, 348 West First Street, Dayton, Ohio 45402.

"A Parent's Guide to Fraternities," North-American Interfraternity Conference, 3901 West 86th, Suite 390, Indianapolis, Indiana 46268-1791.

"Planning for College," Columbus Public Schools Guidance Services, 52 Starling Street, Columbus, Ohio 43215.

"Portfolio Development," The Columbus College of Art & Design, 107 North Ninth Street, Columbus, Ohio 43215.

"Post-Secondary Enrollment Options Programs," Higher Education Council of Columbus, c/o Capital University, East Main Street, Columbus, Ohio 43209.

"Preparing For College Success," Otterbein College, Westerville, Ohio 43081.

"Preparing For the ACT Assessment," ACT Registration Department, P.O. Box 414, Iowa City, Iowa 52243-0414.

"School-to-Work Opportunities," National School-to-Work Opportunities Office, 400 Virginia Avenue, Room 210, Washington, D.C. 20024.

"Section 504," American Council On Education, One Dupont Circle, Suite 800, Washington, D.C. 20036-1193.

"Southwestern Ohio Council for Higher Education," SOCHE, Miami Valley Research Park, 3171 Research Boulevard, Suite 141, Dayton, Ohio 45420-4014.

"The Student Guide," U.S. Department of Education, Federal Student Aid Information Center, P.O. Box 84, Washington, D.C. 20044-0084.

"Summertime Favorites," National Endowment for the Humanities, 1100 Pennsylvania Avenue NW, Washington, D.C. 20506.

"Support for Talented Students, Inc.," Support for Talented Students, Inc., P.O. Box 20308, Columbus, Ohio 43220.

"Taking the SAT/Reasoning Test," The College Board, P.O. Box 6200, Princeton, New Jersey 08541-6200.

"A Technical Manual of the Employment Provisions of the Americans with Disabilities Act: Title I," Equal Employment Opportunity Commission, Washington, D.C., January 1992.

"Tech Prep–What It Takes To Succeed," Ohio Department of Education, 65 South Front Street, Columbus, Ohio 43215.

"Today's College Student," Cleveland Commission on Higher Education, 1162 Hanna Building, 1422 Euclid Avenue, Cleveland, Ohio 44115-1901.

"The Twenty-First Century Nurse," Alliance for Health Reform, 1900 L Street NW, Suite 512, Washington, D.C. 20036 (telephone: 202-466-5626).

"The Ultimate College Experience–1996 Fall Rush Guide," University of Cincinnati Office of Greek Affairs, 221 Tangeman M.L.—136, Cincinnati, Ohio 45221.

"Visual Arts," Otterbein College, Westerville, Ohio 43081.

"Vocational Equity," Ohio Department of Education Division of Vocational and Career Education, 65 South Front Street, Room 909, Columbus, Ohio 43215-4183.

"What Work Requires of Schools," The Secretary's Commission on Achieving Necessary Skills, U.S. Department of Labor (telephone: 800-788-SKILL).

"Women's Panhellenic Greek Community Guide 1996," Ohio University Women's Panhellenic Association, Baker Center 312, Athens, Ohio 45701-2979.

"You Can Afford College and Grad School," Kaplan Education Centers (telephone: 800-KAP-1057).

Organizations

ACT Assessment, P.O. Box 414, Iowa City, Iowa 52243-0414 (telephone: 319-337-1270)

Air Force Recruiting Services, Air Force Opportunity Center, P.O. Box 3505, Capitol Heights, Maryland 20791-9988 (telephone: 800-423-USAF)

Alcoholics Anonymous, 475 Riverside Drive, 11th Floor, New York, New York 10115 (telephone: 212-870-3400)

American Association of Community Colleges, One Dupont Circle, NW, #410, Washington, D.C. 22206-1176 (telephone: 202-728-0200)

American Cancer Society, 1599 Clifton Rd. NE, Atlanta, Georgia 30329 (telephone: 800-ACS-2345)

Amer-I-Can Program, Inc., 1851 Sunset Plaza Drive, Los Angeles, California 90069 (telephone: 310-652-7884).

Arizona College of Allied Health, 1940 W. Indian School Rd., Phoenix, AZ 85015 (telephone: 602-222-9300)

Association on Higher Education and Disability, P.O. Box 21192, Columbus, Ohio 43221-0192 (telephone: 614-488-4972)

Brighten Your Future, P.O. Box 991, Logan, Ohio 43138 (telephone: 740-385-5058)

Career College Association, 10 G Street, NE, Ste. 750, Washington, DC 20002 (telephone: 202-336-6800)

Cleveland Scholarship Programs, Inc., 850 Euclid Avenue, Suite 1000, Cleveland, Ohio, 44114 (telephone: 216-241-5587)

COIN Educational Products, 3361 Executive Parkway, Suite 302, Toledo, Ohio 43606-9844.

College Scholarship Service, The College Board, P.O. Box 6381, Princeton, New Jersey 08541-6381 (telephone: 609-778-6888)

Crime Prevention Association of Philadelphia, Suite 4E, 230 South Broad Street, Philadelphia, PA, 19102 (telephone: 215-545-5230)

Department of Veterans Affairs, 1120 Vermont Ave, NW, Washington, DC 20421 (telephone: 202-691-3030)

Disabilities Organizational Development Services, 5984 Pinerock Place, Columbus, Ohio 43231-2334 (telephone: 614-895-0238)

Educational Testing Service, Rosedale Road, Princeton, New Jersey 08541 (telephone: 609-921-9000)

Enlisted Association of the National Guard of the United States, P.O. Box 261, Groveport, Ohio 43125 (telephone: 800-642-6642)

Federal Trade Commission, 600 Pennsylvania Avenue NW, Washington, D.C. 20580 (telephone: 877-FTC-HELP)

Gender Issues Education, 5625 SE 38th Avenue, Portland, Oregon 97202 (telephone: 503-775-6533)

Higher Education Council of Columbus, c/o Ohio State University, Mount Hall, Room 204, 1050 Carmack Road, Columbus, Ohio 43210 (telephone: 614-688-4610)

Hispanic Scholarship Fund, 1 Sansome Street, Suite 1000, San Francisco, California 94104 (telephone: 877-HSF-INFO)

Keystone College, Counseling Department, One College Green, LaPlume, PA 18440 (telephone: 570-945-5141)

Lake Educational Assistance Foundation, 7519 Mentor Avenue #102, Mentor, Ohio 44060-5410 (telephone: 216-942-5323)

Learning Disabilities Association of Central Ohio, 1422 Taylor Corners Circle, Blacklick, Ohio 43004 (telephone: 614-868-9359)

Lorain County Alliance of Black School Educators, P.O. Box 745, Lorain, Ohio 44052.

NAACP, National Offices, 4802 Mount Hope Drive, Baltimore, Maryland 21215 (telephone: 877-622-2798)

Narcotics Anonymous, P.O. Box 9999, Van Nuys, California 91409 (telephone: 818-773-9999)

National Association of Anorexia Nervosa and Associated Disorders, P.O. Box 7, Highland Park Illinois 60035 (telephone: 847-831-3438)

National Association of College Admission Counselors, 1631 Prince Street, Alexandria, Virginia 22314-2818 (telephone: 703-836-2222)

National Association of Intercollegiate Athletics, 6120 South Yale Avenue, Suite 1450, Tulsa, Oklahoma 74136 (telephone: 918-494-8828)

National College Access Network, 204 East Lombard Street, Fourth Floor, Baltimore, Maryland 21202 (telephone: 410-244-7218)

National Collegiate Athletic Association Clearinghouse, P.O. Box 4043 , Iowa City, Iowa 52243-4043 (telephone: 319-339-3003)

National Institute on Drug Abuse, Community Drug Alert Bulletin—Club Drugs. 6001 Executive Blvd., Bethesda, Maryland 20892 (telephone: 301-443-1124)

North-American Interfraternity Conference, 3901 West 86th Street, Suite 390, Indianapolis, Indiana 48268 (telephone: 317-872-1112)

Ohio Department of Education, 25 S. Front St., Columbus, Ohio 43215 (telephone: 877-644-6338)

Ohio Tuition Trust Authority, 62 East Broad Street, 4th Floor, Columbus, Ohio 43215 (telephone: 800-AFFORD-IT)

Peterson's Education Services, 2000 Lenox Drive, P.O. Box 2123, Lawrenceville, New Jersey 08543-2123 (telephone: 800-338-3282)

The California Family Counseling Center, 5445 Balboa Blvd., Suite 113, Encino, California 91316 (telephone: 818-907-9980)

The College Fund/UNCF, 8260 Willow Oaks Corporate Drive, P.O. Box 10444, Fairfax, Virginia 22031 (telephone: 703-205-3400)

The Compelling Communications Group, 15 Sausalito Blvd., Sausalito, California (telephone: 415-331-6336)

The Education Resource Institute, 330 Stuart St., Ste, 500 Boston, Massachusetts 02116 (telephone: 800-255- 8374)

U.S. Department of Education, Federal Student Aid Information Center, P.O. Box 84, Washington, D.C. 20044 (telephone: 800-4-FEDAID)

Vocational Instructional Materials Laboratory, The Ohio State University, Columbus, Ohio

NOTES

NOTES

NOTES

COPYRIGHT

SYSTEM REQUIREMENTS FOR WINDOWS PC

Windows 95/98 or NT, Pentium 166mhz, 32 MB RAM, sound card/speakers, 8x CD-ROM, 800x600x16 bit color display.

TO RUN ON WINDOWS PC

Insert CD-ROM and wait for autorun to start the program. If the program does not appear, click 'Start' then select 'Run.' Click 'Browse' and select the CD_ROM drive, click on the PC folder then double click on the MainMenu.exe.

MINIMUM SYSTEM REQUIREMENT FOR MACINTOSH

Power PC 166mhz, MAC OS 7.5.1, 32 MB RAM, 8x CD-ROM, 800x600x16 bit color display.

TO RUN ON MACINTOSH

Insert CD-ROM and wait for autorun to start the program. If the program does not appear, double click on the mentor icon on the desktop. Double click on MainMenu.